# *Lovers for Life*

## Creating Lasting Passion, Trust and True Partnership

By Daniel Ellenberg, Ph.D. and Judith Bell, M.S., M.F.C.C.

*Aslan*
PUBLISHING

Aslan Publishing • Santa Rosa, California • 1995

Published by

Aslan Publishing
3356 Coffey Lane
Santa Rosa, CA 95403
(707) 995-1861

For a free catalog of all our titles,
or to order more copies of this book
please call (800) 275-2606.

**Library of Congress Cataloging-in-Publication Data**

Ellenberg, Daniel, 1953-
    Lovers for life : creating lasting passion, trust, and true
partnership / by Daniel Ellenberg and Judith Bell.
       p.  cm.
    Includes bibliographical references.
    ISBN 0-944031-61-7
    1. Man-woman relationships.  2. Communication in sex.  I. Bell,
Judith, 1952-  .  II. Title.
HQ801.E388  1995
613.9'5--dc20                            95-7289
                                         CIP

Cover design by Leslie Waltzer & Stacey Marvel
Cover photograph by Tom Landecker, ©1994 Landecker Photography
Book design by Stacey Marvel

Printed in USA by Data Reproductions Corp., Rochester Hills, MI
First Edition

10  9  8  7  6  5  4  3  2

*To all of you who are relationship pioneers—unwilling to settle for less than is your birthright.*

# Acknowledgements

We appreciate our son, who is a daily reminder of the need to practice what we teach. His delight and joy of life inspires and helps us to be better human beings.

We felt very supported by our dear parents, Ruth and Martin Bell and Anne (Ellenberg) Cohen. Their love and caring, not to mention some editorial feedback, made the project a true family affair. A special thanks to Daniel's sister, Arlene, who added some valuable insight, his brother, Marc for his continual support, and Judith's sister Janis for providing direction concerning women's roles and procuring art.

We are indebted to Bill Keener whose editorial advice and questions helped us clarify and focus the work. A special thanks to Dana Keener for supporting him graciously as he dedicated many of their would-be family hours to the task.

Hal Bennett, our agent, brought the project to us and was a godsend for the mountain of questions we had throughout the writing. His knowledge and humor were very helpful.

Colin Ingram also provided useful editorial work in the earlier stages of this book. He helped congeal some of the material into a more cogent form.

A big appreciation goes to Dawson Church, head of Aslan Publishing and Atrium Publishers Group. Visionary, pragmatist, and lover of life, he stood by us when even we were in doubt. Like a great river rafting guide, he was able to flow with the ever-changing currents of the book.

Special thanks to Brenda Plowman who was part of the original braintrust involved in envisioning this book. Brenda and Dawson, who are married with two children, epitomize the openness and willingness of couples committed to being spiritual mates and lifetime lovers.

We thank all the people at Aslan Publishing and Atrium Publishers Group. They have been helpful and open people throughout the project. We want to acknowledge Joanne Flanagan, who was instrumental in turning the manuscript into a finished book. We appreciate her commitment and patience in this pursuit. Many thanks to Paul Cohen, Veronica LaBeau and the sales staff for their help getting the book out into the world.

We give big thanks to Stan Dale, the founder of the Human Awareness Institute (HAI). Stan has a heart of gold and is a courageous defender of our human right to pleasure. Stan's work helped inspire some healing in our relationship years ago. He was also very generous in providing helpful insights in the book as well.

We thank John Gray for his generous support along the way. He continues to inspire us through this process.

We thank Robert A. Johnson for his intuitive belief in us and the book. As an elder, he exhibits the generativity invaluable for bridging the generations.

We thank Robert Frey and Lori Grace for their generous contributions.

Much love goes to our dear friends who regularly heard "no" to their social invitations yet still waited with open arms when we were available.

In the end, a project of this magnitude involves too many people to mention by name. However, some must be named: Laura Uplinger; Nisha Zenoff; Jeri Marlowe; Carol Roghair; Will and Ailish Schutz; Al Crowell and Richard Cohan. These friends and colleagues helped *Lovers for Life* blossom into a major resource for creating longterm relationships. Thanks to all the people with whom we batted ideas back and forth.

I (Judith) feel tremendous gratitude for Ellen Moore, A. A. Leath, Juanita and Eugene Sagan, and Will Schutz who have been important teachers for me over the years. Their influence is felt throughout the book—as is the influence of my parents who first taught me the importance of an egalitarian relationship. Mom and Dad, I thank you and honor you.

I (Daniel) thank my teachers John Conger and John Enright for their support in times when I really needed it.

I feel deep appreciation for the men who I have co-led *Strength with Heart* men's workshops with—Andrew Michaels, Alan Ptashek, and Alan White. Their love, strength and friendship has made me a better, more conscious and caring man.

I also thank the men who have participated in my weekly men's groups over the last 11 years. While I have been a teacher for them, they have been my teachers as well.

From the bottom of our hearts, we thank the clients who have worked with us over the years and trusted us so deeply. Many of their stories are included throughout the book. Their courageous efforts to create rich and conscious relationships were a continuing source of inspiration as we wrote *Lovers for Life*.

# Contents

# Foreword

Love is one of those great psychological forces that has the power to transform us. It impells us to appreciate others and to honor their importance in our lives. In lover relationships, love opens our eyes to our partner and opens our heart to the potential intimacy between us. We may enter a love relationship with the expectation that our love, as we first knew its intensity and sweetness, would last forever. But it rarely does. In the long run, the relationship can remain energized, nurturing, and co-equal only if we transform our experience of love from "romantic love" to what I term "human love."

Romantic love is a package containing projections, illusions, high drama, impossible demands, and inevitable disappointments. It is essentially a self-absorbed love. Human love, on the other hand, allows us to truly value the individual sharing our life with us, including not only that person's finest qualities but also his or her shortcomings. It is a love based on a daily enjoyment and deep knowl-dege of each other—truly best friends. This book, *Lovers for Life,* can help us make that crucial inner shift from expectations to acceptance—complete acceptance not only of our partner but of our-selves as well.

Most adults find themselves in an intimate relationship, and the very ordinariness of such liaisons has led to neglect. But as this book shows, seeds of immense fulfillment and pleasure may lie in the most ordinary of relationships. *Lovers for Life* weaves a wonderful tapestry from many threads, integrating psychology, sexuality, anthropology, communications theory, subtle Eastern energy systems, addictions theory, sociology, and history along with innumerable personal stories. Daniel and Judith unify these themes into a compelling vision of what it means to sustain an excit-ing and empowering long-term love relationshhip. They do more than describe the splendor of the way life could be; they also provide us with simple, practical tools, replete with exercises that can transmute an ordinary relationship into an extraordinary one.

Undoubtedly, the most challenging (and potentially, the most rewarding) material deals with the topic of sexual shame. Daniel and Judith guide you to uncover how sexual shame (that you might not know exists) can negatively affect the relationship between your lover and you. They also pro-vide ways to heal this shame and take your relationship to new heights.

You will find in these pages an accessible way to understand why it is so vital that we con-sciously examine our life's journey, paying attention to the wounds suffered along the way, and come to know and accept every aspect of ourselves. Only by embracing what lies in our unconscious, our shadow, can we move toward the integration of our total self with both its feminine and masculine aspects. And that clears the way for a human love between real people who can help each other grow for a lifetime.

What touches me most about this work is the openness and courage of these authors, these lovers, who reveal their human vulnerabilities by relating their own trials by fire. They write from the core of their beings, and while they include academic research and reporting, they do not hide behind it. The lessons they share flow from their experience of a flesh-and-blood marriage as man and woman, as well their partnership as two practicing counselors trained to understand the patterns of human behavior and bring new creative insights to intimate relationships. This book rings with authenticity because Daniel and Judith are living its lessons to the fullest every day.

Robert A. Johnson
Encinitas, California
November 20, 1994

# Introduction

*E*veryone wants a lover for life. Someone with whom they can share the joys and sorrows of life. A friend, confidante, partner, parent, sibling, teacher, student, and sexual playmate all rolled into one. Someone who makes the gray days brighter and the sunny days luminescent. Who brings bounce to the dullest moments and makes life worth living. Who is undemanding, yet willing to fulfill every request. In short, a god or goddess incarnated.

Of course, few of us believe we enter lover relationships with these high expectations. Yet our unconscious hopes are larger than most of us realize. How else can we explain the seemingly irrational disappointment we feel when our lover lets us down? Of course, disappointments are understandable, yet the intensity of these disappointments often points to some underlying or unconscious feeling. How many times have you had the uneasy feeling that you failed your partner in ways for which you never signed up?

Relationship dis-ease and failures tend to accumulate over time. As a consequence, expectations tend to decrease as age increases. Experience becomes a teacher. No gods or goddesses have stepped forth. They may have appeared to be the perfect lover once, yet "reality" set in. The hopes of creating a lasting, emotionally and sexually satisfying relationship have been dashed through ignorance, blame, and misunderstandings.

This is hardly surprising given the dearth of relationship training we receive in this culture. Did you learn how to develop and sustain long-term intimacy? Were you instructed in the delicate art of lovemaking? Did you learn how to resolve conflicts effectively, or to illuminate the black times, or to handle other attractions? The answers, for most people, are painfully clear.

Perhaps you are in a great relationship and want to insure its future success. You love your mate, value your relationship, and want to do everything possible to be lovers for life. Or perhaps you have never quite experienced the love you desire. You either feel stuck in an unfulfilling relationship, or you have moved from one partner to the next. Whatever your experience happens to be, the challenges to being *lifelong* lovers are daunting—creating a lasting physical, emotional, and spiritual union. And none of us have received an owner's manual. That's the bad news.

However, there is good news: it's never too late to learn! And *Lovers for Life* may be just the owner's manual you desire. It provides a framework for both understanding what it takes to create a lasting, passionate, and loving relationship and turning that understanding into palpable form. Practical tools are included at every stage of the journey.

If you want to improve your intimate relationship—both the sexual and non-sexual aspects—you must make it an area of exploration and study. Difficulties in any part of your relationship will not be resolved by ignoring or denying the challenges. However, if you address and deal with the issues directly—despite potential pain—you stand an excellent chance of overcoming obstacles and experiencing the pleasure you deserve.

We believe that the surest way to move through lover's obstacles and to develop empowering relationships is through a four-step process:

1. *Become aware of and acknowledge the challenge or problem area.*

2. *Set your intention on creating what you want.*

3. *Apply a powerful strategy.*

4. *Follow through with a high level of commitment.*

*Lovers for Life* provides guidance in this process.

## Choose Your Teachers Well

If you wanted to learn how to build an exciting, long-term relationship, you would not survey people who have been divorced five times and still have not created a fulfilling relationship—or people who remain in an unhappy, long-term marriage. You would seek out people who are already happy—both in and out of bed. And that's precisely what we have done.

We have interviewed many happily-in-love, erotically fulfilled couples, hoping to inspire you to manifest your dream. These are not Hollywood, other-worldly versions of the perfect lover relationships. They are real people who have created satisfying and fulfilling lover relationships. Sometimes they have had to get down in the trenches where the action is—and where the rewards lay waiting. They have learned to pick roses through the thorns. You may find the myriad of challenges faced by these couples mirrored in your own life—and that many of the solutions that worked for them will work for you.

We have also gleaned wisdom from the teachings of many relationship pioneers—from experts in the fields of human relationships, sex therapy, communications theory, the psychology of gender and family therapy, to name a few. In addition, we bring our combined forty years of counseling people to the table.

The book is filled with exercises that are designed to help you develop your ability to be intimate—emotionally, physically, and spiritually—with yourself and with your partner. Although it will be extraordinarily helpful to do the exercises, you can still receive tremendous value just by reading the book. You need not believe everything we say. If you are open to exploring, experimenting, and practicing, we guarantee that you will learn useful things. We trust that you will experience how the physical, emotional, and spiritual dance of relationships is blended together in *Lovers for Life*.

Though the terrain can be rugged at times, we know that your journey can also be fun and enjoyable. *Lovers for Life* will support you in bursting through the bonds of convention to express your deepest desires, and in living a life full of wildness, passion, and creativity.

# Why Another Book on Relationships and Sexuality?

Books abound about love—and sex, and many of them are excellent guides to creating more satisfying relationships. However, the vast majority of books on personal growth and relationships do not address the sexual arena in great depth, and books on sexuality often leave the essential emotional and psychological aspects to relationship experts.

*Lovers for Life* weaves together the emotional, physical, and spiritual strands of relationship—all essential to keeping passion and eros alive in a long-term lover relationship. We have developed a powerful *program* that works over time. As much as *Lovers for Life* is about improving your sexual relationship, it is also about putting love into every aspect of your life. It unites the best of both worlds, bringing sacredness to the bedroom and sensuality to everyday life.

*Lovers for Life* addresses sexual technique, tantric practices, interpersonal communication, *the origin of sexual shame,* healing sexual shame, conflict resolution, and much more. It can help you communicate more effectively with your partner and turn a monotonous relationship into a sizzling theatre of love.

But, perhaps more importantly, *Lovers for Life* is about Lovers—how to open to the Lover within yourself and how to unite with your beloved.

Being a Lover involves far more than the act of physical sex. It includes eye contact, touch, words, sounds, emotional expression, even handling life's practical concerns. Lovers make love on all levels—physically, emotionally, and spiritually. Ultimately, they learn to be in love with life itself.

# Linking in Love

A deeply nurturing and fulfilling union is an egalitarian one. Though many people believe that egalitarian means that couples play identical roles, it actually means that both people are treated as full, equal partners. When one partner dominates and the other submits, or when partners alternate between dominating and submitting, the intimacy people long for can never be experienced. Nor can the ecstatic sexuality intrinsic to our physical, emotional, and spiritual make-up be fully realized.

In non-egalitarian relationships, one person's sexual or non-sexual desires are considered more important than the other's. Consequently, one person will subjugate herself or himself for the sake of satisfying a partner. However, it never works. People who are dominated feel resentful eventually. And they often express their resentment passive-aggressively.

On the other side, it's not exactly a bed of roses being the dominator either. The pressure to always be in control becomes very draining. Studies have shown that men who feel unpressured to dominate, who feel loved and loving, actually live longer. *Lovers for Life* takes on a another meaning here. By shifting out of the dominator model, you will be taking serious steps toward improving your overall health.

Please don't be misled and imagine yourself immune from this dominator model. It affects everyone. The top dog/under dog relationship filters through our entire culture, influencing our behavior from bedroom to boardroom. It turns the potential of being lovers for life into one disappointment after another. It teaches us to deal with conflict—an inevitable aspect of any relationship, including our relationship with ourselves—by either blaming and fighting (dominating) or withdrawing and resigning (submitting).

In the dominator paradigm, conflicts are never fully resolved and relationships never live up to their potential. This leads to resentment between the sexes and inevitable discontent. When we are not satisfied, we begin to treat each other badly. Unable to resolve the conflicts, we treat each other with covert or overt hostility. Though we might not label it as such, most of us experience some degree of abuse in our relationships. We simply have not learned how to treat each other well.

As a culture, we are now beginning to deal with the most obvious manifestations of this abuse: domestic violence. However, we are just in the infancy stage of dealing with domestic violence; it remains below the threshold of public awareness until a dramatic eruption such as the O. J. Simpson case. Domestic violence reveals on a grosser, less common level what exists in many homes—the rampant incidence of verbal and emotional violence.

Fortunately, there's an alternative—the partnership model. In this relationship framework, couples share power through "linking." Both partners care about the other's welfare as they do about their own. They make decisions based on the common good as well as the good of each person. In other words, they are a team in the finest sense. That's the foundation for being lifelong partners.

The entire program underlying *Lovers for Life*, reflects the partnership or linking model. It explores how, paradoxically, power emerges when couples are willing to be vulnerable with each other—to express their deepest hopes, dreams, and fears. To be lovers for life, we must practice this sacred art of vulnerability. It is an art that we will support you in practicing throughout *Lovers for Life*.

Practicing the art of vulnerability is also political work. As we create more conscious, loving relationships, we make the world a better and safer place to live in for our children. As more and more people practice this fine art, we will have less need to foster personal defenses. As the word spreads and people around the world practice and live by the principles described here, nations will have less need to act defensively. Perhaps, we will re-evaluate our need, or perceived need for massive defense spending. Then, no longer feeling the need to defend ourselves, we and all the nations of the world could practice vulnerability. If we as a people do not begin moving in this direction, our chances for planetary survival will be compromised. We know this may sound like naive or wishful thinking, but we believe that if we are not part of the solution, we are part of the problem.

## Leaving the Comfort Zone

To create a great relation-*ship* rather than a relation-*raft*, you must be willing to expand your familiar comfort zone—including your time-tested ways of handling difficult situations. You must practice new ways of being.

We will ask you to question aspects of yourself that perhaps you have never considered. Risks are involved. If it is telling your husband about how you really feel about him sexually, or voicing the erotic fantasies you have never shared, risks are involved. Of course, you choose your level of participation. However, the more willingness you harness, the more value you will likely receive.

Sure, we can make suggestions and even inspire you. However, you must make choices. You must take action to implement some of the strategies we suggest. And to do this, again, you must risk. What stops people from being willing to try new possibilities? The answer is FEAR (False Evidence Appearing Real). Please, don't let your fear stop you from getting what you most want.

When you think about it, life is a risk. Anything can happen—and often does. As the Buddhists say, "All life is change." So there is no true security in holding on—the train of life is always moving.

The question is, how can you find a path through the thick forest, traverse the mountain that lies ahead, or flow with the river? Certainly, you must have your eyes open. It is helpful to pay attention and listen, to utilize all of your senses. Or to seek advice from people who have been there before.

That is what good teachers and coaches really do. They present a possibility—if you take this path and consider some tried and true options, then you, too, can find your way. We hope to be teachers that help you find your own way—not our way.

We would like to introduce ourselves to you in a round about way through a true story about Mahatma Gandhi.

## Practice What You Preach

A worried mother once brought her twelve-year-old son to Mahatma Gandhi for help. She was desperate. Her son was addicted to sweets. He was eating so much candy that it was threatening not only his teeth but his overall health. She implored Gandhi to help her son stop.

Gandhi told her, "Bring him back in three weeks." She was perplexed, but she did not question Gandhi's authority. When three weeks had passed, she returned with her son.

Gandhi looked the boy in the eye. Firmly and loudly he commanded: "Stop eating sugar!"

It jolted the boy. From the look on her son's face, the mother felt sure he would heed the master's words.

After thanking Gandhi, the woman said, "I have only one question. Why didn't you tell my son to stop eating sugar when I brought him to you three weeks ago?"

Gandhi answered, "First, *I* had to stop."

If someone had offered us the opportunity to write this book some years ago, we would have told them to contact us at a future date. Though our relationship was strong, our sex life was lousy. We were hardly candidates to help others with their erotic behavior. We first had to practice before we could preach.

Saying that we wanted our own sex life to improve is an understatement. We were fiercely determined. We were unswerving in our intention and commitment to creating a fabulous erotic relationship. If you have ever watched children learn how to crawl, then walk, then run, you know how dauntless they are in their pursuit of mastery. That's how we were.

In addition to commitment, it took time, energy, sensitivity, ruthless honesty, and a sense of humor to create the sexually satisfying relationship we knew was possible. We have come a long way and the results continue to affirm our sweetest dreams.

As we achieved breakthroughs, we used our new knowledge with many of our counseling clients. And it worked—often dramatically. And so, having gone through the process—starting from the depths and reaching the heights—we finally felt we could write this book.

Sometimes it has been embarrassing, sometimes awkward, and sometimes frightening to reveal our own story. However, we have done it with hopes that by reading about our journey, you will discover the inspiration, courage, and tools to create magic in your own love relationship.

## Your Intention

How about you? What brings you to *Lovers for Life?* Perhaps you have picked up this book because your relationship is good but it lacks the passion you desire. Or you find yourself in serial relationships that are passionate but lack stability or permanence. You may desire a monogamous relationship but find yourself and/or your partner having affairs. Or perhaps you have picked up this book in amusement having years ago decided that being deeply satisfied in a lifelong relationship reflects the remnant of youthful romanticism. Yet still a part of you longs—and hopes—that you were wrong. The part of you that remains open to this possibility is precisely the part we want to address. Your dream can be realized! We will show you how.

Great relationships are like great works of art. They may look fantastic in public, but they can be extremely messy during the creative process. Yet the mess is necessary—it's part of the creative process. If you choose to avoid the mess, you may have a clean palate, but your canvas will be empty.

No mess, no passion. No risk, no joy. If you choose to avoid the mess, you will certainly control your fate: You will not create what you most desire!

The will to succeed urges us to shape the mess into a powerful work of art; it also urges us to shape our love relationship into a thing of beauty and fulfillment. This takes patience, commitment, knowledge, and the courage to openly express our feelings. But, when all is said and done, the rewards for our efforts are majestic beyond our wildest dreams.

Who can benefit from this book? Anyone who has a sincere interest in experiencing deep bliss and intimacy with one partner; anyone who is tired of playing a narrow, limited sexual role and truly wants to be himself or herself—in and out of bed; anyone who is tired of living in the extremes of repression or pornography; and anyone who wants to have more excitement, passion, intimacy, and just plain old fun in his or her love life.

Throughout this book, we extol the joys and advantages we and others have found in being monogamous. In Chapters 2 and 3, we present a blueprint for using your relationship as a spiritual path—through emotional and physical intimacy. Chapters 4 and 5 show how sexual shame develops and erodes intimacy. Chapter 6 focuses on common challenges between the sexes—and offers some potential solutions. Chapters 7 through 10 addresses new ways to experience greater emotional health and spiritual recovery. We describe ways in which partners can support each other in becoming more aware, and in resolving deeply held beliefs and feelings of shame and guilt—thereby opening themselves to heightened pleasure, passion, and intimacy. Chapters 11 through 14 provide a framework for changing limiting patterns, resolving difficulties, and using potent strategies to juice up your love life. In Chapter 15, you will find twenty-four principles of erotic mastery. After each principle, we provide a reference guide to every exercise in the book related to that principle.

Although we, the authors, are a heterosexual couple, we designed this book so that it applies to people in all stages or forms of relationship. This includes new and seasoned couples, as well as heterosexual or homosexual singles. Though we have used the term *partner* or *beloved* throughout the book to refer to your significant other, in many exercises we address "the man" or "the woman," assuming that most of our readers are in heterosexual relationships. We hope that our readers in homosexual relationships will bear with us. However, regardless of whether you have a heterosexual or homosexual orientation, *Lovers for Life* is designed to help you create a more intimate, passionate, and alive relationship.

# Out of the Pits

*I have come to tell you this and to thank you because you are so beautiful. And if it does not displease you, Kamala, I would like to ask you to become my friend and teacher, for I do not know anything of the art of which you are mistress.*

Hermann Hesse, *Siddhartha*

## Her Story

Lying in bed next to him, she felt like a chair—a piece of furniture being moved about for his convenience. He turned her body slightly to get a better angle. With fumbling hands, he stimulated her clitoris and palpated her breasts. She wondered if he had ever been with a woman before. How could he be so artless? Hadn't anyone ever told him what a woman likes?

"Are you enjoying it?" he asked. Why didn't she feel relieved or flattered that he was asking her that? The words seemed to imply that he cared about the quality of her experience. Yet, the queasy feeling in her stomach suggested otherwise. As he continued his clumsy attempts to arouse her, the thought crossed her mind that he was interested only in himself.

But if that were the case, wouldn't he just mount her and seek his own orgasm as quickly as possible? Did he really care about her pleasure, or did he want her to climax simply to prove he could do it?

Again he moved her body, and again she felt like a piece of furniture. She searched herself for what might be missing? For one thing, there was no tenderness, no love coming through his hands. She asked him if he would stimulate her orally, hoping that his tongue would feel more gentle than his intrusive fingers.

He obliged, but to no avail. Usually, when she was aroused, her vagina would be wet and pulsating. Now, it felt as dry and insensitive as cardboard.

The thought came to her again that he was just going through the motions of trying to please her. She had rarely doubted a man's intention or motivation. With many of her past lovers there had been an unspoken agreement to have mutual pleasure—"I love you or at least lust for you, and I enjoy giving you pleasure." Plain and simple. With this man, though, a thought kept nagging her: he was interested only in his own pleasure.

She was usually an active, generous lover. She enjoyed being aggressive and taking the initiative just as much as she enjoyed being receptive, tender, and surrendered. When a man who was experienced and sure of himself took her in his arms, she became like putty. Then the ecstasy of that total surrender transformed her into a passionate, wild beast.

Now, her first time with this new man, she suddenly felt stingy. Certainly, she had felt this previously with some other men. At other times in her life she might have tried to be generous in an attempt to show him how exquisite the act of love could be, to give him an experience that he might never have had. But not this time. Why perform a symphony of lovemaking? Her intuition warned her that such music would fall on deaf ears.

She was disappointed. She had had such high expectations. He seemed so comfortable with feelings and so emotionally available. Earlier, before they were sexual, looking deeply into her eyes, he shared intimate details about himself. He was eager to find out about her. He was attentive and caring. He was funny and intelligent. He was a fiery man and he was sexy. She liked all these qualities. She felt both comfortable and excited with him. He was an enigma. How could such a great guy be such a lousy lover?

With other men in her past, she had had sexual encounters that were disappointing, but none of these were as unexpected. The other men had not been as interested or adept in communicating their feelings. Maybe he was unusually anxious or scared this night or perhaps there was some other reason for his behavior. She hoped so.

The next morning, while sharing a bath, she gently probed, trying to elicit his own feelings about their sexual encounter. His responses confirmed her fear. For him, apparently, this was a typical night of lovemaking.

It disturbed her that this sensitive, caring, passionate man knew so little about the art of lovemaking. Even more troubling than that was how he had treated her like an object. Why was this so? And what should she do about it? She was interested in this man, but she had to bring the matter of their unsatisfactory sexual encounter into the open and resolve it—before she got more deeply involved.

Not certain of how to broach the subject, she decided to wait and think about it until they saw each other again. They parted ways with a promise to see each other in a few days.

## What Are Her Options?

Let's step out of the story for a moment. Perhaps you are thinking that she should get out now before she becomes emotionally entangled—that resolving this kind of problem is improbable, if not impossible. If she cannot accept him as he is, she should leave him alone and find someone with whom sex is natural and fulfilling. But if she still wants to give it a chance, what are her options?

Let's consider the possibility of her talking to him about what she is feeling and perceiving. If she feels angry at him and blames him for not being more sensitive to her, it is likely that he will become defensive. If she uses guilt to manipulate him into being more considerate of her, it may work for the moment. However, because he did not make the decision consciously on his own, the change will not be long-lived. Such covert attempts to change others inevitably backfire. Most people intuitively sense the difference between support and manipulation. Eventually, the targeted person feels unappreciated, unaccepted, controlled—and resentful.

Suppose she tells him honestly what she experienced and how she felt that night, leaving out any analysis or interpretation of his behavior? You might believe that this is impossible. How could she tell him how she feels without blaming him? His feelings will be hurt. He will never forgive her. She will spoil all chances of having a relationship with him. Perhaps, but if she isn't honest with him, how else will she find out whether or not he wants to become a more emotionally connected and skillful lover?

# Contemplating Her Challenge

She thought about him a lot during the next two days. She was impressed with how honest and open he was. When they had looked deeply into each other's eyes, she felt as if she were seeing his soul. How could a man whose eyes showed so much love and tenderness, such depth and empathy, be so egocentric and disconnected? Something did not make sense. She knew he was an unusual man. He was able to communicate clearly and easily. He seemed very self-aware. It was obvious to her that he had done a tremendous amount of work on himself. In fact, he had already told her the numerous ways in which he had consciously changed his behavior and attitudes because he had not been content with himself.

But what about his sexual beliefs, attitudes, and behavior? She knew what it was like to try to change a man covertly. Years before, she had tried that—and had failed miserably. She knew that *she* could not change his sexual behavior. The more important questions were, could *he* change his sexual behavior? And, would he want to?

It seemed unlikely, since most men have so much ego attached to their sexual prowess. It was now four years since the painful and difficult break-up of a long-term relationship with a man she almost married. Since then, she had been dating—waiting for Mr. Right. She could afford to wait longer—no more false starts.

Sighing, she realized that she had already given up the hope that he could be her romantic partner. Maybe if she just told him the truth about how she felt, he might be able to accept it. She imagined that they could become good friends. Whatever the outcome, she knew she would have to be honest and open with him.

# The Moment of Truth

The doorbell rang. Her heart pounded. Was it excitement or nerves? Probably both. How would he react to her feelings, her perceptions, and her decision not to have a sexual relationship with him?

She opened the door and there he stood. She managed a smile and invited him in. "It's not a farewell party," she told herself. "We may not be destined to be lovers, but he is someone I want to keep as a friend."

Before he had stepped through the doorway, she said, "There's something I want to discuss that is bothering me."

"Sure," he said, his brow wrinkling. "What is it?" They walked to the couch and sat down.

She looked him in the eyes and breathed deeply. As she began to speak, she realized she was not going to win any awards for diplomacy. But that was not as important to her as being able to communicate with integrity, honesty and responsibility, no matter what kind of relationship they ended up having.

He listened as she chronicled their previous misadventure in bed together. Without shame or blame, she described what he did, how she responded, what she said, what he said, and how she felt throughout. She ended by saying that she did not want to be sexual with him.

When she finished, his face was solemn and concerned. "Well," he said, "that was hard for me to hear. But what I'm about to say is even harder for me. I thought I had worked on my sexuality," he continued, "but I guess I've got a long way to go. I can understand why you don't want to have sex with me tonight, after what you've said."

He wasn't defensive. He didn't try to refute anything she had told him. Nor did he try to convince her that her perceptions were wrong. He spoke briefly about his background. He discussed some of his feelings of shame and guilt regarding sex. She was amazed once again at his honesty and openness.

How often in the past had she modified and qualified her feedback for fear of offending a man. Now he confirmed her earlier feelings that he was a man of strong character. She knew that it was difficult for him to hear such critical feedback about himself as a lover. Most men would have become angry, defensive, and rejecting. This man's ego was apparently healthy enough to allow him to hear the truth of her experience without overreacting to her message.

It had not escaped her that he had added the time frame of "tonight" to her prohibition on sex. But they had worked through enough for one night. She chose to let it go, knowing that she could address the matter another time if need be.

They had already planned a camping trip for the coming weekend. He stayed over that night and they slept together—but without having sex. They slept well and awoke in the morning, eager to prepare for their weekend camping trip. They separated with plans to reunite only a few days later for their adventure.

## The Next Moment

The weekend came quickly and they headed out of town. Sitting beside him, she felt close and comfortable, once again being with a man she really liked and respected.

Remembering that he had qualified her exclusion of sex, she thought it prudent to discuss it before they left civilization and thus precluded the possibility of procuring condoms (more suitable for camping than her diaphragm). Though she did not want to sleep with him at this point, she did not want to close the door completely. Maybe—given the right circumstance—she would change her mind.

She took a deep breath. "You know," she said, "since I had decided that I wouldn't be sexual with you, I didn't bring my diaphragm. But I was thinking that maybe we should stop somewhere and buy some condoms—just in case."

He was obviously upset. "What do you mean we're not going to be sexual? When did we decide that?"

Just as she expected. Breathe again, she reminded herself. She recounted their recent conversation and added, "Look, I'm willing to leave it open and see what happens between us, as long as you understand where I'm coming from. I'm not willing to have sex the way we did before. It will have to be totally different."

Now *he* breathed deeply. "Okay," he said cautiously. "I'm willing to leave it at that. But I want you to know that I have every intention of being sexual with you. I never intended to say never!"

Later, in the wilderness, they pitched their tent and made preparations for dinner as the sun was setting. They worked together easily. After they ate, cleaned up the dishes, and bear-proofed their food, they relaxed under the stars. By firelight, in the quiet hush of the Sierra Nevada mountains, they looked into each other's eyes. She had the same feeling she had had before, as though they were looking into each other's souls. They drew closer until their lips touched.

The mood was sweet and sensual, and they began caressing each other. Soon, it stopped feeling good. She took a deep breath and said to herself, "Oh well, here I go."

Then aloud, she said, "I want to talk about what's happening."

"What?" he said, obviously surprised by her sudden interruption.

"I was feeling turned on a minute ago until you started touching me that way. It's as though you're not here with me. I don't sense you in your fingertips. It feels to me that you're not touching me in a way that makes it pleasurable for both of us. It feels like you're just trying to get me aroused, and I feel turned off."

He was silent for a while, his eyes cast downward. Then he looked up at her and said, "You're right. I *was* trying to get you aroused. And I wasn't really with you." There was another period of silence. Then he said, "I'd really like you to help me with this."

She stared at him in the flickering light from the blazing fire. As he returned her gaze, she felt surprised, touched, and pleased at his sincerity. "All right," she said, "let's give it a try."

## A Return to Innocence

For three days in the mountains her body and soul served as his laboratory for a crash course in sex and intimacy. He spent hours exploring her body, examining it carefully—this time with the warmth of a lover. He seemed to be innocence itself. Many times, she reminded him to stop, to come back, to be present. Each time, he did. Without resistance, he allowed himself to be instructed in how to give her pleasure.

Even as he touched her clitoris, she kept reminding him to make sure that what he was doing felt good to him as well, that *he* derived pleasure from his touch. She told him that it was much more stimulating for her when she sensed his presence and felt his caring through his fingertips than when he was focused on her arousal or when he was just taking his own enjoyment.

"It's a strange experience," he said. "I've spent much of my life working at getting women aroused so I could enter them, or so I could feel proud that I had brought them to orgasm. But with you, all I need to do is enjoy myself as I bring pleasure to you—the pressure's off."

She was in heaven. It wasn't the kind of glorious lovemaking that she knew was possible—the fireworks displays that sometimes occur. But something magical was happening nonetheless. Every moment was so real and so honest. There were no pretenses, no games. Even though she was the one leading the way, she felt as vulnerable as he. This was the first time she had ever been so clear, so direct, so unattached to the outcome. She felt totally free to say or do anything.

As a result, her patience, her compassion, and, finally, her love flowed as freely as the juices in her vagina. He felt it, too. And as she held him, he cried. Tears of relief, pain, hope, joy, mixed with the tears of allowing himself to be totally vulnerable. She sat with him, holding him, touching him gently, looking at him tenderly. She breathed deeply, taking him into her.

Who was this man she was beginning to know so intimately? She couldn't get enough of him. It had been a long time since she had been in an emotionally and sexually intimate relationship. Her body and psyche were ready. Time disappeared as they stroked each other. She asked him to look in her eyes as he came. And then again as she came.

The orgasms were not nearly as important as his eyes. He was allowing himself to be in deep contact with her—and she with him. She found herself slipping his glistening penis into her even as they sat and talked, her legs straddling his. She wanted to feel this primal connection with him. They dipped in and out of this deep well of physical pleasure as they peeled back the layers to their intimate selves. They were not merely "having sex." They were making love, woman and man, joined as one.

## His Story

The rural, clothing optional, hot springs resort presented a great opportunity to be a legal Peeping Tom. Although he felt some shame in surveying the unclad women, it wasn't enough to stop him. Suddenly, his eyes caught sight of a woman who really grabbed his attention. She was putting on her dress, which initially stimulated him but then disappointed him as her nudity disappeared. Then, suddenly, she was gone altogether. He wanted to meet her and hoped that she would return.

As fate would have it, later that evening he saw her reflection in the mirror as he entered the co-ed dressing room. She was brushing her teeth with only a towel wrapped around her waist. He had intended to grab a towel and leave—that was, until he laid eyes on her.

He felt a sudden urge to brush his teeth also. At the mirror alongside her, he engaged her in friendly and flirtatious banter. Soon, however, his shyness returned and he bid her good night. Yet her image kept appearing before him long after he left.

Early the next morning he awoke with an erection and an accompanying fantasy. This fantasy was unlike any of his typical male fantasies. In this fantasy he was experiencing deep intimacy while making love with this mystery woman. Their eyes and souls were dancing together.

He encountered her shortly afterwards in the hot tubs. Not being the most subtle of men, he quickly told her of his fantasy. She responded, "I'm a very open person, but that's a little fast for me." He smiled at her but wondered inwardly if he had been too forward. Their awkwardness passed, however, as they spent hours together—sharing thoughts and feelings on the deepest level. Intimacy and lust led to mutual arousal. However, his old fear raised its head even as they walked toward her bedroom. She was an intense and passionate woman. Would he be able to satisfy her?

The fear wasn't the worst of it. Women's bodies, however beautiful and desirable, often evoked strange feelings of ambivalence in him. He wanted to be sexual with women, but he also felt ashamed of this desire. Sometimes, when a woman noticed him looking at her lustfully, he turned away quickly, as if caught with his hands in the cookie jar. Although he had acted on his desires time and time again—keeping his shyness at bay—he rarely felt altogether comfortable about the erotic dance.

When it came to the act of lovemaking itself, he always felt a strange sense that there was something wrong with sex—and consequently something wrong with both him and the woman for wanting it. Now, with this new woman, those feelings were re-surfacing. And by the time they were in bed, there was only a glimpse of the emotional intimacy he had previously experienced with her. It was elusive, and quickly gave way to the anonymous sex with which he was familiar.

However, after their sexual encounter, they spent the next ten hours sharing their hopes, dreams, and fears. The feelings of intimacy returned. They decided to go camping together the following week. He certainly couldn't imagine what lay ahead.

On leaving the resort, they made plans to see each other the following evening at his house. They had sex several times that evening and the next morning; however, he felt disconnected from the whole experience. Well, he rationalized, intimacy comes from talking, not sex.

When she left his house that morning, he felt somewhat relieved to say good-bye. He sensed that something wasn't quite right, but couldn't put his finger on it. They were to see each other mid-week, then go camping on the weekend. While he thought of her often as the days passed, he felt both excitement and fear.

Wednesday evening finally came. He arrived at her door and rang the bell. His heart was pounding from both excitement and nervousness. She opened the door and there she stood, inviting him in. Before he had crossed the threshold, she informed him in a serious tone that she had something on her mind that she wanted to discuss. He sensed that she was not altogether pleased to see him.

"Sure," he said, as his heart dropped. "What is it?"

## Hearing the Truth

What followed was the most difficult, wrenching feedback he had ever heard in his life. With a directness that surprised and scared him, she described how he had touched her, how she had responded, what she said, what he said, and how she felt throughout their previous sexual encounters. He felt distraught. All along he had assumed that their sexual experience together, while not phenomenal, was also not abysmal. Now, it was a real shock to hear her side of the story.

It took him several minutes to compose himself. "Well," he said, "that was hard for me to hear. I can understand why you don't want to have sex with me tonight after what you've said."

He wasn't defensive. He didn't try to refute anything she had told him. He felt very trusting of her and spoke vulnerably, describing his background, particularly his feelings of shame and guilt regarding sex. He told her about the negative messages he received about sexuality—how nice girls and boys were not sexual, how penises and vaginas should be hidden.

Although he consciously rejected this shame-based sexual education, he nonetheless felt influenced by these archaic teachings. Therefore, when he touched a woman's vagina, strange feelings of dis-ease came over his body. When that occurred, he started thinking too much, losing touch with his body, and trying to figure out how to arouse the woman he was with. It didn't work very well!

He admitted that even though he had had many sexual encounters, he did not really know very much about being a good lover. He hoped that his ability to bring women to orgasm was proof of his competence. He told her, "I thought that either you have it (the qualities of being a great lover) or you don't—that there isn't much you can learn that will really make a difference." But as their conversation continued, he revealed that the reason he never asked, and never talked to a woman about what she wanted, was due to sexual shame.

He was being excruciatingly honest. He knew that this was a woman who was not just pretending to want truthfulness. She could really handle it. He saw it as an opportunity to get some of these difficult thoughts and feelings off his chest. Also, he was interested in her—more than any women he had ever met. If anything more were going to happen between them, he knew that he must tell the truth. "Rather than admitting that I didn't know how to arouse a woman consistently, I pretended that I was confident and competent. And no one really gave me direct feedback."

## Nocturnal Navigation

This man had grown in many personal areas, yet he had neglected his sexual development. Because he felt shame about it, he kept it as hidden as possible. Since sex is something most people do not discuss with others, it was easy to conceal.

But not with her. He had been with many women before her, but he had rarely received outright criticism. Had they really been pleased or were they simply afraid to voice their dissatisfaction? He hoped for the former; she suspected the latter.

She became an unceasing nocturnal commentator. He was constantly challenged with comments like:

"Please pay attention."

"If you follow the natural movements of my body, you won't have to try so hard."

"Don't get so caught up in what you think you should be doing. Simply let yourself be present."

"Just enjoy yourself without trying to bring me to orgasm."

"Where are you now? You don't seem to be here."

"I want you to hold me less tentatively, like you mean it."

"Are you enjoying yourself now? Your touch feels mechanical to me."

He wasn't thrilled to receive these low ratings. Many men would not have tolerated the type and amount of negative feedback she presented. Many times he felt hurt and angry. He blamed her. He called her a perfectionist and told her she would never be satisfied. He tried to hide his hurt and pain.

Despite his occasional defensiveness, he really listened. Because he was committed to changing, he abandoned his self-righteousness.

## Devouring Illusions

For him, she was like the goddess Kali, a Hindu deity who devours illusions. She was demanding, yet patient; compassionate, yet not co-dependent. She never faked orgasms or pretended pleasure when there was none. She did not stroke his male ego with sweet lies. There were many times when he wished she had! She accepted his woundedness, yet did not coddle him.

He was facing one of a man's greatest fears—being unable to satisfy his lover sexually. However, despite his fear, sadness, and anger, he had a quality that is absolutely essential for anyone who really wants to change: the willingness to learn.

Over time, he started letting go of his shoulds, coulds, and musts. He began allowing himself *not* to know what came next in the lover's dance. In Zen Buddhism, this is called Beginner's Mind. Like a child learning about the world anew, he explored her body with tactile innocence. He felt less and less tentative and afraid of making mistakes. Every missed connection became an opportunity to learn something new.

He no longer needed to be a Don Juan or Warren Beatty. She taught him a vital lesson: If he were truly enjoying himself and not being goal-oriented, then she would also enjoy herself. In fact, it was only then that she would become aroused.

The results were miraculous! Being open and present in the moment and feeling deep pleasure himself, paradoxically, was the path to pleasuring her. Her feedback to him inspired his higher self. Once, he said to her, "I would never have allowed myself to be so vulnerable if I had not felt so safe in your love. That's what has allowed me to open up."

## Happily Ever After

They took the high road together. Instead of being adversaries—trapped in questions of right or wrong—they became allies. Rather than blaming each other, they continually communicated about the challenges they faced. Then, together, they tried to find a solution. They became explorers, students—and partners.

They became engaged several months later. Within a year they were married. The development of their sexual intimacy blossomed. There were setbacks, moments of difficulty, resentment. There were times of bitterness and pain. But, through their love and commitment, they worked through them. She was able to give him the space to work through his fears about his sexual performance, his fears of failure, his fears of not knowing what to do. He, in turn, earned her complete trust, which allowed her also to be vulnerable.

Today, they consider each other fabulous lovers. Together, they enjoy both the firework displays and the subtler joys of sexual intimacy. Because they know that they will both experience sexual satisfaction and emotional closeness in their sexual encounters when difficulties do arise in their erotic relationship, they know how to work through them. What wonderful transformations they have gone through!

They continue to improve their sexual relationship. To support their desire and commitment, they take courses, read books, and practice. They talk about it with each other. They have fun when they make love. They laugh, play—anything goes. They no longer get into bed, dreading that something might go wrong. Their painful encounters are past history, as well as their fear.

# Who Are They?

Are these stories about our clients, friends, or relatives? No. These are our own stories—Judith's and Daniel's. By sincerely dealing with our sexual challenges, we were able to transform the most painful, problematic area in our relationship. In fact, if we had not taken this journey, we would not be together today.

Though our story might make it seem easy, it took a lot of conscious work on both of our parts. The rewards often did not appear as quickly as we desired. Although we had moments of bliss early on, the major changes took place over several years. But when they did materialize, they were magnificent. We trust that you will find the same.

Previously, when I (Daniel) sensed that Judith was not aroused, I tried harder—just lubricate the machine. As you learned in our stories, she didn't respond too well to these maneuvers. Understandably, she didn't like being touched as if she were an object. It's amazing to me now that I used to wonder why she didn't respond. I actually resented her (and past women) for making "my job" so difficult.

It's astounding how different my sexual experience is now. I know how to be present—at least, far more than I did previously. So when Judith has not even begun to consider sex, I know that I can touch her in a way that at least will bring pleasure to me. My pleasure is no longer predicated on getting the appropriate response from her. And generally, my being present and unattached to results, allows the sparks to ignite—and that excites Judith.

We have a ritual that we call "workshop sex." We learned this from Stan Dale, a wonderful man, friend, and the creator of Love, Sex and Intimacy workshops. In workshop sex, we let go of all goals. We lie together simply feeling close. If our touching leads to passionate embraces—fine. If it stays with tender cuddles—fine. If I get turned on and Judith does not—fine. I can always masturbate, with or without her help.

We wanted to tell our personal story, because we want you to know that no matter what you experience in the way of sexual and emotional intimacy, you are capable of improving it—perhaps more than you even imagine! We also want you to know that we, like you, are walking our own paths. We are not distant experts who have not faced challenges of our own. Perhaps, like good mountain climbing guides, we can point out some easier paths along the way. We can also suggest some stunning views.

# The Challenges of Love

Our greatest difficulties happened to have been sexual. That may not be the case for you. Perhaps, sexuality flows with relative ease, but there are thorny communication blocks that stop your love in its track. During these tense times, you or your partner may withdraw or lash out.

In *Lovers for Life,* we will explore the multiple challenges to lifelong love. We will suggest ways of transforming obstacles to intimacy and passion in any aspect of your relationship—including the basics of resolving communication problems.

We hope you will recognize the value of being truthful about your own personal challenges. This book will provide you with ample opportunities to express feelings and concerns you have never voiced before—not for the purpose of lamenting or apologizing, but for the purpose of creating successful, satisfying relationships. By practicing truthfulness and vulnerability, you will be amazed at how much easier and fulfilling your relationship will become.

Together, we will explore what it takes to create a lover relationship that is rich, fulfilling, and pleasurable beyond your wildest dreams. You *can* live your fantasies. That's part of what a healthy lover relationship is all about. We are committed to providing you with the necessary tools for turning potential love into enduring love.

In the next section, we explore ways of sanctifying your relationship by opening up to the spiritual nature of being lovers, and how to develop yourself as a lifetime lover.

*2*

# Eros Unveiled

*Greek philosophers considered eros the prime mover, the motivating principle in all things human and non-human. It was the impulse that made all things yearn and strive for fulfillment. The acorn was erotically moved by its destiny to become an oak. When we limit 'erotic' to its sexual meaning, we betray our alienation to the rest of nature.*

Sam Keen, *The Passionate Life*

## Eros: Lost and Found

Roger and Sally began dating during their junior year in college. She was a virgin even though she had read both popular and clinical books on sexuality. He had experienced intercourse—first with a prostitute and then with two college women—before he met Sally.

They felt an immediate attraction when they met each other. They soon started dating. Almost from the start, they began to date exclusively, but their sex life was limited to heavy petting. In their senior year, during the winter holiday, Sally was finally ready to take the big plunge with Roger. On New Year's Eve she invited him to her apartment, and before the old year was out, they were in bed together.

Sally was nervous at first, but she found lovemaking enjoyable, even though she did not reach orgasm. By the time she moved in with Roger in the early spring, she was having orgasms almost every time they made love. They married one month after graduation.

For the first two years of their marriage they were happy with each other. They had an active sex life, with intercourse three or four times a week. A few times Roger brought home X-rated videos for the VCR, but they both felt the graphic depiction of sex was too dehumanizing.

During their third year of marriage, they began to argue over minor things—whose turn it was to take out the trash, who forgot what appointment. When such petty problems came up earlier in their marriage, they would discuss the issues and work them out. But it reached the point where the issues were not getting resolved. It was never clear to Roger and Sally who started the arguments, although each one believed that it was the *other* person.

However, both of them became equally embroiled and bogged down. Typically, as the argument developed, Roger felt that Sally was acting aloof or sulky. He reacted by withdrawing. That annoyed Sally, and she would put on what Roger called her "Miss Priss Face." He then withdrew even more, prompting her to pick on him about things that happened in the past. Eventually, the arguments would turn into angry shouting matches.

Occasionally, Roger stormed out of the house and drove around until he calmed down. When he returned, there were often periods of icy silence that lasted several days. When they made up, which they did for the most part, they apologized and usually ended up in bed, making love.

On one occasion, Sally packed a bag and went home to her parents. She stayed there for two days. When she returned, they were both contrite. As usual, they made up, vowing it would never happen again.

But it did.

Finally, as the arguments grew more heated, and the intervals between them grew shorter, they decided to seek counseling.

In their very first session, Sally dropped a bombshell: She was bored and unhappy with their sex life. Roger felt sad and hurt but responded only with anger and outrage. "How come you never told me before? It couldn't be *that* bad!" It took most of that session for Sally to acknowledge that she was clueless about how to make their sexual relationship better and about how to deal with her feelings of guilt, shame, and despair. By the end of the first session, Roger was ready to drop his defenses and work on figuring out why Sally was so unhappy.

Relieved that Roger was ready to hear her, she said, "It's always the same. It's totally predictable. We do this, then that, then you come, then I come. I'm bored. Every time I suggest that we take our time or try something different, you react negatively. There are no surprises or real intimacy."

Roger again reacted defensively. "You're blaming me. It sounds as if you're perfect and I'm messed up!" We worked with Roger to find the part of him that was afraid and that even sometimes believed that he *was* messed up. Once he became aware of and acknowledged that hidden fear, he could hear and feel assured that Sally was not assigning blame but was truly interested in improving their sex life. Then he could also acknowledge that their sex was repetitious and unexciting. He had thought that that was normal. Unlike Sally, he had just assumed that sex lost its luster after years of marriage.

We gave them homework to do on their own. Each of them was to take their "arousal temperature"[1] several times a day for the next week. A score of zero meant, "No way," while ten was, "Hot to trot." They were to note where they fell on the scale of zero to ten, as well as what sensations they noticed.

One week later, they returned to therapy pleased and excited. Each of them had been surprised by the experience. Much to her amazement, Sally found herself aroused at seven one morning, while sitting at an outdoor café, drinking coffee, feeling the warm breeze on her skin, and watching people go by. Roger was baffled but pleased. While driving through the mountains enjoying the magnificent scenery and listening to a favorite vocalist, he took his arousal temperature and came up with a six. He had expected it to be zero.

They both realized that their sexual arousal was a stimulus much more elusive than they imagined. They were intrigued. They experimented together, gathering information about what created the erotic element in their relationship.

They reintroduced themselves to some simple things. They went swimming together in a cool mountain lake; then lay beside each other, bathed by the rays of the sun. On a spur of the moment picnic, they watched a family of chipmunks playing a riotous version of leapfrog. And once, in their backyard, a butterfly alighted on Roger's hand. They both remained perfectly still and silent, observing it for several minutes. They watched it slowly open and close its wings. It seemed as if the butterfly was speaking to them, saying "I am life—come join me." Then, suddenly, it flew away.

Their lovemaking was equally affected. Using the same attitude with which they were exploring their world, they began to explore each other's body. They took turns taking the lead, creating environments or situations that they found arousing. They went to a drive-in movie and ended up making love in the back seat of their car. On one occasion they made love on and off for hours without having intercourse.

Roger and Sally's love for each other could not help but be revitalized by their renewed love, appreciation of nature, and willingness to risk being spontaneous. They began in search of satisfying sex, but instead they found eros.

## Snapshots of Erotic Marriage

What does it take to become lovers for life? What does it mean to have a truly erotic marriage? Does your lovemaking need to reach a feverish pitch or cataclysmic heights every night? Do you have to feel turned on to each other all the time? Is sex the most significant part of an erotic relationship? What is the relationship between sex and eros?

When we look at couples we have worked with, interviewed, or known as friends or colleagues, we notice common features in those couples who truly have an erotic union: intimacy, sexuality, and playfulness are woven into the entire fabric of their relationship.

They are not necessarily "having sex" all the time, but nonetheless the erotic element is always there. And when the erotic element goes dormant, they consciously work on restoring it. Rather than taking each other for granted, they explore ways to make their relationship sweeter, more loving, and more exciting.

For most of the couples who have that erotic juice, there is a sizzling aspect to their sexuality. It might not always be in the forefront, but it's there nonetheless. It is part of the glue that holds them together. Sex is viewed as a healthy, enjoyable aspect of their relationship, and it usually has many faces—romantic, loving, lusty, primal, tender. It varies with mood, atmosphere, time, and level of desire.

For some of these couples, sex occasionally takes a back seat. During these times, they are very affectionate, loving, and tender—yet there is still sexual energy between them. They share a relationship that always has a feeling of eros. It isn't always sizzling, but it is sweetly erotic.

Eros is inextricable from life itself. It's part of the feeling that people have when they wake up in the morning, when they kiss each other hello and good-bye, or when they exchange a kiss while walking past each other in the kitchen. There's a vibrancy and aliveness in the silent looks that pass between the people in these couples.

Although these couples tend to be monogamous, there is still permission to flirt with other people. There's an easy acceptance and honoring of their sexual nature. There is also permission and encouragement to feel deep love and intimacy with others. The relationship exists as a haven, not an island or prison.

What separates these erotic couples from most other couples? They allow the current of life to run through them without letting fears and judgments limit their experience of themselves and each other. And when fears and judgments arise—as they inevitably do—they are willing and committed to resolving conflicts, rather than sweeping them under the rug.

Mutual pleasure emerges as a primary value among these erotic couples. The bottom line is— if it's not hurting anyone else, and it's exciting and pleasurable (even though your parents and religion may have warned against it), why not? There is a willingness to experiment, to innocently engage in new possibilities without the burden of performance anxiety.

# Where and What Is Eros?

Many couples feel the absence of something crucial in their relationship. The missing link is often amorphous and indefinable, just as it was for Roger and Sally. Yet when the erotic element is present, problems become challenges rather than nightmares.

The presence of eros cannot and should not be assumed. It must be cultivated consciously. Few of us have had a positive education in allowing eros to inform and guide us as lovers. Opening the door to eros allows the mystery of life to enter and permeate a relationship. We are all capable of far more love and passion than we currently experience.

Eros is the passionate desire to unite with the world. Eros connects us to our bodies, our souls, each other, and a higher purpose. Eros lives where the stone meets the earth, where the river meets the ocean, and where lovers gaze into each others' eyes. Imagine how much more fulfilling all of your relationships will be when you embrace your erotic nature more fully!

Embracing our erotic nature impels us toward wholeness or completion. Every erotic stirring contains the blueprint and key to fulfilling our deepest yearnings. A profound inspiration, if pursued, can lead to great discoveries. However, unattended inspirations lead to feelings of emptiness, meaninglessness, and loss.

The craving for sexual union carries the seeds of deep, erotic satisfaction, in which eros is the motivating force. The desire itself is erotic, but because we have lost touch with our erotic roots, we interpret this yearning as purely sexual. Our desire may express itself through a sexual channel, yet the mere release of this tension never fulfills the soul's yearning. If you have had the experience of having an orgasm, followed by a sense of emotional emptiness and loneliness, you know the longing that comes from unfulfilled eros.

When we experience the sacred aspect combined with our physical expression, we can experience the greatest gifts life offers—a connection with the life force itself. We then experience our erotic nature. Without the sacred connection, our pleasure is fleeting.

We all have a natural sense of what eros is. Although the feeling behind the activity is more important than the activity itself, some activities can more naturally give rise to the experience of eros. Here are some examples.

*Cuddling by a fire in a secluded cabin.*

*Sneaking away while the kids are playing and having a quickie in the back room.*

*A tender embrace after a long day of work.*

*A subtle caress during a dinner party.*

*Deep soul to soul eye contact.*

*Luxuriating together in a hot tub or bath.*

*Making love under the stars.*

*Coming in late at night while all is still and making love before falling asleep, nuzzled in each other's arms.*

Have fun with your partner and take turns completing the sentence, "Eros is." You might learn something about each other as well as get ideas for spicing up your relationship.

# The Nature of Eros

Eros has had several different meanings throughout history. In the current vernacular, it has come to be synonymous with sex, although it previously held a more noble, expansive role. In Greek mythology, eros was the life force itself—the personification of creative power and harmony, the source of all life. When the universe was created, eros was the creative force that brought all forms into being.

In other accounts, Eros was the god of love. As the offspring of Aphrodite and Ares, Eros formed a psycho-spiritual synthesis of their radically different energies. This is not coincidental. Aphrodite was the goddess of love, but a love which lived more in the ether above the heavens than on the ground. Psychologically, women and men who exhibit pure Aphrodite qualities have been characterized as "dance away lovers." They express love for many partners but have difficulty committing to one.

Ares was the god of war and aggression. He was known as the most ruthless of gods, willing to enter battle with mindless hostility. Without the mediating influence of more moderate archetypes, a pure Ares bludgeons others with hostility untouched by empathy. But together, Aphrodite and Ares complement each other. Combining the qualities of Aphrodite and Ares, Eros embodies the ability to love fully, responsibly, and passionately.

In modern times eros is often represented insipidly as Cupid, who targets lovers randomly with his arrows. In reality, this does little justice to the essence of eros—who grounds the love of Aphrodite and tempers the aggression of Ares. Grounded love and tempered aggression are vital qualities in any committed, passionate relationship.

Eros manifests the Lover—the lover of the world, of sensuality, of beauty. Eros can be witnessed in the nurturing mother's great feeling of love toward her child, the gardener's feelings of pleasure toward his beautiful flowers, or the artist's awe toward his inspired creation. Their arrows of love have landed on the targets of their affection. Eros expresses the essence of the feminine principle.

Whether you express your erotic nature through art, through work, enjoying nature, or with a lover, eros embraces our ability to love the world in all its magnificence and splendor.

Jeri Marlowe, a San Francisco Bay Area psychotherapist whose specialty is sex therapy, developed the "arousal temperature," a tool for aiding individuals and couples in discovering their erotic nature. Just as Roger and Sally were surprised at what they discovered by taking their arousal temperature, most people find that their arousal is stimulated by a variety of sources. The primary factor is their own inner attitude. They realize that they, ultimately, are the source of their arousal.

## Exercise #1

### *Take Your Arousal Temperature*

Several times during the day, check in with yourself and rate your level of arousal.

Use a scale of zero to ten with zero meaning you are not at all aroused and ten meaning you are at your peak state of arousal.

Keep a log of your experience noting the numeric value of your arousal level and writing a brief description of all that you are aware of, inside and out.

Share your experience with your partner. Talk about what was meaningful for you and what your partner said that was important, surprising, or touching.

# Unleashing Your Inner Lover

Generally, when we hear the word *lover*, we think of another person—our "significant other." Rarely do we consider that perhaps the most essential lover resides within ourselves. In fact, embracing this inner lover holds the key to unlocking our full erotic potential. The inner lover includes our sexuality, yet goes far beyond the boundaries of sex. The lover expresses primal energy through passion, aliveness, vitality, sensuality, and consciousness. Being in touch with our inner lover inevitably helps us create a love affair with life itself.

By developing our inner lover we are also strengthening our ability to love and be loved.

Contrary to modern beliefs and understanding, we never "fall in love." Love exists before the "other" appears. We love another when we experience our own love in that person's presence. Love is evoked from within.

Without a strong relationship to our own inner lover, we attempt to get the outer lover (husband, wife, one night stand, or anything in between) to fill the void. But the outer lover always falls short. No one can ever bring lasting or deep satisfaction to another. It must come from within.

Fixating on the outer lover without a firm relationship to the inner lover can result in co-dependent relationships, or emotionally or physically abusive ones. Our inability to experience our love of life makes us look to our partner or others to fill the emptiness. This willingness to sacrifice ourselves in the hope that we will find love forms the breeding ground for co-dependence and abuse. We then become irate when our partner is unable to provide the fulfillment for which we are searching. Unable to rely on our inner lover, we become abusive rather than face the pain of our own emptiness and longing.

On the other hand, by embracing our inner lover, we naturally inspire other people's love. We cease to merely be attracted to other people's love and begin attracting love to ourselves.

The stronger our relationship is to our inner lover, the more we love life. As we experience our own natural delight with life, we become mirrors for the aliveness in those around us. As they enjoy these qualities in us, they are reminded of their own inner lover.

If we want to keep passion alive for a lifetime, the best strategy is developing and maintaining a vital relationship with our inner lover.

## Exercise #2

### *Sources of Passion*

*Have your partner or a friend read these directions to you as you go through the imagery, or play back a tape recording of yourself reading the directions. Note that the pauses after each step are merely suggestions and not requirements. Being in touch with eros is about listening to your own natural timing.*

Find a spot where you will not be disturbed and make yourself comfortable. Close your eyes and focus your awareness on your breathing. Take a few deep breaths and let them go, feeling yourself becoming quieter inside and more relaxed. (pause)

Remember the times in your life when you felt most in touch with your erotic nature— alone, with a lover, in nature?(pause)

Choose one of these instances and allow yourself to recall it fully. (pause)

Remember how your body felt, and how you were aware of sensations throughout your body. (pause)

Remember what you saw and the quality of your seeing, what you heard and the quality of your hearing. (pause)

Perhaps you can recall smells. (pause)

Remember what your emotional experience was at the time. (pause)

How did you experience a sense of wholeness, of oneness, and of being connected to all living creatures? (pause)

Now, as you focus your attention on all the sensations and the feelings you experienced while being in this state, let yourself experience these feelings and sensations even more fully. (pause)

Now bring your attention back to your breathing and notice whether you are breathing any differently now than you were before. (pause)

Notice any differences in how your body feels now, compared to when you first started. (pause)

Get ready to open your eyes, but pause a moment. Give yourself as much time as you want, and let your eyes open when you feel ready to.

Do this exercise each day or a few times during the week, focusing on when you felt most alive and vital that day. As you practice, you may find that you become more attuned to and aware of these special moments in your life. The more you practice, the more frequently you will experience these moments of aliveness.

❦   ❦   ❦   ❦   ❦

## The Rhythm of Eros

To develop a more meaningful relationship with our inner lover, we must quite literally slow down. How often do we race through life—impelled toward one goal or another—without "stopping to smell the roses?"

Nadine Stair, at the age of 85, wrote *If I Had My Life To Live Over* [2] in which she simply and eloquently addresses the importance of each moment:

> *I'd like to make more mistakes next time. I'd relax. I would limber up. I would be sillier than I have been this trip. I would take fewer things seriously. I would take more chances. ...I would perhaps have more actual troubles, but I'd have fewer imaginary ones.*
>
> *You see, I'm one of those people who live sensibly and sanely hour after hour, day after day. Oh, I've had my moments, and if I had it to do over again, I'd have more of them. In fact, I'd try to have nothing else. Just moments, one after another, instead of living so many years ahead of each day.*
>
> *If I had my life to live over, I would start barefoot earlier in the spring and stay that way later in the fall. I would go to more dances. I would ride more merry-go-rounds. I would pick more roses.*

Nadine Stair is really talking about her undeveloped inner lover. When we appreciate the beauty and the magic in each moment, we are accessing our inner lover. Happily, the lover is always available, laying dormant, ready for opportunities to turn potential into reality. The lover emerges whenever we bring our senses and consciousness to the present moment. This act alone puts us into a feeling relationship with nature and all of life.

On the other hand, preoccupation with goals and results drives the inner lover underground. Worry and mind chatter create so much noise and static that it becomes impossible to hear the inner lover. Likewise, when the mind is full of strategies and the body full of defenses, the inner lover's dance cannot be felt or sensed.

The artist is often in touch with the inner lover. In fact, creativity is the wellspring from which the lover emerges. Sadly, many of us do not believe we are creative.

Even if we do not have the talent, commitment, or aspirations to become a professional artist, each of us has the potential to live his or her life as a creative art experience. Life itself can be the art form.

If we think of our life as an art experience, our consciousness changes and our sensory awareness becomes more acute. Walking across the room, putting a dish on the table, talking with a friend, crying, making love—become acts of aesthetic and sensory pleasure. A walk in the neighborhood can open our eyes to a wondrous palette of colors, a study of shapes and design, or the wonders of the plant or animal kingdom. If we are quiet for a few moments, the symphony of crickets becomes the background music for a sultry evening. When we find a feather we marvel at its softness as it caresses our skin and feel graced with the gift from its previous owner.

A. A. Leath, a dance therapist and Creative Behavior[3] teacher, describes this approach to life as a "dance attitude."[4] The participant is alert and curious about his or her experience and reactions and is focused on the process rather than the goal. By cultivating an attitude of heightened awareness, discovery, and appreciation of the aesthetic, each mundane activity becomes a wondrous dance.

If we live our life in this way, we would indeed have a love affair with life. Eros would become unveiled. In this state of awakened aliveness, what is most important becomes evident. We find more humor. We are less judgmental and more curious. We are alive and ready for the miracle of the moment.

## Exercise #3

### *Awakening the Artist Within*

Close your eyes and direct your attention to your breathing. Notice how you are breathing right now.

Open your jaw slightly to allow your body to breathe more easily.

Notice the rate at which you are breathing and whether your breath is even or uneven. Pay attention to the parts of your body where you feel your breath moving and where you feel your breath stuck. (pause)

Allow yourself to be fully in this moment with an attitude of "this is all there is." Continue to focus your awareness on your breathing as if nothing else mattered. Let yourself be fully alive in your "breathing dance." (pause)

Slowly open your eyes as you feel ready. Begin to do some ordinary, mundane activity such as walking across the room, looking out the window, getting dressed, writing a letter, eating or drinking—with the same "dance attitude" you just used to follow your breathing.

Continue to do the same activity for as long as you feel curious and engaged.

When you finish, write a brief description of your experience in your journal. Include what you noticed, how you felt, what distracted you and anything else that was important to you.

This exercise is useful to do either alone or with a partner. Experiment to find out what the differences are between practicing alone or with your partner.

If you practice this daily, you will find that your awareness becomes more acute and subtle and that you experience less distractions. As you become more facile with this state of consciousness, you will find that there is a "bleed through" effect. Spontaneously, you will find yourself using a "dance attitude" while doing familiar routines.

## A Lover Loves the World

In the state of "in loveness," the lover moves through the world with grace, dignity, and light-heartedness, experiencing eros through his or her deep sensitivity to the physical world. The lover appreciates the whole world through expressions that many people miss entirely—glistening sunshine through the trees, the music of a great symphony, an infant learning to walk, or a placid lily-filled lake.

The lover's most powerful erotic experience often emerges through lovemaking. This primal, passionate experience becomes a primary vehicle through which the lover opens to the larger world.

The expression "All the world loves a lover" is as true as its inverse: "A lover loves all the world." The lover's ability to enter another's world—and tune into their pleasure and disappointment, victories and defeats—is the true source of empathy. Therefore, embracing our inner lover not only opens us to joy, it can also open us to pain, to feeling the ebb and flow of life. This pain is not bad. It helps create a soulfulness in life whereby we can participate in the full splendor of being alive. Avoidance of pain leads to dullness and lethargy. The lover seeks to live life fully.

## Understanding the Inner Lover

For many of you, this idea of the inner lover is new and perhaps a bit strange. It may be helpful to gain a fuller understanding and appreciation of how inner figures or archetypes manifest within every person. Jungian psychology provides the easiest route to understanding this phenomenon.

Carl Jung, the brilliant Swiss psychiatrist, studied many of the world's religions and discovered that certain mythological motifs appear in all of them. In his well-documented psychology of religion, he named these common mythological motifs "archetypes." Archetypes reside in the "collective unconscious," a part of every person's psyche. Because dreams and myths reveal common figures throughout different cultures—many of which have had no cross-fertilization—the concept of the collective unconscious appears to be valid.

The divine child, the trickster, the wise old man, the warrior, and the earth mother are some common archetypes. Rabbi William Blank, in *Torah, Tarot & Tantra,* describes how the patriarchs and matriarchs from the Bible are archetypal figures, bigger than life, but human enough to be inspirational.[5]

These same archetypes are expressed uniquely within different people. For example, one man may express his warrior energy of moving beyond limits and boundaries through athletics, while another may use those same qualities in scientific endeavors. Likewise, one woman may express her earth mother nature by bearing children, while another may choreograph dances, write books, or grow vegetables and flowers.

Because archetypes are rarely expressed in a pure state within individuals, they can be perceived through what are called "subpersonalities" by Roberto Assagioli (a psychologist known for developing Psychosynthesis[6]) and "self-styles" by Eugene Sagan[7] (who developed the field of Creative Behavior).

Borrowing from Shakespeare's idea that all the world is a stage, and all the men and women merely players, Sagan looked at the individual as if he or she were the stage with many internal players. He described self-styles as the different ways in which we present ourselves—the various characters on our stage. For instance, I might have a self-style that I call Poor Pitiful Pearl (or Paul) which I use when I am feeling sorry for myself or All Powerful Katrina (or Karl) when I am feeling invincible. Regardless of the outer role I am playing, whether it be teacher, mother (father), friend, consultant, when I feel sorry for myself, I move into my Poor Pitiful Pearl (Paul) style and when I feel invincible, I move into All Powerful Katrina (Karl).

# Multiple Personalities

To some people, the idea that they contain different subpersonalities or self-styles may evoke images of "Sybil," or other mentally disturbed persons with multiple personalities. Don't worry, they are not the same. People who have true multiple personalities have inevitably suffered severe physical, sexual, and emotional abuse as children. In these cases, the psyche dissociates one personality from another to protect the individual from unbearable emotional or physical pain. Called "splitting off," this is the individual's attempt to maintain some semblance of control or to create a "reality" that is tolerable.

Self-styles or subpersonalities are not starkly differentiated personalities. They are more like the many facets of a diamond, or the colors produced by light as it refracts through a prism. One facet of a diamond is not better than another, just as one color of the rainbow is not better than the others. Similarly, our tenderness, our playfulness, our eroticism, our lust, and our sweetness are all aspects of us, our sexuality, and our inner lover.

Another way of witnessing archetypes and seeing how we use them in our daily life is through the emergence of "inner child" work. This movement can be understood partially as an attempt to reconnect with the divine child archetype. The divine child exists in a state of "innocence," which in its root means "without harm." Inner child work has been used as a vehicle for healing sexual and emotional abuse.

# Developing Your Inner Lover

Within the context of archetypes or self-styles, the importance of awakening our inner lover becomes apparent. Each of us has an inner lover who is waiting to be discovered and celebrated—to bring more sensuality, love, creativity, and magic into our lives.

However, any attempt to develop the inner lover for the sole purpose of attracting the ideal outer lover will be in vain. The inner lover will not be forsaken for the outer lover—as a means toward an end. The inner lover rejoices in dancing with an outer lover, yet is unwilling to be used as bait.

To have a truly erotic marriage, it will serve you to develop practices for your inner lover without attachment to your partner's response. This is the essence of a relationship which is free from co-dependence. As you share your inner lover with your partner, you will be cultivating your erotic relationship.

## Exercise #4

### *Finding Your Inner Lover*

Get in a comfortable position and close your eyes. Use your breathing to help you let go of any unnecessary tension. (pause)

Imagine a safe place that you know or imagine one where you feel free to explore and discover. Take yourself to that place now. (pause)

Use any or all of your senses—visual, auditory, olfactory (smell), gustatory (taste), touch, and kinesthetic (feeling)—to explore your safe place. Do this for several minutes, for as long as it feels good for you.

Notice any feelings that arise and any changes in the sensations in your body as you explore.

When you are finished, open your eyes. Write briefly in your journal or draw a picture of some aspect of your experience that was important to you.

Now, take several minutes to engage in a similar kind of exploration in your external environment. Use all of your senses to experiment with and discover the world immediately around you. Do this for several minutes, or as long as it feels good for you.

Notice any feelings that arise and any changes in the sensations in your body as you experience your environment in a new way.

When you feel finished, write in your journal or draw something that was particularly meaningful for you.

Any exploration of the erotic is best done with a childlike attitude of innocence. There is little room for sarcasm or cynicism in this sensuous and magical world. Ideally, judgment is suspended so that every sensation, feeling, image, or insight is free to emerge without the fear that you or your partner will be ignored, humiliated or rejected for whatever you experience. However, if judgments do arise, be aware that they are usually hiding an underlying fear. Use your awareness of the judgment as a doorway to discover what the underlying fear may be.

The emotional charge that you feel behind your judgment is commensurate to your own fears about yourself. These fears are best uncovered with an attitude of curiosity, research, and acceptance which we call "emotional archeology." Like an archeologist, we examine everything we find, searching for clues that will reveal hidden aspects of ourselves.

In an innocent and loving environment, you may feel safe enough to celebrate yourself, much like children do spontaneously. Celebration is a lovely and necessary part of integration. It helps us take credit for the work we have done and integrate the change into our newly expanded self.

Since the skill of celebrating ourselves has been conditioned out of us, we must cultivate this skill and practice it frequently. For models, we can look to the optimism and eroticism of the American romantic writers. Walt Whitman's first passage in *Song of Myself*,[8] begins with a true celebration statement.

*I celebrate myself, and sing myself,*
*And what I assume you shall assume,*
*For every atom belonging to me as good belongs to you.*

Whitman is profoundly in touch with the erotic nature, as well as the unity, of all things.

## Exercise #5

### *Celebrating Your Inner Lover*

Write a poem, essay or letter celebrating yourself. If you like, you can use the following form:

*Dear (your name),*
*I love you. I appreciate how you take care of yourself, your sense of humor, your laugh, etc... Thank you for all that you have done. Thank you for...*
*Love,*
*Your Inner Lover*

Put your letter, poem or essay in an envelope, stamp it, address it to yourself, and mail it.

Another option is to give it to your partner or friend with directions to mail it to you in a few weeks, to arrive on your birthday, or at some time in the future as a surprise.

Although your rational (or cynical) mind may discount the value of these types of self-expressions, if you allow yourself to withhold judgment, you may receive immeasurable rewards.

# Erotic Union

The potential for ecstasy is vast when two whole people committed to embracing their inner lovers join together in erotic union. When obstacles emerge to living their dreams together, both partners combine forces to creatively overcome or transform the block. This does not necessarily mean pushing through, using brute force or a laser-like focus. The challenge may very well be to surrender and allow tender feelings to shine through the cracks.

Surrender becomes easier when both partners know who they are and where their boundaries are. Then the process of surrendering those boundaries is an ecstatic experience of oneness rather than an anxiety provoking experience of loss of self.

Lovers are able to rely on each other in the drive to satisfy their life hungers. It helps give them a sense of meaning and purpose. They keep the well-being of each other and the relationship as a whole in mind as they negotiate life's challenges. Lovers freely seek contact or privacy, knowing that each can do likewise without feeling intruded upon or ignored. Their boundaries expand and contract in a constantly fluid manner, respectful of each other as well as themselves.

A poem by Rumi addresses this eloquently:

*Out beyond ideas of wrongdoing and rightdoing,*
*There is a field.*
*I'll meet you there.*
*When the soul lies down in that grass,*
*The world is too full to talk about.*
*Ideas, language, even the phrase each other*
*doesn't make any sense.*[9]

Although this field of grass may not require thought or words, getting there may take some planning and practice. The following exercises may help you evaluate your current situation and create a plan for your journey together.

## Exercise #6

### *Rating Your Erotic Relationship*

On a scale of 1 to 10, 1 being terrible, 10 being terrific, rate your relationship.

Using the same scale,:

*How would you like it to be?*

*What would it take to get your relationship to that point?*

*What would you have to do and what would your partner have to do differently?*

Talk together about how each of you answered these three questions. Discuss the solutions or suggestions you want to implement and how you might go about it.

Before you begin the next exercise, set the scene for a relaxing, uninterrupted period of time. Make sure you will not be disturbed for at least half an hour. Unplug the phone and put on some soothing music, if you like.

## Exercise #7

### *Cultivating Eros With Your Partner*

Make a list of the times you recall when you felt very connected with the earth, with animals, or with one or more people.

Describe what those activities and experiences had in common.

Think about which of these past experiences you believe you can create with your present partner.

Explore some of these experiences with your partner. Repeat those which make you feel close to each other and connected to the life force. Keep a list of those experiences that are the most satisfying and make time for these special experiences as frequently as possible.

One outgrowth of opening to our inner and outer lover is that we experience carry-over effects with other people who are not sexual partners. We are able to have an open heart and express the universal values of love and caring.

# False Images of Eros

Perhaps it may sound surprising that the lover has been repressed in our culture. While the ethos of many religions attempt to de-sexualize aspects of life which are truly sexual, an equally destructive counter-movement exists which sexualize aspects of life which are not really sexual. Advertising and mass media exploit this without conscience. Automobiles, breakfast cereals, and toothpaste become vehicles through which we learn to "improve" our sex appeal. It seems that everywhere we look we are bombarded with images of lovers—from billboards, movies, television, and magazines. Yet these representations focus on image over substance— a distinction that separates the pseudo-lover from the authentic one. These images of the lover are purely secular, having no connection to the divine.

We observe this pseudo lover in modern mythology. Millions of women weep through soap operas and romance novels. Millions of men lust for these secular goddesses in pornography. Yet, the truly erotic component of these lovers is missing entirely. Stripped of the spiritual dimension of eros, these are mere remnants of the lover archetype paraded before us in the guise of false sex gods.

## The Demise of Eros

If eros is so essential to living a passionate and abundant life, then why is its pure expression so uncommon in our experience? Three major influences come to mind: 1) the impact of our dominant religions; 2) the development of the field of sexology; and 3) the rise of materialism.

There has been a tension between what are called moral or ethical religions—Christianity, Judaism, and Islam. According to Jungian analyst Robert Moore and mythologist Douglas Gillette, our major religions have dealt harsh blows to the lover:

> *Christianity has taught more or less consistently that the world—the very object of the Lover's devotion—is evil, that the Lord of the world is Satan, and that it is he who is the source of the sensuous pleasures (the foremost of which is sex) that Christians must avoid.* [10]

The Church has often held artists, innovators, and creators in contempt. The erotic aspect of the lover here has been banished.

In most approaches to Christianity, the body has been viewed as the source of evil and sin. Yet the body is the temple of our being. There is an inherent, irresolvable conflict between these negative beliefs about bodies, sexuality, and instincts—and our potential for healthy erotic expression. Most of us remember the sexual shame taught in our religious backgrounds, which not only eroded eros but actually debased the sacredness of our sexuality.

However, the strong repression of sexuality in the United States was blasted open as a result of the sexual revolution which began in the 1960s. The unspeakable was spoken. The unthinkable was done. The libido of an entire generation of young people was released from the shackles of slavery. But in the revelry of the victory celebrations, eros was often left on the sidelines.

## Preoccupation with the Plumbing

While religion has tried to take the sex out of love, some secular pursuits have attempted to take the love out of sex. What little remained of eros in the sixties became lost in the dissection of sex. Ironically, as George Leonard suggests in *Adventures in Monogamy*,[11] the sexual revolution played a significant part in the demise of eros.

As the sexual revolution opened the door to more innovation and freedom, sex emerged as an area of scientific investigation; soon it was mapped, charted, and broken down into miniscule components. Sam Keen notes that,

> *Anatomy charts detailed the plumbing. Genital engineers explained the angle, thrust, lubrication, frequency, varieties of stimulation, and nature of nerve endings, which, if mastered would produce orgasms—multiple, if not simultaneous.*[12]

Books, audio tapes, video tapes, and training seminars, all aimed at increasing sexual potency and pleasure, proliferated. Some people learned how to communicate sexually and practiced techniques to achieve bigger and better orgasms. But for many of these people, the techniques became more important than the relationship. Sex became a clinical experience that was measurable and definable.

The sixties and seventies were a welcome relief from a time when anything sexual had to be suppressed. Clearly, new knowledge has increased our understanding and hence our ability to treat painfully sensitive challenges like premature ejaculation, impotence, and pre-orgasmic women. The value of the emergent fields of sexology and sex therapy has added to many people's lives.

However, sometimes the solutions provided by such instruction have been only temporary because they missed the larger point. The focus on function and the ultimate goal of orgasm has not necessarily enhanced our erotic potency. Our Western medical approach treats the symptom out of context without taking into consideration the spiritual and emotional aspects of being human.

## Spirituality in a Material World

Spirituality is and always has been the basis of a truly erotic experience. In fact, many cultures have believed that the highest form of love combines spiritual devotion with physical passion. However, today in our culture, the term *spiritual* is often used to mean without substance. Yet, even though it cannot be measured, its effects are powerful. Mahatma Gandhi, Martin Luther King, and Mother Teresa influenced millions by the force of their spirituality.

Often spirituality has been equated with dogmatic religion. The ascetic who scourges himself or the religious zealot who abstains from all pleasure is thought by some to be on a high spiritual plane. But spirituality need not be tied to asceticism or sensory deprivation.

There is an older tradition of spirituality—the female tradition of "the Goddess." Rituals in this tradition honor the earth, its cycles, the universe with all of its life forms, and the sacred nature of the body.

The Goddess traditions also embrace the positive qualities of intuition, healing, and creativity. These qualities, so often attributed to women, are the qualities that make artists, writers, and even physicians and scientists great, whether they are possessed by men or women. The intuitive, creative, and healing qualities are also the qualities of a great lover.

In our culture, by the late eighteenth century—with the rise of materialism brought about by the industrial revolution—these less pragmatic qualities began to fall into disfavor. By the end of the nineteenth century, if you could not measure it, weigh it, buy it, or sell it, it was not worth anything. The indefinable qualities of the spirit seemed meager when measured by the dollars-and-cents standard that prevailed. Spirituality, mysticism, eros, the body—were all debased currency in a material world.

Furthermore, materialism is founded on the belief that fulfillment is external: the answer exists "out there." If you can procure enough money to buy this house, car, or stereo, then you will finally be happy. "When I lose 15 pounds, then I'll be happy." Or "when I go on vacation or get a raise, then I'll be happy." Fulfillment and joy always seem to be over the next mountain—vaguely within range, yet destined to loom forever in the distance.

Perhaps nowhere does this "then I'll be happy" phenomenon function more destructively than in the myth of romantic love.[13] "If I could be with him or her, I'd finally be happy." Have you ever imagined that you would be fulfilled if you could be with a particular person, and then actually formed a relationship with that person? If you are like most people, you discovered that fulfillment did not manifest as you had imagined. Relationships or sex as the focus of a "then I'll be happy" philosophy form the roots of love and sex addictions.

## Sex Without Eros

When the Lover is persecuted—whether by the church, science, or materialism—erotic poten-cy evaporates. Nonetheless, the erotic impulse seeks expression. Sex within the context of an I-It relationship, defined and described eloquently by the brilliant philosopher Martin Buber in *I and Thou* (in which a person is treated as an object)[14], addictive acting out, and "the grass is always greener" phenomenon are all expressions of eros gone astray.

People with dis-owned eros often fall prey to the promise of ultimate satisfaction to be deliv-ered by the next lover. This turns into the endless painful cycle of romantic fascination, carnal explo-ration, disconnected communication and emotional isolation. "Next time it will be better," runs the logic. The next fantasy will fill the bill. It emerges as a co-worker, a film star, someone who drives by, or a picture of someone. These fantasies often flicker through our consciousness as islands of desire discreet from our real life relationships.

## Erotic or Pornographic?

Perhaps the concept of eros has been confused more than any other in modern culture, exem-plified by the pornography industry. Though pornography turns many people on and has been labeled erotic, it is a misnomer. Pornography does a tremendous disservice to the true nature of eros.

Any time people engage in sex without love or caring, when someone is being objectified or used, by definition, the sex cannot be erotic.

Yet, pornography is appealing to many people, perhaps because of our collective desire to expe-rience love, passion, and sensuality.

And no wonder. Living in modern Western society, few among us are taught to be conscious of eros. We are schooled in how to succeed in a material world. We become adept at dissociating our-selves from our feelings so that we can function in a culture rampant with violence, poverty, and social inequities. Sadly, we have accepted the alienation that ensues.

However, despite our lack of awareness, attention, and education, eros thrives. Erotic by nature, we seek fulfillment—but often down the wrong roads. Some of us look to affairs to fulfill the long-ing dulled by the routine of our daily lives. Others read romance novels, or watch soaps and movies, hoping to vicariously experience the thrill of being in love, the sensual pleasure of an abundant uni-verse, and the feelings of wholeness that our beings know are possible.

## Wounds of Love and Eros

Surely, the lover has been wounded. No longer luxuriating in the innocence and beauty of love, the lover—embroiled in shame and doubt—struggles in despair. Erotic marriage cannot exist in this state.

Something is missing. There is a profound sense of loss and lack of fulfillment that permeates most of our experience. We keep searching for the answer to a question we can barely articulate. As in all the great spiritual traditions, the answer lies within ourselves, not "out there." We must revital-ize and nurture our lovers, inner and outer. We must return the inner lover to the garden. There we can meet our beloved.

As you practice and develop your erotic nature, you will probably experience a difference in the way you view yourself in relation to all life. Perhaps you will feel a sense of fullness or richness for which you had been longing. Perhaps you will feel a greater sense of belonging—with your partner, other people and with nature. You might find yourself feeling more connected to your spiritual nature. You may even experience glimpses of the numinous presence of God.

# Envisioning Your Erotic Relationship

By envisioning our goals, we start a chain reaction that will help us create them. We limit ourselves primarily through our lack of imagination. People who succeed in any endeavor start out with a vision of what they want to achieve. It is the beginning blueprint for success.

Relationships are no different. If you want to achieve a successful relationship, you will need a blueprint, too. The first step is to develop a vision of the kind of relationship you want. The following exercise may help you pave your path.

## Exercise #8

### *Envisioning Your Relationship*

Close your eyes and take a few deep breaths. Make yourself comfortable and let go of any unnecessary tension in your body.

Allow images, feelings, or sensations to emerge of how you want your relationship to be. Imagine your relationship to embody all that you have dreamt to be possible. Think of normal, everyday circumstances as well as special occasions. Do this for several minutes.

Ask yourself the following questions, and make your answers specific. After each answer to a question, open your eyes and write your answer in your journal. Then proceed to the following questions:

*How will your partner relate to you, and you to your partner?*

*What will our lovemaking be like? (You might want to include different possibilities, rather than viewing it as static.)*

*How will you face challenges and resolve conflicts?*

*How will you experience nurturing, both giving and receiving?*

*What activities will you enjoy together?*

*How will you include/exclude other friendships?*

*How will you communicate with each other?*

*How will you play together?*

*How will you handle outside attractions?*

*How will the erotic element be woven into the fabric of your everyday life?*

When you have finished your writing, share it with your partner and discuss how you might implement some of your ideas.

By becoming aware of the characteristics of your ideal relationship, you are far more likely to create what you want. If you can imagine it, you can create it.

You can use the vision of your desired erotic relationship to refer back to throughout the book—and, more importantly, throughout your life. Whenever challenges to your erotic fulfillment emerge, use your vision as a source of inspiration. This inspiration can give you courage to go through the difficulties which emerge along the way. It is this commitment that determines how successfully you will walk your path and realize your dreams. Don't let circumstances defeat you. You've got to have heart!

🌿     🌿     🌿     🌿     🌿

The next chapter shows you ways to spice up your erotic relationship and also provide a deeper context for opening up both emotionally and spiritually. By embracing Eastern wisdom, you will be able to enliven your relationships in ways that may surprise you. So let's continue our journey.

# 3

# Eastern Sex for Western Lovers

*Our culture has lost the understanding that sexual energy is a physical expression of spiritual power. In truth, the desire to unite sexually with another human being is a reflection of an underlying spiritual need to experience wholeness and complete intimacy. It is a need to return to...a oneness within the self.*

Margo Anand, *The Art of Sexual Ecstasy*

If you have ever seen Eastern erotic art—sculpture and paintings in which bodies twist and engage at seemingly impossible angles, you may have assumed that these poses were exclusively for sexual yogis. It's hard not to be intrigued or intimidated, or even to wonder what pleasure would be possible if only you were capable of performing at this level. Alas, for us mortals, the missionary position is still tried and true.

But what if it were possible to learn some basics of "tantra"—the practice of these erotic arts—without studying for endless years or having to transform yourself into a human pretzel? That's precisely the intent of this chapter! We'll give you some new tools and attitudes that can help you expand your erotic repertoire and take your lovemaking to new heights. The intent is also to provide you with a spiritual framework for your erotic relationship.

The next three exercises are designed to be done sequentially. At first glance they may not seem like tantra, but you will experience important tantric principles from these basic practices.

## Exercise #1

### *Ready, Get Set, Go*

Choose a piece of music that you and your partner enjoy dancing to (or two different pieces of music).

Make sure you have enough space to move around or dance without bumping into anything.

Begin to move your body in a way that feels good to you, not necessarily relating to your partner.

As you dance, focus your attention on the sensations in your body and on your breathing. If you find that you are breathing shallowly or have stopped breathing, take a deep breath and let it go.

Continue to dance, feeling your energy move through every part of your body. If there are parts of your body that you cannot feel, focus your attention there and notice what happens.

As you continue to dance, squeeze and release your pubococcygeus (PC) muscle—the same muscle you use to stop yourself from urinating. It is located between the anus and the genitals. But if you are unable to isolate it, just squeeze and release the muscles around your entire genital area. Pay attention to the sensations that this generates as you continue to squeeze and release while dancing and breathing.

Now, as you continue to dance, begin to make contact with your partner through your eyes or touch. Notice what happens to your energy, the sensations in your body, and your feelings. Continue to breathe deeply.

After you have danced for at least five or ten minutes, sit down and face each other.

*This leads directly into the next exercise.*

## Exercise #2

### *Heart to Heart*

Facing your partner, stand about one and a half feet apart so that you can easily gaze into each other's eyes.

Without talking, breathe easily as you gaze softly into each other's eyes without staring.

Place the palm of your right hand on your partner's chest (the heart center) directly between the nipples. Place your left hand on top of your partner's hand over your own heart center.

Maintaining a soft gaze (it is okay to blink or close your eyes briefly to sense yourself) as you exhale imagine that you are breathing love from your heart into your partner's heart. As you inhale, imagine that you are breathing in your partner's love.

Continue to do this for several minutes. If you feel uncomfortable or want to avert your partner's gaze, close your eyes for a few moments, breathe deeply into your belly, and then open your eyes again.

When you are through, talk together about your experience, sharing any feelings, images, somatic (body) sensations, fears, etc.

*When you are finished sharing, move on to the next exercise.*

## Exercise #3

### *The Power of Truth*

Sit facing your partner. Take turns asking the question, "What do you want from our relationship?" When your partner answers the question, you say, "Thank you."

Keep your answers short, such as, "I want all of me to feel accepted in our relationship." "I want more intimacy with you." "I hope to feel more alive."

Keep going back and forth for five to ten minutes. If you feel that you have no more to say, keep going for several more minutes to find out if there is anything else that arises which might feel more vulnerable or scary to express.

When you are finished, talk about what was the most important, touching, or surprising thing that your partner told you. Add anything that you thought but did not say.

We hope you and your partner had some satisfying experiences as you tried these exercises. If you found that you had difficulty, thought they were silly, or began to quarrel with each other, please don't be discouraged. If you work with this material, you will find that you are able to uncover, address, and even heal some of the wounds that create problems between you.

If you and your partner sailed through these exercises easily or found that they heightened your intimacy or erotic union, you will be happy to know that we have barely scratched the surface.

Yet before we get too far ahead of ourselves, let's learn more about the philosophy of tantra. This foundation will provide a context for understanding why the practices we recommend later in the chapter are so central to experiencing a fabulous erotic relationship.

🌿 🌿 🌿 🌿 🌿

## Eastern Perspectives

Erotic art actually serves an important function in tantra—to engender a state of holiness within you. For practitioners of tantra, *becoming sexually excited is not in conflict with holiness—it is an aspect of it!*

To understand tantric art, we must learn to love our feelings—including our feelings of sexual arousal—to respect them as an artist who captures the beauty of the trees, clouds, and rolling landscapes.

By loving rather than denying our feelings, we can approach the act of love as we would approach a holy act. In tantra, everything is holy.

Everything we do is, or can be, a meditation, a prayer, a spiritual act. The sexual act of love is considered a divine expression. That is why erotic art is displayed in tantric temples.

The holy atmosphere or energy people sensed in these temples was created through erotic art—not

*Khadjouraho, India; Temple of Kandariya Mahadero (ca. A.D. 1000)*
*Erotic reliefs from Indian temple. Giraudon/Art Resource, NY*

through sermons espousing religious concepts, dogma, or devotion to a god. In these temples, the practitioners, upon seeing pictures of the act of love, were brought to a holy state of being just as many Westerners are affected when entering an awe-inspiring cathedral.

The technology of tantra is ancient and has much to offer Western lovers. From India, China, and Tibet in the far East to Persia and Palestine in the Middle East, tantric approaches provide a context for creating and experiencing the sexual experience as sacred. Sexual interactions between part-

*Couple in relief; unknown temple, India.*
*Couple from an erotic relief. Berkson/Art Resource, NY*

ners are perceived as having the potential to be profoundly healing and to facilitate the spiritual experience. Tantric practices are precisely designed to aid the practitioner in experiencing the numinosity—the mystery—of God.

Sexual energy is viewed as the vital, supreme life force. It is the force that has kept our species on the planet for many thousands of years. Using this force for our own personal healing, for bonding with our partner, for feeling deeply connected with God and the universe is an essential aspect of tantra.

## The Inner Male and Female

Tantra, as a spiritual tradition, embraces the notion that the universe and everything in it is permeated by a secret energy which emanates from the source of all being. This energy or power, although singular in form, manifests itself in three ways: 1) static or receptive energy (the feminine principle); 2) dynamic energy (the male principle); and 3) the union of the two.

The female-male polarity reflects the universal principles of yin and yang. Yin expresses the more receptive, surrendering, intuitive female energy of the moon, whereas yang expresses the more initiating, thrusting, and dynamic male energy of the sun. Together their harmonious union forms the foundation of wholeness.

Tantra recognizes that each person has an inner male and an inner female, similar to what Jung called the "anima" (the female aspect of a man) and the "animus" (the male aspect of a woman).

A primary purpose of tantric practices is to enhance the play between these opposite principles and to create what is known as the divine androgyne—the marriage between the inner male and the inner female. Sex is recognized as a yearning for completion—a movement toward balancing the male and female within oneself.

Consequently, tantra gives permission for men and women to act in both male and female roles during the sexual experience. It helps people access parts of themselves that they have chosen to suppress because it hasn't fit their gender image. For example, heterosexual men who express their inner woman often access whole new levels of sensuality, openness, and sexuality.

Since the nature of the energy work taught in tantra focuses on inner male and inner female, some tantra teachers say that it is as valuable for gay couples as for heterosexual couples. According to Tiburon, California, tantra teacher Lori Grace, energy flows in similar ways in male and female bodies. However, some variations in body position and visualization are necessary for homosexual couples, and they need to be even more aware that both male and female energies lie within. One person may take on the male role (yang) and the other the female role (yin), although this is not essential to a satisfying Tantric energy exchange. Tantra is suitable for relationships of any sexual orientation.

# Sacred Acts of Love

Many people raised in our Judeo-Christian culture are skeptical of the notion that sexual practices are not only sacred but are also pathways to experiencing the divine. Others are offended or shocked. A new client of ours expressed this doubt: "I can accept that sex is natural and it's important to heal my shame about sexuality, but it's going too far to call it spiritual." Is it?

What if you viewed your partner as a sacred aspect of the divine and that loving him or her expressed your love for the divine?

Most of us find it challenging, if not impossible, to powerfully merge with an abstract concept of God or a higher power. A focal point or entrance into the divine is necessary.

For most of us, that focal point is through the expression of one of the highest spiritual values—the experience of love. And person-to-person love is the primary forum that we human beings have for learning to love. Almost everyone has felt the strength and power of these emotions when they have experienced deep love. It is that same energy which provides an entrance or door to opening ourselves up to something greater than ourselves.

The act of love, for most of us, will be the prime area in our lives where we can transcend the small, individual boundaries of our self and merge with something beyond ourselves. When our ego boundaries dissolve, we open to the spiritual experience of surrender. Giving to our beloved is an expression of love and devotion. This experience includes lovemaking, yet also embraces every aspect of life and relationships. Thus, the essence of tantra is loving another with the entirety of our being. In the state of love, our hearts open, our normal ego boundaries dissolve, and we expand into each other.

Similar to the state of love, according to Rabbi William Blank, "the experience of God involves breaking the ego's normal boundaries and altering the distinction between self and other." He goes on to say that "any human experience is perceived through the body. The experience of God is no different. All sensations are perceived, all emotions are felt, and thoughts realized, in and by the body."[1] Every human experience, from sexual behavior to feelings of love to the experience of God, can be described in terms of the changes in the body. These changes have been identified and described by the spiritual masters throughout the ages. They have been used in tantra to guide practitioners in moving energy through the body for the purpose of opening to the spiritual experience of God.

*Erotic scene on ivory plaque from India.*
*Werner Forman/Art Resource, NY*

# Chakras: Sacred Energy Centers

In India and China, physiological changes in the body were described in terms of energy centers known as *chakras* (Sanskrit for "wheels").[2] Though Western science and medicine insist that there are no identifiable structures at the site of these chakras, Eastern practitioners are able to perceive and evaluate the level of vital energy in a given chakra. The chakras are like psychic sense organs which contain and radiate energy. Interestingly, they are located at the center of nerve-ending clusters such as the solar plexus, or the site of important glands, such as the thyroid.

The Eastern system of *chakras* maps out seven energy centers located in a vertical plane through the body:

1. The first or lowest chakra resides at the base of the spine (or at the feet) and is commonly called the "root" chakra.

2. The second chakra is located at the genitals and is called the sexual *chakra*.

3. The third chakra is located at the solar plexus, just above the navel.

4. The fourth is at the heart area.

5. The fifth lies in the throat.

6. The sixth is centered between the eyebrows (the "third eye").

7. The seventh or highest radiates from the crown of the head.

Various Eastern tantric traditions include additional energy centers. The Japanese *hara*, another energy center known to many Westerners who study the martial arts, is located at the spleen, below the navel.

According to the sacred tantric texts, the vital energy called Kundalini (Sanskrit, "serpent power") waits like a coiled snake in the lowest chakra during our normal resting state. As we move closer to the experience of God, our physiology, psychology, mental and energetic states change—the Kundalini rises into the higher chakras. This enables us to experience life in extraordinary ways.

The sacred system of tantra is an ancient art of transforming physical energy into spiritual energy. By moving the Kundalini up the spine through the chakras, lovers are schooled in techniques which transform the sexual experience from a purely physical act to a spiritual experience of oneness—potentially culminating in the experience of oneness with God.

The following exercise will give you an experience of your energy centers. We are going to explore eight energy centers altogether. There is no "right" sensation for you to feel. Just pay attention to your experience as you explore moving and focusing your energy. If you want more information about the chakras, you can refer to the detailed description in the Appendix.

Crown

Third Eye

Throat

Heart

Solar Plexus

Sex

Root

**The Chakras**

## Exercise #4

*Experiencing Your Energy Centers*

*Clear a space for yourself where you won't bump into anything if you move in a large circle.*

### The Root (Survival) Chakra: Walking

✻ Walk slowly around the room. After a few seconds, focus your attention on your first chakra—the chakra at the base of your spine. (You can also try this focusing on your feet.) Notice what happens to the pace and the way you are walking. Now squeeze and release your anal sphincter, just as if you were trying to hold back a bowel movement. What effect does this have as you walk or when you are stationary?

### The Sexual Chakra: PC Squeeze and Release

✻ Stand with your feet about shoulder width apart, toes pointed forward. Bend your knees slightly to keep stress off the back of your legs and to allow your pelvis to drop into alignment.

✻ Tilt your pelvis forward (creating a little arch in the small of your back), then backward several times (rounding your back slightly) until you find a comfortable rhythm.

✻ Now, as you inhale and rock your pelvis forward, squeeze your pubococcygeus (PC) muscle, just as if you were trying to stop the flow of urine. As you exhale and rock your pelvis backward, release the PC muscle and allow your perineum (the area between your anus and your genitals) to soften. If that is hard to feel, imagine that your genitals are bulging.

✻ Keep squeezing and releasing as you breathe and rock, allowing yourself to focus on the sensations in your pelvic area.

✻ Keep your awareness on your anus as well, so that you are bringing the vital energy up from the root chakra. (By this time, you may be feeling warmth and tingling in your genitals and pelvic area. If you do not, just attend to your own experience and keep breathing.)

### The Hara: Pelvic Circles and Fluid Power

✻ Keeping the same stance, begin to rock your pelvis from side to side several times until you can do it easily.

✻ Combine these movements with the pelvic rock so that they make a circular pattern: front, side, back, side, etc. Keep circling your pelvis until you are making a continuous, fluid circle (like a belly dancer).

✻ Focus your attention on the area below your navel in the middle of your belly, allowing your energy to radiate from your anus through your genitals as you continue rotating your pelvis. Experiment with keeping your anal sphincter and PC squeeze and release going while you rotate. (The squeeze happens as your pelvis rotates forward and you release as you are rotating backward.) Notice what happens to the quality of your movement, the sensations throughout your body and any thoughts or images that occur.

✻ Now, widen your stance so that your feet are slightly more than shoulder-width apart. Keeping your knees slightly bent, shift your weight from one foot to the other several times. Notice how you are maintaining your balance.

❀ Still focusing your attention on your "hara," imagine that the energy stabilizing you is emanating from that point. Continue shifting your weight from one foot to the other, but allow one foot to move forward, backwards, or diagonally.

❀ Feel the warmth of your vital, sexual energy spreading up from your genitals, into the middle of your belly. Again, notice any differences and pay attention to how you maintain your balance and sense your power.

### The Solar Plexus: Self-Assurance

❀ Once again, stand with your feet shoulder-width apart. As you inhale, allow your ribcage to rock forward. As you exhale, allow your ribcage to rock backward. Continue breathing in this way, amplifying the forward and backward motion of your ribcage.

❀ Now, extend your arms out in front of you as you inhale and exhale, as if your were reaching for your beloved. Continue breathing, letting your ribcage rock. Pull your beloved into you, bringing your hands to rest on your solar plexus, above your navel.

❀ Allow your vital, sexual energy to move up from your anus, through your genitals, through your belly, into your solar plexus. Notice the sensations, feelings, colors, and images you experience.

### The Heart Chakra: Heart Opening

❀ Stand comfortably with your eyes closed and lay your hands, one on top of the other, on your chest between your nipples. Allow yourself to rock or sway in any way that feels good to you. Remember or imagine a time when you felt deeply loved. Focus your attention under your hands and notice what happens.

❀ Now begin to think about someone you love, imagining your love radiating out like rays of the sun. Extend your arms as if you are sending your love out while focusing on your heart chakra. Repeat this pattern several times, spreading out from your heart chakra and back, until you find yourself breathing in and out easily as you do it. Notice what happens.

❀ Experiment with adding your anal sphincter and PC squeeze and release as you inhale and exhale, breathing the energy up through all your centers.

### The Throat Chakra: The Song Bird

❀ Sit or stand in a comfortable position. Let your jaw drop slightly open and begin to sing "ah" sounds. Sing as loudly and as fully as you are willing. Continue singing while focusing your attention on this chakra in the middle of your throat and notice what happens.

❀ Once again, experiment with bringing your vital sexual energy up through all of your centers into your throat as you inhale. Then, imagine all that energy being released through your voice as you sing.

### The Third Eye: The Inner Guru

❀ Sit in a comfortable position and close your eyes. Take a few deep breaths and let them go. Allow your belly to soften as you exhale.

❀ As you inhale, imagine that you are breathing from your anus and genitals and pulling your breath up through all of your energy centers, up to your third eye, the space between your eyebrows. As you exhale, maintain your focus on your third eye. Repeat this several times, adding your PC squeeze and release.

❀ Allow your breathing to fade into the background and focus your attention on your third eye. Do this for several minutes and notice if an image or vision or a sense of knowing becomes present.

### The Crown Chakra: Experiencing Oneness

❀ Breathe from the base of your spine all the way up to your crown chakra, a few inches above your head. Imagine that your breath emanates from the base of your spine, travels up your spine through all of your energy centers, hovers a few inches above your crown, and returns down into the base of your spine.

❀ As you continue to breathe in this way, maintain your focus on the crown chakra. Notice any images or sensations that occur without trying to control them.

Learning how to move your energy from the base of your spine up to your crown takes practice, but if you do this regularly, you will be well rewarded. As you master this, your sexual ecstasy will no longer be only genitally focused but you will feel sensation spreading throughout your body. It is also a key to experiencing blissful union with your partner as well as experiencing the oneness of the universe.

Margo Anand uses the metaphor of music when describing this flow of energy through the chakras.[3] The Inner Flute is the name she gives the passageway through energy centers up to your crown. As your sexual energy moves up through your Inner Flute and opens— energizing each center—you and your partner can learn to play the most ecstatic music.

🌿    🌿    🌿    🌿    🌿

# In the Flow

Regardless of our religious background or our spiritual proclivities, tantra has much to teach us about the use of sexual energy for spiritual growth. Tantric sex is not about the licentious release of our animal lust but, rather, about joining together to experience God. But enjoy it we will!

Tantra is related to the Taoist term *wu wei* which means "to be"—to be in the natural flow of life—without forcing it. Imagine how lovemaking could be if the pressure to perform or co-dependently care for your partner were entirely removed.

No matter what we recommend for you to practice in this chapter or elsewhere in *Lovers for Life*, nothing is more important than being gentle and compassionate with yourself and your partner. Because we come from a culture which is so focused on *doing*, it is important to give yourself and your partner a big margin of error while you are in the process of learning how *to be* in the flow.

The practice of tantra is inclusive rather than exclusive. Most of us learn that who we are and what we feel is not acceptable, and consequently, we learn to distrust and deny our experience. This is not so in tantra.

Tantric practices are based on trusting the naturalness of your feelings and movements and staying true to yourself.

Learning how to surrender to and go with your feelings or sexuality—rather than to control or be controlled—becomes the foundation for deep pleasure and spiritual growth. This is at the core of tantra, beyond exotic positions and challenging postures. Rather than taking control of or being controlled by your powerful internal forces, tantra teaches that control comes from being in the flow.

## Attitudes About Practice

Now that we have outlined some of the philosophy behind tantra, it is time to move into actual practice. Notice what feelings arise as we begin more hands-on exercises. Are you excited, scared, angry, happy—all of these or anything else? Remember, there is room for all of your feelings. You need not be a true believer—only receptive. If you have an open attitude and are willing to experiment, you are likely to receive tremendous value.

Changing lifelong habits and patterns will probably not be accomplished overnight, however by changing a little bit at a time, a whole new organism (or should that be orgasm!) can develop. As you explore the exercises in this chapter, remember that you are experimenting and learning. You will find that if you re-visit these exercises and practices later on, you will develop greater intimacy, satisfaction, and mastery.

## Rituals for Lovers

Our culture is practically bereft of meaningful ritual—ceremonial forms that touch us deeply. Those rituals that do exist suffer from consumeritis or lack meaning in some fundamental way. Many people have repudiated organized religion and consequently, all ritual, because of the hollowness and seeming hypocrisy. This is a grave error. We have thrown the baby out with the bath water.

Creating a sacred atmosphere is vitally important in tantric lovemaking because it can turn an ordinary sexual exchange into a sacred experience. Since we have not been trained in the use of ritual to create sacred space, we can borrow rituals from other traditions that strike a resonance within us or we can develop our own. Whichever we choose, we must stay attuned to the effect of the ritual on us, our partner, and our experience together.

Here are some guidelines to bear in mind when you are choosing or creating rituals:

*Keep it simple.*

*Appeal to your sense of aesthetics and beauty.*

*Engage your senses.*

*Be flexible. Change the ritual if it isn't creating the atmosphere you desire.*

*Use ideas, symbols, objects, or movements that come easily and naturally to you.*

Rituals help to nurture us. They need not be formal. There are simple things we can do to nurture and love each other. We can share a shower, hot tub, or massage, or we can chant, dance, or create music. Many lovers like to begin with a prayer or shared meditation. The deep relaxation and quieting of the mind that ensues shifts our consciousness from the mundane to the experience of our essential selves. Some enjoy dancing together and moving the Kundalini energy up the chakras. Whether subdued or energetic, rituals create the space for lovers to join in a shared experience.

Remember, the intention behind the ritual is to shift your consciousness from the material plane to the spiritual plane.

Sometimes, just stating your intention is enough to transform the energy. In many religions, there is a blessing that precedes every action—from basic functions like eating food and urinating to the more exalted—like entering into marriage or engaging in sex. Much like the Buddhist idea of mindfulness, the purpose of this blessing or prayer is to awaken us and remind us that every act can be a doorway into the experience of God.

## Exercise #5

### *Creating Ritual Space*

Remember or recognize what has given you deep pleasure—a walk in the rain, a majestic view, dancing, meditation, a warm bath.

After you and your partner have agreed upon an atmosphere or activity that you want to do together, decide what, if any, sacred objects will be present (for example, these could be your favorite rocks, vases, candles, statues, or flowers).

After creating your environment, determine your intention by telling each other what you hope to experience.

Then, find out what emerges in this space without expectation or pressure (if you do feel pressure, breathe deeply, communicate with your partner, and give yourself permission "to be").

Perhaps one or both of you would like some special attention; allow yourself to ask for it (for example, a neck massage or reading a poem or telling a love story).

If you and your partner become aroused, it's fine to follow your impulses. Regardless, allow yourselves to appreciate what you have experienced together in the ritual space that you have created.

# What's In a Name?

Even more important than literally creating a ritual space is adopting an attitude that sanctifies the act of lovemaking. If you begin to believe that your sexuality is sacred, then the way you think about sexuality changes, the way you talk about it changes, and so does the way you practice it.

That does not mean you can't have quickies if you enjoy them. And it's just as easy to sanctify a secluded cove on a deserted beach as it is your bedroom. It all depends on your attitude. Are you exploring the breadth and depth of your erotic nature or are you engaged in lewd behavior? Which attitude will lead to greater fulfillment?

Since language directly reflects our beliefs, it is important to be aware of how we talk about sexuality. The language of our culture tends to denigrate sexuality. The language of tantra celebrates our erotic nature and sanctifies sexuality.

The terms used to talk about our genitals exemplify this wherever the teachings of tantra are an accepted part of the culture. There are many names for the penis and the vagina, all of which have dignity. The Sanskrit name for penis is *lingam,* meaning "tongue." A Tibetan term, *vajra,* means "thunderbolt" or "scepter of power," as well as penis. Other names used in the East include the Peak, the Warrior, the Hero, the Emperor, the Jade Stalk, and the Magic Wand. Common usage for the vagina is the Sanskrit word *yoni,* which means the vulva or the Womb of Creation. Other Eastern names include Valley of Joy, Great Jewel, Pearl, Lotus Blossom, Moist Cave, Ripe Peach, Enchanted Garden, and Full Moon.[4] Rather than asking his beloved to "do it," a man might say, "The Emperor would like to visit your Moist Cave tonight."

How much more dignified and erotic if your wife were to whisper, "My Enchanted Garden awaits your Magic Wand." As you practice these basic tantric exercises, experiment with names that create a sacred atmosphere as well. You can also use pet names that you create—as long as they are not derogatory. Have fun and let your imagination soar.

# The Essence of Presence

Surrender is central to the experience of intimacy. We all long for intimacy in which our eyes, souls, and bodies meet and join. When we feel known, appreciated, and loved, we relax our guard and meet our lover unmasked. In the intimate experience, we let go of our chronic separateness, our boundaries dissolve, and we blend with our lover—a truly sacred experience.

If intimacy is what we desire, it is vitally important to know how to create it. Since feeling seen, heard, and understood is central to intimacy, knowing how to create an environment which supports you and your lover in this experience is paramount. Being present with your partner is a primary ingredient. Whether through physical activities or meditative forms, tantra helps center you in the present moment. Where else can life be fully lived?

To be fully present in the presence of your beloved is a truly erotic experience. This presence is felt most profoundly through deep eye contact. The eyes are the windows of the soul. This is why in tantra the majority of lovemaking is done with open eyes—looking at your partner, breathing deeply, and moving freely. One aim is to be able to climax with your eyes fully open, fully in contact with your beloved. Certainly, you can close your eyes for periods of time if this allows you to tune into your own sensation, but the focus on keeping your eyes open can help you to stay present with your partner.

Yet for some, looking into your lover's eyes or being seen by your lover produces anxiety. If we probe the anxiety, we find feelings of fear ("What if you really see me and do not like what you see"), or sadness ("No one has ever taken the time to really pay attention to me"), or shame ("I wish I could disappear"). Whatever the underlying feelings, real intimacy is possible only when those feelings have permission to come to the fore, be felt, and expressed.

How to be present or to communicate presence to your lover may seem apparent to some but nebulous to others. We have included a few exercises to support you in exploring presence—what it is and how to create it—so that you can experience the effect that increased presence has on your relationship.

## Exercise #6

### *The Eyes Have It*

Give yourself at least fifteen minutes for this exercise the first time you try it.

Sit at a comfortable distance from your partner so that you can gaze into each other's eyes easily.

Take a few minutes to breathe together.

Simply look into each other's eyes without trying to do anything; remember that there is nothing (no thing) to do.

If you sense yourself searching for recognition or approval, or trying to communicate acceptance or love to your partner, pull your energy back to yourself and allow yourself to simply be present.

If fear, anxiety, or negative feelings arise, notice them and keep focusing on your breath and your connection with your partner.

When and if feelings emerge that could take you out of contact with yourself or your partner, simply notice them, keep breathing, feel whatever you are feeling, and maintain eye contact.

Do this portion of the exercise for at least five minutes the first time. When you are finished, make any kind of physical contact that feels good for both of you. Then, share your experience with your partner.

When five minutes of soul-to-soul eye contact feels easy, extend the time period to ten minutes and so on.

Allowing yourself to be seen, as you feel or express intensely vulnerable feelings, may be an emotional stretch for you. If so, remember that this process is not about perfection. Often people experience feelings of shyness, fear, self-doubt, shame, or anger when they first do this exercise. Please do not judge yourself for this. We have huge prohibitions in our culture about meaningful prolonged eye contact. We are also conditioned to hide behind masks, even in our most intimate relationships.

With this kind of eye-to-soul contact, we peel away the layers of masks and reveal our authentic selves.

If you have spent years wearing your own mask, and colluding with others to maintain their masks, really looking and being seen can be frightening. Be patient with yourself and with your partner. Revealing yourself to your lover becomes easier as you experience the small pleasures that come with increased trust and intimacy.

As you begin to feel comfortable making intimate eye contact, here are several ways to experiment:

*Lie together, caressing each other while you maintain eye contact.*

*One partner caresses or stimulates the other. The person on the receiving end does nothing but experience what it feels like to be touched while maintaining eye contact.*

*While sexually joined, maintain eye contact continually.*

*Maintain eye contact while coming to orgasm.*

As you experiment with this kind of soul-to-soul eye contact over time, notice what the effect is on your relationship with yourself and with your partner.

# A Touching Presence

Just as eye contact is a means of being in contact with another, so is touch. If the eyes are the window of the soul, then touching someone is touching their soul. And just as many of us do not have much experience simply being present with another through eye contact, most of us have had little experience being present through touch—even if we have had hundreds or thousands of sexual encounters. When someone is emotionally present when he or she touches you, it makes a world of difference. Most of us are starved for nurturing physical contact. Sadly, many people have had such negative experiences with physical contact that they associate pain with touch.

People who have been physically abused (from violent assault to spankings) have these negative associations with touch in their cellular and sensate memory. Similarly, people who have experienced sexual abuse often have negative associations with touch. Whether or not you have been abused, you have probably experienced some touch as manipulative or controlling. Everyone has used touch to try to get something. Few of us have received touch that communicates, "I am here with you. I want nothing from you. You need not do anything or change in any way. I love you exactly as you are."

Being present to your lover through touch can be a profoundly healing experience in which the two of you feel bonded, the person touched feels fully met, and the toucher lets go of unnecessary and co-dependent feelings of responsibility.

## Exercise #7

### *Touching Your Lover's Soul*

One person (the receiver) lies down in a comfortable position. The other person (the toucher) sits at the receiver's side, facing him or her.

Breathe together for a few minutes. If you want to, make eye contact with your lover.

*Toucher:* Place your hands on your partner's body slowly and gently as if saying, "Hello, soul. I'm aware that I'm entering your space. I respect you and honor you." Let your open palms rest quietly without doing anything other than being aware.

*Receiver:* Breathe into the place where your partner is touching you and experience what it feels like to be touched.

*Toucher:* As you listen with your hands, allow your breathing to synchronize with your partner. When you feel your partner relax under your hands, or when you feel his or her breath moving into the region where your hands lie, slowly remove your hands and place them elsewhere on your partner's body.

*Receiver:* Keep tuning into the sensations, images, and feelings that arise within you as your partner touches you with presence. Direct your breath to the region under your partner's hands and notice any areas that you feel are restricted. If your partner moves his or her hands before you feel ready, ask your partner to remain in that place longer.

*Toucher:* Do not touch your partner's genitals unless you receive permission and are able to maintain your focus on presence rather than sexual stimulation.

Continue to touch with presence for ten minutes or more. Talk about your experience—somatic, emotional, memories, images. This is not a critique of your partner.

Then switch roles and repeat the entire process.

You can use this practice to develop your ability to sense yourself and another. As the toucher, you can ask whether your partner feels your presence, or senses when your mind strays. You can ask if you should change your touch in any way. Remember, this is *not* about perfection but about learning how to be with each other more consciously and lovingly. For me, Daniel, this has been an invaluable practice in my own erotic awakening.

As the receiver, you can verbalize your perceptions and find out if they are accurate—"I just felt a shift in your energy. I don't feel you as present. Did anything change from your point of view?" If you do this as an experiment, you can benefit greatly. However, if you begin to get adversarial because you feel hurt or misunderstood, stop the process, make eye contact, breathe together, re-establish your intention, and then talk about the feelings that arose.

After you get comfortable with touch that has no intention other than to be present, it will become easier to be present with sensual and sexual touch. Throughout all the following exercises, we recommend that you check in with yourself, noticing if you are truly present—be it visually or through touch—or if your attention is focused elsewhere. Being present itself becomes a spiritual practice. Without shame or blame, you can bring your attention and presence back to your partner.

One way to help yourself stay present with your partner is to make sure you are present with yourself. In order to be present with yourself you must know how to listen to yourself. This requires an awareness of your internal experience—be it emotional, physical, spiritual, or cognitive—and knowing how to contain or express whatever you are experiencing in a productive manner. Both of these are accomplished more readily by becoming more aware of your breath.

🌿　　🌿　　🌿　　🌿　　🌿

# The Importance of Breath in Tantra

Nothing is more important in tantra than breath. Breathing lies at the core of all emotional states. We breathe differently depending on whether we are afraid, joyous, sad, angry, at rest, or sexually aroused. If you have ever noticed your breathing during lovemaking, you are aware that it varies radically depending on your level of sexual excitation.

Ironically, as most people become increasingly aroused, they breathe in ways which minimize their sexual pleasure and decrease their excitation. This is usually unconscious and can be changed when brought to consciousness. However, surprising and conflicting feelings often arise as people begin to change lifelong habits.

When the breath stays in the shallower regions of the chest rather than moving into the belly, the possibility of enjoying deep sexual satisfaction greatly diminishes.

One of the reasons that people tend to breath shallowly during sex is that, with excitation, the preexisting tension in the pelvic floor becomes more obvious and may be uncomfortable. By breathing shallowly, we do not confront this discomfort. Unfortunately, we also stop ourselves from releasing the tension and experiencing deep, sustained pleasure and surrender.

# Surrender and Love

How we live in, hold, and move our physical bodies reflects and affects the state of our emotional, psychological, and spiritual being.

If you are unable to fully let go and surrender on a physical level, you will be unable to fully let go and surrender emotionally and spiritually. Therefore, working on one naturally influences the other.

As you learn to relax your body and let go of physical tension, you will correspondingly be learning to surrender emotionally and spiritually.

Many of the exercises in this chapter are designed to help you let go of chronic tension and increase your flexibility while simultaneously opening yourself to deeper levels of sexual pleasure and spiritual union.

## Exercise #8

---

### *Belly Breathing*

Sit with your back erect or lie on your back with your knees pointing toward the ceiling and your feet flat on the floor.

Put your hands on your lower abdomen so that your little fingers rest just above your pubic bone.

Breathe deeply and easily into your belly.

Allow your belly to rise as you inhale and to fall towards your spine as you exhale.

Relax your anal and genital muscles.

Imagine and sense that as you inhale, the air you breathe in makes your anus, perineum (the space between your anus and genitals), and genitals bulge out.

Relax and rest as you exhale.

Do this several times with the quality of attention that you would use if you were practicing meditation. Let your belly soften more and more as you breathe.


As you practice belly breathing on your own, you may find that feelings arise seemingly out of nowhere. Allow your feelings to move through you as if you were being washed by waves that roll onto shore and then recede back to the ocean. Holding your breath often occurs because of fear and is an attempt to stop feelings from moving. Paradoxically, in trying to prevent pain, we stop the natural flow of our feelings and by so doing, we create pain, stress, and distress. Resistance is a great source of pain. So whenever you become aware that you are holding your breath, refocus your attention on your breath and allow the feeling to flow through you.

Just as our breathing allows us to connect with the core of our being, it also is the conduit for connection between people. When people are attuned, their breathing is synchronous.

The ancient tantric practices were developed with the awareness that breath could be used to bring two people together and, ultimately, closer to the Godhead.

Kathryn Dedman, a counselor and tantra teacher in Marin County, California, uses breath work as a basic building block for couples who are attempting to rekindle their passion. She finds that many couples who are estranged sexually and emotionally have difficulty breathing synchronously together. She uses "spooning" combined with breathing to help couples feel bonded and joined.

## Exercise #9

### *Spoon Breathing*

Begin by creating a sacred space and setting your intention. Take a few minutes to share your appreciation of each other and to open your heart chakra. Play soft background music if you like.

Lie on your side with the back of one person curved into the front of the other. Allow your knees to bend at whatever angle is comfortable and find the most comfortable resting places for your arms.

To maintain a straight alignment of your spine, make sure that each of you has a pillow under your head. Also use smaller pillows between your knees and your ankles if you want to.

Begin to breathe together without trying to control your breathing in any way. Just notice what happens.

After several minutes, if you are not breathing in the same rhythm, try speeding up or slowing down to find a pace that works for both of you. (Sometimes, if one person breathes more slowly than the other, a two-breaths-for-one-breath pattern can be established in which the couple feels joined.)

Experiment with communicating nonverbally, "Hello. I'm awake and here with you." Throw one leg over your partner's, caress a hand or thigh, press your foot against your partner's.

Take turns with one of you in front and the other behind to find out how each position feels. Notice if you have a preference.

After you have spooned for about fifteen minutes, talk about what you felt, thought, and experienced in your body.


Because many people tend to become unconscious and may even drift off to sleep in the prone position, it is important to develop tools for staying conscious and awake. Try squeezing a hand or changing your position slightly every five minutes.

If and when you find that your breathing becomes synchronous, experiment with your focus of attention. For instance, imagine that you are sending and receiving energy through your chakras, one at a time. If your breathing does not become synchronous, try softly playing a piece of music that has a steady beat.

🌿　🌿　🌿　🌿　🌿

# Breathing Opposites

As we have discussed previously, the idea of balancing polarities has been of utmost importance in all the ancient and esoteric traditions. These polarities are described in terms of yin/yang, feminine/masculine, magnetic/electrical, moon/sun, and receptive/active, to name a few. In tantra, supporting the harmonious union of opposites is addressed in a variety of ways.

Since each person has both a positive and a negative charge, moving energy through one's body for the purpose of creating harmony underlies many tantric practices. This is important between partners as well as individually. One avenue is through the breath.

## Exercise #10

### *Yin-Yang Breathing*

As you inhale, imagine that energy rises up from the base of your spine, through your genitals, flows up the back of your spine and over the top of your head. Squeeze your PC muscle as you inhale as if you are sucking up energy. (For women, it is often easier to imagine that your vagina is doing a sucking motion.)

Place the tip of your tongue lightly against the roof of your mouth. If it is comfortable, try placing it at the point where the hard palate becomes soft.

As you exhale, send the energy down the front of your body. Release your PC muscle, allowing it to bulge out as you exhale.

Continue to bring the energy up the back on the inhale, and down the front on the exhale for five minutes or longer.

According to Marin County, California, tantra teacher Robert Frey, moving energy up the back expresses the positive or male active energy, while sending it down the front expresses the negative, receptive female energy. The reason to send the energy down the front of the body is to ground and disperse the charge. A complete out-breath is very important for men, as it aids in the process of letting go and surrendering.

Men tend to focus easily on bringing the energy up their spine—which is exciting and powerful—but they tend to forget the feminine dispersal of energy down the front.

The more a man lets go into the feminine, the more he will let go into his partner. Frey notes and advises,

> *A gift that a man can bring into lovemaking, into the intimacy is his ability to move energy up his back, building the charge and then remember to release the charge down his front as he exhales.*[5]

By practicing the yin/yang breath, even on your own, you are indirectly working on the connection between yourself and your partner because emotional and spiritual union occurs during the out-breath.

You can also practice this yin/yang breath with your partner—while embraced standing, sitting, or reclining. Both of you breathe up the back of your spines simultaneously, and then exhale, sending the energy down the fronts of your bodies. As you practice this breathing pattern with your partner, allow yourself to build a charge on the in-breath, and then surrender and energetically, fall into your lover on the out-breath.

If a man deeply lets go on the exhalation, a woman who is very sensitive will feel it. She feels met, received and joined—in the deeply feminine core of her being.

Women can often feel the vibration—the basis of the connection. Most women are better at feeling this connection than men because they are more in touch with the receptive, magnetic energy. However, when men experience this surrender, they also feel a sense of wholeness, integration, and union.

The deepest nonverbal sharing takes place on the exhalation when lovers surrender to each other. When practicing the yin/yang breath while sexually joined, people often experience a full-body orgasm at the end of the out-breath—the body shakes, undulates, and vibrates spontaneously—particularly when they have been tantric practitioners for one year or longer. When a man and woman experience this simultaneously, it feels like a quivering rush that moves through both bodies simultaneously.

## Exercise #11

### *Tantric Embrace*

Stand facing your partner, gazing softly into each other's eyes.

After a minute or so, move toward your partner until the two of you are embraced. Put one hand on your partner's spine at the level of the heart, and the other hand as low on the spine as you can reach comfortably.

Allow yourselves to breathe together for a few minutes, feeling your energy blend with your partner. Squeeze and release your PC muscle as you breathe.

Now change your breathing pattern so that one of you inhales while the other exhales and vice versa. Establish a rhythmic pattern together so you can do this comfortably. When you get the pattern established, add your PC squeeze and release.

**Women:** As you inhale, imagine that you are receiving your partner's energy through your genitals. With your breath, bring your energy up your Inner Flute to your heart center. Then, as you exhale, send your energy to your partner from your heart center.

**Men:** As you inhale, imagine that you are receiving your partner's energy through your heart center. With your breath, move your energy through your Inner Flute down to your genitals. Then, as you exhale, send your energy to your partner through your genitals.

Do this for several minutes. Imagine that your energies form a continuous circle that goes in the female genitalia, up her spine through the Inner Flute, through her heart into his heart, down his spine, through his Inner Flute, and through his genitalia back into hers. Imagine that your energy blending with your beloved's is like two instruments harmonizing to make exquisite music.

When you are ready to stop, make eye contact with each other for a few minutes before speaking about your experience.


You can vary the tantric embrace by changing your positions. Experiment together by breathing in this way when you are lying together in each other's arms or when you are sexually joined. Try sitting with the man cross-legged with a pillow in his lap and with the woman sitting on the pillow, straddling the man. This position is known by practitioners of tantra as the yab/yum position—the union of mother and father.[6] If that is not comfortable, find an armless chair that is low enough for the woman's feet to rest on the floor while she straddles her partner. Whether you sit on pillows on the floor or on a chair, any of the exercises we suggest can be varied by using this position.

In tantra, it is common for the woman to be sitting on the lap of the man while the couple is sexually joined. This is the pose that we often see in Indian art. Practicing in a vertical plane gives a

*Indian album painting. Late eighteenth century.*

*Tantric practitioners regarded sexual intercourse as the essential rite of initiation enabling them to accede to knowledge. The two principles Shiva (male) and Shakti (his wisdom, embodied by the female), merged in the couple and transcended the sexual embrace. The yab/yum position (union of the mother and father) allows the couple to move energy in the interior while their bodies remain motionless.*

Werner Forman/Art Resource, NY

slightly more meditative quality to the sexual experience than lying down. It cannot be duplicated by lying down on a bed because the horizontal position creates a different energetic experience.

      🌿     🌿     🌿     🌿     🌿

# The Orgasmic Spine

When your breath is moving freely through your body, your entire body is affected. If you watch a baby or young child breathe while sleeping, you can see how the entire spine ripples with the inhalations and exhalations. Try an experiment right now to feel how your spine moves in response to your breathing.

## Exercise #12

### *Spinal Breathing*

Sit cross-legged on the floor. (If this in uncomfortable for you, sit on a bench or hard chair with your feet flat on the floor and your spine straight, not touching the back of the chair.)

Take in a long, slow, deep breath and notice how your spine lengthens and your head begins to tilt backward.

Now exhale and continue to exhale until every ounce of air is out of your lungs. Allow your spine to move in response and notice how it folds or curls down, bringing your head down as well.

Continue to breathe in this way, exaggerating the movement of your head as it drops backward and forward.

Allow your spine to find the fullest range of movement possible. Continue until you feel your spine undulating gracefully in response to your breath.

Now stand with your feet shoulder width apart, knees slightly bent. Once again, inhale and allow your spine to lengthen and arch. As you exhale, let your pelvis tilt back and your spine round.

Continue to breathe, allowing your spine to undulate.

Experiment by adding your PC squeeze and release to your breathing undulation.

This slow undulation is the same movement that your spine moves through during the powerful wave-like undulation of orgasm. If you find that your spine does not undulate easily, do not give up. After years of shallow breathing, the muscles of the spine tighten as well. The next exercise will help you stretch and loosen these muscles as well as strengthen them.

Wilhelm Reich, a colleague of Freud and a pioneer in body oriented psychotherapy, understood the effect that breathing had on the sexual and emotional response. He found that when a person's breathing was restricted and there was little spinal movement, the person's emotional and sexual expression was equally limited. Reich developed exercises to free the breath as well as the spine.[7] Many practitioners, aware of the efficacy of this work, have adapted his teachings. This next practice is one such adaptation.

## Exercise #13

### *Opening to the Orgasm Response*

Lie face up on the floor with your legs bent, knees pointed to the ceiling. Rest your hands comfortably on your abdomen.

Allow your pelvis to rock forward as you inhale, creating a little arch in the small of your back.

As you exhale, allow your pelvis to rock backward, keeping your abdomen soft. (Slightly press your feet into the floor which enables your legs to support your body and permits your pelvis to rock freely.)

As you practice this pelvic rock, imagine that your breath is creating the impetus for the movement. On the exhale, as your pelvis rocks backward, exaggerate this movement and allow your pubic bone to move forward and upward in the direction of your knees. Keep exhaling until you have released all the air from your lungs.

Then, as you inhale, allow your pelvis to tip forward, creating a small arch in your lower back.

When you develop a comfortable rhythm, add a PC squeeze on the inhale and a release on the exhale. Continue to do this for at least ten minutes, allowing your breath to transport your vital, sexual energy to each of your energy centers through your Inner Flute.

As you continue to practice this pelvic curl, you will find that you increase the flexibility of your spine. With increased flexibility, your spine will undulate more freely when you experience orgasms. The result, we are happy to relate, will be increased sensation and pleasure.

As your body becomes freer to surrender to the pulsing sensations flowing through you, you will also experience greater emotional surrender. Also, by "offering up your pelvis and your genitals to your partner, you can enhance the experience of release and surrender."[8] In the following exercise, by combining the yin/yang breath with the pelvic rock, you and your partner can experiment with this idea.

## Exercise #14

### *Rock Yourself to Love*

Sit in a yab/yum position with your partner (one person straddling the other) on the floor. You can use pillows or an armless chair that is low enough for the top person's feet to rest on the ground.

Breathe fully and easily (inhale through your nose and exhale through your mouth). As you inhale, bring your energy from your tail bone up your spine to your crown and as you exhale, down the front of your body.

Allow your pelvis to rock back and forth as you breathe. Since many men in our culture have tight pelvic musculature, you may find that the woman has more flexibility when you first try this. If you practice this regularly and gently, and if the man practices the pelvic rock (from exercise # 13) on his own, this will change over time. The reward will be greater pleasure for the man—full body orgasms.

Imagine that as you both inhale simultaneously, you are gathering energy and that as you exhale, you are offering yourself to your partner.

Add your PC squeeze and release, gathering or tightening your genitals on the inhale and allowing them to soften and bulge as you exhale.

Also experiment with embracing each other so that you are in full body contact but separated enough to maintain eye contact.

Continue practicing this for at least 10 minutes.

After completion, share with your partner what you experienced (remember that sharing isn't about what the other "should" have done differently, but rather about your own sensations, feelings or thoughts).

Now, let's re-visit touch. As we described earlier, being present as you touch your partner is vitally important. Of equal importance is being able to touch your partner in a way that he or she experiences feeling loved. However, because the experience of feeling loved originates from within your partner, not from you, you can only support your partner.

Clear, direct communication is essential so that you and your partner know what each other likes in order to feel loved. None of us is a mind reader!

In the following exercises, please tell your partner how you enjoy being touched and how she or he could touch you in a way that you would enjoy even more.

## Exercise #15

### *Loving Hands*

*Preparation: Take a shower or bath and prepare a sacred space using flowers or music, if you desire.*

One person (the receiver) lies down in a comfortable position. The other person (the toucher) sits facing the receiver.

Breathe together for a few minutes. Make eye contact with your lover, if you desire.

***Toucher:*** Place your hands on your partner's body slowly and gently as if saying, "Hello, soul. I'm aware that I'm entering your space. I respect you and honor you." Let your open palms rest quietly without doing anything other than being aware.

Imagine that there is a direct connection between your heart and your hands and that you are sending love to your partner through your hands.

***Receiver:*** Breathe into the region under your lover's hands and notice any feelings that arise.

***Toucher:*** Using your open palm, begin to glide over your partner's body, feeling the contour of the curves. Use long, continuous strokes over the entire back, buttocks, legs, down to the souls of the feet. Keep focusing on sending your heart energy through your hands.

***Receiver:*** Give your partner feedback in the way of sounds if you feel pleasure, or ask your lover to touch you more softly, slowly, etc. If you merely "put up with it, " you will only end up feeling resentful.

Keep genitals off limits until you both feel more comfortable with this kind of loving, sensual touch.

After an agreed upon time, ten minutes or more, talk about your experience and then reverse roles.

As you and your partner feel comfortable touching with presence and love, you can move on to touch with arousal. If you or your partner suffer from performance pressure or if your sexual relationship feels dark and difficult, we recommend that you practice this next exercise with patience, compassion and a sense of humor. As you progress into the book and read the chapters in the section entitled "From Healing to Ecstasy," you may find it useful to return to these exercises with increased awareness and skill. This is true with all the exercises in this chapter.

## Exercise #16

### *Erotic Massage*

*Begin in the same way as above in "Touching the Soul" and "Loving Hands." Take a shower or bath and create a sacred space.*

**Toucher:** As you put your hands on your lover's body, begin with presence, move into the sensual gliding strokes of love, and then begin to caress your partner, using your fingertips rather than the open palm of your hand. Maintain your long strokes and avoid the genitals until you and your partner feel that your whole body has become an erogenous zone. Use lots of massage oil on the body and water-based lubricant on the genitals when you get there.

**Receiver:** Your only responsibility is to stay aware, breathe, let your pleasurable sounds come out, and give your partner feedback. If something does not feel good to you, ask your partner to touch you differently. Also communicate what does feel good. Expressing appreciation keeps the heart energy open and fluid. As you are massaged by your beloved, practice your PC squeeze and release. Use your breath and your focus of attention to send your energy through your Inner Flute, letting your sounds come out like the music of your pleasure.

As you practice erotic massage, maintain eye contact. As you attend to your breathing, make sure that you are breathing deeply into your belly. Include any of the breathing techniques you have practiced and found valuable.

Experiment with different kinds of touch. Find out what feels arousing to your partner. Remember: There is no right way. What matters is that your strokes are pleasurable and arousing to your partner.

#### For Men as the Giver

Most women become aroused when their entire body is stroked lightly before moving to their pelvic area and before focusing on their genitals. When you get positive feedback from your lover—from sighs or moans of pleasure—keep doing what you are doing. As you stimulate her entire body, watch for signs that she is wanting you to move toward her genitals. Many women will begin to undulate their pelvis, make slow pelvic circles, or arch their pubic bone toward you. Move slowly toward her genitals, taking your time, allowing her arousal to build. When you begin to massage her vagina, begin with the labia, then slowly, circle toward the clitoris. Keep listening and watching for feedback. Do not change your stroke if you are getting positive feedback, since that means her arousal is building.

Rather than bringing your beloved to an orgasm when she becomes aroused during your first round, encourage her to bring her energy up through her Inner Flute to her crown. Allow her to rest for a few minutes, then begin to arouse her again. Follow this sequence two or three times before you maintain your stimulation through to orgasm, if she is ready and desires an orgasm. The focus of this exercise is arousal, not orgasm. So, there is no need to pressure yourself or your partner to reach orgasm.

### For Women as the Giver

Do not be alarmed if you are massaging and caressing your beloved's body and he does not develop an erection. Most men need direct stimulation of the shaft of their penis to achieve an erection. One way to help your partner experience his entire body as an eroge- nous zone is to caress his entire body, gently brushing over his penis as you move past it to different areas. Before stimulating the penis directly, massage and stroke his inner thighs, belly, scrotum, perineum, and his anal area. Use plenty of lubrication. When you begin to stroke his penis, use long strokes all the way up and down the shaft of the penis, applying firm pressure. When he develops an erection, vary your strokes, making sure to ask him what he likes if you do not know. While he is in a state of high arousal, vary your focus between stimulating his penis and caressing the perineum, anus, scrotum, belly, thighs, and spreading out over his whole body.

Bring him to a high state of arousal, then spread the energy through his body with your hands as he breathes and directs his energy through his Inner Flute up to his crown. Repeat this sequence two or three times before he has an orgasm, if he so desires.

If your partner is about to ejaculate, you will see his testicles draw up against his body, and his thighs and buttocks begin to contract or he will say, "Stop." To help him control the urge to ejaculate, you can press against his perineum as he inhales deeply, puts his tongue on the roof of his mouth at the point between the hard and soft palate, looks up, and squeezes his PC muscle.

### For Both Partners as Givers

Before you finish, allow your hands to rest on your beloved. Breathe together and embrace or do spoon breathing together. As in the previous exercises, talk about your experience and change roles. Now the giver becomes the receiver.

If you found that you did not know how to stimulate your lover, or that the communication between you is troubled, you might return to this exercise after having completed the exercises in Chapters 9 and 10. In Chapter 11, we include techniques which help both men and women experi- ence fuller, more intense, and more satisfying orgasms. We specifically address stimulation of the "G" spot or "sacred" spot in women and the anus and prostate for men.

# The Power of Sound

Our culture has taught us to suppress our sounds and keep them to a minimum—except when rooting for our favorite sports team. However, sound plays an important role in healthy sexuality. It allows energy to move through your body by creating vibrations. It facilitates the throat chakra open- ing, which supports your expressiveness and creativity. As your own sound resonates in your body, it creates a feedback loop which furthers excitation and arousal on a cellular level. When your lover hears your sounds, the positive feedback is often immediate. A synergistic loop is set up that sounds something like this:

Partner 1: "Aaah…Oh…Aaah." The message: "This feels good. What you're doing is arousing me."

Partner 2: "Mmmm…Ah, yes." The message: "I'm glad that you're aroused. Your arousal excites me. I want to arouse you and pleasure you even more."

Partner 1: "Oh…Oh…Oh…Ohhh" The message: "Wow, you're turned on by my pleasure. Now, I'm feeling even more pleasure. I want to turn you on too."

Sadly, most women and men make very small, soft sounds if at all. This suppression actually cuts off the vital energy and dampens excitation. So, if you want to enhance your erotic experience, begin to let more and more sound pour forth.

Here are some practices which can assist in your transition from suppressive to expressive eroticism.

## Exercise #17

### *Sounds Good*

*Since sounds are so taboo, give yourselves permission to experiment making sounds alone and together (you might become very hesitant, especially after some sounds escape your lips).*

Begin to breath together and make eye contact.

Make a big AAAAHHHHH sound together as you exhale.

Keep doing this as you let your jaw drop and your aaah sound emanate from your belly.

Whether you are sitting, standing, or lying down, allow your spine to undulate while breathing and letting your sound emerge. (As you exhale, and let out your aaah, your spine rounds as your pelvis tilts back slightly.)

Allow your sound to be as low and guttural as feels good to you.

Women will experience great value by opening their jaw and throat, and making lower sounds than usual. When women do make sounds, they tend to tighten their throat and make high, screechy sounds which are culturally considered to be more feminine. Many women feel shy or conflicted about making strong, low, guttural sounds since they feel ashamed of their earthy sexuality and they fear that powerful, guttural sounds will be threatening to their man.

On the other hand, most men in our culture have been raised to suppress their feelings—to be the strong and silent type. When they are having sex, it's fine to enjoy themselves, but they have to hold themselves together and not make too much noise. Finally, when they do climax, they permit themselves an ejaculatory grunt.

The man then comes across as being in control and able to handle a lot of sexual feeling, without getting too carried away. However, by maintaining such control, he loses out on the pleasure of surrender. Furthermore, the woman doesn't really know how the man is feeling. She doesn't receive the benefit of hearing his sounds of arousal, which are actually quite exciting to her—and are a non-verbal form of communication. Furthermore, the man doesn't experience the bodily power that making sound and creating vibration can have on his sexual sensations.

## Exercise #18

### *To Sound or Not to Sound*

Do any movement without making sound.

Then do the same movement while making sound that emanates from your breath. (Most people find a tremendous difference in the power and energy they experience in the latter.)

Try different movements such as the pelvic rock, pelvic circles, and the spinal undulation or any other movements that you consider erotic. Again, first do them without making sound and then do them while making aaahh or ohhh sounds on your exhalation.

Now re-visit loving hands or erotic massage, doing it without sound for several minutes and then letting your sound out.

The next time you are aroused and ready to climax, experiment with letting go—free your sounds. Find out how you experience orgasm differently as you let more and more sounds pour forth.

Talk about your experiences together and any feelings you have of embarrassment, self-consciousness, shyness, fear, or anything else.

It's wonderful for couples to play and discover the difference. You have probably now discovered the power of sound to enhance your erotic experience and build energy.

# Opening Your Erotic Channels

Practitioners of tantra are aware that each chakra has a different energetic and psychological meaning. Remember that tantra was developed for the purpose of raising consciousness to a spiritual level so that we may experience God. For this to occur, we must free up all restrictions so the Kundalini can rise all the way to the crown chakra.

Thus, opening the chakras are essential if we want the vital life force of the Kundalini to flow through the body.

The key to opening and connecting the chakras naturally involves attending to or focusing on the energetic space between them. Tantric practices teach people how to build, circulate, and manage their vital force by moving energy through the chakras. It has been well documented and tested that where awareness goes, energy follows. For example, if you put your awareness on your elbow, and we measured the galvanic skin response before and after you focused your attention, there would be a measurable change.

Since most of us have learned the cultural lessons well, we are adept at shutting off the signals and messages of our body. We are experts at taking our attention away from our bodies. Tantra requires that we re-learn these lessons—that we tune into what is happening inside us. However, focusing our attention and developing awareness takes practice, patience, and persistence. If you feel awkward or incompetent, have compassion for yourself and keep practicing.

## Exercise #19

### *Awakening and Integrating the Lower Chakras*

Sit opposite your partner on the floor or on a pillow with your legs crossed. (You can also practice this alone.)

Breathe quickly through your mouth, pursing your lips so that the air whistles as you inhale. Do not exaggerate your breathing so much that you get lightheaded. Make sure that you exhale as well as inhale.

Imagine that you are breathing through your anus. (Contract your anal sphincter muscle as if you're holding back a bowel movement.)

Tighten the anus while you do this quick breathing. (If done with your partner, both partners do this at the same time.)

Then begin to breathe into your genitals, which can be experienced by squeezing and releasing your PC muscle.

As you run energy back and forth from your anus to your genitals, keep your attention on both of them for maximum healing power. (Visualize a line running between your anus and penis or clitoris.)

Now, use a relaxed, quick breath to stimulate your entire pelvic area. Bring your energy up into your belly, right below your navel. Keep running the current up from your anus to your genitals and into your belly, then back to your genitals and out your anus. (You will not necessarily feel sexually aroused, but there will probably be a feeling of warmth or sensitivity.)

Stop squeezing and releasing your muscles, but continue with relaxed, quick breathing.

Go into a more relaxed breathing pattern and allow the energy you have built up to run through the pelvis. Visualize this energy running through your pelvic area by imagining streams of light and energy running out through your hips and back.

Do this for about 10 minutes.

Now imagine the energy moving downward from your hara to your genitals, and to your anus.

You may experience a slight metallic taste in your mouth and feel a bit uncomfortable after doing this. According to Berkeley, California, somatic educator Thomas Cooper, "men often resist the feeling of this grounded discomfort. So it is essential that a man's desire to heal be stronger than the discomfort he will probably experience."[9] Through the willingness to plow through the discomfort, men will feel more grounded in life and lovemaking. Women will experience a stronger man as a result of this grounding.

A woman will often have orgasmic-like releases in the general pelvic area when doing this exercise. Men can also have this experience, but it often takes increased sensitivity, patience, and awareness of non-genital orgasmic releases.

Another important connection to establish is between the sexual chakra and the heart chakra. There is an ancient technique to help join sexual passion and love which involves masturbation. Focusing on the path between sexual passion and love will actually strengthen and enhance this connection.

## Exercise #20

### *Tantric Masturbation*

Lying on your back, begin to caress and massage your genitals.

With each inhalation and exhalation, breathe a little more deeply and slowly.

When you inhale, imagine that there's a movement of sensation going from your genitals up to your heart.

Every time you exhale, release from your heart down into your genitals.

Breathe sex pleasure up, and breathe love back down, so that love joins with sexuality.

Now, use one or both hands to trace a pathway between your genitals and your heart center, including your nipples. Continue with the same focus of attention as you massage your heart area and nipples, connecting the energy between these chakras.

After you have done this exercise alone, try doing it with your partner. Let your beloved watch you masturbate first so that h/she can see what you like and how you arouse yourself. If this is uncomfortable for you, know that you are not alone. Many people feel shy and embarrassed about masturbating with their partner. However, as you move through your discomfort, masturbating in the presence of your beloved can greatly enrich your erotic relationship.

Under the loving gaze of your partner, your tantric masturbation can fuel the fires of eros by decreasing shame, increasing arousal, and showing your partner what you like.

It is also a great way to address difference in desire. The more desirous person can still express his or her sexuality in the presence of their partner. But don't take our word for it. Find out for yourself.

After your partner has watched you masturbate, she or he may be ready to try his or her hand at it, so to speak. When your lover is stimulating you, it is incumbent upon you, as the receiver, to give your partner feedback that will help you maintain your focus of attention. Tell your lover to touch you more slowly, more firmly, or whatever feels good to you. The intent is for both of you to be working together with your energy.

As the receiver, the more you know your body and are in touch with your feelings, the more satisfying this will be. It is also important that the giver be aware of his or her energy. Maintaining eye contact also helps people bring their heart and genitals together.

Another variation of this exercise is for you to stimulate your own genitals while your partner stimulates your heart area, or vice versa.

## Exercise #21

### *Loving Genitally*

Breathe together for a few minutes.

*Toucher:* Begin to stimulate or massage the genitals of your lover.

After a short while, take your other hand and gently move up from the genitals to the heart.

Gently caress both of your lover's nipples with the intention to help open the energy of your lover's heart.

Gaze deeply into your lover's eyes during this experience.

*Receiver:* Breathe deeply as you focus on sensing your energy moving between your genitals and your heart.

As you receive, you can practice running energy all the way through your body. Let your sound out as you bring your energy up through your throat chakra. Continue circulating your energy back down your body to your root chakra, then all the way up until it rests at your third eye, and then finally at your crown.

After a period of time that feels right for both of you, talk about the experience and change roles.

Tantric philosophy teaches that the physical area of the heart is truly connected to your feelings of love. Reichian and bioenergetic work provides evidence of this connection. In addition, some research has shown a relationship between heart attacks and people who shut down their feelings of love.[10]

How remarkable that the practice of opening our hearts has a healthy impact not only on our love relationships, but also on our bodies—what a great combination.

## Exercise #22

### *Giving and Receiving Love*

*Play some sensual, erotic music during this process, if you like.*

Begin to breathe deeply while standing or moving in order to get your energy flowing. Use your PC squeeze and release as you breathe and allow your sexual energy to circulate.

Sit in the yab/yum position on pillows or on a narrow, armless chair.

One person, the sender, energetically projects love and warmth to the other person who will focus on receiving it.

Each of you places your hand over your partner's heart or on the back at the level of the heart.

Then reverse.

A variation of this is to stand and rock your pelvis (with hands on each other's hearts) at the same time that you are giving or receiving love; the pelvic movement intensifies the fire within and between you.

As you practice, over time you will be able to run energy all the way up your Inner Flute, through your chakras, while doing this.

As you do these exercises, remember that what is most important is that you stay conscious, present, and patient. There is no race. There is no goal other than being as alive as you can be in each moment. The next two exercises bring the work you have already done together. Enjoy!

## Exercise #23

### *Erotic Embraces*

Breathe fully and deeply throughout this entire process.

When you are joined in sexual union, look directly into your partner's eyes.

Allow all of your feelings to be present, not only your so-called positive ones. Fear, shame, anger, guilt, and sadness are also welcome.

Let your partner see into the deepest parts of you without trying to hide. If you feel yourself beginning to hide, simply breathe and be present without judging yourself for it.

Allow yourself to see deeply into your partner. If judgments arise, simply notice them without trying to deny them or focus attention on them.

Whenever thoughts emerge which take you away from the immediate experience with your partner, keep using your breath and intention to be intimate as a way to bring you back to the moment.

**Exercise #24**

### *The Morning and Evening Prayer*

*This is practiced reclining, usually with the man on top. However, if the woman feels trapped or her vagina is shallow and the man's penis is long and thick, she may want to be on top.*

When you are sexually joined in a high state of arousal, make your movement more and more subtle until you are hardly moving.

Breathe the energy up your Inner Flute to the third eye (in the middle of your forehead between your two eyebrows), and then down the Inner Flute to your genitals as you do small, subtle pelvic rocks together.

Visualize each of your chakras connecting with your partner's corresponding chakra.

Focus your attention on the movement of energy and internal sensations rather than the movement of your bodies. Experiment with what happens when you remain perfectly still. Allow yourself to relax totally.

If your arousal level drops, begin your PC squeeze and release. Then, relax again. The intention here is to join your energies, not to move through to orgasm. Move just enough so that the man can sustain or regain his erection.

The Taoists call this The Morning and Evening Prayer because they recommend starting the day with this when rising, and ending the evening with this before going to sleep. As you practice this, you will experience a joining of your energies that is deeply bonding. If you feel that nothing is happening, focus your attention inward to sensations and the movement of energy. In our culture, we tend to look for athletic sexuality which is more *yang* rather than the more internal *yin* of The Morning and Evening Prayer. However, if you practice this regularly, you will surely reap benefits. You will be training yourself to hear and play all the music—the harmony as well as the melody.

🌿   🌿   🌿   🌿   🌿

# Transitioning to Tantra

Transitioning from your common sexual practices to tantric lovemaking may seem like an impossible leap. If you find yourself feeling intimidated by this information—please take heart. Like learning anything new, it takes time. In the meantime, perhaps you might find some simple practices more to your liking.

Before you begin the next exercise, make sure you will not be disturbed for at least half an hour. Create a time when both of you will be uninterrupted. You might start with thirty minutes and extend it as you feel comfortable. Unplug the phone, relax, and put on some soothing music.

**Exercise #25**

### *Cultivating Your Erotic Garden*

Take turns creating non-goal oriented together time—touching, playing, being sensual, nurturing one person at a time, focusing on the entire body as the erogenous zone rather than the genitals, massaging, bathing together, sharing fantasies, looking into each other's eyes, covering your partner's face and body with little kisses.

Your imagination knows no bounds, so allow yourselves to explore, experiment, and enjoy!

## Exercise #26

### *Basic Tantra*

After you have been making love and reached a high level of arousal, stop your motion.

Quiet yourselves and let your partner know in some way how much you care for him or her.

In silence, look in each other's eyes for a few moments or longer.

Then begin to move again and increase your arousal level, attempting to keep eye contact. Repeat this pattern two or three times before moving to a regular ejaculation or climax.

If you want to, you can have an awareness that the back of the spine corresponds with the chakra system.

If you are in the missionary position with the man on top, the woman can help the man bring energy up from the base of the spine up to the heart, by placing one hand on the base of his spine (or as far down as she can reach)—which helps stimulate a certain amount of passion—and with her other hand she can trace a line up his spine.

You might say to your lover as you gently massage around the heart area on the back, "Let's take this moment to sense and feel our hearts connecting."

# Timely Interludes

Being intimidated by tantra is not the only reason you might shy away from these practices. Time—or more precisely, the lack of time—is another reason. These days time is of the essence. Couples, particularly parents of young children, are often hard pressed to make time for eros in their frantic schedules—especially when their sexual experience is less than ecstatic.

We do not want to give the impression that tantric lovemaking always takes several hours. A profound experience need not take a long time. However, if you begin to experiment with these practices, you may find good reasons to create more time.

## Exercise #27

### *Tantric Quickie*

While making love in ways that are satisfying for you, take a minute to become quiet, breathe and move the energy up from your genitals to your heart area, or to your third eye.

When and if you want to, move into orgasm.

# Prelude to Healing

However fantastic and effective these tantric practices can be, they will be far less valuable or effective if you do not confront the obstacles to passion, love, intimacy, and spiritual development. Besides the lack of education, the problems that most people encounter when beginning to explore and experiment with these practices are a result of sexual shame.

The exalted states we know are possible seem distant and unreachable when the ugly face of shame rears its head. Because of the pervasive damage caused by shame in our culture, we focus the next two sections of this book on shame: first, on raising awareness about the negative impact of sexual shame; and second, on healing sexual shame individually and in your relationship. Even if you think that sexual shame has little or no impact on your relationship, you will probably be surprised by the subtle influence it exerts.

Most tantric practices involve eye contact as a pathway to experience greater intimacy and passion. Whatever difficulty you may have experienced with eye contact during lovemaking is most likely related to shame. In shame, the eyes are cast downward, because the shamed person—and that's practically all of us—consciously or unconsciously believes that his or her soul is tarnished. We feel embarrassed when maintaining prolonged eye contact or even meeting the gaze of others. These experiences, so common to many of us, reveal the deep shame we feel.

The next chapter, *The Wounds of Sexual Shame*, shows how sexual shame develops and how it can turn the potential for lasting love sour. It may help you understand some of your enduring questions about why you are the way you are.

We must confront sexual shame if we intend to have the sexual fulfillment and spiritual union we desire and deserve. The highest heights can only be reached if we are willing to explore the lowest depths. Let's forge ahead and learn how to overcome some of the limiting patterns of shame.

*4*

# The Wounds of
# Sexual Shame

*Perhaps no aspect of human activity has been as dysfunctionally shamed as much as our sexuality. Sexuality is the core of human selfhood. Our sex is not something we have or do, it is who we are...Our sexual energy (libido) is our own unique incarnation of the life force itself. To have our sex drive shamed is to be shamed to the core.*

John Bradshaw, *Healing the Shame That Binds Us*

## Shame Catches Fire

Shame has recently caught fire in the world of psychology. Professionals are finally starting to listen to and understand what many people have known all along: that shame dominates their lives. A mere glance from a person can set off a chain of painful, physiological reactions—sweaty hands, palpating heart, a clenched stomach, and, what feels like an immediate drop in IQ. These reactions are often accompanied by experiences of shyness, self-consciousness, anxiety, preoccupation with other people's perceptions, and a desire to hide.

Perhaps you have wanted to crawl under a rock, yet you were painfully aware of your visibility? If you have felt inadequate, out of place, or like a fool, you may be familiar with the experience of dread which often accompanies shame. Or you might simply avoid eye contact with others—a clue that shame is present.

The purpose of this chapter is to help you learn how sexual shame harmfully impacts your lover relationship in ways that you have probably not realized. Those disturbing fights or misunderstandings—in or out of the bedroom—are often surprisingly related to sexual shame.

## How Shame Develops

The development of shame is not intrinsically related to specific feelings or behaviors—shame can be conditioned into any feeling or behavior. Parents and significant others can shame children for expressing sadness, fear, anger, or even joy! For example, most of us learned in our families that anger (at least our own) was not an acceptable emotion to exhibit. We were taught this either overtly ("How could you speak to your mother that way? What's wrong with you? Go to your room!"), or covertly. (Our parents would become cold and aloof, give us dirty looks, or simply pretend that we were invisible.)

The emotions and behaviors for which we were shamed became replaced with more "acceptable" feelings like depression, guilt, sadness, confusion, fear, or the pretense of happiness—whatever our family deemed more desirable. The "covering" emotion could have been anything.

Essentially, our parents, grandparents, or siblings try to eliminate what they consider to be undesirable behavior. Of course, there need not be anything problematic about the child's behavior other than that the parent dislikes it for whatever reason. This unwarranted dislike can lead to shaming the child's expression of this unacceptable feeling or behavior.

Shame, which the mother, or parent figure projects onto the child, becomes conditioned or bound together with the "unacceptable" feelings. If a child's experience of joy is shamed enough, the child will experience shame every time he or she starts feeling joyous. Shame then automatically accompanies the unacceptable feeling and/or behavior.

Children get the message that their real feelings are not acceptable, and therefore, they themselves are not acceptable. These essential feelings which were not respectfully heard, seen, or recognized by our parents, significant others, and the culture at large, become woven into the fabric of shame.

Robert Karen, in writing about shame, describes it like this:

> *"An unconscious feeling of unworthiness often crystallizes around some hectoring, negative view of the self: One is ugly, stupid, impotent, unmanly, unfeminine. One is phony, grasping, ignorant, boring, cheap. One is insignificant, immature, unable to love."*[1]

Men and women tend to feel trapped by different tendrils from shame depending on the cultural values. Men succumb to experiencing shame over feelings of neediness, incompetence, weakness, or sexual inadequacy. Women fall prey to feeling ashamed of being unattractive, unable to control their emotions, or unable to relate well with others. Neither gender has a monopoly on any of these issues as you may well know.

When our natural and vital impulses are pushed underground, we create and adopt belief systems to help ourselves fend off undesired feelings of inadequacy. A classic male belief epitomized by the statement, "People shouldn't need help from anyone; they should be self-sufficient," develops from early shaming about their dependency needs. Only sissies need help. When a man who operates by this traditional male belief system wants help—even when he stops himself from asking—he experiences shame just for having the desire.

When we fail to adhere to or measure up to the image ideal of whatever our belief systems—which invariably happens—the experience of shame ensues. The familiar feeling arises: We rarely understand it, but we feel inadequate, unacceptable, and unworthy.

These feelings, associated with shame, affect spontaneity, decision making, self-esteem, creativity, and more. The shamed child matures, becomes a shame-based adult and subsequently, a shaming parent. It is in this way that shame is passed on from generation to generation.

## The Shaming of Eros

In a culture that glorifies independence and condemns dependence, even toddlers stand the risk of getting shamed for wanting closeness with Mom—or even desiring physical and emotional comfort. Reaching out for love, asking for nurturing—whether to be held, touched, or noticed—can become negatively associated with intense pain. These experiences reflect the wounds of eros:

A six-year-old boy reaches out to his preoccupied mother, wanting to be hugged, only to be met with a cold response: "Don't bother me now." After repeated experiences of a similar nature, the boy learns to associate reaching out with pain; he represses the desire for closeness and develops the belief, "I don't need anyone."

A girl toddler has her hand between her legs and her mother admonishes her, and slaps her hand—all without explanation. Pre-cognitively, this innocent little girl is already learning that the area between her legs is a dark, forbidden territory—to be avoided at all costs. Yet she also has experienced the pleasure of her hand on her genitals. As she grows older, she will experience greater pleasure through sexual stimulation—both by herself and through the aid of others—yet she has also learned to associate shame (pain) with this pleasure.

A brother and sister, three and five years old, are standing next to each other; the boy's pants are pulled down and the girl's skirt is pulled up. They are looking at each other's body and laughing happily. Their mother walks in, gasps, spanks both of them, and warns them never to do such a thing again. They are punished for their innocent explorations into gender awareness. Invariably, the meaning the young child gives to this experience is that their behavior (and hence they) are bad and wrong.

An eight-year-old girl asks her mother, "What's fucking?" (having heard the word at school) and receives a hard slap on her face. She literally did not know what the word meant. Little sense can be made from this maddening experience.

A four-year-old boy touches his penis. His parents pull his hand away. The boy places it back there. They slap it away and yell at him. He places it there again. The yelling becomes louder and the slap harder. Pain (shame) is being conditioned into touching his penis, so that he learns to associate shame with the natural pleasure of his penis. Instead of associating only pleasure with his genitals, he develops an ambivalent relationship with them. He learns to associate pain and loss of love with touching his penis.

A father tells his nine-year-old son, "Your mother says you're spending a lot of time in the bathroom. Make sure you're not doing anything you shouldn't be doing!" The father's shaming message about masturbation which, incidentally, the boy is not doing, unconsciously lays a bulwark. Later in life when the boy begins to masturbate, he already has the blueprint for sexual shame; pain and pleasure become hermetically sealed.

Sexuality, however, does not disappear. These types of humiliating experiences drive people inward. Their sexual curiosity, desire, and awareness drop below the surface. A tug of war ensues. Which side will win out? Sadly, for many people, the natural pleasure of sexuality verses the conditioned pain of shame is experienced as an enduring battle. And the possibility of being lifelong loving partners receives a severe blow.

# Shame Based Sexual Conditioning

It is probably apparent that, in all of the above examples, these children were expressing innocent childhood sexual curiosity and behavior—hardly grounds for harsh punishment. However, when parents have strong prohibitions against sexuality because they have not healed their own shame, they respond inappropriately to their children. Even though their motivation may be well intentioned, the results are disastrous. Their children develop beliefs that their sexual feelings are aberrant.

Perhaps the last examples seem extreme to you. Or maybe you have had experiences that make these pale in comparison. In either case, you have probably felt misunderstood and shamed by people you cared about.

If, as children, we feel that our desires and emotions come up repeatedly against stone walls, we develop the belief that something is wrong with us for having these desires or emotions. Often, we try to dig a hole and bury the offending feelings. However, left underground they start growing toxic roots, ready to poison the entire garden. We then lose the purity of the experience or emotion which, if directly expressed, could have led toward resolution and fulfillment. Instead, we tend to experience the feeling of shame which clouds the original desire. That's why many people hardly know what they want.

Perhaps you can remember times in your life when you felt strongly about something or someone and you were told that you did not or should not feel the way you felt. If that person were your mother, father, priest, teacher or another significant person, the shame generated can be profound. These feelings of shame continue through adulthood unless addressed.

It's remarkable how often we, as adults, disavow and condemn (if only subtly) our precious sexuality (or other aspects of ourselves), because as children, our budding erotic nature was abused by people who were important to us. As children, when we expressed our natural curiosity about our bodies and bodily functioning, and adults treated us with disdain or disgust, we got the message that something was wrong with us. Because these are expressions of our core erotic being, we incorporated the belief that we, ourselves, were aberrant. Thus the shame cycle commences.

## Exercise #1

### *Uncovering Shame*

Get in a comfortable position and close your eyes. With your attention focused inward, follow your breath as it moves through your body. When you feel your mind and body quieting, begin to remember back in time to your childhood.

Scan your childhood and adolescence for any scenes in which you experienced:

*acute embarrassment*

*desires to disappear*

*fear of being caught in the act*

*self-conscious awkwardness*

As you review these scenes, how does your body feel? What images do you see in your mind's eye? Are there any sounds or words that accompany these images? Or smells?

What kind of action do you imagine yourself taking as you review these old memories?

What did you actually do when these events occurred?

If you told anyone about them, how did those people respond?

What decisions did you make at the time about yourself—about what you would do, feel, think, etc.—in the future?

Take a deep breath and let it go. If you become aware that you made childhood decisions which no longer serve you, remember that awareness is the first step to change.

When you feel ready, write about any memories or images you had that are important to you. Share these with your partner or a friend when you so desire.

The instinct to avoid pain is built into the deepest levels of our biological and psychological make-up, thus reinforcing a difficult-to-resolve paradox: The very experiences that make life enjoyable and pleasurable—emotional and physical intimacy with loved ones—become tinged with extreme pain. No wonder that both intimate relationships and the healing process seem so mixed with confronting the things in life we most dread.

🌿   🌿   🌿   🌿   🌿

# The Unconscious Forces of Parental Shaming

It's so easy to take things personally. Most of us do this our entire lives. We believe and feel that we are the problem, that we are the cause of our parents' problems. We are not!

Parents are rarely aware of their unconscious motivations in child rearing—particularly regarding sexuality. However, children must adjust to the situation, no matter how distorted the parents behavior may be.

What unconscious forces motivate parents to act so blindly? When children begin to express their sexuality (or what is perceived as sexuality), it unconsciously reawakens the parents' experiences of having had their own sexuality shamed as children. Although parents usually have the best intentions, their own archaic, unhealed wounds make it nearly impossible for them to fully support their children's sense of freedom to be sexually healthy beings.

Shaming the child's innocent sexuality (as well as other bodily functions and impulses) is far more damaging than simply stopping the premature expression of sexuality. The humiliation occurs when the parents show contempt for the child's instinctual wishes and desires. In effect, the parents voice admonishes: "How could you want to do something so disgusting as be sexual?" These shaming parental messages often pierce the soul of a child's blossoming sexuality.

# The Shaming of Adolescent Urges

I, Daniel, slept nude when I was both a child and an adolescent. My mother disapproved but lacked the means to stop me. However, on those occasions when we chanced to meet in the hall on nocturnal bathroom jaunts, she motioned toward my penis, made a sour face, and asked rhetorically, "Do I have to see that?"

The rebellious youth in me responded with, "If you don't want to see it, don't look." But in fact, it made me shrivel up inside, and I began trying to hide the manifestations of my maleness. Subconsciously, I was picking up the message that there was something bad about my penis, about sex, and about *me*.

Then, when I was seventeen years old, I had a classic experience regarding sexual shame. I had cleverly arranged—or so I thought—a way to sleep over my new girlfriend's house. Her parents' trip out of town provided an exciting opportunity. It didn't take great insight to know that my mother would not approve so I concocted a reasonable adolescent plan. I told her that I was sleeping over my friend Barry's house. I told Barry that if my mother called his house, he should answer the phone and tell her that I would call her after getting out of the bathroom. Then he would call me at the girl's house and I would calmly return my mother's call. It sounded like a great scheme to me. However, there was one slight problem.

When my mother called, my friend didn't make it to the phone as fast as his mother. The truth came out. I hadn't slept there. My friend then called me at my girlfriend's house with the grave news. "Your mother knows. She wants you home right away!" Terrified, I hurried home. When my mother saw me, she glared at me with that angry-hurt expression I knew so well. Then she spoke: "Why would you want to do something like that?" (This meant, why would you want to sleep over a very attractive girl's house and have sex with her?) She was absolutely incredulous that I had these desires.

Her question implied two things to me which were already encrusted in my erotic self: that I should not even have sexual desires and that my sexual desires were aberrant. Even my stepfather surprised me with a comment I will never forget: "A stiff cock has no conscience." For me, since the word conscience is usually associated with morality, not having a conscience implies that I was, or would be, acting lewdly. And there was a part of me that already believed that anyway.

I grew up with a deep-seated shame about sex. This was manifested in my fear and, hence, unwillingness to ask questions about sexual things I really wanted to know. I was even reticent to discuss sex with anyone—including my friends. That has largely changed now—my relationship with Judith and my own inner work have helped immensely—however I still do personal work on healing sexual shame.

## Parent's Erotic Needs—and Their Children

If a father feels inadequate or unresolved about his own sexuality, then quite possibly, he would not want to be confronted with a son who exuded sexual confidence. In cases like this, which are quite common, whenever the son expresses his healthy sexual identity, he meets with emotional rejection—and maybe even physical abuse—by his father.

Unconsciously clinging to his father's love and acceptance, the son might easily manifest shame and inferiority feelings about his sexuality to protect against his father's rejection—an example of the strange adaptability of shame.

Thus, the unspoken telepathic agreement or psychic contract (as unconsciously expressed) by the father may run something like this: "I'll love and support you as long as you don't feel good about your sexual identity. Then I won't have to face my own inferiority feelings so directly."

For the son: "I'll subvert a healthy relationship to my sexuality to avoid emotional abandonment and/or physical abuse by you, dad."

If dad could acknowledge and deal with his own erotic pain, he would not need to project his inadequacy onto his son; this would mean dealing with the wounded child within himself—an initial step toward developing his own sense of healthy sexuality.

Another common and equally disastrous pattern occurs in many families when a young girl enters puberty. If the spousal relationship does not have a healthy erotic element, both parents often act inappropriately toward the emerging woman, damaging her fragile sense of sexuality. The father, feeling frustrated and unfulfilled in his marriage, may begin to direct his sexual energy and attention toward his daughter. The daughter, in need of positive mirroring regarding her burgeoning sexuality, feels flattered by the attention yet is somewhat ashamed, aware that something is amiss. She is also keenly sensitive to her mother's jealousy and anger, knowing that she is receiving attention that would more appropriately be directed toward her mother.

The mother, also unfulfilled in her marriage, may feel some relief that there is another woman to absorb some of the heat which she may not want from her husband. Selfishly, she sacrifices her daughter to save herself. Even if she does experience some relief, she is also furious at her daughter for being young and pretty—and able to elicit a man's attention. She may become physically and emotionally abusive. Some mothers take revenge by becoming seductive with their daughter's boyfriends.

# Confused Identity: Am I Your Daughter or Girlfriend?

The following story is an example of how the unconscious erotic needs of a parent can affect a child—even into adulthood.

Elizabeth, a thirty-six year old woman, had never been married nor had she been in a relationship for more than one year. She complained about not trusting men and believing that they were interested in one thing—sex.

She had recently met a man and fallen in love. She was fearful that she would repeat her pattern. In a group meeting, she asked the other members for help. As she uncovered buried feelings and fears, the following story emerged:

Elizabeth's parents were divorced when she was twelve years old. Prior to the separation, Elizabeth had overheard many arguments and had determined that her father was having an affair because he was unsatisfied with her mother. Elizabeth felt torn between the two as she had a close relationship with her father and a strained relationship with her mother.

Subsequent to the divorce, Elizabeth's father frequently took her out to dinner when he had visitation. If they happened to meet someone, her father introduced her as his "girlfriend!" As they were eating or walking after dinner, her father continually commented on the good-looking women he noticed. Occasionally, he pinched her behind and winked!

Elizabeth, a typical adolescent, remembered feeling confused as all this happened. She liked the attention, felt flattered, beautiful and sexy, yet she also felt ashamed of herself and angry at her father. She felt responsible as she had never told him to stop nor had she ever talked about these incidents.

As an adult, she always felt as if she had to take care of men's fragile egos. If she did not feel sexually attracted to someone whom she thought was attracted to her, she avoided them or acted mildly hostile. If confronted, she smiled and responded with a platitude such as, "I like you but I don't have time to develop new friendships right now." If pushed, she often became angry and blaming.

Inside, she felt cold and cut-off from her feelings. Men accused her of being cold and heartless. They felt dismissed by her. They accused her of being seductive and of putting out sexual cues. Then, when they responded, she cut them off and acted as if they were lecherous. She never admitted to feeling sexually attracted to them or of being seductive.

As Elizabeth unraveled this complex web of feelings and memories, she began to feel anger toward her father for his inappropriate behavior, anger toward her mother for not protecting her, and tremendous sadness for her lost adolescence and sexual innocence. By pursuing an emotional archaeological approach, Elizabeth began to see how, unconsciously, she used her sexuality to draw men toward her. Then, feeling ashamed of herself, she projected her feelings onto them. She accused them of objectifying her as a sexual object and of not being appreciated for herself.

Elizabeth soon became aware that this behavior pattern kept her from feeling her underlying fear—perhaps she wasn't worthy of a man's attention if she were just being herself. She knew she could get attention if she created conditions in which he felt sexually desirable—and flirting did just that! She knew how to make a man feel like a real man!

But what a price—for her and for the unlucky recipient! To Elizabeth's credit, she was determined to heal her sexual and gender wounds which prevented her from having lasting intimacy with a partner. By the end of her experience in the group, she had become involved with a wonderful man with whom she did not play her seduction–rejection game. They are engaged to be married within the year.

# Wounds from Sexual Abuse

Since sexuality is a core facet of our being, it often elicits our greatest vulnerability. Our sensitivity and sensibility are at stake. Being sexually touched is perhaps the most vulnerable experience we have as human beings—touching someone's body is touching their soul. To be physically and sexually violated cuts to the core of our being—affecting our ability and desire to trust, be aware of, and be open to ourselves and to others.

The incidence of childhood sexual abuse and adult rape—an outgrowth of this abuse—is startling, overwhelming, and far reaching. There are few people who are not affected by this experience either directly or indirectly through a family member, friend, or partner who has been sexually abused. Between 40 and 60 million Americans are estimated to have been sexually violated! The numbers are staggering. Groups for sexually-abused people are growing as fast as any types of personal growth groups.

Awareness of how prevalent these abusive experiences are has only risen to the surface and gained national exposure recently—even though sexual abuse has existed for thousands of years. We finally started taking it seriously in the 1980s.

Though sex offenders are now being punished and sometimes rehabilitated, there is relatively little attention focused on why sexual abuse is so rampant in our culture. We do know that people who sexually abuse others have been abused themselves. However, what is not addressed is the level of repression and shame that spawns sexual abuse in the first place.

Our culture is so afraid of sexuality that many people think about sexuality as being on a continuum that ranges from licentiousness to abuse. They place normal sexuality somewhere in the middle. Nothing could be further from the evidence. With sexual repression comes both licentiousness and sexual abuse. With sacred sexuality comes an honoring and respecting of the body and sexual contact. We propose a continuum that places sacred sexuality at one end and repression—with abuse and licentiousness—at the other.

As we resolve sexual shame, we are better able to experience greater intimacy and sexual ecstasy. There is another positive by-product as well: we will experience improved self-esteem. And as a culture, when we heal our sexual shame, sexual abuse will become an artifact of our past.

# The Paradox of Sexual Abuse

According to Bradshaw, "sexual abuse is the most shaming of all abuse. It takes less sexual abuse than any other form of abuse to induce shame."[2] Sexual abuse can devastate a person's ability to develop a healthy sexual identity. Paradoxically, the victim inevitably feels responsible for the abuse and ashamed of it—if not consciously, then unconsciously.

The abuses can be direct as in the case of a parent or caretaker being sexual with a child. Or it can manifest through threats—as in David's case. When David was fourteen, his father threatened that he would hit him with the buckle end of a belt if he found or heard of him being sexual with a girl. David developed a very shaming inner voice about his sexuality. ("You're disgusting for even looking at that girl.") However painful David's shaming voice was, it did help to protect him from potential physical abuse—he wasn't sexual at all throughout his teen years.

After he left his father's house, he finally got up the nerve to ask women out on dates. Eventually, with great trepidation, he ventured into a sexual relationship. His reason told him this would be fine: "My father can't stop me now!" Yet a strange development occurred—or rather, did not occur. He could not develop an erection.

The critical voice, now David's own, was still blasting messages about how perverse he was and how dangerous it was to be sexual with women. His penis continued to obey his father's commands. Only by first developing awareness that his "performance" in bed was being influenced by archaic voices, did he begin the process of healing.

When we get to the bottom of why our reactions are so distressed and disturbed—we no longer remain imprisoned by their impact. Alice Miller stresses the importance of awareness :

*"Things that we can see through do not make us sick; they may arouse our indignation, anger, sadness, or feelings of impotence. What makes us sick are those things we cannot see through, society's constraints that we have absorbed through our mother's eyes."³*

You, yourself, may have been sexually abused or have a partner (past or present) who has experienced this. You might also be a perpetrator. It's impossible to ignore the feelings that stem from these experiences, whether you are consciously aware of them or not. When someone enters the inner chamber and does damage to the throne, everyone suffers. Everyone shares the challenge of healing.

# Covert Sexual Wounds

The greatest incidence of sexual wounds emerge from families in which sex was considered aberrant—either the parents never mention sex, or they outwardly disparage it. Either way, the message is clear: Sex is bad. We have heard many people say, "I can't imagine my parents having sex." Others say, "I know they must have done it once," referring to the hard evidence of their own birth.

Few people realize the incredible harm done by avoiding the topic of sex. In one men's therapy group, I (Daniel) broached the subject of covert sexual wounds through a guided meditation. In this meditation, I called it covert sexual abuse for the following reason: Although a parent's intent is rarely to abuse the child, the denial of sexuality severely limits a person's ability to develop healthy sexual identity. Although it may not be malicious, it is certainly abusive.

One man acknowledged shortly after the meditation that he was internally defending his family: "My parents weren't abusive. They were good people," etc. etc. After his internal argument with me, several different feelings and images of his childhood and adolescence emerged—feelings and images so dissonant with his memories that he felt jarred. This fifty-three-year-old man realized that the lack of overt sexuality in his family caused him to develop discomfort with his own sexuality. He had a lifelong pattern of sexual shame and could never tie it back to negative messages he received about sex. In fact, he had not received any verbal messages at all. And that was the problem.

Another dimension of covert wounds develops from covert incest. One client named John had a very close relationship with his mother. She would confide in him how disappointed she felt in her husband—John's father. His mother told him repeatedly how much she wished her husband were more like John.

John had some really eerie feelings during these interchanges. He felt both special and terrified, appreciated and guilty. He sensed that his father was angry and frustrated with his mother, and carried the fear that his father would take his frustration out on him.

He was hardly paranoid, because his father did just that. In John's words, "My father sensed the tight bond between me and my mother. Needless to say, he did not approve. He called me derisive names like mama's boy and pansy."

Now, at the age of thirty-six, John is working hard to reverse the damage that had made it difficult for him to establish a healthy, long-term relationship with a woman.

# A Family Legacy of Shame

The critical inner voices you hear and the fears, feelings, and beliefs you harbor about your self-significance, competence, or lovability are often connected with the legacy of shame you inherited from your family.

In the words of Alfred Ells,

*"Perhaps the most hurtful legacy many families leave their children is shame. This painful emotion is at the root of most codependent and compulsive sexual practices. Where guilt says, 'I made a mistake,' shame says, 'I am a mistake.'"*

He goes on to say that,

*"Shame is often an excruciating and punishing awareness of one's own insufficiency and inadequacy, and it is probably the most painful emotion one can experience."* [4]

Shame begets shame. When parents experience shame but do not consciously deal with it themselves, they pass it along to the next generation. The good news is that, beginning with awareness, the chain can be broken.

# Shame, Lovemaking, and Intimacy

As we have seen, shame can have a profoundly negative impact on lovemaking. It also pervades the sacredness of intimate connections, acting as a buffer to intimacy—both in and out of sexual explorations. In fact, shame silently poisons the garden of love. When shame is lurking, the last feeling a person wants to experience is vulnerability. And vulnerability is necessary for intimacy.

Always looking to rear its head, shame leaps forth at the most inopportune times. Have you ever wondered why you have gotten so hurt or angry over the seemingly smallest event? Or why your lover has reacted so intensely to your mildest transgression? The answers lie in the web of shame.

# A Typical Scenario

Lorraine and Phil have been trying to improve their sexual relationship. Lorraine has found a new book of sexual exercises and is eager to try them with Phil. When they're together at night, she says, "Honey, let's try one of these exercises, okay?"

Phil is wary. "Well, I'm not so sure. You always want to be in charge—like you're the teacher and I'm the student."

Lorraine feels hurt by his remarks but tries to take a positive attitude. "Look, Phil, I was only trying to suggest something that might be good for both of us. Don't you think that you are over-reacting?"

Phil is sensitive to being accused of over-reacting, something they both know. As if on automatic pilot, he feels his face and neck growing hot—a sure sign of irritation. But this time, he swallows it: "Okay, okay, let's try it."

Lorraine then reads from a passage in the book where the man is supposed to arouse the woman by caressing her sensuously. Phil tries it but his heart isn't in it. "This is taking all the spontaneity out of it, Lorraine."

"Well you haven't given it much of a try. I think I deserve at least that much consideration."

"What are you saying—that I'm not considerate?"

"You're not really interested in pleasing me."

"Damn it, Lorraine. I do want to please you. Why can't you be satisfied with what we have? You're never really satisfied with anything—there's always something wrong."

Lorraine is tempted to scream, "Maybe that's because you're so concerned about taking care of yourself when we make love!" But she suppresses the urge and, instead, says, "Come on, Phil, just try it, okay?"

Phil sighs. "Okay, honey, okay," and he begins to stroke her.

There is no response from Lorraine. Finally, he asks her, "How does this feel?"

"Well, it's okay. Um, actually, it's a little too hard—would you do it softer?" He does and then after a moment, Lorraine says apologetically, "Uh, harder now, do it harder."

"Oh, geez, Lorraine, here I'm trying to please you and you can't even make up your mind— what do you want, harder or softer?"

Lorraine begins to cry. Phil stops, exasperated. Out of frustration she says, "I can never say anything right with you. I knew I should have just kept quiet."

She turns away from him; he turns away from her. The tension is high, but they are both silent and remain that way for the rest of the night.

## What Happened?

This couple has been married for many years. They both want to have a wonderful marriage, great sex, and please their partner. Yet this type of painful misunderstanding threatens their relationship.

How can loving experiences turn sour so fast—from a passionate embrace to a screaming argument or tense, angry silence in the space of a few minutes? Why do misunderstandings that may amount to little in other circumstances become so overblown and dramatic in bed? Let's look at what really happened with this couple. A brief glimpse into their history may prove helpful for this understanding.

Lorraine and Phil met in their junior year in college and began going steady. They married shortly after they graduated. Sex was awkward at first but they fell into a routine which seemed to work well—except that neither of them had ever resolved the feelings of shame they had about sex and about themselves. Though they had both repudiated their religious upbringing, both considered themselves spiritually inclined. Neither of them had ever talked about or acknowledged the myriad feelings they had regarding sexuality.

Unconsciously, Lorraine fell into a role similar to that of her mother. She normally enjoyed sex but had become bored with their routine. She put up with it silently. Phil, also acting unconsciously, did what came naturally to him—just as his father had instructed him. Their sexual relationship almost exactly replicated that of their parents—the only difference being they practiced birth control, so sex was supposed to be solely for enjoyment.

As their children grew up, Lorraine avidly read self-help books. Her interest had shifted from parenting to herself. Now, with the children out of the house, she was interested in cultivating her sexual relationship with Phil. Hence, the scene at the beginning of this chapter.

Lorraine was brought up to make do with whatever she had. Though she hungered for more— pleasure, abundance, joy, and intimacy—and believed more was possible, unconsciously, she felt ashamed of her desires. She did not let herself ask for more until she could no longer bear the pain of her longing and feeling that she was missing something. When she finally addressed the issue with Phil, she was already critical of herself—"why can't I just be content with what I have?"—and ashamed for having done so. When she broached the subject, she gave mixed signals to which Phil unconsciously reacted. Sensing her critical attitude, he imagined that she was critical of him, unaware that her critical judgment of herself was fueling the fire.

Phil compounded the problem because of his own feelings of shame. At the time they married, he was ashamed that he was an inexperienced lover—but he kept this to himself. He continued to feel ashamed, believing that he knew nothing about sex. Phil also felt ashamed of himself when he believed that he fell short of perfection. He prided himself on being able to solve his own problems. So when Lorraine suggested anything new, the story he told himself was that he had fallen short, was not enough, and could not solve the problem. The shame he felt about his inadequacies was unbearable.

Hence, Phil also gave double signals when responding to Lorraine, which she also picked up unconsciously. The story she told herself was that he wasn't eager to experiment and improve their sexual relationship because he didn't love her enough. She often thought that he put work and friends ahead of her and this became another example of how he didn't value her. Sometimes, she worried that she was boring and wasn't really worth paying attention to. She felt ashamed of herself when she thought this, believing that she was selfish and self-important.

As we unraveled the complex dynamics of Phil and Lorraine's relationship, it became apparent to both of them that shame about themselves as sexual beings played a large part in their acrimonious exchanges. Difficulties also arose because of unconscious beliefs they had regarding their roles as a man or woman. Unconscious feelings and beliefs they had about themselves—fears about their significance, competence, or lovability—also contributed to their sexual difficulties. When any of these painful feelings arose, they both felt intense shame.

By helping Lorraine and Phil address their shame—all aspects of it—they were able to find their way out of the spiders' web.

So it behooves us to find out how our religious, cultural, and family backgrounds influence us currently. If we find positive influence, we can acknowledge and appreciate it. However, if we find negative influence, then we have the choice to change it if we so desire.

## Exercise #2

### *Your Religious Background & Sexuality*

*Create a space where you will not be disturbed for at least 10 minutes. If you like, play music that takes you back to your early religious experiences or cultural roots.*

Close your eyes and bring your attention to your breathing. Notice how you are breathing and listen to the rhythm of your breath going in and out of your body.

Allow yourself to go backward in time, remembering experiences from church, religious school, sermons, with the clergy, or within your family having to do with sexuality and religion.

What messages did you receive, overtly or covertly, verbally or nonverbally?

What messages did you receive because of omission—subjects that nobody mentioned or did anything about?

In your religious upbringing, what part was sexuality supposed to play in life, marriage, or relationships?

What was considered normal and healthy sexuality and what was considered aberrant?

What were the rewards associated with healthy sexuality and the punishments associated with aberrant sexuality?

How were girls and boys supposed to learn about sexuality?

What were the different roles designated for males or females regarding sexual behavior?

Bring your attention back to your breathing and notice if it has changed since you first began this exercise.

When you feel ready, describe some of the potent images or experiences you remembered by writing or drawing them. If you are in a primary relationship, take time to share your memories and any insights you may have had with your partner.

🌿 　 🌿 　 🌿 　 🌿 　 🌿

# The Shadow of Shame

An interesting and disturbing dynamic occurs in religions that teach an anti-body philosophy and use shame to control their adherents. When we consciously learn to identify our bodies, sensuality, and sexuality as bad and other than who we are—the not-me—we unconsciously adjust our self-image and identity. We identify with what we believe is good and push into the shadow all attributes that don't enable us to believe that we are who we hope to be. The not-me aspects are attributed to other people and, in fact, are readily seen in others.

James Hillman, an erudite Jungian analyst, believes that, "whenever we're talking about anything in a Christian culture, the shadow is always sexual."[5] Because sexuality is so taboo and hidden in most branches of Christianity, it naturally rears its head through the shadows.

The *shadow*, a term coined by Carl Jung, reflects the parts of ourselves we find unacceptable and therefore want to hide. The more we experience these parts as unacceptable, the more we hide them; the more we hide them, the more unconscious they become. We *dis-identify* with them.

Certainly our culture and the time in which we live greatly influence what we identify with and what we *dis-identify* with and, therefore, put in the shadows. Another important and potent influence is our family of origin. The attitude and approach each family holds toward the cultural mores, religious dogma, and its own generational norms affects what each family member unconsciously or consciously decides is me or not-me. The more rigid the family's beliefs about which behaviors, thoughts, or feelings are acceptable or unacceptable, the more children must hide parts of themselves in the shadow. The more severe the consequences for acting outside those norms, the deeper into the shadow they are hidden.

The more social systems, whether relationships, families, religions, or nations, rely on authoritarian rule—dictating how people should behave, think, or feel—the greater the shadow. And the more likely that shame will be used to keep people in line.

# Shame Fuels the Shadow

Shame fuels the development of the shadow. Let's say that I have come to believe that feeling lustful is wrong, and I have been so successful at pushing my lustful thoughts and feelings away that I rarely feel sexual. On the rare occasion when I do feel sexually attracted or even attractive to someone, I feel deeply ashamed. Then, I try to push the thoughts and feelings away even more.

Inasmuch as I am successful—and I usually am quite successful because it is just too painful to feel the initial feelings or the overlay of shame—these aspects of myself become my shadow. Lust becomes part of my shadow. I am no longer aware that it is a part of me. In fact, I may even identify myself as being asexual. I don't believe that I have lust or that I am seductive. (Naturally, I have lost awareness of these parts of myself which are hidden in the dark closet, because it is too painful to be aware of them.)

Perhaps you know the pain of constantly fantasizing about sex and concurrently feeling ashamed of any sexual feeling. So, you can see that the shadow gets larger as you dis-identify with more and more so-called unacceptable parts of yourself—believing the myth that they no longer exist.

# Persona—Our Face To The World

Contrasting with the shadow, the persona highlights the image we try to project to the world. Most of us want to be seen as attractive, kind, intelligent, and faithful, while few of us want to be recognized as mean, hostile, uncaring, or stupid. Our persona is what we identify with as me—who we consciously strive to be.

Despite our best attempts to project a positive persona and keep the shadow at bay, the shadow still powerfully influences our actions from behind the scenes—often at the most inopportune times. Slips of the tongue and behavior, hostile or fearful statements embedded in so-called humor, dreams and fantasies that are considered not-me, and projections onto others are all expressions of the shadow. They are also ways of recognizing or becoming aware of it.

The following exercise can help you become aware of your own sexual shadow—which by definition is unconscious. Since much of our early childhood sexual education—by commission or omission—occurred in our family of origin, let's revisit our childhood and adolescence to get a glimpse of what may be lurking in the shadows.

## Exercise #3

### *Me and My Shadow*

Make yourself comfortable and focus your attention on your breathing. Allow yourself to relax. If you like, put on music which is quieting but non-intrusive.

Think about someone who you find to be too sexually provocative, free, or licentious. Pay attention to how your body feels as you think of this person. Imagine how your mother would react to this person, verbally and non-verbally? Your father?

Now think about someone who you believe is sexually repressed or prudish. Notice how your body feels, paying particular attention to any changes in sensations. How would your mother act toward or talk about this person? Your father?

Imagine someone you feel is extremely sexually attractive. Once again, notice how your body feels. Now imagine how your mother and father would react to this person.

Think of some kind of sexual behavior that you would like to do but have stopped yourself from doing. Pay attention to your bodily sensations. What would your mother say if she knew? Your father?

Lastly, imagine a sexual activity that you would never want to do, that you imagine to be disgusting or repugnant. Pay attention to your bodily sensations. And once again imagine what your mother and your father would say about this fantasy.

Bring your attention back to your breathing and notice how your body feels now. When you feel ready, write some of your reactions on paper, draw, or sculpt some of your feelings.

If you are in a primary relationship, take some time to share what you have imagined with your partner. If you feel fearful that your partner might react negatively, talk about your fears first.

🌿    🌿    🌿    🌿    🌿

## The Devastating Effects of Shame

The following story is an example of how the unacknowledged shadow of shame can destroy a relationship and a family. This family happens to practice Catholicism though it could have been any religion in which sexuality is denied.

Barbara and Jack had been married for 26 years, had raised four children, and had never seen each other naked. They would take turns going into the bathroom, changing into their pajamas, and slipping quickly under the bed covers.

Both were actively practicing Roman Catholics, and they had learned their lessons well. Sex was for procreation, not recreation. Barbara had never had an orgasm. In fact, she had never come close to being highly sexually aroused.

When their fourth child entered high school, Barbara returned to college to finish her degree. She decided to major in Psychology because she found the information stimulating to her and she enjoyed the students who attended these courses. Most of them were twenty years her junior and so had been raised in a culture that was much more liberal sexually. In and out of class, Barbara listened as these younger women talked about their experiences with men, with other women, moving in and out of relationships.

She had mixed reactions. She felt excited that marriage and sex could be more fulfilling, sad that she had spent so many years feeling isolated, alone and unsatisfied, angry that her husband was not at all interested in changing, talking, or learning, and afraid that she would never experience the emotional or sexual intimacy of which these younger women spoke.

With much trepidation, Barbara finally got up the courage to broach the subject of sexuality with Jack. She was not prepared for Jack's reaction when she finished telling him how she felt about their sexual relationship and what she hoped they could create together. Without a word, he stood up, walked out of the room, and moved into the guest room. Jack refused to attend couple's counseling. Their marriage never recovered.

Before the year was out, Barbara was having an affair with Charlie, a recently divorced man whom she had been friendly with for years through church. For the first time in her life, she was naked with a man with the lights on. She experienced a new kind of sexuality—they caressed each other, they kissed and touched—giving and receiving pleasure became a reflection of the love they felt. She had an orgasm for the first time in her life. Much to her amazement, she found that she consistently had multiple orgasms without any effort.

Barbara left her marriage and began to rebuild her life. Her relationship with Charlie lasted only one year; he was ten years her junior and wanted to have children. They parted amicably and continue to be friends many years later.

## The Twisted Remnants of Shame

Some parents attempt to override, transcend, and/or deny their sexual shame by acting as if they are sexually free and uninfluenced by repressive religious doctrines. These parents are permissive and often over-educate their children, giving the children information that they do not want and for which they are not ready. Overemphasizing sexuality is the flip-side to repressing it.

The story of Lisa exemplifies how confusing and damaging it can be for a child to be exposed to adult sexuality. Lisa, now a woman in her thirties, remembers visiting her girlfriend's house when she was six, seven, and eight years old. Her girlfriend, Christie, was the same age. Christie's mother was divorced and frequently entertained her current boyfriend while the girls were playing. The couple engaged in sexual intercourse, including oral sex with their bedroom door wide open. The girls, naturally curious, saw everything. And as curious children do, they copied the adults to the extent that they were able—laying on top of each other and giving each other oral stimulation.

When Lisa returned to her home, she remembered feeling very confused and anxious. Not feeling comfortable spilling the beans but knowing something was wrong and wanting help, she reached out by telling her own mother, "Lisa's mother walks around the house naked." Her mother, who wanted Lisa to be exposed to people from varied socio-economic classes replied, "Oh! That's different." She never asked Lisa how she felt about it, or how often the mother did this, whether she had male company, etc. She never called the mother to discuss it. This entire scenario happened many times. Lisa did not tell anyone about her experience for thirty years, though she felt ashamed and confused by it.

## The Double Life of Shame

Whether expressed through sexual repression or licentiousness, shame never completely eradicates sexuality. Since sexuality is natural and instinctual, but the expression of it is rife with taboo, we learn to express these impulses in indirect and circuitous ways. In extreme cases, people who are burdened with sexual shame carry on double lives.

For example, the man whose persona is nice and kind to all, and who is particularly courteous and gentle with women, may be filled with sado-masochistic fantasies about women in his inner life. (Accounts of mass murderers often reveal stunned reactions from neighbors or fellow workers: "It couldn't have been Mr. Jones! He was such a nice, quiet man.") He might be morally upright in his public life and a child molester in his private life. Perhaps this may explain the Michael Jackson molestation case, if indeed he is guilty of the accusations. The stronger the persona identification with piousness and anti-sexuality, the greater the negative sexual shadow will become.

Perhaps this can partially explain the shocking event that rocked the nation in the summer of 1994. Though viewed as a hero by millions, and a nice guy in the truest sense, O. J. Simpson was accused of the brutal slayings of his ex-wife and her male friend. "Say it ain't so, O. J." could be heard on many street corners. Disbelieving and dismayed, people couldn't reconcile his image (persona) with his violence (shadow). Scores of people stepped forth and attested to the myth of his persona: O. J. was a great guy. But 911 calls revealed a different side. So did his first wife who referred to him as "a beast." Abusive, insecure, hostile, and controlling, O. J. was filled with rage—explosive rage. Whether or not O. J. Simpson is ever found guilty, few people were not stunned by the incidence of spousal abuse.

You may be aware of dramatic differences between your own shadow and persona. There are countless examples of this chasm. John, a participant in one of my (Daniel) men's groups had a strong Christian background. He turned away from the church during his late teens—although as he later discovered, the church still lived within him. He gravitated toward Eastern religions where he imagined his natural spirituality could blossom. He "tried" to be spiritual. For John, this translated into dissociating from his body—after all, his religious training taught him that the body could never be holy. He meditated. He prayed. He wanted nothing more than to absolve himself of obsessions of the flesh.

Yet he still fell prey to sexual fantasies—women dancing provocatively before him. He frequented strip-tease shows, became aroused, masturbated, and later, experienced tremendous shame. He had brief sexual affairs and then felt ashamed. His internal conflict culminated in horrific herpes attacks which he believed were retribution for his sinful behavior. Needless to say, there was an internal war waging between his sexual impulses and his spiritual aspirations. This war was fueled by shame.

The shaming of sexuality so evident in ascetic religions drives sexuality to clandestine corners. Hidden in the darkness are all the parts of that person which were deemed unfit when he or she was still small. As sexuality becomes more and more hidden, these disenfranchised and ignored aspects become ferocious, twisted, and aberrant. Over the years the pressure builds and then, seeking release, erupts in an aberrant form.

# The Shadow of Shame in Fundamentalist Christianity

An extreme case of how sexual denial or disidentification creates strange shadow developments can be witnessed through one of America's most popular televangelists, Jimmy Swaggart. He was obsessed with sexual profligates whom he considered to be the scorn of society and a blemish on humanity. He sermonized against the evils of the body, sexuality, and pornography for many years. He had even written a 300-page book espousing the sins of sexuality in general and pornography in particular. (Of course, the research entailed a review of pornography!) Yet, irony of ironies, Swaggart, the fundamentalist Christian, was "caught" with prostitutes and pornography at least twice. He had succumbed to the very sins he was warning others against.

Although many people were shocked that this seemingly moral man was caught performing less than "religious" acts with a prostitute, shining light onto his shadow reveals a rather different story. After all, the shadow never lies. The shadow teaches us that any obsession hides an underlying repression. The stronger the repression, the more likely it will eventually emerge in an aberrant form.

Swaggart's persona was identified with a moralistic, dogmatic religion, where there was no room for sexual impulses. Having to exist somewhere, these impulses were projected onto other people—the sinners and perverts. By denying and disowning his own sexual impulses, his shadow became more and more twisted.

Like pulling a weed and leaving the roots intact, his attempts at squashing his lustful impulses centered around constructing a moral philosophy of good verses bad, rather than on integrating his natural sexuality. Had he consciously worked on accepting his sexual impulses instead of projecting his negative shadow onto others (sinners), his shadow would not have wielded such force.

Denial of reality leads toward perversion. The preaching and anti-pornography book reflects a massive cover-up, an attempt to control his own shame about sexuality. Surely, he felt ashamed of his own sexual impulses because of his own religious upbringing. And so, he used religious dogma to control these impulses. As we know so well, it didn't work!

# Projection and Displacement: Futile Attempts

In Jimmy Swaggart's and in other extreme cases of sexual repression, sexual desire becomes so deeply repressed that adherents to fundamentalist religions are literally unaware of its existence. However, Swaggert and others like him, are remarkably disturbed by other's sexuality. This irritant brings to the foreground what they have pushed to the background. The irritant, or those displaying it, must be eliminated. Though unconscious, other people's sexuality is experienced as too threatening. For if you regard sexuality as healthy, then you have to evaluate your own belief system. If you can "cleanse" the sexuality out of others, then you do not have to face it within yourself.

Unknowingly, we accept the myths of our culture. Then, having internalized the anti-erotic values, we react defensively when someone or something inspires the erotic feelings we are unsuccessfully trying to ignore. We feel victimized (projection), we become angry (displacement), or we feel sorry for that person and try to "help" him/her (projective identification). We may use denial, confusion, or intellectualization to try to rid ourselves of the unwanted feelings.

David Steinberg, a pioneer and expert on healthy eroticism, calls this the erotic shadow.

*"In its more extreme forms it operates as a dangerous cultural and political force, threatening our most fundamental values of freedom and diversity. Those who most misunderstand and fear the power of the erotic impulse label eros the work of the devil."* [6]

And sadly, most of us have been severely wounded by the shadow of patriarchal culture and religions. We have learned that our sexuality, severed from the sacred, is nothing save gross, disgusting animal impulses. Is it really surprising that we have such an ungodly preponderance of sexual shame in our culture?

Let us return to our present culture and look at how the shame, inherent in modern religions and states, has created and perpetuated sexual aberrations, pornography, violence toward women, and what is often called, "the war between the sexes."

## Talk Dirty

We need look no further than our language. Words are powerful. When we hear them, we form images, experience sensations, and form ideas. Talking about our sexual organs as "pieces of meat," a "cock," a "cunt," reflect our cultural beliefs that sex is base, dirty, and demeaning. How can we expect young children to develop a healthy attitude toward their genitals or about sexuality if we use language that is derogatory or degrading?

When giving encouragement to one another about having sex, young men say to the would-be lucky man, "Sock it to her!" A rather violent approach! Afterwards he is asked, "Did you score?" as if he were winning some kind of competitive game.

We go yet another step in attaching violence and degradation to sexuality. Our most derogatory curse words use the very same words as our slang words for genitals. We can not say anything more degrading to someone than to spit out, "You cunt," "You pussy," or "You cock sucker." Doesn't it seem strange that we refer to the act of lovemaking as "getting screwed or fucked," yet the worst insults we can hurl are, "Screw you!" or "Fuck you!" These words hardly stimulate a sacred sense of sexuality. So changing our language is essential to changing even a subtle debasing of our sexuality.

## Why Should I Look Into the Shadow?

Why not learn as much as we can from life's lessons? Whenever we feel a strong emotional charge, whenever our buttons are pushed, we know that a shadow aspect lays waiting to be discovered. If we take the time and energy to explore this shadow aspect, we are sure to uncover great treasures. Anytime we put an attribute into the shadow, the positive qualities are denied along with the negative. However, the longer it remains in the shadow, and the more buried it is, the harder and scarier it becomes to look at it. However, if we are patient and persistent, it is sure to pay off. Here lies the gold.

Unfortunately, when Swaggart was exposed, he claimed that he had been overtaken by the devil. He kept the enemy outside himself, thus attempting to remain pure and virtuous. By refusing to look into himself to uncover his fears, feelings of shame, or unacknowledged aspects, he failed to take responsibility for his shadow. He also failed to learn a valuable lesson or be a model for others.

Learning can often be maximized by viewing extreme cases. That's why the case of Jimmy Swaggart is so valuable. We all have some degree of Jimmy Swaggart in us—someone inside who becomes self-righteous, even preachy when we are denying a fear or feeling about ourselves. Even being disgusted by Jimmy Swaggart or other hypocrites can point to our own shadow. Who among us has never fallen to hypocrisy?

# Shame and Secrecy

Jimmy Swaggart is just a blatant example of people who have secret sex lives—from feeling controlled by sexual fantasies, to surreptitiously visiting brothels, to perpetrating sexual abuse. The numbers are in the high millions. The growing awareness of sex and love addiction has spawned new groups and programs nationwide.

This population is not primarily composed of social outcasts. It includes ordinary people as well as some of our most "upstanding" and "outstanding" citizens. The public-at-large reacts with shock and disgust as respected luminaries and clergy are exposed with striking regularity. Yet, considering our social milieu regarding shame and sexuality, these developments are not surprising. The secrecy itself is indicative of sexual shame.

*"A person may react against this powerful negative feeling by becoming shameless. Shameless sexual practices— promiscuity, prostitution, rape, incest, masochism, voyeurism, and pedophilia—violate personal and moral boundaries and cause hurt to one's self and others."* [7]

Although common public perception imagines these people as free from shame, a closer look reveals a different profile. That's why most people engaged in these practices maintain an air of secrecy. They fear how other people would react if their practices were to become known. Their secrecy fortifies their shame and a vicious cycle ensues.

Where secrets and taboos lie, fascination grows and fixation takes hold. So it goes with sex. Titillation and fantasy are guided by the hidden and the dark. Sexual expression ceases to be a full-bodied journey, but instead revolves around the clandestine—the dark caves and jutting peaks of the body.

## Exercise #4

### *Sexual Secrets*

Close your eyes and allow your breath to move easily in and out for a few minutes.

Remember back to your earliest memories of exploring your body or your sexuality (including experiences of masturbation or touching yourself sexually).

Go through your life, from childhood until the present, remembering ways in which you have kept your sexuality secret. These secrets may include thoughts or fantasies you have never shared with anyone or "acted out" yet still maintain as a secret (e.g., engaging in a trio.)

Write these down in your journal or on a pad. Next to these entries, write two imagined responses—one from an internal critic or judge and the other from an aspect of yourself that is loving, supportive, and nurturing of your essence.

If you are willing, reveal any or all of these to your partner or a friend (revealing secrets is one of the best ways to heal shame.)

❧   ❧   ❧   ❧   ❧

Perhaps you wonder how the natural pleasure available through our erotic natures could go so far astray. What are the ancient forces which propel us toward sexual shame and away from natural pleasure? When and how did bodies become viewed as mere carnage? What purpose did this anti-body philosophy serve, then and now? How have these contributed to the challenges we face these days?

The next chapter, The Roots of Sexual Shame, will address these questions. You may be wondering, "What do these questions have to do with understanding and overcoming my personal feelings of shame?" You may find that getting a fuller picture or sense of the grand impact of sexual shame, you can unburden your personalization of shame, and take greater stock of your available options. This can open up freer, more exciting possibilities between you and your lover.

# 5

# The Roots of Sexual Shame

*History is not just the evolution of technology; it is the evolution of thought. By understanding the reality of the people who came before us, we can see why we look at the world the way we do, and what our contribution is toward further progress. We can pinpoint where we come in...the longer development of Civilization, and that gives us a sense of where we are going.*

James Redfield, *The Celestine Prophecy*

## The End of Paradise

We are all familiar with the story of Adam and Eve in the Garden of Eden. Perhaps no story has such wide-ranging and profound implications. For most people, this story lays the foundation for sexual shame and original sin (for which people feel shame). These are no small matters! Drilled into our psyches from before the time we could reason on our own, these "morals" condition shame and sin into the deepest fibers of our beings. It's hard to forget these words,

*And the Lord God commanded the man, saying, "Of every tree of the garden you are free to eat; but as for the tree of knowledge of good and bad, you must not eat of it; for as soon as you eat of it, you shall be doomed to die."* [1]

First there is Adam, then God makes Eve from one of Adam's ribs. They exist in paradise, naked and unashamed. God warns them not to eat from the Tree of Knowledge (of good and evil), but the snake tricks Eve into eating the fruit. She offers some to Adam, who also eats. Suddenly aware of their sexuality, they cover themselves with fig leaves. When God finds out that Adam and Eve have violated the prohibition, he punishes them. Eve will have pain in childbirth and Adam will have to work hard for his entire life. Worse still, they no longer reign as immortals. They fall from grace and are banished from the Garden of Eden.

How many of us grew up believing that when Adam and Eve became aware of their nakedness, they felt ashamed? Or that they hid from God because they felt ashamed? Certainly we thought that God was angry at them for disobeying him and for doing something sexual. Exactly what remained a mystery. Yet, we knew it must have been serious because they were punished and exiled forever from paradise.

But questions remained. Were they really ashamed of their nakedness? Did they hide from God because of this or because they were afraid of his reaction to their disobedience? Is Eve (and therefore all women) blamed for the exile from the garden because she listened to the snake and then influenced Adam? Were they punished because they disobeyed or because they did something sexual? Is the moral of the story "Do not disobey authority," "Do not be sexual," or "Do not follow your curiosity?"

What if the moral of the story has to do with accepting responsibility for our curiosity, knowledge, and actions? Or what if we view this story as an attempt by Biblical editors (all of whom were male) to impress upon the ancient Hebrews that the fearsome God Yahweh was more powerful than his 30,000-year-old predecessor, their beloved Goddess, "Queen of Heaven," "the Mighty Lady, the Creatress"—known as Queen Nana, the Goddess Nammu by the Sumerians, Astarte or Asherath by the Canaanites and Hebrews? [2]

If you grew up in this culture, the likelihood is that the meaning you gave to this story included an interpretation which led you to believe that sexuality is shameful. Even now, as adults, most of us believe that the story of Adam and Eve is about falling from the grace of God because of something having to do with shame, sexuality, and disobedience. We rarely question whether the meaning we are deriving today comes from the interpretations given to us as children. This unconscious acceptance of sexual shame—that the body and sexual impulses are the antithesis of holiness—is the greatest foe to healing it.

Shame about who we are and who we are not, shame about our sexuality, about our inadequacies—this shame fuels the fire which creates seemingly unresolvable conflicts.

## The Politics of Shame: Religion, State, Sexuality, and the Body

If we are to discover the roots of shame, we must take an investigative approach to the story of Adam and Eve in the Garden of Eden. In *Adam, Eve, and the Serpent*, Elaine Pagels reveals how the interpretation of this story has changed throughout the course of Christianity. She shows how ideas and beliefs about sexuality and human nature that we take for granted were introduced subsequent to the life of Jesus.

For instance, the idea of original sin was introduced by Augustine in the late Fourth and early Fifth Century. Until that time, Jews and early Christians believed that the real theme had to do with moral freedom and responsibility. The story was to teach us that we are responsible for the choices we freely make—good or evil—just as Adam and Eve were. Using historical research, Pagels shows that up until that point, contrary to the claim made by the radical Christians, the majority of Christians believed that Adam and Eve's sin was one of disobedience, not sexual indulgence. In fact, contemporary belief was that conscious participation in procreation is 'cooperation with God in the work of creation.' [3]

But Augustine argues that Adam and Eve's disobedience occurred because of their inability to subjugate the body, the "inferior part," to the rule of the rational soul, the "better part of a human being." He asserts that spontaneous sexual desire is evidence of original sin. Arousal functions independently of the will's rightful rule, and "Because of this, these members are rightly called 'pudenda' (parts of shame) because they excite themselves just as they like, in opposition to the mind which is their master, as if they were their own masters." [4] Augustine assumes that since we experience arousal spontaneously, apart from will, that it is *against* our will. How would absorbing this belief affect your experience of sexuality? It then stands opposed to anything sacred.

Believing that semen transmits original sin, Augustine asserts that all beings save Jesus Christ (because he was conceived without semen) are born into original sin. Because of humankind's corrupt nature, he concludes that we are incapable of self-governance. Thus, his theocratic position endorsed the use of "commands, threats, coercion, penalties, and even physical force,"[5] by both the church and the state.

Within two centuries of his death, Augustine's interpretation of the Garden of Eden story became the predominant Christian viewpoint. The effects of this view of human nature have confounded healthy sexuality.

The impact of this philosophy is notable in Roman Catholic teachings. Many of our clients who have been raised by the catechism tell painful stories of how nuns and priests instilled the fear of God in them—a tactic certain to stop them from succumbing to their bodily impulses. One client told us, "I was ashamed to touch my penis even while I was urinating. I was afraid that it might be enough for God to get the wrong message." Another client, a sixteen-year-old girl, remembers her mother taking her hands out from between her legs where she was keeping them warm, scolding and shaming her as if she were doing something sinful. Children learned that tarnishing themselves in this way would earn them a place in hell.

Satan, they were told, rules the world of the senses. Deriving pleasure from bodily sensations—particularly sexual sensations—was a sign that you had succumbed to Satan. Even in the privacy of their own beds, many children were terrified of exploring their own bodies. However, usually they did succumb. These children, now adults who label themselves as "recovering Catholics," sometimes recount derisively how eager the priests were to hear the details and nuances of their transgressions during confession. The recent uncovering of sexual abuse among many priests reveals a chilling sequence of repression leading to abuse.

All of the major religions possess their own approaches to shaming sexuality. Since the body and everything having to do with the body belong to the world of gross matter, transcending it becomes paramount. Just as succumbing to bodily pleasures is considered evil, transcending bodily urges is considered the ultimate spiritual act—true holiness.

There are countless examples of how major religions—from both the east and the west—teach that the body and sexuality are the very essence of evil, keeping us from the holy path. In these religions, only by suppressing sensual delights can one hope to attain enlightenment or be insured of a place in heaven. The words of Krishna to Arjuna in the *Bhagavad Gita* exemplify this position. He first warns us of the evils of sensuality:

> *When a man thinks of sensuous things*
> *He becomes attached to them,*
> *From that liking springs desire*
> *And from desire comes anger.*
>
> *From anger comes utter confusion*
> *From confusion, wavering of memory,*
> *From wavering of memory, loss of reason,*
> *From loss of reason, he is lost.*

He goes on to instruct us on the benefits of controlling the senses:

> *But he, by ranging over objects of sense*
> *With senses self-controlled, cut off*
> *From desire and dislike, himself governed,*
> *Attains a clear quietness of spirit. (2.61–64)[6]*

The philosophy that has developed from this is: the spirit is good; the body is bad. The body obscures the spirit. To follow the spiritual path, even to be a "good" or "holy" person, one must control and subjugate the body's impulses.

After hearing this "morality" preached from the pulpit, and seeing it reflected in family behavior and cultural symbols, people begin to feel debilitating shame about their sexuality and bodily functions. Some fear that they are dirty—even aberrant or evil. With this preponderance of negative feelings and beliefs, the life of the body—desires, natural impulses, even awareness of sensations—must be forced underground.

## Questions and the Collective Unconscious

Several questions keep arising for us regarding this philosophy:

When, historically, did the body and sexuality *begin* to be viewed as dirty, evil, and shameful?

Why did it occur? What was happening—economically, politically, and culturally—that desecrated and disdained what had been sacred and revered for millennia?

What purpose did this anti-body philosophy serve, then and now?

How has it been maintained?

What can we learn from history that can help us solve our current problems?

You may be asking, "What do these questions have to do with my personal feelings of shame?" Consciously, perhaps not much. Unconsciously, probably a lot. Why?

One answer lies in what C. G. Jung called the "collective unconscious." In his study of cultures, religions, mythology, his patients and those of his colleagues, he found that people shared themes, images, visions, myths, and what seemed like memories that they had not experienced in their lives. Information was passed down through generations and across cultures in an undetermined manner. Striking similarities across cultures which obviously had no physical contact or communication bore testimony to a common psycho-spiritual reality. For example, major archetypes such as the Lover, the Crone or Wise Woman, and the Golden Child are found in all cultures, even those that have had no apparent cross-fertilization. Jung asserted that we are all influenced by this collective unconscious. Consequently, we are affected by past events and patterns which existed long before we faced our own individual challenges.

Another answer lies in the transmission of culture. As stories are told and retold, their symbols pass along moral, ethical, social, and political values. Bible stories are a good example. Similar stories were told by the Greeks. The *Oresteia* trilogy, written by the brilliant playwright Aeschylus, dramatized the new patriarchal values when it was performed on important ceremonial occasions. Its audience included all segments of the society: adult and child, men and women, free people and slaves. Today, children's stories such as Cinderella and Sleeping Beauty communicate enduring beliefs held by our culture.

Though comprehensive answers go beyond the scope of this book, a cursory answer is necessary if we are to understand the roots of shame. Perhaps by viewing history from another angle, we can glimpse the images which shape and guide our unconscious. Perhaps we can make more sense of the complex feelings and attitudes about sexuality which pervade our culture. Only then can we change what no longer serves us. The writer James Baldwin eloquently reminds us that "the great force of history comes from the fact that we carry it within us, are unconsciously controlled by it in many ways, and history is literally present in all that we do."[7]

If we believe that human nature is and has always been evil, as Augustine depicted, then we have little hope—unless fighting continually against our evil impulses represents hope. However, if we had evidence that what we have been witnessing for several millennia was, in fact, only one potential aspect of human nature, we could have hope for a more positive evolution. Hence, our inquiry into our distant past.

## The Roots of Shame: A Glimpse Back

Riane Eisler, an internationally acclaimed scholar, futurist, and activist, indirectly sheds light on the questions posed regarding shame and sexuality in *The Chalice and the Blade*. Eisler addresses issues such as why we persecute each other, why there is so much inhumanity to man—and to woman, why we are moving toward destruction rather than actualization. By using the newest archaeological research, she helps us understand how and why civilization shifted from a matrilineal, partnership society in which social relations were based primarily on linking (cooperation, teamwork, empathic and supportive relationships), to a patrilineal, patriarchal, dominator model in which the ranking of one half of humanity over the other is the organizing principle.

As she recounts history from a unique perspective, quite different from the one we were privy to (our history books were written primarily by men within the context of a dominator perspective), it becomes quite clear why and how sexuality has become a forum for power and control, violence and shame. The pervasive misogyny in our culture, the ubiquitous level of sexual shame, the increasing level of violence, and why we struggle with what is often labeled the battle between the sexes, begins to come into perspective as Eisler helps us understand the myths of our time—the last 5,000 years—and the preceding myths—30,000 years prior.

Of particular interest to us is why and how women and sexuality, which were venerated for almost 30,000 years during the partnership societies in the Paleolithic and Neolithic eras, became denigrated and repudiated during the shift (which occurred approximately 3,200 years ago with the fall of Crete). What we can learn from history can help us inform and direct our future. We must know what existed before the shift, how the shift occurred and took root. With that knowledge, we can develop a better strategy for healing society's ills which have been created and perpetuated by the sexual shame, repression, and aberrations we now face.

Perhaps we can also catch a glimpse of an ancient culture that embodied what we now only envision to be possible—egalitarian relationships between men and women, reverence of nature including sexuality, and social laws based on cooperation rather than domination.

## Goddess Worship

Prior to the rise of Christianity and patriarchal religions, all religions included Goddess worship. As far back as 30,000 B.C., (32,000 years ago), Paleolithic art gives evidence of extensive Goddess worship. And the Neolithic cites of Catal Huyuk and Hacilar (founded 8500 years ago) reveal a continuity in religion with the Paleolithic which become the great Mother-Goddess religions of archaic and classical times.[8] "The supreme power governing the universe is a divine Mother who gives her people life, provides them with material and spiritual nurturance, and who even in death can be counted on to take her children back into her cosmic womb."[9] These gynocentric (or Goddess-based) religions flourished until approximately three thousand years ago.

These were not primitive, unsophisticated cultures. The art and artifacts of these gynocentric cultures show highly developed societies in which unity among all things in nature and life are revered. There is equality between the sexes, parenthood is traced matrilineally, and there are tremendous cultural advances in the arts, agriculture, building, law, metallurgy, writing, dance, and theater, to name several. The more advanced Minoan art seems to express even more strongly "a

view in which the primary function of the mysterious powers governing the universe is not to exact obedience, punish, and destroy but rather to give."[10]

Just as life was celebrated, the destructive forces of nature were also addressed ritualistically and ceremonially so that people could contain and control their more fearful processes. In this way, these societies were able to bring out into the open people's greatest fears—rather than hide them (in the shadow) and pretend no fear.

In these ancient cultures, the goddess, or Great Mother, was recognized as the earth itself, as well as the stars, the elements, intelligence, life, and death. Goddesses were attributed with the ability to create, sustain, and take life. Birth, life, and death were viewed as three aspects of a cycle which perpetuated itself.

Aging was revered, as it brought wisdom and creativity. Sexuality was regarded as sacred, and women, since they were thought to be closest to the goddess, were thought to be endowed with the ability to impart the life force to their partners through the sacred act of sex. The ancient religions treated sexuality as a powerful sacrament in which physical unification with another mortal led to connection with the goddess.

Just as night coexists with day, images of the Great Mother included the "beautiful, sensual, divine giver of birth, light, love, and nurture,"[11] as well as rejection, abandonment, and death.

As Barbara Walker describes, early peoples and early religions understood that

*"...it is the Mother Goddess who reigns alone on the deepest level, since ...the basic fear of any young mammal is abandonment by the caretaking mother, on whom it is totally dependent. To be rejected by her is to die."[12]*

Two gold serpents coil about the arms and extend from the hands of this delicately carved ivory and gold Goddess from Crete. (Late Minoan I, ca. 1600-1500 B.C.) Gift of Mrs. W. Scott Fitz, Courtesy, Museum of Fine Arts, Boston

Recognizing that their human mothers provided everything necessary for life— warmth, nourishment, protection, tactile, and kinesthetic stimulation—just as the goddess, women were also imbued with the attributes of the goddesses. They were high-priestesses of the Temple, they were healers, sages, and counselors. Just as they were midwives to birth, they cared for the sick, comforted the dying, and were funerary priestesses. In life, women fulfilled all the roles that were attributed to the many-named goddess—the Creator, Preserver, and Destroyer— the original Holy Trinity.

This trinitarian pattern of the goddess can be traced to cultures and religions ranging from India to the Middle East into northern Europe. Understanding this, ancient religions, including early monotheistic Judaism, held the goddess in the highest place of reverence.[13] Love of the great goddess was widespread in all of the cradles of civilization.

*Cast of Upper Paleolithic Venus figure (ca. 25,000 B.C.) from Willendorf, Austria Giraudon/Art Resource, NY*

# Partnership Versus Dominator: Relationship Possibilities

Before we look at how the shift occurred from gynocentric cultures which valued partnership to patriarchal cultures in which one group of "strong" men dominated the rest of society, let's first lay out language that more accurately describes these ideas, values, and principles which are inclusive of men and women. (These terms will also help us more accurately define and describe the nature of social and intimate relationships which are shame-based versus self-actualizing.)

To describe the kind of society which has existed since the fall of Crete through the present—a social system ruled by force or the threat of force by men—Riane Eisler proposed the word *androcracy,* from the Greek root words *andros,* or "man," and *kratos,* or "ruled." Inherent in these societies are domination hierarchies based on ranking.

We want to emphasize that the androcratic or dominator model does not imply that all or even most men are dominating or abusive. Rather, it is the relatively few men who have seized power and help create conditions where domination and control become the focus of relationships.

To describe partnership cultures, an alternative social structure to that of ranking and domination, Eisler has coined the word *gylany,* pronounced with a hard *g,* accented like progeny. *Gy* comes from the Greek root word *gyne,* or "woman," *an* from *andros,* or "man."[14]

If we could step out of the cultural mind which we all inhabit (that is, steeped in androcratic symbols, images, and myths), it might be possible to imagine a society in which linking and life nurturing values were the norm. In this image, the only hierarchies that exist are those that promote actualization—those in which there is a progression toward more evolved and sophisticated functioning. If social structures exist which support the actualization of higher functioning of individuals, families, communities, and nations, rather than supporting domination, suppression, and restriction, we could imagine that shame could not find a stronghold. (Since shame is a control tactic used to suppress any variation from the dominator's status quo.)

Before looking at how the goddess cultures were suppressed by the warring, dominator tribes, let's explore how these two divergent paradigms exist inside each one of us. Remember, gylanic or androcratic tendencies can be expressed by either men or women.

## Exercise #1

### *Your Relationship Paradigm*

Most of us have elements of both paradigms—partnership and dominator—within our relationship. Use the following scale to rate the amount of each of these characteristics in your relationship. Then rate your parents' relationship as you remember it from your childhood. If you grew up with stepparents, rate each of the parental relationships separately. The more you include what is really happening in the shadows as well as the persona of your relationship, the more you will learn about how you and your partner embody these characteristics.

Using the following scale, choose a number that reflects how much your relationship (or your parents') embodies each characteristic.

Not at all          0          1          2          3          4          5          Completely

| Partnership Characteristics | PARTNER A | | PARTNER B | |
|---|---|---|---|---|
| | current | parents | current | parents |
| Men and women share attention, power, and love equally. | | | | |
| Partners interact (attend, feel, and act) in I-Thou relationship. | | | | |
| Relationships feel harmonious. | | | | |
| Sexuality is considered sacred. | | | | |
| People trust each other. | | | | |
| Diversity is appreciated. | | | | |
| Property is owned jointly. | | | | |
| Finances are joined and shared. | | | | |
| Generosity flows between partners. | | | | |
| Sharing is rewarded. | | | | |
| Cooperation is normal. | | | | |
| Decision making is shared. | | | | |
| Change is organized, meaningful, and paced. | | | | |
| Communication is open, honest, and direct. | | | | |
| High self-esteem is fostered. | | | | |
| Children are valued, educated, loved. | | | | |
| Child abuse is rare (including spanking). | | | | |
| Partners feel a sense of connectedness and belonging. | | | | |
| Partners consider the other's welfare as much as their own. | | | | |
| Conflicts are resolved. | | | | |
| Partners feel free and self-determining. | | | | |
| Partners feel appreciation and gratitude for each other and for what they have. | | | | |

*I add up my scores and write the totals:*   _____   _____   _____   _____

| DOMINATOR CHARACTERISTICS | PARTNER A | | PARTNER B | |
|---|---|---|---|---|
| | current | parents | current | parents |
| One gender dominates the other and commands more fame, power, or love. | | | | |
| Partners attend to, feel, and act toward the other as an object. | | | | |
| Relationships are disharmonious with overt fighting (verbal and physical) or covert hostility. | | | | |
| Partners are viewed as sexual objects. | | | | |
| Partners feel fearful or mistrusting. | | | | |
| Diversity is discouraged, sameness is desired. | | | | |
| Property is held individually. | | | | |
| Finances are separate or secretive. | | | | |
| Taking is normal. Giving occurs out of obligation or fear. | | | | |
| Hoarding is normal and rewarded. | | | | |
| Overtly & covertly, partners feel and behave competitively. | | | | |
| Decision making is authoritarian. | | | | |
| Change is rapid, arbitrary, and uncontrolled. | | | | |
| Withholding and lying are normal. | | | | |
| Low or shaky self-esteem is normal and instilled. | | | | |
| Children are punished, unvalued, and mistreated. | | | | |
| Child abuse is common (verbal and physical). | | | | |
| Partners feel alienated and alone. | | | | |
| Partners have a me-first attitude. | | | | |
| Conflicts fester and go unresolved. | | | | |
| Partners feel enslaved and oppressed. Partners are addictive, ungrateful, and always wanting more. | | | | |

*I add up my scores and write the totals:*  _____  _____  _____  _____

## Understanding and Using Your Scores

To get an idea of the extent to which you perceive that you are relating from a partnership or a dominator paradigm, you compare your score to the highest total possible: 110. A score closer to 110 means that you perceive your relationship to have more attributes of that paradigm than a score closer to 0. For example, if your Partnership Total is 62 and your Dominator Total is 45, the most general piece of information you can receive is that, according to your perception, your relationship tends to be more based on partnership than dominance.

Next, look at the individual scores for your relationship to find any patterns. You might notice that you have scored characteristics in similar areas similarly. For example, all the items having to do with decision making and money may be higher in the Dominator Paradigm, whereas the items having to do with children are higher in the Partnership Paradigm.

Notice your emotional and somatic reactions to your scores. These reactions are more important than the actual number because they signify that you have strong feelings about this particular characteristic of your relationship. You can use your reactions to the scores to develop a plan for changing aspects of your relationship in which you experience dissatisfaction. Compare your scores with those you gave for your parents' relationship to gain understanding of your own scores.

Next you look at your partner's scores. Use the differences in your scores as a catalyst for discussing your relationship: how each of you view it; what you like; what you don't like; what you want to change; what you want to work toward.

# The Rise of Shame, the Fall of Eros

How is it that the prevailing ideology shifted so radically from a gynocentric perspective with a reverence for the generative, nurturing, and creative powers of nature (which includes sexuality), symbolized by the chalice, to a patriarchal perspective in which the lethal power of the blade became glorified? Archeological evidence shows that people lived peacefully together for thousands of years, enjoying humanity's early peak of evolution.[15] But, approximately seven thousand years ago, by the fifth millennia B.C., there is evidence of invasions from warring nomadic tribes from central Asia as well as natural catastrophes such as earthquakes and floods causing large-scale destruction. "At the core of the invaders' system was the placing of higher value on the power that takes, rather than gives, life. This was the power symbolized by the "masculine" blade, which early Kurgan cave engravings show these Indo-European invaders literally worshipped."[16]

With the invasions came the symbols, myths, and experiences of a totally different culture—a culture in which might makes right, physical strength means power, women are reduced to the status of mere male property, the purpose of life becomes paving the way for the soul's journey after death, the body, as well as everything natural is denigrated while the spirit and the mind are venerated.

Images and sculptures of the life-giving goddess are replaced by fierce gods of war and destruction. Rather than celebrating the planting and harvests, historic art venerates the ravages of war—depicting massacres, looting, rape, sacrifice, and slavery—art now created by men from the warring tribes. Inventions for torture replace advances in pottery-making, and the arts in general. Artifacts from tombs reflect the new social order.

The strongest, most destructive men rose to the top of the social hierarchy, while women, as a group unable to compete with men on a raw physical level, were subjugated. Ultimately, women became nothing more than another piece of the male technology used to produce, and to reproduce.[17]

Sadly, as we know too well, this story also includes the denigration of everything having to do with the natural order—the body, sexuality, and women—since women are attributed with the ability to create, sustain, and take life, and are perceived as being closer and more connected to the natural cycles.

# The Goddess Will Not Die

However, these patriarchal and authoritarian religions had such great difficulty convincing people to give up their worship of the great goddess that the Christian church fathers finally succumbed by instituting the cult of Mary in the goddess's Ephesian temple in A.D. 432. Early monotheistic Judaism underwent a similar struggle that was resolved by including the feminine face of God—the Shekhina—with the celebration of the Sabbath. When the feminine Hindu trilogy was replaced by a masculine trilogy, Hindus maintained that at death, the male deities would return to the feminine cosmos.[18]

This unrelenting desire to pay homage to a nurturing, life-giving goddess is testimony to the strength of this 30,000 year old bond that both men and women have with the Great Mother—the goddess.

Perhaps, our devotion to the Great Mother has to do with a desire on the part of men and women to live according to the gylanic values of partnership and cooperation which are attributed to her. However, since those in power are threatened by the egalitarian values of true partnership, throughout history, movements toward those values have been met by greater androcratic violence and repression. The witch hunts, which lasted for three centuries, are a prime example.

# Witch Hunts: The Denunciation of Sexuality

Nowhere in history is there a better example of the war waged against the body and its inherent wisdom, sexuality, and, hence, women, than in the period called the Renaissance. Few of us learned in European history that the witch hunts were created, produced, executed, and funded by the Church and State.[19] In 1484, Pope Innocent VIII declared witchcraft a heresy and extended the power of his Inquisitors. In 1486, two Dominican Inquisitors published *The Malleus Maleficarum* ("The Hammer of Witches") that became the Inquisitors' bible for the next two and a half centuries.

Many thousands, by some accounts millions, of women were sadistically tortured and killed by men based on three primary charges:

1. that they (the midwives and healers) were practicing medicine without a license (licensing had just come into being and was reserved for the new male physicians);

2. women were meeting together to worship Pagan goddesses (which was a threat to the Church);

3. and the most common and revealing charge—that they were too sexual by nature.

This accusation was upheld by the descriptions of witchcraft in *The Malleus Maleficarum,* which declares that the devil acts through women since they are the "carnal source of all evil." It further states that "All Witchcraft comes from carnal lust which in women is insatiable."[20] Because of this belief and fear that women's sexuality was the work of the devil, many women, accused of witchcraft, were tortured until they confessed that they had, indeed, consorted with the devil and that "his member was as long and thick as a man's arm."[21] Many children saw their grandmothers and mothers burned at the stake for an offense no greater than engaging in or enjoying sex—with their husbands.

## The Past Lives On: Shame as Control

Let us remember that this genocide of women was planned and orchestrated by a handful of powerful men and continued for almost three centuries,[22] through, what is called ironically, The Age of Reason, in our history and philosophy books. Remembering Baldwin, "History is present in us today," we can assume that the memories, feelings, beliefs, and assumptions that could create and perpetuate such vilification of woman and sexuality, only three centuries ago, live in us today.

We have all been born of women, and, those of us who have been truly mothered have been nurtured and swathed in untainted, sensual delight. To turn against women, therefore, is to turn against all that is life-giving, nurturing, of the flesh, and sensual. And it follows that the ascetic religions, which, by definition, repudiated anything having to do with the flesh or comfort, of necessity, denigrated women.

The patriarchal, androcratic religions and states reworked people's psyches with myths, using violence, fear, and shame to change the old mind that had created and existed in the garden for 30,000 years. All remnants of goddess worship as well as the values of the gynocentric cultures—egalitarian, nurturing, and life supporting—had to be erased and replaced with the values we know so well today. Because the feelings, thoughts, or actions having to do with the flesh, sensuality, or sexuality are rooted in the deepest aspects of our being, shame—which is about who we are rather than what we do—has been used easily as a means of control.

According to Swami Nostradamus Verato, publisher of *New Frontier* magazine, director of The Nepal Institute, and a leader in the field of Tantric Sexuality for many years, every fundamentalist country has used sexual repression to control people. Speaking of the former Soviet Union, in which the Communist party's attitude was that sex was sacred only in marriage, he says, "This is similar to what was done in Hitler's Germany. This suppression allowed them to control the people. If you control a culture's sexuality, as is done in any despotic nation, you also control people."[23]

## Towards a Healing of Sexual Shame

Our intention in laying out this material has not been to rub salt in your wounds. Nor has it been to depress you or contribute to feeling helpless. Rather, it has been to help empower you to take actions that will lead toward healing—toward creating the intimate and erotic relationships you desire.

By understanding the scope and magnitude of what you are dealing with, you can truly take stock of your potential options—not simply act from unconscious conditioning. Developing healthy sexuality while facing shaming parents, religion, state, and school is extremely challenging. "Just say no" will not suffice.

The following chapter, *Love, Sex and the Gender Dance,* takes us into the world of gender—how men and women learn and practice the lovers' dance. These adventures—or misadventures—have been dramatically influenced by the dominator model. Its effects are mind boggling.

You will learn how many obstacles to being lifetime lovers develop from both the inadequate and dissimilar erotic educations that men and women receive. Sexual shame looms large in both accounts. It clouds our potential to develop true partnership and lasting passion. Also, our gender conditioning, if unchallenged, makes a truly erotic and intimate relationship impossible to sustain. By learning more about gender differences, you will increase your ability to handle conflicts as they unfold—rather than resort to fruitless judgments of men or women.

# 6

# Love, Sex and the Gender Dance

*That so much human struggle seems to take place in sexual terms is somewhat misleading. The ambiguity and uncertainties of fulfilling oneself as a man or as a woman sometimes mask the more profound anguish of simply being human.*

Sheldon Kopp, *If You Meet the Buddha on the Road, Kill Him*

## Splendor in the Grass?

A group of thirteen-year-old boys stop at an empty lot on their way home from school. Within moments of their arrival, each boy finds a private spot in the tall weeds, pulls his pants down, and begins to masturbate. Phillip is among them. He mouths words like "beating my meat" and "jerking off," liberally mixed with "fuck," "shit," and "goddamn." There is laughter and joking.

Jack teases Ted, "Hey, Ted. Have you got it up yet?"

Ted yells back sarcastically, "Why? Do you want to help me?"

Their behavior is raunchy—intentionally so. Like the other boys, Phillip has been told that masturbation is wrong, so he makes sure his words and behavior match the deed. No sissy girl stuff, here. This is meant to be gross—and fun.

## An Insider's View

Looking into the weeds from the outside, it seems that the boys are shamelessly rejoicing and pleasuring themselves—immersed in male camaraderie and play. However, when we peer beneath the surface, this wild male ritual reveals a soft underbelly of hidden pain and confusion. Though the boys curse with practiced ease as their hands move rhythmically on their penises, they each harbor secret shame, fears, and insecurities:

"I wonder if I really know what I'm doing."

"I feel guilty about this. What if someone catches me here? My parents will kill me."

"What's wrong with me? No one else seems to be scared."

Two of the boys cannot even get their penises hard. Ted is one of them. His earlier comeback to Jack hides his deeper fear: "Maybe Jack knows I'm a wimp. Will I ever be able to get it up? Will I ever be a real man?"

Their fears are veiled by uproarious laughter. Better not let the others know. Though none of them are aware of it, they share this unspoken bond of fear and shame. Few boys do not feel the uncertainty of this age, yet there is no one to talk with openly about it—certainly not their friends.

Phillip is confused, excited, and ashamed all at the same time. He knows that in spite of everything he has been told about masturbation being bad, orgasms feel good; in fact, they feel terrific. But he cannot shake the accompanying feelings of shame. Again, he has no one to talk to. Most boys have their first masturbatory experiences in even greater isolation than Phillip—emotionally and physically separated from every other person. Sexual shame is at work here.

Although he does not articulate it, Phillip also knows that he is making himself feel good all by himself—no girl is necessary or even desired. But, as we shall see, this self-absorption is changing rapidly. During the next few years, most of the boys will begin to relate to girls in a new way. Some day, while holding hands, dancing, or participating in other activities that bring him physically close to a girl, Phillip will experience a familiar feeling.

He may not know anything about romance, but he knows what it feels like to have an erection. He may be frightened of trying to have intercourse. What if he finds himself incapable of attaining or sustaining an erection? He only knows that the urge he feels when he is close to a girl is similar to the urge he has when masturbating.

In the throes of this awakening, girls will suddenly become sought-after companions. In fact, they will mysteriously acquire enough power over boys like Phillip to arouse both intense excitement and anxiety. These blossoming young women will start to exert a pull on them that is strong enough to drag them away from their buddies. Not only will girls become magnets for their attention, formerly close friends will become potential rivals for the affections of these girls. Sexual competition among the boys will intensify.

Their boyhood competitive games will be transposed onto a sexual playing field. Who will "score" with the prettiest girl? Who will get to first base (kissing), second base (fondling breasts), third base (manual stimulation), and even hit a home run (intercourse)? The mix of the physical need for sexual release and the psychological desire to acquire social status propels the advances of males. As boys encounter girls (and later, women), their desires meet serious obstacles.

## Inside the Girl's Room

How about the girls who are Phillip's classmates? They are spending time in each other's bedrooms, endlessly fixing their hair, rubbing each other's backs, putting on make-up, trying on clothes, and dreaming of future loves. Laurie is one of them. She likes Phillip. He also likes her.

Laurie and her girlfriends share a collective dream. Each hopes to meet a handsome, charming, and bright young man who will know exactly what to say and what to do. In Laurie's fantasy, this boy will treat her like a queen. With him, she will feel special, beautiful, and loved. Without her needing to ask, he will provide her with exactly the right atmosphere to be swept off her feet.

Her girlfriends sigh in dreamy and blissful agreement as Laurie describes the romantic moonlit walk on the beach and the words of love and commitment she longs to hear from Phillip. Each girl hopes to find this special love.

Laurie talks about her excitement and anxiety regarding the party which she and her friends are throwing the next day. Her body is warm. Her face is flushed. Her heart feels like it is melting into her whole body. She hopes that Phillip will ask her to go steady. Her girlfriends assure her that he will, since he has already shown an interest in her.

The girls talk about their hopes, dreams, and fears until the wee hours of the morning. They express their self-doubts, tell each other whom they like and find sexy. They describe in great detail how each of the boys they like will kiss. They compare their movie and music idols and share their fantasies about them, too. While they are fantasizing, they are also relating to one another, fixing each other's hair, lounging on the bed, and munching on popcorn. Finally, they fall asleep, warm and content.

## Adolescent Advances

On the night of the party, Laurie and Phillip find themselves alone together. They walk down a path to a lovely, private spot in the garden. Phillip cautiously draws Laurie close to him and Laurie, just as cautiously, surrenders to his embrace. Laurie's eyes are closed. Phillip kisses her gently but eagerly on the lips. Laurie's lips are ready and meet him expectantly. After a few minutes of kissing, Phillip gropes in the dark for Laurie's budding breasts. She gasps slightly as he touches her, but lets his hand rest on her blouse. After all, she is hoping to go steady with him, and she imagines that at any moment he will say the magic words.

Those magic words are the last thing on Phillip's mind right now. His sexual tension has been building—urging him to seek release. He now has a chance. His physical and emotional desires prod him to risk going further with Laurie. But what should he do? He knows that it feels good to touch his own genitals where most of his sexual sensations are centered. He knows that Laurie's genitals are also between her legs, but he doesn't know much more than that. If it feels good to him, would it not feel good to her, too? He's terrified to make the next move—but he surely does not want Laurie to know that. Phillip has learned that girls like boys to act confident and self-assured. He pushes out his chest as he tentatively, with both apprehension and eagerness, lets his hand slide off of Laurie's breast, down her stomach, to rest between her legs.

## Shock Waves in the Garden

And what a reaction! Laurie recoils in horror and disgust as she tells Phillip that he is crude, that what he is trying to do is wrong. Is he some kind of pervert? She is a "good girl" and how could he think that she would do such a thing?

Phillip stiffens! He is scared, hurt, and angry—all at the same time. He feels crushed. He has taken a giant risk and has been sorely rejected. Laurie's romantic bubble has been burst. Her dream of being romantically swept away exploded abruptly when she felt Phillip's hand reaching between her legs. She, too, is experiencing many different feelings simultaneously. She is disappointed, angry, scared, and strangely excited.

They have both learned a great deal from this episode. Phillip concludes that Laurie has the power and makes the rules in matters sexual. He feels similar emotions to those he had when he was a little boy and his mother was in control. He is the supplicant; his need to touch Laurie is greater than her need to be touched. If Phillip wants to touch her again, he will have to let her decide when and how she will be touched. His hope is that if he "behaves" then sometime, maybe, she will allow him another chance.

## The Inherent Dilemma of Male Strategies

How can Phillip accomplish his goal? He is desperately trying to figure out what he should do to attain sexual success—yet he is not sure what will bring him the desired results. If he wants to keep seeing Laurie, and she is still willing, he must swallow his pride. Another option would be to dump her and try to find a girl who is easier sexually. He considers two different strategies—to be nicer, sweeter, more thoughtful, and most of all, less pushy, or whether to be cooler, louder, more demanding, and callously unconcerned.

No matter which he chooses, he is in a terrible bind. His body demands that he be sexual, but he bitterly resents the bargain he must make in order to satisfy his desires. His adolescent psyche pushes him to score, to prove to himself and his peers that he can succeed, but he resents his friends for the pressure he feels and Laurie for the obstacle she presents.

Subconsciously, the situation with Laurie catalyzes another problem. Her reaction activates Phillip's sexual shame, whose internal voice chastises, "She's right. You are an animal. What's wrong with you? You're not interested in anything but sex." Afraid of rejection, another voice chimes in, "Why don't you quit now, before you make an even greater fool of yourself?"

How will he satisfy his intense sexual drive and his compulsion to prove himself, without alienating the girl, arousing his feelings of shame, or his fears of being an inadequate male? As long as Phillip sees only these options, he is doomed to failure.

Phillip must reconcile his shameful feelings about sexuality and his intense desire to have sex with the realization that Laurie refuses to have sex. Again, this puts him in a terrible bind. If he views her as a complete, feeling human being, and he pushes her to be sexual with him, he would feel guilty for forcing her into a situation in which she may feel debased or violated and he would feel like an insensitive lout. If he develops an empathic connection with her, and tries again, he is afraid that he will get turned down again. Having no role models of egalitarian relationships based on true partnership, he comes to believe that he cannot fulfill his sexual needs with a direct, humane, and loving approach.

Given Phillip's sexual urgency, his limited life experience and lack of positive role models, his desire to avoid pain and gain pleasure, the strategy that he inevitably chooses is consonant with androcratic, dominating values—he *must* perceive Laurie as a "sex object." If he can objectify her as a means toward an end—sexual release—then he can remove the obstacles to success in the same stroke. First, he can fortify himself against the pain of rejection, because it is far less painful to be rejected by an insignificant object than by a whole human being—one who he regards as his equal or even superior. Second, he can quell his own shame, because he would be disregarding an object's protests rather than a real person's stated wishes. Third, he can feel powerful and stand up to her if he can strip her of the control and power he attributed to her as a mother figure.

## The Girl's Plight

Laurie, not surprisingly, perceives the situation quite differently. She has a similar experience of feeling powerless, ashamed, and inadequate—but for different reasons. She wonders what she must have done to lead Phillip on and fears that she should not have let him touch her breasts. She resents his forward behavior and at the same time feels afraid that he may stop liking her. The geni-tingles she felt and the sensations of warmth spreading through her body were pleasurable, and she is curious to pursue them but also feels ashamed of her desires. Also, she is a product of our androcratic society so she has been inculcated with attitudes of deference, dependence, and passivity. However, if she does what he wants, she will be going against her mother's and, possibly, her father's wishes as well.

So Laurie, too, is in a bind. She wants to explore her sexuality, but she feels ashamed and afraid to pursue it. She also dearly wants a boyfriend, but if she is to have one, she must walk a fine line. She must give him some of what he wants, or he will part company with her and get it elsewhere. At the same time, she must not develop a reputation as a "loose" girl, or he will use her and then dump her for a more "respectable" girlfriend. She believes that she must give him some of what he wants sexually in order for her to get the romance and emotional intimacy she wants. Yet, she must constantly put the brakes on her sexuality to minimize her own feelings of shame and guilt.

Laurie also faces peer pressure, but hers is vastly different than Phillip's. Her friends have taken over her mother's role—they police each other to maintain their "good girl" status. Laurie dare not venture over the line lest she lose the respect of her girlfriends. In fact, she must not even reveal the extent to which she wants to be sexual.

Besides her feelings of sexual desire, shame, fear of parental and peer disapproval, and dismay at having her romantic bubble burst, Laurie experiences a disquieting yet exciting possibility. Sensing the urgency of Phillip's desire and witnessing the impact of her rejection, she realizes how much he wants her. This is an ace in her hand. If she plays her cards well, she can keep him interested, keep her reputation, and keep her girlfriends. Yet, to do this, she pays a price. Rather than practicing the interpersonal skills of being genuine and vulnerable—with all of her fear, excitement, and disappointment—she hones the widely used, but highly dysfunctional, skills of manipulation, indirectness, and dishonesty.

# The Potential for Erotic Expansion

And so, boys and girls meet sexually and romantically as though from different worlds—with contrasting assumptions, expectations, and desires. In subsequent years, we learn to bridge our differences through compromise. Like Laurie and Phillip, we accommodate in order to get something we want. Yet many of us still do not fundamentally understand our differences or our similarities.

If we were to understand our differences, we would be able to bridge these differences by expanding our repertoire of possibilities. As a result, we could begin to think like this as follows: "When I truly understand and appreciate you and your qualities, then I begin to empathize with your position. I also have the opportunity to taste those qualities in myself. When I expand my repertoire of possibilities to meet you and your possibilities, I grow personally—and you and I connect. A bridge is formed. When I allow myself to be affected by you in this way, I develop some of the attributes that you have more fully developed in yourself. In this way, I use our relationship to embrace more aspects of myself, and I become a richer, more whole person."

Sadly, most of us feel threatened by each other's differences and regard these differences within a right-wrong context—believing that we must be wrong if they are right, and vice versa. Women and men rarely take the time and effort to understand what motivates the other sex to feel, think, and behave in the ways that they do. Nor do many of us fully understand ourselves—our own conscious and unconscious motivations for feeling, thinking, and behaving as we do. Through experience men and women do learn to accommodate to each other erotically, to a degree, but many of us still do not understand our fundamental differences. Nor do we know how to begin bridging these differences.

By gaining insight into what men and women undergo in their erotic educations, we can develop greater compassion for ourselves and each other. We can grow beyond justifying ourselves and judging each other. We can relinquish our limited model of right and wrong so that we can dissolve our conflicts. We can truly mature.

If we are to arrive at such a state, we must begin by learning about each other. We must discover how men and women are similar and we must understand our differences. Let's begin to build the bridge by delving into our erotic education remembering that this is happening within a dominator paradigm.

# Erotic Education

We have all been given inadequate and misleading information about our erotic natures. What happened between Philip and Laurie—their mutually intense pain which she experienced when he reached between her legs and he felt when she rejected his advances—is part and parcel of their skewed and limited erotic educations.

Our own ignorant and paltry erotic educations have fostered unnecessary pain. They have contributed to subtle, even gross, abuse of ourselves and each other. They have influenced how we relate to each other in every erotic dimension: meeting, dating, looking, talking, touching, kissing, intercourse, emotional intimacy, communication, and long-term intimacy. Unfortunately, we were never taught that "making love" is natural, healthy, and intrinsically human.

Just how are we coached in developing our erotic nature? How does our distorted education impact the joining together of hearts, spirits, and bodies? Let's take an in-depth look at how men and women learn about eros in our culture.

# Sex Education in the Dark

Our sexual education and background hardly prepares us for the challenge of developing healthy eros. An uncomfortable father foists a clinical book about sexuality onto his teenage son, hoping against odds to teach him about the "birds and the bees"—itself an indirect symbol of sexuality; a half-hour class is given in a dark high-school classroom, supposedly to enlighten students about their upcoming urges; a flustered mother informs her newly pubescent daughter that she finally has the "curse" and warns her to keep her legs shut. Locker room banter and boasting—which veil the fears of confused adolescents—become the guide for other confused and fearful adolescents.

Perhaps, as you did the exercises in *The Wounds of Sexual Shame*, you remembered your own introduction to sexuality. Were you taken aside by a parent and educated in a loving and shame-free manner? Were you taught about how to merge your personal and spiritual development with your natural instinctual desires? Was there a celebratory rite-of-passage that marked your passage out of childhood and initiated you into young adulthood? It is highly unlikely. You probably learned about sexuality by groping in the dark, literally and figuratively.

# Men's Erotic Education: What We Call "Normal"

What kind of coaching have males received in the art of lovemaking? Have they been taught by compassionate elders who took them under their wings as boys and instructed them in the expression of healthy sexuality? Were they welcomed into a community where any questions about their budding sexuality were heard? Were they clued into the physiological and psychological changes which would occur after they reached puberty? Were they taught anything about being an erotic being? The answers are painfully obvious.

Rather than learning to trust their impulses, to rely on their senses, and to open their hearts in lovemaking, young males learn to externalize their inner world—performance, achievement, and the right equipment become the yardsticks of erotic success. Males float in an ocean of ignorant and limited social stereotypes—learned both verbally and nonverbally—completely disconnecting sex from heart and spirit. They receive mixed and crazy-making messages:

*You should naturally know exactly what to do.*
*You should be ashamed of your penis and sexuality.*

*You should flaunt your sexual prowess.*

*You should control your sexuality.*

*If you have to ask for help, you must be incompetent.*

*You should never be confused or uncertain; you should be completely confident.*

*You should never have a limp penis; you should always be ready to have sex.*

The list of contradictions goes on and on. There's no way for boys to make sense of these mixed messages, and there's rarely anyone knowledgeable and mature to guide them. In essence, adolescent males are emotionally abandoned in regards to eros.

Throughout history boys have been initiated into manhood by mature adult males. Introduced into the male mysteries by these elders, boys learned by direct instruction to fulfill the male sex role as well as to rejoice in the sacred qualities of masculinity. This instruction in the sexual arts was elaborate and grounded—eliminating the ignorance so common among modern men. Without glorifying these male initiation rites, which were usually brutal, including circumcisions and subincisions, the boys did learn directly from more knowledgeable men.

How have fathers or older males fulfilled this role in our culture? Here are a few representative examples we have heard:

George's father told him to get in the car so they could have a talk—something they never did. George recognized the unusual situation and the thought dawned on him, "Oh no, my father is going to try to teach me about sex." George—who was fifteen at the time—was right. As they drove over the Golden Gate Bridge, George's father asked him in a stilted voice, "Um, do you…have any questions about…sex?" George recalls, "The real message was that I better not have any. He just needed to ask to fulfill his obligation." George responded, "No." His father said, "Good." That was the beginning and end of George's erotic education by older males.

Matt never heard a word about sex in his family. Sex didn't exist.

Dave's father foisted a clinical book about sexuality on him when he was 16 years old and told him, "This should answer any questions you have."

Brian's mother told him that she hoped he wasn't having any sexual feelings (he was sixteen years old), but if he had any questions, he should ask his father.

At the other extreme, Hank's father took him to a brothel to visit a prostitute. He warned Hank, "Don't tell your mother." After the experience, which was terrifying and disorienting to fourteen-year-old Hank, his father slapped him on the back in "good old boy" camaraderie, and laughed, "Now you're a man." Hank didn't feel like one.

Obviously, the lack of healthy erotic education by older males is a situation that needs to change, but let's not shame or blame fathers and older males for this plight. After all, they also learned little from their elders. Erotic male education has been absent for many generations. The lack of teachings by older males is not the only reason for erotic misinformation. Let's take a look at the school yard where older braggarts often occupy a significant yet inappropriate role initiating young males into the art of sex.

# Boys as Sexual Initiators of Boys

When we consider who are the sexual initiators of boys in our culture, we confront a disturbing reality—they are often other boys. Sauntering through the playground, these "initiating" boys have mastered the coolest swagger—irresistible qualities to the other boys, hungry to become potent, attractive males themselves. In other words, many boys model themselves on other boys, thinking, "If I can learn to be as cool as Jerry, then I'll have a chance with the girls." What invaluable lessons do these cocky boys pass on about how to be a sexually potent male? Here's what one of our clients was taught:

"Hey, dick head, want to learn how to do it? This is how you do it. You take the girl into a dark place. Then you start kissing her. Then you put your hands down her dress. If she says no, it's just a game. You have to show her that you're stronger than her 'no.' Don't worry. If you don't take no for an answer, she'll eventually say yes. And don't blow it, asshole."

Even though most boys do not receive this crass lesson so overtly, they do receive the underlying message: hide your fears of rejection, don't take no for an answer, and feign confidence and assurance. The androcratic principles have already made their mark. Dominance means power. Women are objects in a game. Sexuality is a thing to be had. If you ever wondered how date rape and rape in marriage could be so widespread, you need not wonder any longer.

# Daniel's Erotic Education

My (Daniel) erotic education was as pathetic as most. No older male took me aside and taught me anything about sex. A schoolmate gave me a porno magazine when I was twelve years old that utterly fascinated and turned me on. Of course, I hid it, knowing my mother would hardly approve. My brilliant hiding place was a small space between the stove and the dishwasher. Needless to say, she found it. She then stared at me in horror, asking rhetorically: "You're not interested in this—are you?" What could I say? I just looked straight down—scared and dumbfounded. No acknowledgment from her that I might be interested in nude women—just disbelief.

My male initiation (in the most superficial sense of the word) through older boys occurred when I was fifteen or sixteen. These boys had found some "loose" girls from another town whom they called "The Slaves" (an androcratic image). The guys would take these girls into houses under construction where the girls would either masturbate or perform fellatio on them. One day, they invited me to join in their escapades.

I remember being terrified, but determined to hide my fear. I pretended to take things in stride—just like the rest of them. When my turn came, I went into the room and sat down on the bench. One of the girls unzipped my fly and started masturbating me. She looked in my eyes and I avoided her gaze. I felt so uncomfortable that I could hardly breathe. After I ejaculated, I quickly pulled my pants up and left the room—barely a thank-you or good-bye.

The older boys were waiting as I joined them. "So D Bird (my nickname), how was it?"

"It was great," I responded, my nose growing longer.

They laughed and jived me, "So, are you in love?"

"Get out of here," I rejoined, hoping they would not notice how flustered I felt.

The only erotic lesson I received here was how to objectify females. Although I felt proud to be included with the older guys, I felt little caring or compassion from them. All in all, it was a forgettable experience that I will always remember.

Like most other boys, I was searching for ways to develop erotic confidence. Naturally, I looked to other males who seemed to embody those classically male attributes. And when the purveyors of those masculine qualities are on the big screen, they seem bigger than life.

## Sex Stars, Media, and Erotic Initiation

These icons are everywhere you look—revealing the latest images of male erotic power. Their images from the movies, playing fields, and billboards leap straight into our psyches. Through the larger media we learn what is sexy and what is not. In this nation of rugged individualists, we emotionally buy into mass-produced images embodied by false idols.

For most men, their primary fantasy is to be with a beautiful woman. Advertisers know this and exploit it to the hilt. They present images of male success and juxtapose a beautiful woman as a coup de gras. The fancy car, the big house, or the important job will insure him of his most precious commodity—a sexy woman. So men have the success equals sex ratio drilled into their psyches from a very early age. It's part of the rampant objectification that happens between the sexes: women are *sex objects,* but men are *success objects,* according to Warren Farrell. It's part and parcel of the dominator paradigm.

Farrell, author of *Why Men Are the Way They Are* and *The Myth of Male Power,* and a pioneer in male-female relations, used the movie *The Outsiders* to demonstrate a related twist to this dynamic between the sexes. Matt Dillon portrayed a greaser type, whom Farrell labels as "Most Likely to Be a Psychopath." Farrell describes a classic scene in the movie where Dillon, the handsome tough guy, comes onto a beautiful cheerleader at a drive-in movie:

He comes on. She resists. He comes on stronger. She pulls away. He puts his face and body in "her space," pushing her menacingly, putting her down every time she gets turned off. She's trying to keep her cool, but the viewer can cut her fear with a knife as she anxiously scouts for a way out.

How scared was the cheerleader? She reveals the depth of her fear to Dillon's buddy. "Keep that guy away from me, you hear? You hear? I don't ever want to see him again, never."

"Why?" Dillon's buddy asks.

"I'll fall in love." [1]

With the film's success, Dillon became the heartthrob of young girls across the nation. At first glance, it seems bizarre that this abusive male—who will stop at practically nothing to get his way—became an erotic ideal of girls (and women) from every socio-economic background. No girl would feel terribly proud to bring this guy home to her parents, yet he fulfills a primary romantic fantasy. What is it about Dillon's character that inspires the adulation of females and the envy of males—beyond his good looks? What role does this male persona play in the illusions between the sexes? Are females attracted to him for a different reason than males imagine, and if so, does this difference contribute to confusion between the sexes? What are boys and men supposed to think when they see this rude, violent teenager become desired by females of every age and class?

The meaning males usually ascribe to the popularity of this image—similar to the image of cultural heroes like Rambo, Dirty Harry, and the Exterminator—is that male sexual appeal is inextricably bound to physical toughness and violence. Unconsciously, males are conditioned to believe that the ability to be violent—or at least physically tough and potentially violent—is utterly male and sexy.

Boys and men incorporate these attitudes and behaviors into their erotic repertoire. Guys who learn not to take no for an answer are merely following an age-old male script. They wonder when no really means no or whether the girl or woman really means yes—if only you push a little harder. They emulate these characters based on their interpretation of what women want—a guy who is tough, single-minded, supremely confident, and will not take no for an answer. They do not comprehend the deeper female psychology which underlies why many girls (and later women) succumb to the tough male persona. Males have become confused by this attraction—especially when the emerging message since the 1960s is that men should be vulnerable, empathic, understanding, and sensitive. Most men still don't know what women want.

## Women's Erotic Education: Paucity as "Normal"

What kind of coaching have young females received in the art of lovemaking? Even less than their male counterparts! Rather than learning to trust their impulses, to rely on their senses, and to revel in their luscious sexuality, girls also learn to disconnect their sexuality from heart and spirit. The messages females in our culture receive influence them to keep their true sexual nature in the shadows. They are schooled in developing the aspect of eros that is love, but the sexual aspect of eros is sorely neglected. They receive massive mixed messages about their sexuality, because of unconscious sexual repression:

> *You should not feel or be sexual.*
>
> *You should not know what to do, and if you do know, you should not reveal how you learned. At least, you should know less than your male partner.*
>
> *You should be proud or ashamed of your breasts (depending on their size) and you should be ashamed of the smells, secretions, and shape of your vagina.*
>
> *You should be seductive but restrained.*
>
> *You should control yourself sexually.*
>
> *You should not give in to a man easily.*
>
> *You should never allow a man to directly know that you want him sexually or emotionally.*
>
> *You should have orgasms quickly and easily during intercourse and without much stimulation.*
>
> *You should fake orgasm so that your partner's ego is not bruised.*
>
> *You should make sure a man loves you before engaging in sex with him.*

This list is by no means comprehensive. And just as the boys are abandoned, the girls, as well, have no mature, experienced, and knowledgeable women to answer their questions and help them solve their dilemmas.

This has not always been the case. In the goddess-based religions which lasted millennia, until A.D. 200, girls served as priestesses to the goddess. The young girls were introduced to sexuality, to the mysteries of the female and male body by women—called *qadishtu,* the Akkadian name for "sanctified women" or "holy women"—who were familiar with the sacred sexual customs.[2] By direct instruction, they were taught how to be skillful lovers and to rejoice in the sacred qualities of the feminine.

The extent to which this cultural paradigm differs from our current model is reflected in the attitude of the people toward the *qadishtu.* These priestesses were revered, and were sometimes women of wealth and high social status. Even their children, whose paternity was unknown, were given the same social status and the girls often became *qadishtu* as well. When these women got married, they were said to make excellent wives. Serving the goddess in this way was an honor and privilege rather than a sin; therefore instruction in the sexual arts was elaborate and widespread.

How have mothers and older women, crones, fulfilled this role in our culture?

When Sharon was thirteen years old, her mother slapped her across the face when she found bloodstains on Sharon's underwear. "That will teach you not to be a slut," her mother chided. She asked if Sharon had any questions. Ashamed and afraid, Sharon said no. Her mother ended the conversation warning her, "Well, make sure you don't get knocked up. And if you do, don't come crying to me."

When Cynthia began to menstruate, she was afraid that she was bleeding to death. She ran to her mother, crying. Her mother explained to her that now she had "the curse." After showing her how to use a menstrual pad, she said matter-of-factly, "I suppose I have to tell you about the birds and the bees." She then proceeded to give her an anatomical description of intercourse, devoid of any feeling. When she was finished, she told her, "Wait until you get married. Then your husband will tell you everything you need to know. You probably won't like it at first, but it gets easier. They (men) don't want to do it as much when they get older." Her mother warned her against using tampons because it could call into question her virginity.

To make matters worse, we are finding that many young women are initiated into sexuality through various forms of sexual abuse. More and more stories of incest by fathers, uncles, brothers, cousins, and even mothers are surfacing. The number of girls and young women who suffer their first sexual experience at the hands of those who use them for their own gratification is staggering when you add the priests, neighbors, and older boys who also molest and abuse them. Of course, many boys have also been sexually abused as well.

Certainly, there are many saner, less traumatic stories of girls learning about sexuality at the onset of menses, but few that impart the natural beauty and sacredness of sexuality. Women frequently tell of their mothers sitting them down to tell them the facts of life. But many mothers gave their daughters a book to read to save themselves from the embarrassment of talking about this very uncomfortable topic. Few women have fond or joyful memories of the beginnings of their sexual education.

Equally pathetic are the stories told by our mothers regarding their sexual education. I, Judith, was a "diaphragm baby." I was conceived before my parents intended because my mother had never been taught how to use her diaphragm!

The truth is, erotic education for men or women has been absent for many generations. When the goddess-based religions were suppressed and the patriarchal, dominator-based religions prevailed, sexual education ceased, as did the passing on of sacred customs. The patriarchy did not want women to engage in sexuality with any man other than their husbands. Why? They wanted to trace lineage through paternity, transferring money and land through the hands of the fathers. The only way to be certain of paternity was to limit women's sexual autonomy and make it a crime and a sin against God for her to be sexual outside of marriage. Remember, up until this time women who served the goddess during special celebrations were revered—prior to marriage and even within a monogamous marriage.[3]

The lack of education from the elders is not the only reason for erotic misinformation. Girls are given the message that they should not learn about their own sexuality. Boys are expected to masturbate, even if there is shame surrounding it, but young girls are not. In fact, until this generation, many girls and women had never masturbated. Even now, in the nineties, I (Judith) have worked with adolescent girls and young woman who are brought up with sexually repressive religious training, who would not dream of masturbating because "It's dirty."

Thanks to a great deal of literature on the subject, this is changing. Starting with the publication of *Our Bodies, Our Selves*[4], the new field of women's erotica, and books on menopause, women now have access to knowledge that had been hidden. More and more, young women are following the example of pop star Madonna—their sexuality is rightfully theirs and it is something to celebrate. The fantasies contributed to Nancy Friday's latest book, *Women on Top,*[5] attest to the fact that young women feel differently than their elders about masturbating and about taking an initiatory role in sexuality.

# Boys as Sexual Initiators of Girls

Without female elders to initiate them into the sacred customs, and for many, without their own sexual explorations, most young girls are initiated into their sexuality by their male peers—the boys. Though girls learn morals from their girlfriends and are policed by them, they learn about their sexuality from their first boyfriends—who are the same age or slightly older than the girls. Though many girls talk to their girlfriends about how far to go with their boyfriends and describe in detail what actually transpired, they rarely practice "sex" or masturbate together. Some women describe practicing "French kissing" with their girlfriends but I (Judith) have not yet heard many stories about groups of young girls masturbating side by side. For the most part, girls learn about sexuality from their boyfriends.

Since the boy's coolness and confidence mask their ignorance (except in the area of masturbating themselves), the education most girls receive from them is paltry and male-centered. More often than not, the girls are focusing their energy on preventing the boys from going too far, on avoiding pregnancy, or on helping the boy feel like a man.

# My Erotic Education

My (Judith) erotic education was better than most. Though my mother sat me down to talk about sex when I was an early adolescent (I think prior to menses, though she and I are not certain), I had no use for her knowledge. I informed her that I already knew. I had been going to a girl's camp since age eight and with the help of the counselors who were eighteen and older, all the questions my girlfriends and I had, were amply answered. Between the camp counselors, "trash magazines" (more aptly called romance magazines), and my older sister, I had all the sex education I needed, thank you, Mom.

So, though my mother offered to teach me after I already knew the facts, so to speak, she had a very important and positive role in my sex education. When I began to menstruate, she welcomed me into the world of women. With a feeling of celebration, my coming of age was honored. She instructed me in the use of menstrual pads but after one cycle, I protested and asked to use tampons. She showed me how to use them. With the help of a mirror and my fingers, she showed me which hole was which. There was no shame in my family about bodily functions, so this part of my education was easy and fun.

I became the local expert for several of my girlfriends who were not allowed to wear tampons, or who were afraid or ashamed to ask their mothers to show them how. For girls who felt ashamed and awkward, I stood outside the bathroom door, describing what my mother had taught me directly. With other girls, I played my mother's role, showing them where to insert the tampon.

Though I had my share of young boyfriends who groped around while I tried to make sure they didn't go too far, I was blessed with the good fortune of meeting Hal, a young man four years my senior. When I was a junior in high school, Hal was a junior in college.

Hal was an excellent initiator and teacher. He respected my desire to retain my virginity, so I had no need to protect myself. Together we examined his genitals and mine. He told me what felt good to him and how different parts of his penis and scrotum provided different sensations. As we explored my genitals, I also described my sensations and told him what felt good to me. More than anything else, I learned that it was okay, even necessary, to talk about what I wanted, what felt good, etc. We expected to explore what felt good together; this was part of the joy of being sexual together. He knew about the different rhythms of men and women and without making one better than the other, showed me how to harmonize our rhythms.

He taught me that my satisfaction was as important as his, that respecting each other was more important than any goal. In fact, he taught me that there was no other goal than to have fun. Because he was not ashamed of sexuality, his or mine, he helped me to heal some of my shame. He also taught me, in no uncertain terms, that he, and by inference other men, loved the feeling, sights, smells, and tastes of women's genitals. Thank you, Hal!

Though Hal graced my life during my later high school years and began to turn around some of my earlier notions of sexuality, the role models I had grown up with were slanted toward the sexual man and the romantic woman. Like the boys and girls my age, I was strongly affected by the media. I felt ashamed of how sexual I was! Secretly, I feared that I was over-sexed.

## Sex Stars, Media, and Erotic Initiation

Just as our young men emulate movie heroes as models of sexual prowess, young women look to the screen for their script. And what do they find? Sexy, empty-headed bimbos. Women who use their looks to trap a man. Women who are covert and deceptive to catch the man of their dreams. Women who are looking for a man who is going to take care of them—even better than their parents did. Women who feel lovable when a man who is good-looking, powerful (in this context, tough), and has social status desires them. Women who believe that their fulfillment will come by pleasing others. Our models of femininity have been women who are taught to be emotional caretakers and not to ask for anything themselves.

Recently the media has begun to portray women as competent and sexy, maternal and sexy, or smart and sexy. Yet in the sexual arena, we still see the man taking the woman, the woman surrendering in ecstatic abandon. How often have we been given models of women, sexually autonomous, economically independent, and emotionally mature, taking the man?

And what of the issue of violence and force? Why is it our young women find the Rambo-like characters sexually appealing? Why do we have such a large incidence of date rape? Why do so many women write love letters to jailed mass murders—often killers of women—and sometimes marry them in prison? How is it that rape in marriage is legal in many states? Why is there so much wife battery, a problem largely neglected by our legal system?

## Taken and Ravished: A Female Fantasy

As we mentioned earlier, the young woman believes—consciously or otherwise—that a strong man will take care of her. She will be able to depend on him and ultimately, she can surrender to him. Her attraction to his toughness or violence lies not in his brutality per se—which men often misunderstand—but that his willingness to fight for her demonstrates how *important* she is to him. Not only that, his willingness to fight for her also shows that he must *love* her—his intensity proves it. Since she is also a product of a dominator society, she has been steeped in the myth that force and power are synonymous. Because he is so courageous and fearless, she sees him as powerful and she believes that he will be seen as significant and competent by other people—and therefore she herself will be elevated in the eyes of others.

Further, when he looks at her as if she is the most beautiful, desirable woman in the world, she becomes the fairy tale princess. He wants her! He will stop at nothing to get her. His determination to win her will overcome obstacles of every kind. His unswerving faith communicates his confidence. The prince will always find a way.

Many women steeped in liberation philosophies of the last thirty years will gasp at this presentation. They want to believe that the myths of Prince Charming are dead and buried. He <u>is</u> gone for some women, but for many others, his image still rides through their fantasies—consciously or unconsciously. Old beliefs die hard and new possibilities do not easily replace them.

Although our new belief system tells us that sensitivity and tenderness are masculine—that sexiness and sensitivity are no longer exclusive—our androcratic thought patterns, three thousand years in the making, still equate roughness with sexy masculinity. Though many changes have occurred through consciousness raising, many unconscious beliefs and behaviors still linger. Movie ratings don't lie! Nor do police, hospital, homicide records, and court reports of battered wives.

The fantasy falls apart when their partner's confident swagger turns to domineering threats and violence—against them. And then they have difficulty getting out due to religious convictions, fear for their lives, lack of adequate legal or police protection, and societal norms which make husbands the rightful authority of their wives.

What follows about male violence toward women represents the extreme pole similar to that of gross sexual abuse. Just as most children are not overtly sexually abused by their parents, most women are not physically violated by their husbands. Similar to how our exploration of Jimmy Swaggert and the shadow (*The Wounds of Sexual Shame*) highlighted the relationship between repression and shadow projections, our exploration of male violence toward women will highlight the relationship between the dominator model and male violence. Our purpose for exploring the extremes of sex role conditioning is to get a clearer sense of what we are really facing. But first a few words about how most people experience androcracy.

Actually, most men will scoff at the notion that they are dramatically influenced by androcratic principles. They don't beat their wives. Sometimes they don't even yell. They take out the garbage, try to pick up after themselves, fix a few things around the house, and attempt to be helpful, decent people. And most of them are good, decent people. However, there are unconscious assumptions which fly in the face of egalitarian relationships.

Fran and Allen have been together for eleven years and married for eight. They have two children. Coming of age in the 1960s, they were determined to rid themselves of rigid sex roles. They believe they have a very conscious, egalitarian relationship. However, when we peer beneath the veneer of their conscious agreements, we notice a striking dissimilarity in the responsibilities they actually hold. Although they both work full-time, Fran cooks dinner most nights while Allen plays with the children. After dinner, Fran does the dishes most nights (Allen does occasionally), and Allen reads to the children or goes to the gym. Fran does the lion's share of the cleaning and Allen cleans the sink once in a while. Fran feels resentful at times, but eventually gets over it.

When they have dinner guests, the women usually jump up after the meal and clear the table. They wash dishes and prepare the dessert. The men sit and talk, oblivious to all the work going on around them. Liberation has meant all the prior responsibilities and a full-time job.

Money is a prime mover in all relationships—it is power. Who holds the purse strings controls much of what happens in the relationship. Often, when the husband is bringing in all the money or more money when both spouses work, he feels entitled to control the bottom line. Add to this the difference in earning power between men and women and you come up with an unbalanced equation. Women, economically disadvantaged and tied to their children, become financially dependent on their husbands. This power imbalance is integral to androcratic societies. Women stay put if they are financially dependent.

Furthermore, there are still assumptions that a woman should give a man sex whenever he wants it. This represents part of the complicity between men and women. These agreements, while familiar, ultimately erode trust and compromise the ability to create lifelong love.

Many people, especially women, believe that if women feel powerless, then men must feel powerful. However, nothing could be further from the truth. That's the irony of the situation. Most men lead lives of quiet desperation. Even though they are raised to be the dominators in the androcratic paradigm, few men feel a sense of control over their lives. In addition, there are role reversals in some relationships, where the woman is more dominating and the man is more passive. Instead of finding fault, we must release ourselves from this unhealthy paradigm. Perhaps the most disastrous aspect of the dominator paradigm is how sexuality and violence are connected.

## Male Violence Toward Women

In *Rape in Marriage,* Diana Russell exposes the extent to which violence—beating, emotional and physical torture, rape, and threats—is an aspect of many women's sexual experience, in and out of marriage. The results of her study researching rape in marriage were so staggering that she developed a typology of men in relation to violence and sexuality. The range spanned and included men who *only* engaged in sexual behavior in which they took the woman by force, those who preferred violence but also engaged in sex with consent, to men who were not at all interested or aroused by using force. Equally astounding was the acceptance by many women that violence and sexuality were bound together. We have only to look at our courts and the Bible for substantiation of this union.

Historically, our courts have refused to consider the testimony of many wives who have been battered when the violence occurred within the context of sex. "That was part of the sex play," they ruled. As first delineated in the Old Testament of the Bible, the new rule legitimized rape by making the woman the man's property after he had raped her. Inherent in this relationship as well is the power differential. Though in the United States, women are not legally viewed as their husband's property, the fact that many men rape their divorced wives—long after they have been separated—speaks to the notion of rightful ownership.

In 1981, when *The Hite Report on Male Sexuality* was published, a male respondent wrote about rape, "I would never think of taking it by force—except from my wife. I don't think I could get it up in a rape situation. It so appalls me that I couldn't do it."[6] This man, and many like him, feel justified in raping their wives. Legally, in many states, they are entitled to do so based on what is commonly referred to as "the marital rape exemption." According to these laws, rape in marriage is a legal impossibility in that they define rape as *the forcible penetration of the body of a woman, not the wife of the perpetrator.*

The origin of this exemption is traced to a Chief Justice in England in the seventeenth century who made a name for himself by presiding over witchcraft trials. Published in *History of the Pleas of the Crown* in 1736, Matthew Hale decreed the following:

"But the husband cannot be guilty of a rape committed by himself upon his lawful wife, for by their mutual matrimonial consent and contract the wife hath given up herself in this kind unto the husband which she cannot retract."[7]

This idea, of course, is based on the dominator view that wives are the property of their husbands. As late as 1980, many states did not recognize wife rape. In fact, "thirteen states had quietly extended the privilege of husbands to rape their wives to men who are cohabiting with women with whom they are not legally married."[8]

In her study of 930 women living in San Francisco which excluded women who were in institutions, shelters, or living on the street (where the prevalence of wife rape is likely to be the highest), Russell found that fourteen percent of the women in her study admitted to being raped by their husbands. However, many others not included in that group "saw it as their 'duty' to submit to sexual intercourse with their husbands, even when they had no desire for sex or were repulsed by the idea."[9] Others made it clear that they were unwilling to admit experiences of forced sex with their husbands.

In another study on violence in marriage by sociologists Finkelhor and Yllo, women who were raped by their husbands did not resist as forcefully as women raped by strangers for the following reasons:[10]

114

*Lovers for Life*

a. They felt they could not deter their partner's aggression no matter how hard they tried.

b. They perceived their partners as very strong. (There was usually a considerable size difference).

c. They believed they were somehow in the wrong.

d. Unless they were prepared to leave, they knew they had to face their partner the next morning or later that day.

e. They wanted to keep the peace.

f. They wanted to make things more tolerable for themselves.

These reasons, given by wives who admit to being raped by their husbands are similar to the reasons many battered wives do not seek medical attention after being beaten. And those who do seek medical help are often met with doctors who collude—ostensibly believing women's cover-up of their husband's abuse. Is it that they do not want to get involved or they are part of the androcratic paradigm in which men and women believe that husbands have the authority and the license to rule and abuse their wives?

Perhaps this tendency to look the other way can partially explain why police and the courts did not take more serious action against O. J. Simpson in regard to Nicole's now famous 911 calls—and his subsequent conviction of battery.[11] Perhaps it also relates to our cultural denial of our "hero's" foibles. The consequences of this myopia can be dire. Perhaps there has been too much general acceptance that violence is a justifiable way to resolve problems of any kind. Although the Wild West is dead and gone, the dominator model is alive and kicking.

It is apparent that the result of our cultural views which connect masculinity with violence and make violence an acceptable means of resolving conflicts is disastrous. And equally, if not more disastrous, are our views which legitimize a husband's authority over his wife—in sexual matters as well as every aspect of daily life. Intimacy and sacred sexuality cannot exist when a man says, "I can do what I like, she's my wife."[12] In this model, if a husband has sexual desire, it is his wife's duty to oblige him. If she does not, she is viewed as disobedient and warranting punishment. Of course, most men do not resort to violence.

As long as we groom young girls to be passive, dependent, and deferential, young boys to be fiercely independent and believe themselves superior, we will perpetuate violence toward women in marriage and maintain a patriarchal model for relationships. This kind of objectification of women is obvious in cases of marital rape, battery, and psychological violence, but it can be seen in relationships that do not involve overt violence at all. These kinds of cases are far more common. In the following case, notice how both the man and the woman respond stereotypically—and how their responses create unnecessary problems. Both men and women lose here.

# Abdication of Responsibility

Maggie is thirty-eight years old and has never been married. She is a capable and accomplished lawyer in the public defender's office. She pays her bills, owns and maintains her house, and in general, acts responsibly in most areas of her life. She was dating Jim, also an accomplished and responsible lawyer, and became pregnant. When a friend asked her why she hadn't used a contraceptive, Maggie said, "I didn't plan on having sex with him until it happened. He was really sweet and romantic and before I knew it, we were making love. It would have broken the spell if I had stopped to ask him if he had a condom or if I had gotten up to get my diaphragm."

When Maggie told Jim the news, he became irate and accused her of trying to get pregnant. His response to her questions concerning why he had not used a condom or why he had not inquired into her form of contraception left Maggie astounded. "I don't like how intercourse feels with a condom," he said, "and I assumed that you would take care of yourself if you were worried about getting pregnant."

Both Maggie and Jim were handling the sexual part of their relationship in an adolescent manner within a dominator society. Maggie, eager to be swept away in romance and "taken," had abdicated her responsibility for the sexual act, for her body, and for the possibility of conceiving a new life. If she is swept away, she can maintain the illusion that she is "Mommy's good girl," innocent and chaste.

But to maintain this illusion, she must pay a price. She must not choreograph the seduction, initiate sex, plan for contraception, tell her partner what will give her pleasure, or inquire as to what would give him pleasure. If she did, it would mean that Maggie admitted, accepted, and appreciated being a woman with sexual desires. And if the sex is less than wonderful, well, it's the man's fault. After all, he was the one in charge.

Maggie has not learned to distinguish between sex and love. Like the adolescent girls, sexual arousal is associated with feelings of love. Love is great, lust is not. As a result, all her sexual encounters are laden with hopes and expectations of love and commitment.

Jim, quite able to distinguish feelings of sexual arousal from feelings of love because of his adolescent experiences masturbating and learning to manipulate girls, is nonetheless still functioning sexually as an adolescent. He does not want to use a condom because it will reduce his sexual pleasure. Like the adolescent boy whose primary concern is dissipating his sexual charge, Jim is concerned with his own pleasure at the expense of his partner. He "assumes" that the woman will be responsible for contraception. Creating a life is not his responsibility. So Jim has abdicated his responsibility in relationship—with his partner and a potential new life. Maggie has abdicated responsibility for sexuality—with herself and her partner.

In both cases there is a faulty connection between love and sex. Whereas the man has a problem connecting the two, the woman has a problem distinguishing between the two. If your genitals and your heart are disconnected, sex takes place in the context of an I-It relationship, in which you objectify, or use the other. On the other hand, if they are irrevocably merged so that sex means love, then you cannot fully experience the pleasure of your own or your partner's sexual nature. Just as this creates problems in a dating relationship, similarly, it creates problems in long-term, committed relationships, as the following example shows.

# The Morning After

Ted, a sales executive, and Marie, a dental hygienist, who have been married for nine years, had a wonderful, transcendent night together. They became enraptured by each other's bodies and by having brought each other to states of sublime ecstasy. That night, sex—each caress, each word, each look—was a mutual work of art, a celebration of eros. Finally, exhausted and deeply satisfied, they fell asleep in each other's arms.

In the morning, Ted, whistling, bustled about getting ready to go to work. In between sips of coffee, he punched away at his laptop computer, mentioning to Marie how he just thought of a great idea to land a new account.

Marie listened halfheartedly, trying not to show her disappointment. They had been so close, so exquisitely intimate during the night, and now he was acting as if it had never happened. How could he be so uncaring, after she had…had opened herself up so completely to him? She asked him what time he would be home for dinner, hoping that he would show some affection to her before he left.

"Late. I have a business meeting," Ted responded without looking up from his computer. "But you said we were going to have time together tonight," Marie shot back, unable to hide the complaint in her voice. Ted quickly closed his computer and got up to go. "I was wrong!" he retorted as he walked out of the house. Marie yelled after him: "All you care about is work and sex!"

Marie felt hurt and angry. She didn't want to climb out of the deep pool of togetherness she had experienced the night before. She wanted to hug Ted forever and never let him go. On her way to work she listened to sorrowful love songs on a country radio station, identifying with an unrequited love which the lyrics expressed so poignantly.

Marie spent her day in uncertainty, wondering when Ted would call, wondering if he really loved her or if he were really just interested in sex—and resenting his lack of sensitivity and seeming independence. Throughout their marriage, she often felt invisible with him. This feeling was exacerbated after they were physically intimate. Instead of sending flowers or leaving sweet messages, Ted often forgot to call her when they had been particularly close. Today was no exception. This morning, he seemed to be even more oblivious of her than usual. She was fairly unproductive that day, using her energy to go over again and again in her mind what had happened the previous night and that morning.

Ted also felt hurt and angry. Somewhat unnerved by the intensity of his feelings the night before, he also felt vaguely frightened. He was not used to feeling so vulnerable or dependent. He was also disturbed by the spat with Marie—unsure whether he was insensitive and uncaring, as she had accused. Once in the car, he quickly made a business call, eager to get to work. He knew that once he started working he would forget about the little tiff.

Work was important to Ted. His sense of success and identity—of who he was and where he was going—was definitely tied to how well he performed. Today it was important for him to be successful, partly to reduce the nagging tension he felt in his stomach when he thought about Marie's parting words. He also needed to feel successful in the workplace to prove to himself that he didn't need her, that he really was independent, and to prove that he was competent.

Unlike most days, Ted did not call Marie at all. He poured himself into work and had a fairly productive day. After all, he had been groomed to focus his attention on work. He knew that not calling her was making a statement that she couldn't control him—that he didn't need her. He didn't feel good about it, but he thought it was necessary to make a point.

## Irreconcilable Differences?

What's wrong here? Beyond the obvious problems Ted and Marie have communicating with each other vulnerably about their feelings, both have issues with dependence and independence. Marie's sense of self is tied to Ted—if he pays attention to her, then she feels important, significant, and worthwhile. If he does not behave in a way that shows her he appreciates her, she feels invisible. And so, both Marie and Ted label her "dependent."

Ted's sense of self is tied to his work—if he is successful, he feels competent, significant, and lovable. Take away his achievements and he feels like a nobody. He resents any demands on his time from Marie or anyone else—with the exception of his boss. Ted's workaholic behavior receives praise from his boss. He is proud that he is "man enough" to make work his first priority and that he is not a "hen pecked" husband. Both Ted and Marie call him "independent."

And so, Marie wants Ted to be more like her and Ted wants Marie to be more like him. Both feel misunderstood and unappreciated. Neither understands what the other is unconsciously trying to accomplish in their dependent or independent behavior. They attribute their differences to gender, as if genetically men are insensitive and women are clingy. Though it is clear that boys and girls are different—as evidenced by watching two and three year olds play—perhaps Ted and Marie's differences have more to do with how men and women are raised.

## Fundamental Interest

"Women are brought up to love people and men are brought up to love things," said family therapist Carl Whitaker, addressing an audience of several thousand people in the early 1980s. Though this is not necessarily how it has to be, we do witness it on a daily basis. Men tend to be better at *doing,* whereas women tend to be better at *being.* Men talk about business, politics, and sports; women talk about relationships. Sure, it's a generalization, but it's also true for most people in our culture.

This basic difference in interests generally holds in sexual matters as well. The man is the doer or controller, more focused on results. He occupies the "instrumental" role. As the complement to his role, the woman is the done-to or responder. She assumes the "expressive" role—more interested in being and experiencing her emotions. In all the erotic ads and displays, it is always the woman, her eyes closed, her lips parted in ecstasy, who is feeling sexual passion.

At first glance, this seems contrary to society's prohibition against women fully expressing their sexuality. Look again and you will notice that in all these pictures, she is being taken by a strong, self-assured and competent man. He is in total control. She gets to lose control and enjoy temporary amnesia—forgetting about her sexual shame or guilt. She has already forgotten about being the "good girl." She is the mistress—the whore aspect of women's sexuality.

Try to imagine an erotic movie poster or the cover of a paperback romance novel where the woman is pressing herself against the man, his head thrown back, his eyes closed, his lips parted in almost painful passion. It feels strange, even alien because we are trying to reverse long-held beliefs about men and women.

But this is happening. Regardless of what we may think of her, Madonna (the performer) herself is pushing us to change our views as she aggressively flaunts her sexuality for all to see. The Crones, women who are in menopause, are writing about their experience as sexual beings, helping us to change these old and out-dated beliefs. In TV and movies, until quite recently, the sexy woman was always the girlfriend or mistress, never the wife. For the first time, there are sexy, married couples on TV. Hopefully, this means that we are beginning to admit that women can be sexual and nurturing, that men can be powerful and nurturing. We are beginning to restore aspects of women and men that were severed when dominator religions and culture became entrenched. Perhaps it is the beginning of seeing woman and men as whole beings—creative, intelligent, powerful, nurturing, and sexy.

Men's roles are changing slower than women's. Witness the traditional roles that leading men assume in entertainment media: they are supremely confident and always know how to drive women to these passionate states. The woman has no choice, and surrenders to his advances. Some male heroes do show more vulnerability than previously, yet the changes are relatively small.

For a man in the audience, the utter competence of male stars is unnerving and intimidating. He knows that his sexual advances, strategies, and success pale in comparison. Women have rarely writhed in uncontrollable passion through his expert maneuvers. He feels inferior and insecure about his sexual competence—and he surely doesn't want to be confronted with it. This shows the hidden side of many men. They feel insecure, inadequate and anything but strong, yet have learned to hide doubts at all costs.

So if his partner even indirectly suggests ways to change or improve his sexual repertoire, he will usually react with defensiveness, fearing that his competence is suspect. Since men are traditionally the do-ers and fixers—fixers are people who fix other things, not themselves—they react negatively when a woman tries to help him in the sexual arena.

## The Advisability of Advice

Sarah generally enjoyed making love with her husband Owen. He was considerate and could excite her—even after many years. Intercourse rarely lasted quite long enough for her though, since Owen could not maintain his erection as long as she wanted. She was often straining to push herself to orgasm before he went limp. Sometimes she made it, sometimes she didn't.

One night, she tentatively made a suggestion based on something she had read recently. Explaining that he might be able to maintain his erection longer, she suggested that he deliberately try to relax the muscles around his genitals during their foreplay. Owen said nothing. She was puzzled at his silence so she repeated herself, trying to be helpful; "This will allow *you* to prolong your pleasure." Again there was no response from Owen. Although he didn't say anything to Sarah, he was having an intense internal reaction. He thought to himself, "Nag, nag, nag!" Owen felt that his sexual competence had been attacked, without welcome or warning.

## Nag, Nag, Nag

An old stereotype casts women as nags. What this means is that women will keep reminding men—time after time after time—until they get what they want. Much of this is due to how many men react to a request for change. While many women are inclined to do what is asked of them without making a big deal out of it, many men resist suggestions—particularly by a woman, especially in bed.

In a business situation, if a man is asked to respond to a suggestion, he would not dream of ignoring the request, whether from his boss or an underling. If he were to ignore it, and the request were repeated, it is doubtful he would think of the other person as a nag. So when he fails to respond to his wife's suggestion, and she says it again, it is hardly fair for him to think of her as a nag.

But why doesn't Owen respond? He did not even acknowledge her advice. He remained mute. Owen did what many men instinctively do. He is not adverse to trying something new, but he is waiting until sufficient time has passed so that it doesn't appear that he is following orders—particularly from a woman.

When a woman asks a man to do something differently, he often perceives her request or suggestion as if he were the identified patient, or the one who can never do it right, rather than as a way to make a situation better for both of them. For so many men in our culture, help implies that he is doing something wrong and that he is not good enough.

According to John Gray, author of *Men Are from Mars, Women Are from Venus*: "To offer a man unsolicited advice is to presume that he doesn't know what to do or that he can't do it on his own."[13] However strange it may appear to women, trying to "help" a man usually evokes strong feelings of insecurity in him. Men tend to view suggestions as an indictment against their competence—the core of their masculinity. You don't fix something unless it's broken. Something must be wrong if it could be made better.

He reacts from an internal scenario that goes something like this. "She doesn't think I'm a good enough lover. She's right. I've finally been discovered. Who does she think she is, anyway, to tell me what to do." Unconsciously, at the self-concept level, any fears he harbors about his own competence or feelings of inadequacy have been activated. Though it is a defensive behavior and highly dysfunctional, it feels more familiar and less vulnerable to resist being controlled than to feel or express the unpleasant feelings or fears of inadequacy.

Instead of looking upon the suggestion as something that could possibly improve a situation, and create positive results for his partner and further his own growth, he interprets it either as a personal attack or an insult to how he currently is or an imperious order. Either way, he resists.

# Indirect Directions

Women tend to believe that things can be improved, especially if it concerns someone whom they care about. When Sarah suggested to Owen that he try to relax his genital muscles, she believed that he would certainly try it if he understood her request. Since she knows that he loves her, she believed that he would want to please her, not to mention experience greater pleasure himself. Because she enjoys learning about herself and working on self-improvement, and she believes he does also, she thought that he would want this new information. To point out a potential improvement is for Sarah and most women, an act of love and caring.

Are women so naturally benevolent that they want to "help" their men out of pure altruism? Absolutely not! Trying to help their partners is often more acceptable, less risky, and therefore easier, than making a direct request for themselves. Sarah's attempts to help Owen are the result of her own coping or defense mechanisms. Sarah didn't primarily focus her suggestion on what she really wanted—greater sexual satisfaction—but told Owen that "his" pleasure would be prolonged. Designed to protect her from feeling her own fears of insignificance, incompetence, or unlovability, this mechanism provides her with another payoff. As the "helper," Sarah feels important, competent, or lovable because she is contributing and therefore needed.

Her helpful behavior also reflects how well she has learned her lessons of indirectness and compliance in the dominator paradigm. Traditionally women are taught that, "Trying to help your man directly will usually evoke strong feelings of incompetence, insecurity, and judgment in him. If you want to be successful, you should be indirect, tactful, and complimentary." No matter that she is treating the man as if he has a fragile ego, or that she is colluding with his dysfunctional male scripting. No matter that she is being co-dependent, or that she isn't taking risks and growing herself. No matter that she isn't confronting her own fears, or that together they are missing an opportunity to become more intimate.

# Mixed Messages

A man often hears indirect, confusing, and contradictory communication from a woman. She might say, "I know you aren't happy about this. I'm doing this to help *you*." However, he intuits that she means something other than she is saying. He can't quite put his finger on it though. He feels criticized by her altruism. Why is he feeling so diminished when she is being so "generous" and "loving"? He looks and feels like a fool when he ignores her reasonable suggestions or reacts strongly to them. He feels a bit crazy because he cannot validate his position or justify his intuition.

Surely, a part of his defensive reaction stems from his own fears of inadequacy, but he's also sensing her mixed message. Her request, "Dear, will you please touch me more gently?" might very well carry a covert criticism: "You are such a clod! Are you ever going to learn how to touch me?" If he reacts defensively as if he's been put down, she can always point to her indisputably innocuous words. She would be right—in a court of law. There's no way to *prove* the discrepancy between her verbal content and the nonverbal message. He has no rational defense. He often then reacts with anger—the great equalizer. Of course, this scenario could be reversed, where the man gives the woman a mixed message. Whichever direction, confusion and obfuscation in communication are major factors here.

Many people attribute these communication problems between men and women to gender differences. If gender were the sole factor, we would not see these same issues emerge when men interact with men, or women with women. Yet we do. Let's look beyond gender differences for understanding and solutions.

# Nature vs. Nurture

Those on the nature side of the controversy say that women are more desirous of emotional closeness and have an innate propensity toward care-taking because of their biological and psychological make-up related to their ability to bear the children. They conjecture that men tend to be more focused on external matters because of their biological and psychological make-up related to spreading their seed and protecting the mothers and children. Those on the nurture side of the controversy contend that these behaviors are learned and passed on from generation to generation to maintain culture.

Regardless of which is true, or if both are true, what is most important is that we bridge the differences that seem to exist between men and women. We believe that many people use gender issues and gender differences to avoid taking responsibility for their feelings and behavior, to avoid risking vulnerability and revealing their fears and their perceived or real inadequacies. If we were to take off the masks, drop the pretenses, stop playing games to protect and defend ourselves, we would see how similar we really are. Our differences would become less problematic.

Rather than make allowances for or cater to our "gender differences" as a way of building a bridge, we have found the strongest structure for bringing us together is communication based on awareness, vulnerability, and openness. Perhaps this doesn't sound like such a tall order but our experience shows us that it is. Men and women have grown up learning to hide who they really are. Our reasons vary. Some of the more common rationalizations we have heard are as follows: "I don't want to hurt other people." "I'm too much. I'm too intense. People can't handle me." "People won't like me." Whatever the stated reason, conscious or unconscious shame plays a key role.

Because shame is about who we are, it is more painful to feel or acknowledge than guilt, which focuses specifically on our behavior. And because shame about our sexuality (which is related to gender shame) touches us in our deepest core, we must uncover the roots of this shame. We can treat the symptoms of shame without understanding its origins but it will crop up again and again, necessitating an ongoing shame-control sentry—dedicated to spotting and eradicating all suspicious symptoms. This takes a great deal of energy and vigilance and doesn't create an environment which fosters intimacy or eros. However, if we want to live without shame, we must understand what creates and perpetuates our shame.

Blaming or shaming men for androcratic tendencies is not the answer. Many men who are trying to rid themselves of the dominator model, feel ashamed of their masculinity—as if being male innately means that they are abusive. They have been shamed by certain radical feminists who blame men for every atrocity on the planet. These particular women do not take responsibility for their own tendency to be abusive—their own unique manifestation of domination. There's even been a backlash among some men who feel consumed with shame, that they should eradicate everything male within them—hence a book by one of the more zealous members of this movement entitled, *Refusing to Be a Man*. [14]

# Last Thoughts

Our intention has not been to point the finger at men or women in this chapter. Rather, it has been to take a hard look at how adrocratic principles influence men, women, and sexuality. In so doing, our intention is to awaken ourselves to more empowering, pleasurable possibilities. Gender problems are not innate. Solutions to gender madness lie in men and women understanding the beliefs, fears, and hopes that motivate themselves and each other. Once we understand ourselves and accept how we came to be who we are, then we can look toward changing that which no longer serves us. In the next section, we focus on reconciliation, healing, and expanding the possibilities between lovers. Although there are specific suggestions for men and women throughout, any two people can receive value from doing the exercises, regardless of gender.

Perhaps the best way to reconcile conflicts and increase love is by working through sexual shame. To this end, we are providing you with a 5-step path to healing sexual shame: 1) gaining awareness about the reality of your situation; 2) accepting it and committing to take positive action; 3) developing a personalized healing program and following through with it; 4) developing new patterns of relating with your partner and others with whom you are intimately involved; 5) and confronting the parts of yourself that are opposed to change. We don't promise you that all will change overnight; however, we guarantee that sexual shame will influence you less and less as you follow through with this work. Also, the skills you develop are transferable to all other aspects of your life.

The first step takes us into developing awareness because there can be no meaningful change if people are not aware. So let's move onto the next section to discover some powerful and creative ways of becoming more emotionally vulnerable, creating more intimacy, and healing sexual shame— starting with developing greater awareness and then accepting yourself.

# 7

# The Power of Awareness

*Harmony is a beautiful state but not nearly as powerful as awareness.*

Arnold Mindell

## Sculpting Away the Shame

The cool, moist clay became a penis, then changed to feces; then a penis again, and back to feces. Back and forth, until I felt satiated. Then my shame got the best of me. I (Judith) remolded the clay into its original shape as it had been given to me by A. A. Leath, my Creative Behavior teacher.

When he had put the lump of clay in my hand, he had told me to work with it for as long as it felt good to my hand, and to stop when I had enough. My hand was in a brown paper bag so I could not, nor could anyone else, see the clay. Still my shame was tremendous. How perverted I must be to form such things with the clay!

As other students displayed their shapes, unusual bowls, even animals were revealed. No penises. No feces. I was disgusted with myself and embarrassed. At least I'd been smart enough to squash the evidence of my oversexed psyche.

But a voice inside me whispered, "No. There's nothing wrong with you. It was all right." I reached for a black and a red crayon and a large roll of newsprint. I began to write furiously, scribbling and pounding out my inner dialogue. The shame was thick.

My sexual feelings weren't so aberrant. A small voice inside me that supported me, my "angel voice," fought off the critical voice of shame. My angel asserted that other people probably experienced similar feelings. They were either too afraid to allow themselves to play with the clay, or they falsified the evidence, as I had.

Anyway, for a while I had fun doing exactly what felt pleasurable for my hands. And why not? It was only natural. Besides, it didn't hurt anybody. There was nothing wrong with having sexual feelings, my angel voice kept telling me.

The part of me that longed for freedom and self-acceptance was sick of the war that had been waging inside me since I was a child—the war between my curiosity and my shame.

Though I had played doctor, participated in a game my sister, friend, and I called "Boss," and had pulled my pants down in a closet with my boyfriend who lived across the street—also five years old—I had always felt somewhat ashamed and fearful of getting caught.

Even though my curiosity was strong enough to propel me into exploring my world, shame always took its toll, curbing my free spirit.

But on that fateful day in 1970, my healthy sexuality was the victress—despite the shame, I finally sensed a way out. Though still a small voice, that day I knew from deep within me that my sexuality was okay.

I was not oversexed. Nor was there anything to be ashamed of.

My experience with the clay and the subsequent dialogue I had with these two conflicting parts of myself became a reference for me over the next decade. Little by little, my shame dissipated until I felt free to feel whatever emerged. Free to behave however I felt inspired. Free to feel entitled to receive pleasure. Free to ask for exactly what I wanted. Free to express the energy of the Goddess Kali[1] and destroy anything that was not life-giving. Free to give as passionately, tenderly, and generously as I desired. Free to be a sweet kitten one moment, a passionate lioness the next.

# Original Innocence

Who cannot relate to being in a painful conflict over their sexuality—like the war that raged within Judith? A deep part of her knew that healthy, pleasurable sexuality was her birthright, and yet she—like most of us—learned that her sexuality was flawed and shameful. Sadly, most of us continue to live in an ambivalent relationship with our sexuality—banished years ago from paradise.

We were all born into the world in a state of "original innocence"—uncorrupted and unscarred by shame and abuse. The word *innocence* itself means "without wound"; without the wound, before the fall there was no shame; infants are born into a shameless state, a state of grace—simply being. Everything is so new, so pristine. But the golden child becomes the wounded child through the wages of shame—usually the accumulation of other people's shame. We have explored the impact of taking on other people's sexual shame in *The Wounds of Sexual Shame*. In this one, we will work on gaining awareness about our sexual shame—a major step to healing our shame and having the glorious, erotic relationships we desire and deserve.

# Re-mything: From Shame to Pleasure

It takes a revolution of consciousness to consider how life could be different than how it has been. Experience, symbols, and myths chisel grooves in our memory, and through time, these grooves become our blueprint of "reality." However painful and difficult, they become our comfort zone—familiar and known.

The grass may be greener elsewhere, but home is home.

Perhaps we can learn from the re-mything of the old gylanic mind of the Paleolithic, Neolithic, and Cretan people to the new androcratic mind of today. It took centuries of a new priesthood, biblical editing, Greek theater (which everyone attended and participated in), Greek literature, and the educational and legal systems to move the psyche from the gylanic images of a nurturing goddess, a unified natural order, equality between sexes, and among ethnic groups and races to our current images, symbols, and myths. In other words, it took centuries to carve new grooves that even considered the rationale that "might makes right," that God is a punitive, angry force to be feared, and that the body and everything associated with natural impulses including sexuality is sinful.

Healing means creating new grooves in our memory again. This time, grooves of empowered, pleasurable, loving, and expansive eroticism.

A more alive place to call home. A place where men can be proud of their masculinity and women proud of their femininity. The only way we can create new grooves is by trying on new experiences which can bring us to realize, "I like being this way. I like feeling freer with my lover. I like feeling proud of my erotic nature. And I deserve this!"

For some of you, simply reading this may bring on feelings of embarrassment, shame, anger, or fear. Others may feel hopeful. Still others may feel disheartened or hopeless, resigned to your lot. Whatever your experience, as you work with the material in the next few chapters—if you are open to new possibilities—you are certain to uncover a world of riches.

## The Challenge of Healing

If you are willing to bring all of yourself forth— what you appreciate and dislike about yourself—you can heal yourself. However, what you do not bring forth will damage you or those around you. The first step is awareness.

Our intention in this chapter is to help you become aware and then bring forth what is within you. For your part, you will need a strong focus to confront old patterns and beliefs. You will probably be pushed beyond the edge of your comfort zone—challenged to explore your sexuality in ways that may radically conflict with what you were taught by your parents, clergy, and teachers.

## Understanding as Potential Power

In the last section, we showed some religious, cultural, and familial influences that produce shame about the life of the body and sexuality. The forces of sexual shame are so potent and the faces so varied, that to heal it, we must first uncover it and then transform it. Healing requires that we deal in realities by understanding and acknowledging where we are right now—beginning at ground zero—without putting up the facade that "everything is fine the way it is." We must dig deep into the roots of sexual shame or we will be like gardeners who leave weeds free to grow.

If you can understand the source of your pain, you are in a far better position to heal it. Where awareness flows, positive action can follow.

Without awareness, we simply set forth doing what we have always done by continuing old habits and not considering new possibilities—like mice who keep going back for the cheese long after it has been eaten. We look for sunrises in the West and sunsets in the East. Just as the last section dealt with gaining awareness of the impact shame plays in our lives, this chapter deals with gaining awareness about our own particular history and patterns of handling sexual shame.

Paradoxically, in order to heal, we must become aware of what has been unconscious—what we have put in our shadow. There are tools that aid us in reclaiming what we have previously placed outside of our awareness. Feeling that you have the right tools to work with shame can give you enough confidence to practice and heal your sexual shame. But, before you experiment with tools to develop your awareness, let us clarify what we mean by awareness.

## What Is Awareness?

Total awareness is the state of having a 360-degree focus of attention—outward and inward— a divine state. Since few of us have achieved this state, we use awareness to mean that our senses are open and that we are tuned into our body, mind, and spirit. We are present to our surroundings without being preoccupied. Our full senses are operating—hearing, smelling, tasting, feeling, and sensing. Our intuition is working as are our cognitive facilities. In short, we are cognizant of what is happening inside ourselves and what is happening outside ourselves.

Sometimes awareness is painful—like being aware of sexual abuse, shame, or some other disturbing experience. It is a well known psychological fact that people use defense mechanisms to push painful emotional material into the unconscious. This, as we discussed earlier, is partially how we develop our shadow. Originally, this material does not become unconscious through conscious choice. We do not say, "Gee, this is too painful to remember. I will repress it." However, it is an unconscious choice. If the feelings associated with certain thoughts, feelings, or behaviors seem too painful to experience—for whatever reason—we unconsciously push them out of our awareness.

# Choosing Awareness

While losing awareness may not be a conscious choice, gaining awareness can be. We must break through our denial—the foe of awareness. By moving through our denial and confronting our demons, a magical process will occur. Our demons transform into angels. The poet Rilke offers words of wisdom that inspire the self-searching required:

*"Perhaps all the dragons in our lives are princesses who are only waiting to see us act, just once, with beauty and courage. Perhaps everything that frightens us is, in its deepest essence, something helpless that wants our love."*[2]

Rilke was aware of the fear most of us harbor about looking deeply into ourselves. Yet, he was also aware of the value in shining light upon the shadow, befriending the demons. He knew that if we do not uncover that which frightens us, we become a slave to it. Living in the shadows will not suffice.

As we have witnessed in our exploration of the shadow *(The Wounds of Sexual Shame)*, simply because something is out of our awareness, its influence on our lives is not mitigated. In fact, then it is most likely running the show. So often we hear people exclaim, "I just don't understand why I do the things I do!" "Why can't I control my eating?" "Why am I so inhibited?" "Why do I feel embarrassed when an attractive person 'catches' me looking at them?" "Why is sex always my last priority?" "Why does something as pleasurable as sex arouse such strong feelings of shame in me?" "Why do I constantly think about sex—whether I'm at work, going out, or at home?"

Conscious or unconscious shame often lies behind the quagmire. The following inventory can help you become aware of sexual shame which may be influencing your life unconsciously.

## Exercise #1

### *The Sexual Shame Inventory*

Use the following scale to evaluate your responses

*0-Never   1-Rarely   2-Occasionally   3-Often   4-Always*

Place a number that best expresses your feelings about the item either at the left side of the item or in your journal.

_____   Not asking specifically for what I want sexually from my partner.

_____   Feeling shy or embarrassed about being seen naked by my partner and/or other people.

_____   Making my partner wrong or using blame to say what I want or don't want sexually.

_____ Withholding my sexual dreams or fantasies from my partner.

_____ Not feeling desire or lust for anyone.

_____ Feeling desire or lust but attempting to push the thoughts out of my mind.

_____ Feeling disgust for my bodily functions or particular body parts.

_____ Believing that my genitals or breasts are the wrong size.

_____ Believing that masturbation is wrong, immoral, dirty, or perverted.

_____ Always making love in silence, in the dark, or under the sheets.

_____ Making love or climaxing without making any sounds.

_____ Having engaged in sexual behavior earlier in my life which I keep hidden and secret.

_____ Avoiding someone's gaze if they look at me with lust or sexual admiration.

_____ Avoiding the gaze of others when they "catch" me looking at them with lust or sexual admiration.

_____ Feeling denigrated, offended, or violated if someone finds me sexually appealing or attractive.

_____ Fantasizing constantly about sex.

_____ Never fantasizing or thinking about sex.

_____ Engaging in silly or childish talk and behavior as sexual activity begins.

_____ Choosing clothing which will hide my body.

_____ Choosing clothing which is provocative, regardless of the context.

_____ Finding myself in situations in which sexual activity is beginning and I am questioning whether or not I should be doing what I am doing.

_____ Feeling rejected or humiliated when my partner turns down my sexual advances.

_____ Receiving feedback that I am being seductive when I am not consciously intending to be.

_____ Doing push-pull behavior—attracting someone to me, then pushing him or her away as soon as he or she shows interest.

_____ Becoming emotionally distant after making love.

_____ Needing reassurance, becoming clingy, or feeling depressed after making love.

_____ Using sex to feel loved.

_____ Using love to get sex.

_____ Feeling afraid of my erotic desire and focusing only on my spiritual connection to my beloved.

_____ Censoring my expression of lust toward my lover.

_____ Censoring myself from speaking about sexual organs or intimate body parts by name.

_____ Believing that oral or anal sex is wrong, immoral, dirty, or perverted.

_____ Engaging in crude and crass sexual joke telling.

_____ Feeling offended by a joke that has any sexual innuendoes.

_____ Engaging in sex to appease a lover or avoid conflict.

*Now add up your total score from the 35 items and then divide by 35 to give you an average per response.*

It is probably clear that 0 indicates a low sexual shame score, whereas 4 indicates a high sexual shame score. Your average will give you a sense of where you fall along this continuum—provided you have responded with awareness and honesty. Beware of shaming yourself because you have sexual shame—this just heightens the shame cycle. Just being aware that shame may be influencing your behavior can bring positive changes.

Most people belittle themselves and their partner for behaviors which emanate from unconscious shame. Just considering that many unbeneficial behaviors stem from shame can help you find compassion for yourself and your partner.

# Family Legacies

By becoming more aware of how your mom and dad experienced sexual shame, you will have a direct inroad into how it was passed on to you. Here are some questions to consider as you explore how and to what extent your parents were/are operating from sexual shame.

Though we use the word *parents* in the following questions, answer for your mother and your father separately as individuals if appropriate. Oftentimes we receive different and sometimes conflicting messages from the two of them. If you grew up with a grandparent or nanny present, you might answer the questions for them as well. If you were adopted, you might answer for your biological and adoptive parents.

## Exercise #2

### *Question Your Parents*

*In your journal or on a newsprint pad, write your responses to the following questions. Also, write a list of the attitudes your parents had about sexuality, bodily functions, and the body, or more specifically, their bodies and your body that were not addressed in the question. Next to each item, write a plus if you regard it as a positive value and a minus sign if you regard it negatively. If you are unsure, put a question mark.*

Did your parents ever speak about sex?

How did your parents speak about sex in general, or your sexuality, specifically? With derision, disgust, resignation, fear, joy, pleasure?

What nonverbal messages did you receive from them about sexuality?

How did they encourage you to develop a healthy, natural, and joyful sense of sexuality?

How were you encouraged to ask questions about your sexuality?

How were you introduced to the biological changes which occur during and after puberty?

What do you remember about feeling as if you needed to hide your sexuality, e.g., masturbation, being sexual with others, or even your desire to be sexual?

What overt or covert messages did you receive about your genitals or other body parts related to sexuality?

What were your parents' views about oral sex? about pre-marital sex? about homosexuality? about adultery? about pornography? about marital sex?

What was considered kinky by your parents?

What are your mother and father's family histories regarding incest, rape, pedophilia, or other forms of sexual abuse?

It is probably obvious which responses indicate sexual shame. Whenever there is a sense that there is something bad, wrong, unnatural, or disgusting about sexuality, it highlights the presence of sexual shame. By naming the beast accordingly, you can begin to extricate yourself from the shaming conditions in which you were raised.

Going back into your personal history can help you identify decisions you made as children which are unconsciously guiding your behavior now. The following exercise is designed to take you back into your personal history to uncover the events—both positive and negative—that shaped you.

## Exercise #3

### *A Timeline of Sexual Shame*

Supplies needed: the largest drawing paper you have available or a roll of white shelf paper as well as colored pens or markers.

Get in a comfortable position and close your eyes. Focus your attention on your self as a child and begin to recall the events which shaped your beliefs and feelings about your body and sexuality.

Remember when you were young, year by year, up through your adolescence, into your college years and to the present. Think of events from your family life, school, church, friends, or work.

Think about the sexual behaviors you engaged in for which you felt ashamed. (For example, did you play doctor when you were a little boy or girl, or did you ever pull your pants down in front of someone?)

Perhaps an adult criticized you for saying "naughty" words when you were a child.

Were you ever caught masturbating?

If you are a male, were you ashamed when you thought someone knew you had an erection because of a bulge in your pants?

If you are a female, were you embarrassed when your breasts began to develop, when someone noticed you were wearing a bra, or when you began to menstruate?

As an adolescent, what was your experience masturbating? Was there permission for masturbating in your house? Were you caught and if, so, what happened? How did you hide your masturbation if you did?

As an adolescent or an adult, did you ever make sexual advances that later made you feel ashamed?

As an adult, what experiences have you had that contributed to the feeling of, "I will never do *that* again!"

When you feel finished, draw a time line on which you record or symbolize each event that feels meaningful for you. Some people draw representational pictures, others use color or design.

After you record all the pictorial or symbolic events, write words, phrases, or a brief description of each event in your timeline or on separate paper.

If you enjoy using your body to express your feelings, use some of the important events as a focus for improvisational movement.

Another way to use your timeline is to find family photos that most closely match the time periods of the events you have noted. Allow yourself to look at the photos and associate freely to them. Notice what images, feelings, and reactions you have. Write your impressions in phrases or words next to the photos.

Once you are aware of the negative and positive beliefs, attitudes, and feelings you have toward your body and sexuality, you can begin the process of choosing which serve you, that you want to keep and which do not serve you, that you want to release. When you strip away the negative conditioning that has held your shame in place, you are free to discover your own positive, natural feelings about sexuality.

Then you can begin the task—sometimes joyful, sometimes difficult—of replacing your old patterns and attitudes with the new.

If you have a primary partner, take uninterrupted time together to share what you have uncovered. It is rich and rewarding to hear about your beloved's past—particularly when the remnants of that past affect you. However, when that past involves many painful experiences, it can sometimes feel overwhelming to your partner, especially if he or she tends towards solving problems alone or feels responsible for your feelings. A useful guideline to remember for the listener: Breathe, listen, stay present, and feel your own feelings. That, in itself, is supportive. If your partner wants feedback, talk about how you felt as you listened.

🌾     🌾     🌾     🌾     🌾

# The Power of Beliefs

The experiences we explored in the last few exercises create conditions in which we develop sexual shame. If we keep learning that something is so, we naturally develop the 'belief' that it is so. A belief is a feeling of certainty about the meaning of a particular experience, situation, or feeling. The certainty we carry about what is possible helps us set our sights on potential goals.

For thousands of years people believed that the earth was flat. They were certain, but they were wrong.

Many limiting beliefs about sexuality have been conditioned into the deepest fiber of our being—no more accurate than the earth being flat. However erroneous, beliefs seem to be written in stone—simply as the way it is. The more unconscious and unquestioned the belief, the more power it wields. Unconscious positive, empowering beliefs are no problem. However, with unconscious negative beliefs, it is quite another story.

This next exercise can be a vehicle for you to become more aware of your unconscious and conscious beliefs about sexual shame.

## Exercise #4

### *Erotic Stories*

To prepare for this exercise, get a pen or pencil, your journal or writing paper. You will be asked to imagine a variety of scenes and to write a sentence or two describing what you imagine, your reactions to the scene, and your feelings about each of them.

Take some deep breathes, and focus on relaxing on the exhale.

When you feel relaxed, read Scene A, close your eyes and get a picture in your mind, hear the sounds of the imaginal environment, smell the smells, and notice your somatic reactions. After a few minutes, write down your description, reactions, and feelings.

When you are done, read Scene B and continue with the same process until you are finished.

When you are done, write one word or phrase next to each scene which sums up your reactions. These might be something like disgusting, sensual, looks like fun, etc. Do not censor yourself. Write down any words that emerge.

Scene A: A heterosexual bar scene with men and women.

Scene B: Teenagers engaging in sexual behavior.

Scene C: Lesbian women being sexual, engaging in oral sex.

Scene D: Homosexual men engaging in anal sex.

Scene E: A heterosexual couple engaging in oral sex together, e.g., 69.

Scene F: Paraplegics or quadriplegics engaging in sexual activity together or with a non-injured partner.

Scene G: An elderly couple enjoying a sexual encounter.

*As you think about what you have just completed, notice how much of the time you felt embarrassed, ashamed, angry, excited, naughty, aroused, bored, curious, or disgusted. Notice if you had other feelings than those mentioned above.*

As you review your reactions to these scenes, your underlying feelings and beliefs about sexuality are probably becoming more conscious to you. For some of you this might be exciting, for others anxiety provoking and upsetting. Some of you might even feel angry at us and want to shut the book.

Uncovering what has been unconscious, shedding light on feelings which have been hidden in the shadows can be uncomfortable and disquieting. So, please remember, this is not the end of the journey. The rewards come but not until the prohibiting beliefs are cleaned out and new, more permissive and expansive beliefs replace them.

One way to aid yourself in this process is to become aware of the specific verbal and nonverbal injunctions and prescriptions you received as a child. Often unaware, we follow these internalized messages even though we may not intellectually agree with them. The following exercise is designed to help you uncover the family of origin messages that you still follow consciously and/or unconsciously.

## Exercise #5

### *Injunctions, Prescriptions, and Declarations*

Get in a comfortable position and close your eyes.

Take a few deep breaths while focusing on the exhalation. Allow yourself to become more and more relaxed.

Remember back to your childhood, scanning for incidents, remarks, or behaviors having to do with your body image, bodily functions, and sexual behavior.

Recall any injunctive messages you received such as, "Don't touch yourself down there." "Don't dress provocatively."

Also remember prescriptive messages you received such as, "If you partially cover yourself, you are more sexually appealing." "Remember, it's the girl who sets the limits."

Now do the same for declarations such as, "Your private parts are dirty." "Your breasts are too small." "Your penis is too small."

If you have raised children or spent time with them, recall incidents, remarks, or behaviors in which you have conveyed similar injunctions, prescriptions, or declarations about body image, bodily functions, and sexual feelings and behavior to your children.

Think of similar experiences in which you heard or saw your own parents relate to their grandchildren or other children.

Get your journal or writing paper and make three columns headed Injunctions, Prescriptions, and Declarations. Under each column heading, list the injunctions, prescriptions, and declarations you received about your body and sex. Include verbal and nonverbal communications.

When you finish, review your lists, looking for conflicting messages and consistent messages among the three lists. For instance, you might become aware that you heard the injunction, "Don't act sexy." However, nonverbally, you received prescriptive messages to, "Act Sexy." You also heard declarations such as, "Sexy girls are sluts."

| injunctions | prescriptions | declarations |
|---|---|---|
| Don't act sexy. | Act sexy. | Sexy girls are sluts. |
| Don't masturbate. | Take care of yourself. | You'll get warts if you masturbate. |

By becoming aware of the conflicting messages you received or the consistency of the messages, you can gain a deeper awareness and understanding of the attitudes and beliefs you developed about your body and sexuality.

You may find that you begin to notice these messages during your everyday life when, previously, they would have been unconscious. We know that it can be quite unpleasant and uncomfortable to become aware of feelings, thoughts, and behaviors that seem to be out of your control. Indeed, they feel as if they are controlling you! However, the benefit is that you can choose to change them only once you are aware of them. So remember, awareness is the first step—a giant step.

# Your Body, Your Self

As you recalled important and possibly traumatic events from your life, you may have been aware of somatic responses such as shortness of breath, tightness in your chest, or some other physiological sensation.

Because all of our experience is remembered in the sensory memory of our cells, it makes sense that our somatic reactions would tell the body's version of our life story. If we allow ourselves to listen to this story, we can profit from our body's wisdom.

When people tune in to their somatic wisdom, they have a variety of experiences. Some people become acutely aware of physical sensations, other people begin to see visual images, while others feel emotions or hear voices. While having their body touched during a massage or body work with a therapist, many people experience flashes of memory. Still others, while engaging in authentic movement,[3] find themselves symbolically re-enacting traumatic memories.

Because our bodies hold a wealth of information about our unconscious feelings, attitudes, and beliefs about sexuality and bodily functions, the following exercise is designed to help you uncover some of that wealth.

## Exercise #6

### *My Body, My Sexual Self*

*Supplies needed: Large drawing paper or a piece of butcher block paper that is a few inches longer than you are tall; colored pencils, markers, crayons, paints, or pastels.*

Make an outline drawing of your body on your drawing paper. Or, if you have butcher block paper, have someone trace you as you lie on your back on the paper.

Use symbols, colors, and designs to represent the feelings, memories, and attitudes you have about all the various parts of your body.

When you have finished, look at each area of your drawing and add words, phrases, or brief descriptions that express your reactions. You can write on your drawing or in your journal.

Standing, sitting, or lying down, focus your attention on each part of your body that you have colored. As you do, allow yourself to move in reaction to the feelings that emerge. Each time, before going on to the next, find a movement that symbolically expresses your feelings.

You probably have a whole range of reactions to your different body parts—from appreciation to disgust, from feeling apathetic to being flooded with feelings, images, associations, and memories. You may like your eyes and legs, yet feel repulsed by your stomach or your hair. These feelings are based on experiences which you have had that were painful or traumatic.

Your traumas—be they minor or major—may have occurred within the family, at school, at camp, or at work. The perpetrators could have been family members, friends, acquaintances, or even strangers. The incident could have occurred once or repeatedly. It could have been delivered with the intention to inflict pain or it could have been delivered with a positive intention by someone who was unaware of his or her negative impact.

I, Judith, remember an incident that occurred when I had just started puberty. We were at a family gathering to celebrate a holiday. I had just greeted my favorite great aunt and was standing next to her. She was sitting on a sofa. She reached up, ran her hand over my chest and with delight in her voice exclaimed, "Oh, you're developing!" I wanted to sink through the floor.

Whether the incident was meant to be positive or negative, if you suffered pain or shame, or if you experienced pleasure and pride, you used these experiences to make important decisions about your body and your sexuality. Many of these incidents are indelibly etched in our memory. However, sometimes, the pain is so great that we forget or repress the actual incident.

Nonetheless, our feelings and subsequent decisions and attitudes are based on those long forgotten events. Bringing the feelings and possibly the events into awareness is a first step to healing these wounds of sexual shame—wounds that touch the deepest core of the soul.

Oftentimes, because of these wounds, we are discontent with ourselves, longing to be other than who we are. Some people are haunted by waking or sleeping images about who they are, who they would like to be, or their ideal partner. They spend much of their energy wishing they were different, or languishing for their ideal other. The following exercise is designed to help you become more aware of the conscious and unconscious images you hold about yourself that keep you from enjoying who you presently are.

## Exercise #7

### *Erotic Collage*

> *Supplies needed: A variety of popular magazines with pictures of women and men; scissors; glue; paper; or pasteboard for backing; colored marking pens.*

Look through your stack of magazines, cutting out images—pictorial and words or phrases—that speak to you about who and how you are—your feelings about your body and about yourself as an erotic, sexual being,

It is important to follow your spontaneous reactions without censoring yourself even if the images do not make sense to your logical mind or are disturbing to you.

Some people find that they want to make a separate collage or an overlay to distinguish between the exterior, social persona and the more private interior.

Do the same for images about how you would like to be, putting these pictures and words in a separate stack.

Make a third stack for images of your ideal partner that represent your masculine or feminine ideal in a partner.

Now take your picture and word images and place them on your backing paper in any way that fits your personal aesthetic. There is no right way except for what looks or feels good to you.

Feel free to add words, phrases, your own drawings, even symbolic objects onto your collage.

You can either glue your images as you build each collage or wait until you feel finished with your layout, and then glue everything in place.

When you are finished, write descriptions of your collages in your journal. Include what you learned about yourself, any surprises you had, what you like and do not like about your images, and anything else that is important to you.

Some people feel disturbed by some of the images that emerge. These images are part of the shadow—what we have dis-identified with because they conflict with our self-image. We don't want to think of ourselves as *that kind of person!* So, once again, let us remind you that though becoming more aware of our shadow aspects can be painful and disruptive, healing the shame that has kept them in the shadows is immensely liberating.

Some of the more disturbing images that may arise when doing these collages have to do with desires to seduce, manipulate, or violate someone as well as feelings of being inadequate, victimized, or powerless. Though uncomfortable and scary, bringing these images to the light, ironically, is the beginning of healing them. Remember, the longer that aspects of ourselves stay hidden in the shadow, the more aberrant and potent they become.

## Seduction and Victimization

The word *seduce* comes from the Latin *seducere,* meaning "to lead away." When we lead someone away from their self so that we may gain something solely for ourselves, we are not honoring the other persons' humanity—in essence, we are reducing them to an object. This is the I-It relationship Buber names in *I and Thou* which we refer to in Chapter 2, *Eros Unveiled.*

It is also the product of an androcratic mindset that thinks in terms of ranking and personal gain rather than linking and mutual pleasure—that teaches us to use people rather than view relationships as sacred. And being a product of this culture, we all have this androcratic mind to some extent. If we want our culture to become gylanic—where women and men are linked for the common good and resolve conflicts rather than using violence and fear to force submission—we must first become aware of the covert and overt, subtle and gross ways in which we oppress and victimize others.

You may be saying inwardly, "I am not a perpetrator. I do not victimize others. I feel like a victim—a victim of my past, a victim of this culture." However, if you identify as a victim and do not recognize the part of you that is or has been a perpetrator, as a shadow aspect, the victimizer will slip out in unforeseen and surreptitious ways.

The fact is that all perpetrators have been victimized at some point in their lives. You have to learn it somewhere. If you feel like a victim without recognizing your ability to oppress, there is a greater likelihood that you are already victimizing others unknowingly. It's challenging to recognize the vicious cycle of victim and victimizer, especially because no one wants to see themselves as a victimizer or perpetrator of others. Although it can be painful to perceive oneself as a victim, it is often more painful to perceive oneself as a perpetrator.

Let us first look at the range of behaviors that might fit the label perpetrator. Granted, there are heinous crimes such as rape, incest, child molestation, and other forms of sexual abuse that occupy one end of the continuum. These are clearly cases of one person dominating another, objectifying the other as an It.

However, on the other end of the continuum are many behaviors we take for granted in our culture which could be called seduction—a more mild form of perpetration. Women are taught to dress provocatively to catch a man. Men are taught to say the right line to win a woman's heart and to get her in bed. Women are taught that sex will get them the affection and attention they crave. Men are taught that being loving and attentive will buy them the sex they desire.

All of these and more are ways in which we manipulate each other to try to fill our own needs—not really keeping the other person's best interest in mind or heart.

However, unpleasant and painful it may be to become aware of how you have subtly or blatantly used others in the arena of sex, love, and eros, it is essential to the healing process. If you do not become aware, there is still a part of you that unconsciously feels ashamed. The following processes can help you become more aware of when you have been either the victim or perpetrator of sexual wounding. There is generally shame experienced in either position. In order to uncover those ways in which you have engaged in I-It relationships—as the victim or the perpetrator, the seduced or the seducer/seductress—we ask that you be painfully honest with yourself. (Painfully, because most of us do not like to admit to being a victim or to harming others.)

## Exercise #8

### *You, the Victim*

Make yourself comfortable and close your eyes. Take several deep breaths, let them out, and feel your body let go of tension.

As you look back into your past, please, have compassion for yourself. You did the best you knew how to do to take care of yourself.

Begin to think about your romantic and sexual relationships from adolescence through adulthood.

Remember times when you felt used, betrayed, cheated, seduced, or abused—be they little or big hurts.

Pay attention to how your body feels as you recall these events, noticing any changes in your breathing, tension in parts of your body, feelings of lightness or heaviness, or any other sensations.

As you recall these events, notice if you remember any clues or signals about anything that you ignored at the time.

Think about the story you told yourself internally that made it desirable or necessary to ignore those signals.

When you realized you had been seduced, betrayed, or violated in some way, what were the stories you told yourself about why such a thing had happened to you?

Take a few deep breathes, let them out, and let go of these images, memories, and feelings. Which memories were the most painful? Which events were easy to recall and which were more illusive? What themes did you notice emerging in the stories you told yourself about why you should ignore suspicious signals and why you were being victimized?

When you feel finished, write about these images, memories, and feelings in your journal. Include any insights or surprises you had.

## Exercise # 9

### *You, the Perpetrator*

Now remember times in your life, from your early memories until now, when you subtly or overtly seduced or violated someone.

Include events when you tried to allay your fears of sexual inadequacy through your partner?

Remember times that you engaged in sexual activity even though you may not have totally desired it —to gain attention, control or power, or to feel loved.

Pay attention to how your body feels as you recall these events, noticing any changes in your breathing, tension in any parts of your body, feelings of lightness or heaviness, or any other sensations.

Think about the stories you told yourself that made it desirable or necessary to get what you wanted surreptitiously.

As you recall these incidents and the story you told yourself, remember any fears you had about yourself or feelings of inadequacy.

Once again, take a few deep breaths and let them go. Which memories were the most painful? Which events were easy to recall and which were more illusive? What themes did you notice emerging in the stories you told yourself about why you were being victimized and why you needed to seduce?

If you want to go further into these images—to gain awareness, understanding, self-compassion, or to integrate what you have learned—and you enjoy doing creative art projects, we suggest any of the following activities. Using the focus of victimization or perpetration:

*Make a collage of yourself.*

*Write a story or a play, using real or imaginary characters.*

*Make a home video or audio tape, choosing scenes of pieces of music that capture the feelings you experienced.*

*Choreograph or improvise a dance.*

*Write a song or a poem.*

*With your unaccustomed hand and your eyes closed, draw a picture of yourself or of the other—your victim or your perpetrator. As you draw, focus on the feelings you experienced rather than how you think your drawing should look.*

Having done many of these exercises, you probably are more aware of your sexual shame—some that you had been conscious of and some that had been unconscious. Chances are you are experiencing some discomfort—few of us like uncovering feelings of shame. However, as you continue exploring the exercises in the chapters ahead, our belief is that your discomfort will go through a metamorphosis—until, like a butterfly, you can catch the joy as you fly. After awareness comes acceptance. Putting yourself down for who you are only creates more shame and more hiding.

Pushing yourself to change so that you will not hate yourself usually backfires. The following chapter contains material that will help you accept your sexual shame—and your whole sexuality at the same time—rather than hide from it, feel resigned to live with it, or try to deny it. Acceptance sets the stage for being able to decide how you would like things to be and to design a strategy for moving in that direction. Let's keep moving!

# 8

# Freedom Through Acceptance

*When we change our attitude from shameful compulsive indulgence to joyful, choiceful experience, our entire sense of aliveness is liberated and extended.*

Omar Garrison, *Tantra: The Yoga of Sex*

## Acceptance: Reality On Its Own Terms

There's a Buddhist word called *tathata* which expresses acceptance beautifully—*as it is*. Not as we wish it were, dream it could be, or fear it is. Simply, as it is. There is tremendous freedom here. What a relief—to finally face the dragon—and discover how much vitality is freed through simple acceptance. Often dragons are not nearly as frightening as the fear of dragons. When so much energy amasses around shame—trying to hide, deny, cover-up, avoid—then little is left for living and loving.

Acceptance can only occur after awareness for obvious reasons: you must be aware of what you are accepting. If you possess the belief that accepting sexual shame is a death sentence, please know that nothing could be further from the truth! Acceptance does not mean that you accept shame as an experience you deserve. It simply means that you accept the fact that you have sexual shame—or any other challenge for that matter.

Acceptance is a vital link in the healing process, like this 40-year-old man revealed:

*"For my whole life, I ran away from admitting that sexual shame controlled me. It made me ruin every potentially healthy relationship I've ever been in. It's made me hurt every women who has ever really loved me. Now that I've become aware of my sexual shame, and more importantly, have accepted it, I'm finally dealing with reality. I'm no longer running away from it. And you know what, I feel exactly the opposite of how I had imagined. I feel peaceful. I'm being kinder with myself and other people. And my sense of humor is even better."*

This man was not a personal growth neophyte. He had consciously worked on himself for many years, yet he had not confronted the most important obstacle of all. Once he became aware of sexual shame, the next step was to accept it. As he came to accept his sexual shame—not begrudgingly or with additional shame—but in a state of innocence, he was able to create changes that had eluded him for years.

You were also born into the world in utter innocence—not carrying a gunnysack of unresolved shame. Acceptance can lead to the realization that *you* are not the original cause or source of your sexual shame—that you are merely reflecting the hurts and fears that others have projected onto you, and you, innocent and believing, took it in.

Such was the case of Cheryl, a woman we worked with who entered therapy with the intention to heal her sexual shame. Her mother recommended to her that if she ever wanted to feel what sex was like, she should put a garden hose up her vagina and turn on the water. Her mother described sex as "dog-on-dog," canine-like, dirty, evil, and immoral. Even though her sexual conditioning was so negative, Cheryl fantasized that sex would suddenly become wonderful and blissful once she got married.

Cheryl's mother spoke with disgust and repugnance about menstruation, her genitals, and how messy and dirty it was to be a woman. Not surprisingly, as a young woman, Cheryl had a hard time accepting the beauty of her own genitals and body fluids—from regular vaginal discharges to the lubrication of arousal to her monthly menstrual blood.

Cheryl's mother believed in what is called "the Cloaca Concept." *Cloaca* is Latin for sewer. The entire genital area is looked at as a sewer—and all the smells and liquids are sewage. How can a young woman think highly of herself and enjoy her genitals if she is repulsed by the smells and sight of her own genitals?

Consonant with this attitude, Cheryl's mother told her that sex meant that men would service themselves upon her. As a result, throughout adolescence, Cheryl imagined sex as a man driving up and using her like the pump at a gas station.

Cheryl's attitudes about sexuality were also formed as she watched and listened to how her parents related to her brother. Her brother started masturbating in the bathroom at about age twelve. He had discovered his father's hidden *Playboy* magazines.

One day, their mother found the *Playboy* magazine in the bathroom. Both parents had noticed that he had been spending more time in the bathroom than previously. When their mother found the *Playboy* magazine, she also found some toilet paper in the wastebasket. She looked at the paper, looked at the magazine, and stormed out of the bathroom, hurling accusations. "What are you doing in this bathroom? This is disgusting, this magazine. Where did you get this magazine?" Hearing this, Cheryl and her brother realized that their father had never told their mother that he was buying this magazine. She continued, "I never want you to do this again! Don't you know that masturbation can send you to Hell? This will make you blind."

Her brother was really frightened, as was she. Her mother had a rolled up magazine in her hand as she was yelling. When she stopped yelling, she told Cheryl's brother to hold out his hand, and she slapped him with the rolled up magazine. Neither Cheryl nor her brother ever told her mother that the *Playboy* magazine was their father's. They were too scared.

A similar shaming of masturbation was done to Cheryl, yet communicated far more subtly. Cheryl remembered an incident that happened when she was a little girl playing with her genitalia in the bathtub. Her mother came in and gave her a very disapproving look, and told her not to play with herself. She was not punished nor yelled at—the look was enough—and she definitely got the message that this was forbidden. She stopped masturbating for many years and when she resumed the practice, she knew that she had to keep this very private and hidden.

Cheryl slowly worked through her conflicts about her sexuality. Already aware of a profound level of sexual shame, she became clear that many of her attitudes came directly from her mother. She realized that they no longer served her. She longed for a feeling of freedom, for a sense of pride about her body and her genitals, and for a feeling of pleasure with sexuality, unencumbered by guilt or shame.

Cheryl felt angry at her mother and at how these convoluted attitudes affected her capacity to experience sexual sensations and emotional intimacy. As her awareness grew and she saw how shame pervaded her life, she was able to give these attitudes back to her mother, so to speak, and say, "These are yours. I'm getting them out of my system. I'm me, I'm going to be a fully alive, sexually passionate human being. That is how I choose to live my life. I am going to surround myself with people who believe the same thing."

Cheryl's anger subsided and transformed into compassion and acceptance when she realized that her mother was a daughter as well and was merely passing on the legacy of her mother. Her intentions were good, though misdirected. Cheryl once again felt love for her mother, accepting her as she was, though no longer bound to follow her conscious overt and unconscious covert expectations.

Over time and with a lot of hard work and persistence, Cheryl developed a healthy attitude towards her sexuality and towards her body. As she accepted how damaged she was, she came to realize how she wanted to feel and behave. By practicing exercises similar to those in this chapter and throughout the book, Cheryl came home to herself. She now enjoys her sexuality and experiences sexuality as an integral, joyous aspect of intimacy.

# Loving Your Shame

One aspect of accepting sexual shame has to do with accepting who you are now—and loving yourself—shame and all. Most people hold their self love out as a promise. They will love themselves after they have healed or resolved certain life issues.

This never works. It's like putting the cart before the horse. It makes self-acceptance impossible because it always exists out there, not in the present. The key is to love who you are currently, not who you are going to become. No more waiting to be deserving of your love. If we remember the poet Rilke's words, perhaps we can accept our shame as a part of ourselves that is "in its deepest essence, something helpless that wants our love." Imagine, loving your shame! Even appreciating your shame as an important part of you that has served a vital function—trying to insure that you will be the kind of person you were brought up to be. Misguided, at times, certainly. Evil, at core, certainly not!

If you can accept the fact that you are merely a link in a multi-generational legacy of shame, you are on your way to changing the legacy—and becoming the last link.

## Exercise #1

### *Accepting Sexual Shame*

Write a list of ways you experience sexual shame. You can refer to the Sexual Shame Awareness Inventory in the last chapter or any other exercises you have done so far. Let yourself write your list without censoring what you put on it.

With each of your sexual shame items, choose a modality with which to take the next step. For example, for one item you might want to tell a story, for another, manipulate clay; or another, make a collage. For instance, if you always wear clothing that hides your body, you might exaggerate this or you might venture into a store with the focus of trying on clothing that reveals your shape but that you do not intend to buy. You are free to work in any modality that helps you to contact and to stay with your feelings.

Begin by choosing one item and pursuing it in a way that deepens your experience of it.

When you have done this, write a description of your experience in your journal, allowing yourself to express all your feelings. Continue working through your list, choosing whatever modality seems appropriate for you.

Share what you discovered with your partner, a therapist, or a close friend. If you continue to pursue this, allowing yourself to be creative and ingenious as you pursue each item, you are sure to find greater and greater acceptance. You are on your way to healing your shame—and bringing more love and openness into your relationship.

🌾   🌾   🌾   🌾   🌾

# Accepting Imperfections

The path of healing is rarely a straight path. When we become aware that we are off the path, we are at a critical choice point. The first choice is the attitude we take towards ourselves for having veered from the path. We recommend compassion. Shame, guilt, and blame only make the task of getting back on course more difficult.

The second choice is how to get back on the path. Often, simply the awareness that we are off the path, together with the desire and commitment to be on the path, is enough to bring us back on course.

An analogy for this self-correcting mechanism is found in flying. As naive passengers, we imagine that our jet is flying perfectly on course to our chosen destination. Yet the knowledgeable person will tell us that jets are "off course" over 90% of the time. The actual flight plan is a straight line whereas the pilot's route is a series of zig-zags.

Because wind and other weather factors cause the plane to move off the path, the pilot must constantly make adjustments to bring the plane back on the path. How efficiently and effectively the pilot can do this determines the actual path flown and the time of the flight.

So, when you become aware that you have veered from the path, without shame or blame, guide yourself back. Most people feel better when they are back on the path than when they are beating themselves up for having fallen off! Daniel Casriel, author of *A Scream Away From Happiness*[1] used a vivid metaphor to make this point:

> *When you fall off a pony, you can either walk behind the pony or get back on the pony.*

## Exercise #2

### *Getting Back on the Pony*

*Supplies needed: your journal or a newsprint pad and crayons.*

Write a list of the phrases with which you harass yourself internally when you veer from your path.

Now, write a list of phrases and statements that a loving, compassionate, and supportive friend, therapist, or parent might say.

Put each of the statements from the second list on cards that you keep in your pocket or purse, put on your bathroom mirror, your refrigerator, your desk, etc.

When you become aware that you are using your first list, berating or flagellating yourself, take out one of your "Get Back on the Pony" cards from the second list, read it and say it to yourself silently or out loud.

Remember, you are simply getting back on the path. There is no need to punish yourself for veering off the path. Celebration is in order for noticing that you have veered off and that you are once again on the path.

🌿   🌿   🌿   🌿   🌿

## Your Body Is Beautiful

Perhaps there is no more basic acceptance than accepting your body. By accepting all levels of bodily functioning—from sexual desires to body odors to physical elimination—you embrace yourself as a person. Accepting the sacredness of your body, as we have explored throughout this book, helps you feel connected with the erotic sacredness of life.

When we attune ourselves to our erotic nature, it teaches us to live a spiritual life—a profound interconnectedness with all life—fully within the body. Metaphorically, eros is the marriage of heaven and earth, of spirit and matter. The body is our sacred home, the foundation through which higher possibilities exist.

In our culture we have attempted to separate the spirit from the flesh, from our bodies. Sensuality, including all aspects of physical pleasure, is often considered inferior to the soul or spirit. But to be a truly spiritual person, we must live fully within our bodies. Hence we must be in contact with our sensuality. How can we experience our spiritual nature fully if we are cut off from our senses?

For eros to flourish in our relationships, we must develop and maintain a healthy relationship with our bodies: taking care of, nurturing, loving, respecting, and appreciating our physical manifestation.

Like Cheryl and her brother, many of us received verbal and non-verbal messages about our bodies that were less than positive. Because our mother is the primary care giver in the first year of our life, it is she who gives us our first impressions and lays the foundation for our attitudes about bodily functions.

Hindu sages realized long before modern day psychologists have shown—that all forms of love begin in the relationship between mother and child. They called the complex interactive web of sensuality, body language, compassion, play, reassurance, tenderness, verbal and non-verbal communication, and other facets of mother-child bonding, "karuna," or "mother love." They were aware of what has been proven again and again in our own time: that development of adult sexuality and sociability depends largely on mother-child interaction in early life.

Adult sexual behavior often patterns itself after infantile practices like breast sucking, pet names, cuddling, and baby talk. Sexual relationships sometimes revert to the period when the infant was learning to relate to the world through his or her relationship with mother. And our bodies have been the vehicles though which we have assimilated this way of being.

Your body is a major facet of who you are—and the cells of your body hold the memory of your early relationship with mother. It is the ground wherein you began developing erotic wounds. Therefore, accepting your body is integral to healing sexual shame, to feeling greater freedom in the sexual arena and all areas of your life, to experiencing more sexual pleasure, and to experiencing greater intimacy. It also increases the possibility of experiencing lifetime love with your partner. The following exercises are designed to help you accept your body as beautiful. They will likely be quite challenging.

## Exercise #3

### *Mirror, Mirror on the Wall*

Stand in front of a full-length mirror and look at yourself without any clothes on.

Look at the specific parts of your body. Which parts do you like and which parts do you dislike?

Talk to each of these parts, especially the ones you dislike. Be as compassionate as possible.

See if you can view the parts you dislike as if they were unwanted or neglected children in need of love.

How would a loving parent speak nurturingly and lovingly to those parts? If, for example, you are a man who dislikes what he believes is his undersized penis, try saying, "Poor penis. You have been so neglected. I've been ashamed of you all my life because I always thought you were too small. I am so sorry. I know you are essential to my sexuality and I will give you the respect you deserve."

## Exercise #4

### *Your Body: A Luscious Landscape*

Completely naked, sit or recline in front of a mirror. Close your eyes, breathe deeply, and imagine that you are in a foreign land which you have never seen.

Open your eyes and with a soft, relaxed focus, look at your body as if you were an unusual landscape. Do this for only about one minute.

Turn away from the mirror and draw your body as a landscape, with mountains, forests, gulleys, etc. You may draw with your eyes open or closed. If you have a tendency to put down your artistic abilities, we recommend drawing with your eyes closed, as your pathological perfectionist has less hold on you.

When you feel finished, open your eyes and look at your landscape. Write a description of your experience and what you see, feel, and think as you look at your drawing.

Another version of this is to first look in the mirror, then to close your eyes and feel your entire body with your hands as if you were a sculptor, and finally, to mold a landscape using clay or paper maché.

Ala Judy Chicago, you can also use a drawing focus of flowers. Look at your genitalia for about one minute or longer, and then draw the exotic flower that you behold or imagine. You can also do this with your partner, each of you drawing the other.

Many people have an easier time accepting the shapes, textures, and colors of their bodies than the smell or taste of their secretions. Because there is so much shame about bodily functions, many children hear only derogatory adjectives about their bodily processes—the *cloaca* or sewer phenomena.

Bowel movements are called smelly, disgusting, dirty rather than talked about as a precious part of the cycle of digestion and excretion. As adolescents begin to develop underarm odors, once again they are told that their smell is offensive and they are bombarded with ads about antiperspirants which will eradicate their foul odor. Smelling like a pine forest will insure success in finding a sexy girlfriend or boyfriend.

Menstrual pads and tampons are perfumed as are many brands of toilet paper. Young women and men can find sprays that will get rid of any crotch odor. When I (Judith) was in college, I knew a young woman who used six different sprays: hair spray, mouth spray, underarm deodorant, crotch spray, foot spray, and finally, perfume. It seems that personal hygiene has gotten confused with trying to smell artificial. This reflects the shame that pervades our culture about bodily functions and subsequently, sexuality.

If men and women believe that their bodily secretions are disgusting, it is no wonder that many women and men are reluctant to engage in oral sex.

The following exercise is designed to help you accept the smells and tastes that are yours as a human being.

## Exercise #5

### *Your Body: A Garden of Earthly Delights*

*Supplies needed: Your journal or a newsprint pad and large crayons.*

This exercise is best done when you first awaken, or at the end of the day—in both cases, before you shower. It is helpful for women to do this at different times of their cycle since their secretions vary so much.

One at a time, put your fingers in each orifice of your body. Experience the sensation of having your finger there.

Then, allow yourself to taste or smell your bodily secretion (excluding your anus).

Write your reactions without censoring them in your journal or on a newsprint pad.

Continue to do this until you have smelled or tasted every orifice (excluding your anus).

Repeat this exercise every few months. Use your reactions to measure change in your attitudes and feelings about your body.

If you do these exercises several times a week or every day, you will notice a change in the way you perceive yourself and relate to your body. This is due to the fact that acceptance, in and of itself, brings about change.

# Your Fantasies Can Set You Free

Most people frame their fantasies within a moral framework—"Is this an acceptable fantasy?" They might not verbalize it as such, but the moral question is still there. The problem is not only that "acceptable" falls within a very narrow range, but posing the question as a moral issue attests to the the controlling influence: shame.

Is it okay for a woman to fantasize about seducing a man while masturbating?

Is it okay for a man to want to submit sexually to a powerful woman?

Is it okay to fantasize about the same-sexed partner?

When Nancy Friday began her research into women's sexual fantasies in the late 1960s, she could not find a single reference for the topic in the card catalogues of the New York Public Library, the Yale University library, or the British Museum library. In millions upon millions of books, not a single word was mentioned about the sexual imagery of one half of humanity.[2]

When she tried to find a publisher for *My Secret Garden,* in which she told the fantasies of women courageous enough to admit to having them, almost every publisher in New York returned it to her. "As late as June 1973, the same month *My Secret Garden* was published, permissive *Cosmopolitan* magazine printed a cover story by the eminent and equally permissive Dr. Allan Fromme, stating, "Women do not have sexual fantasies. The reason for this is obvious: Women haven't been brought up to enjoy sex. Women are by and large destitute of sexual fantasy."[3]

The time was ripe and within months, advertisers were using women's erotic fantasies as a selling tool. Now, we could not even imagine that women were without sexual and erotic fantasies. However, accepting that we, men and women, have erotic fantasies does not necessarily mean that we accept or appreciate the fantasies.

We have seen many people who have shamed themselves mercilessly for their sexual fantasies—unrelated even to actual sexual practice. One heterosexually identified client of mine (Daniel) had fantasies about being sexual with men for over 20 years. He never acted on them. In fact, he never even talked about them.

As a prior alter boy and ministry student, his fantasies aroused tremendous shame in him. When he came to see me in counseling, he was wrought with pain and self-recriminations: "What's wrong with me?" "I don't want to be having thoughts like that." "It drives me crazy!"

I asked him what was wrong with having thoughts about being sexual with men. He told me, "It's sick." He thought that something must be really wrong with him if he were having gay fantasies. Little did he know that a high percentage of heterosexual men have also had homosexual fantasies. Many have even acted on them.

This was a man who did not take a moral stand against homosexuality. He was politically to the left and absolutely in favor of gay rights. He believed that people should be allowed to follow their own inclinations. Yet when it came to him, it was quite a different story.

All the years of fighting against the fantasies had left him feeling desperate. After exploring his fears in therapy, over time, he came to accept these thoughts without railing against himself. He gave himself the freedom to fantasize without blaming or shaming himself. Paradoxically, as he gave himself more freedom to fantasize about men, he thought less and less about being sexual with them. In the end, he never acted on his fantasies, yet he reached a peaceful state of mind. He rarely fantasizes about men now. Such is the power of acceptance.

In his case, acceptance led to the cessation of fantasies. In other cases, it may lead to continued fantasies and a healthy acceptance of them—perhaps even acting on them. The act of acceptance creates changes that are unimaginable when the struggle, shame and fear are present. Stan Dale, director of the Human Awareness Institute and author of *Fantasies Can Set You Free,* describes fantasies like this:

> *"Fantasy is the mind at play, the highest form of mental activity. Fantasy is as real as life itself and as valuable; without fantasy life would not be worth living. Deprived of it we would be that dread thing, a human vegetable."*[4]

What stops people from accepting their fantasies? The simple answer is fear—fear that they will be discovered and judged as aberrant, sick, weird, perverted, over-sexed, etc. We have found that as people feel better about themselves, that is, they realize their self-worth, competence, and lovability, they can accept their sexual fantasies more easily. Judging or condemning any sexual titillation does not make it disappear. Most of us are so busy pushing away what seems disturbing and unpleasant, that we eventually get clobbered by it.

As the saying goes, "that which we resist persists." By consciously working with erotic material and bringing it forth from the fangs of shame, valuable energy will be unleashed for pleasure and healing.

# Psychic Erotic Imprints

Accepting sexual fantasies, dark or light, can be stimulated through understanding. And understanding what we call *psychic erotic imprints*—images, feelings, and sensations that arouse us sexually—can help us de-pathologize our fantasies. Strong early experiences involving erotic material create psychic erotic imprints. The following story will help clarify.

Harry, a man in his forties, aroused himself with a fantasy that involved a psychic erotic imprint from his early childhood. When he was six through ten years old, he had a babysitter who was sexually inappropriate, repeatedly. The adolescent sitter, Nancy, would ask Harry to put his hand in her pants to feel her pubic hair and her vagina. She would also touch his penis. Harry sensed that something was inappropriate but also felt intrigued. He never told his parents.

Years later, Harry found that he became aroused when he fantasized that an adolescent girl was stimulating his penis while he lay in bed, pretending to be asleep. This fantasy aroused him yet also disturbed him as he did not really want this to happen. He felt great shame and guilt. When he came to understood that this abusive experience had created a psychic erotic imprint, and did not mean that he was perverted, he could welcome and accept the fantasy.

If Harry were seeking teenage girls to act out his fantasy, then the treatment of the fantasy must change—he would be endangering the welfare of others. But since Harry simply stimulated himself through this fantasy, and was not hurting anyone else, he could simply enjoy it. Accepting the fact that early experiences help paint our erotic landscape can help free us from unnecessary guilt and shame.

The following exercise can help you continue your journey to self-acceptance.

## Exercise #6

### *Honoring Your Fantasies*

*Supplies needed: Your journal or a newsprint pad and crayons. Optional: soft background music.*

Get in a comfortable position and close your eyes. If you desire, put on soft music. Breathe deeply and let your body release tension each time you exhale.

Begin to think about the various fantasies you have had that are sexual, erotic, or romantic. They may be fantasies that you use while masturbating, making love, walking down the street, sunbathing, etc.

Pay attention to your somatic responses as you think about each one.

When you have reviewed fantasies from your childhood, adolescence, and adulthood, slowly open your eyes and get your paper.

Write a description of each fantasy, your somatic and emotional responses to it, and your judgments of yourself. Please, do not censor what you write. If you feel ashamed, write about your shame. Have acceptance and compassion for yourself.

## Exercise #7

### *Revealing Your Fantasies*

Close your eyes once again. Notice how your body feels.

Imagine telling these fantasies to a group of people.

Who are the people?

What are their reactions?

What are your reactions?

Now imagine telling your fantasies to your lover, your parents, your friends, your clergy, your boss. Fantasize with people who are or have been authority figures, people you respect or admire, people who love you. Each time, notice how you feel, how your body responds, and how you judge yourself.

When you feel through, open your eyes and slowly come to standing. Take a bow for the hard work you have just done.

If you feel that you have the courage to tell your fantasies to some of the people you just imagined, we highly recommend it. One of the best ways to heal shame is to face it squarely. Tell your first truth first—that you are afraid of what this other person might think of you, how you want them to respond, etc. If you want support to accept your fantasies or to broaden your horizons, reading the following books may be beneficial: Nancy Friday, *My Secret Garden, Forbidden Flowers, Men In Love,* and *Women on Top;* Stan Dale, *Fantasies Can Set You Free;* Lonnie Barbach, *Pleasures: Women Write Erotica,* and with Linda Levine, *Shared Intimacies;* Bernie Zilbergeld, *The New Male Sexuality.*

                    🌿    🌿    🌿    🌿    🌿

# Freedom Through Tolerance

For people who have a heterosexual orientation, it is important to explore overt and covert homophobia. Homophobia literally means "fear of the same." Addressing your homophobic fears not only broadens your mind and makes you more tolerant of others, it also frees up your own sexual fantasies. Exploring your fear does not mean you need to act out homosexually.

Simply accepting that other people can have a different sexual orientation can help you feel freer to explore aspects of your own sexuality that you have previously judged. Even accepting any little fantasy you might have about being sexual with someone of the same sex and allowing that to be an okay, natural, or normal thought to pop up in you mind at times, is going to enhance your overall capacity to bring passion and excitement into your relationship.

Shame shows it face through intolerance to your own fantasies or other people's sexual expression. Part of overcoming shame is developing a greater tolerance for other forms of sexuality—excluding behaviors that are abusive or non-consensual, such as sexual abuse of children. If it is not hurting anything but your sensibilities, then it is time to re-examine and change how you limit yourself unnecessarily. By broadening your perspective, you create new options and greater freedom for yourself.

All those moralistic, religious judgments and self-righteous attitudes about sexuality are cover-ups for shame and fear. Whether they are projected onto other people or whether we feel them about ourselves, we prevent ourselves from experiencing the pleasure and intimacy of healthy sexuality.

## Exercise #8

*Erotic De-Sensitization Process*

*Supplies needed: Your journal or a newsprint pad and crayons.*

Get in a comfortable position, close your eyes, and take a few deep breaths.

Imagine people whose sexuality or sexual expression has activated judgments in you.

(This exercise is *not* about sexual expression that is abusive, in which there was a minor, lack of consent, or that was emotionally or physically hurtful to someone).

What bothers you about their sexuality?

What might be pleasurable about what they are doing?

What stops you from doing the same?

Imagine giving them permission to be exactly as they are. What happens inside of you? What fears about yourself emerge? What somatic reactions do you notice?

Slowly open your eyes and write about your experience. Include the sexual behaviors which you judged negatively, your judgments or opinions, your fears about yourself, and how you would like to feel about those particular behaviors.

You can use this exercise to measure change in your attitudes towards sexuality if you revisit it and do it every few months. Though you may choose not to change your own behavior, by dropping your prejudice, you will probably feel less self-righteous or arrogant. What a relief! You will probably feel freer and experience more joy.

I (Daniel) remember being at a large party fifteen years ago attended by numerous members of a spiritual group. Unlike many spiritual groups, they supported full sexual expression. Many clusters of hugging, fondling adherents adorned the furniture. I was highly judgmental. Who do these people think they are? However, when I got off my high horse, I confronted the bottom line of my irritation: These people were enjoying themselves and I was not!

I wanted to be in one of those clusters—although I wasn't admitting this to myself at the time. I was using judgment to protect myself against my feelings of insignificance. I realized later that I was telling myself a disempowering story: if I were more important, attractive, or lovable then I would be invited into one of those clusters. By opening to my insecurities, I allowed myself to acknowledge what I really wanted—instead of protecting myself behind a shield of judgment and self-righteousness. This helped open the door for me to create more physical nurturing and contact in my life.

🌱　🌱　🌱　🌱　🌱

# The Next Step

If you have been doing the previous exercises, more than likely, you are well on your way to healing sexual shame and experiencing a deeper level sexuality. When you become aware of the feelings of shame that lurk in the shadows, and view them with compassion and acceptance, you are profoundly engaged in the healing process. The next step involves the sometimes painstaking, yet ultimately joyous task of re-creating yourself—fulfilling the highest vision you hold of yourself.

If you are determined and persistent, as in learning any new skill, you will experience successes. (The last chapter, *Erotic Mastery* focuses on this.) The more you believe in your ability to change, trust your own pacing, and have compassion for yourself, the easier your path will be. The following chapter will provide you with advanced tools for transforming challenges with yourself and with your lover.

# *Awakening Your Erotic Self*

*Divine am I inside and out, and I make holy whatever I touch or am touched from.*

Walt Whitman, *Song of Myself*

## Developing a Personal Healing Program

Most of us wish for a magical, immediate recovery. However, committing to a well devised strategy will more likely bring desired results. What is a good strategy for healing your sexual shame and becoming lifetime lovers? First, it must address the primary areas of your life—your relationship to your self, to your intimate other, and within groups or community. Second, it must contain tools for confronting the opposition—internal and external. And last, it must support you in integrating your new attitudes, feelings, and behaviors. This chapter, *Awakening Your Erotic Self,* naturally leads into the next chapter, *Healing with Your Beloved—and Beyond.* Evolution starts at home, so let's take care of ourselves first.

## Self-Work

The clearer your idea of both how you would like to be and how you do not want to be, the easier it is to develop a plan for change. It is not necessary that you know all the steps along the way. However, if you are aware of the payoffs or secondary gains you receive from your current attitudes and behavior, you have a better chance of implementing the changes.

Most people do not like to believe that there are any positive payoffs for feeling or behaving in undesirable ways. We frequently hear, "That's just the way I am. I don't like it but I can't help it." When asked to find a positive payoff, a common response is, "Why would I want to do something like that? There's nothing positive about it. I would be crazy to choose something so stupid." The fact is that most of us behave in limiting ways that we would dearly love to change, but the negative patterns somehow persist. We have so much trouble ridding ourselves of undesired attitudes and behaviors because they serve us in ways that are out of our conscious awareness.

At first, most people who have worked with us express shameful feelings from which they cannot imagine receiving any positive payoff. However, when they question themselves more deeply, some of the embedded payoffs we have heard are: "I hate feeling ashamed but it's better than feeling like a slut." This woman discovered that the payoff from her shame was that she could be sexual and still keep her belief that she was virtuous—and the feeling that she was a good person. A male client complained and bragged, "If I didn't feel ashamed, I would take every woman to bed." For this man, the payoff was that he maintained a Don Juan stance which helped him to feel sexually desirable and virile—cloaking an underlying fear that he was less than attractive.

It is fairly easy to become aware of the payoffs if we assume that there must be some good reason—otherwise, why would we do it? One way to become conscious of the payoff is to complete these statements—you fill in the meaning of *this:*

*When I feel or act* this *way, I believe I am a* _____*person.*

*If I did not feel or act* this *way, I'm afraid I would feel or act* _____.

*By feeling or acting* this *way, I believe that other people feel or think* _____*of me.*

*By feeling or acting* this *way, I am trying to accomplish* _____.

The following exercise will help you become clearer about what you want, what you do not want, and how you currently prevent yourself from fulfilling your erotic desires.

## Exercise #1: The Erotic Inventory*

This is how I feel about my erotic self right now:

*Awful*    0    1    2    3    4    5    6    7    8    9    *Great*

### *My Ideal Erotic Self*

*I shut my eyes and imagine the erotic person I want to be. I write a description of the person I imagined, placing one characteristic per line. More specifically, how this person…*

**Looks & dresses**

_____ __     _____ __

_____ __     _____ __

_____ __     _____ __

**Feels**

_____ __     _____ __

_____ __     _____ __

_____ __     _____ __

**Thinks**

_____ __     _____ __

_____ __     _____ __

_____ __     _____ __

*This form is adapted from *Element E: Self Esteem Instrument,* Will Schutz Associates

**Believes**

_____  ___  _____  ___
_____  ___  _____  ___
_____  ___  _____  ___

**Practices or does**

_____  ___  _____  ___
_____  ___  _____  ___
_____  ___  _____  ___

**Moves**

_____  ___  _____  ___
_____  ___  _____  ___
_____  ___  _____  ___

**Communicates**

_____  ___  _____  ___
_____  ___  _____  ___
_____  ___  _____  ___

**Feels about and acts toward his or her body**

_____  ___  _____  ___
_____  ___  _____  ___
_____  ___  _____  ___

**Other important characteristics**

_____  ___  _____  ___
_____  ___  _____  ___
_____  ___  _____  ___

## My Unwanted Erotic Self

*I take a deep breath, erase my ideal erotic self from my mind, and shut my eyes. I now imagine the erotic person I do **not** want to be. I write a description of the person I imagined—one characteristic per line. More specifically, how this person…*

**Looks & dresses**

_____  ___  _____  ___
_____  ___  _____  ___
_____  ___  _____  ___

**Feels**

_____    __    _____    __

_____    __    _____    __

_____    __    _____    __

**Thinks**

_____    __    _____    __

_____    __    _____    __

_____    __    _____    __

**Believes**

_____    __    _____    __

_____    __    _____    __

_____    __    _____    __

**Moves**

_____    __    _____    __

_____    __    _____    __

_____    __    _____    __

**Communicates**

_____    __    _____    __

_____    __    _____    __

_____    __    _____    __

**Feels about and acts toward my body**

_____    __    _____    __

_____    __    _____    __

_____    __    _____    __

**Other important characteristics**

_____    __    _____    __

_____    __    _____    __

_____    __    _____    __

I circle the number that best expresses how I feel about my erotic self now:

_Awful_     0     1     2     3     4     5     6     7     8     9     _Great_

I return to the descriptions I wrote and read over each statement I made about my ***Ideal Erotic Self*** and my ***Unwanted Erotic Self***. I place a number on the small line to the right of each statement indicating to what degree that statement is true of me, on a scale of 0 to 9.

*I am not at all this way* ➡ **0   1   2   3   4   5   6   7   8   9** ➡ *I am exactly this way*

Then I circle the lowest numbers in the ***Ideal Erotic Self*** description and the highest numbers in the ***Unwanted Erotic Self*** description.

**Looking over these items I consider:**

*What fears or beliefs are keeping me from being my ideal?*

*Who or what, internal or external, keeps me from being my ideal?*

*When did I begin to feel this way?*

*What positive payoffs or secondary gains am I getting from being or feeling this way? If nothing comes to mind, just make a guess as to what it might be.*

Below, I list items with the lowest ***Ideal Erotic Self*** scores and the highest ***Unwanted Erotic Self*** scores. Under each one, I write my *Fears* and *Payoffs*.

| **Characteristic** | **Fear** | **Payoff** |
| --- | --- | --- |
| | | |
| | | |
| | | |
| | | |
| | | |
| | | |
| | | |

When you finish doing the Erotic Inventory, you are clearer about the payoffs you receive for your undesired attitudes and behaviors, or for not becoming the erotic person you would like to be. This has prepared you to face your fears, and risk getting your primary needs and desires met more directly. If this sounds foreboding, know that it will become less so as you continue on your personal program of erotic transformation.

Many people stop themselves from moving forward by being unable or unwilling to let go of the past. Self-recriminations and regrets keep them stuck in the past, wishing they had done it differently, punishing themselves for not having done it better.

For some people, forgiveness is the way out of the labyrinth. Sometimes, simply telling yourself that you did not know any better or you were just trying to survive is enough to elicit self-forgiveness and compassion. Sometimes, self-responsibility is the key. This path leads you to examine your motivation for acting in a certain way, and to discover what the payoff was at the time. This often leads to the same compassionate position—that you did the best you could then. Regardless of which path you choose, it is imperative that you come to terms with past feelings or behavior so that you can enjoy the present and move freely into the future.

## Exercise #2

### *Making Erotic Amends (Self)*

Write a list of all that you have done in the erotic realm for which you feel shame. Your list could include ways you have treated your body, times you have engaged in sexual behavior that didn't feel right for you but you did it anyway, clandestine flirtations or affairs, or actions you have taken toward your partner or past lovers that you regret, such as how you ended a relationship—anything you have done in the sex and love arena.

When you are finished writing your list, reread one item, and think about what you were experiencing at the time of that incident. Ask yourself these questions: Of what was I afraid? What do I imagine would have happened if I had done it differently? How was I feeling about myself at the time that prevented me from being aware of or choosing another option?

Now, close your eyes and take a few deep breaths. Either find a compassionate part of yourself or think of someone you know or imagine who is very compassionate and loving.

Talk to yourself, either out loud or silently, using such phrases as, "I did the best I knew how at the time. Even though somebody felt hurt, I am still an okay, lovable human being."

Continue working through your list until you are complete. Notice the ones you easily come to terms with, and those that give you difficulty. Re-visit the items for which you were not able to fully forgive or make peace with yourself by looking for a deeper level response to the questions above. Once again, find the compassionate, forgiving figure to help you out.

# Return to the Garden

Making amends with ourselves, accepting that we are human and therefore, perfect in our imperfection, moves us closer to a state of innocence. Once we acknowledge that we have acted in undesirable ways, but we were trying to survive the best way we knew how, we can take responsibility for our actions without incriminating ourselves.

We can accept that we have done something hurtful without becoming a heinous villain, without feeling that we are bad at our core. We can even look at that part of ourselves—and love it as a self-aspect that, in some way, was reaching out for love. Every expression can then be seen as communicating love or asking for help.

To heal shame and experience erotic freedom, we must return to the state of innocence into which we were born. Sam Keen suggests this return by revisiting your childhood and reclaiming what was lost.

> *"Those virtues, or graces, by which we are healed- trust, hope, and love—all depend upon seasoned innocence, openness to novelty, the willingness to be refreshed. Refurbish your memories of childhood and you will find fragments of an old map that will lead you to a treasure hidden in your future."*[1]

By returning to the shaming events of our past, and experiencing them differently—looking at them with fresh eyes, hearing with new ears, making sense of what we could not understand when we were young—we can return to our innocence.

Shame emerges from harmful family legacies and co-dependent or compulsive sex often results. Consequently, we need to revisit experiences in which we felt shamed in order to be healed.

To change our future script, we must rewrite our past one. Only then can we experience our erotic nature free from the strains of sexual shame. There is no right way to be as we become explorers or emotional archaeologists of our pasts, but if we have the intention of uncovering hidden jewels—we are more likely to find them.

Can you fathom what life would be like if you were born into a state of "original innocence," rather than original sin? Imagine that from the time you were born, your body was treated as a temple, your curiosity about your body and your environment was considered healthy and was sanctioned.

All of your bodily functions—from eating to defecating to masturbating—were regarded as sacred and honored. People looked at you with love in their eyes, spoke to you with interest and caring in their voice, and touched you with reverence and tenderness. You were held when you wanted comfort and closeness. Your sexuality was considered a vital part of your being—spanning the heights of spiritual union and the depths of animal pleasure.

## Exercise #3

### *Revisiting the Garden of Innocence*

Make yourself comfortable, close your eyes, and take a few full, deep breaths.

Imagine what it would feel like to be healed of your sexual and erotic wounds, to experience the state of innocence that is your birthright.

Imagine how you would feel about your body (pause), your genitals (pause), your desires (pause), your curiosity.

How would you communicate your desires—what you wanted and what you did not want?

How would you feel about other people's bodies, about their desires?

Imagine being loved for who you are.

Imagine loving others, fully trusting them and their intentions.

Bring your focus back to your breathing and to the sensations in your body. Notice if they have changed at all since you began to imagine returning to a state of innocence.

*When you feel ready to, write a description of your experience in your journal or on a large, newsprint pad.*

If you want to experience this state of innocence more deeply, use it as a focus for a collage, dance, poem, play, photographic essay, or any other creative expression. If you find that you feel sad, allow yourself to cry and to mourn for what you did not have. Then, go back to your return to innocence.

If you feel angry, first find out who is the object of your anger. Then do the following exercises in this chapter, starting with *Moving Through Your Anger* (#4). You may then be able to imagine being in a state of innocence more easily.

# Transforming Your Anger

We have seen many people become stuck in a state of anger, blaming the important people of their past for their current problems. Though it is healthy to feel and express anger in a constructive or productive manner, to use it as a springboard to self-empowerment or as a passageway into mourning, it is not healthy to wallow in it.

But many people, particularly men, would rather feel angry than sad. Focusing your energy on the enemy out there may help you to mobilize yourself, to feel righteous, or even powerful, but, in the end, it will not help you to heal your shame, feel your true potency, or get on with your life. In fact, it can become an impediment.

If you find that you get stuck in anger and blame and are unable to move through it easily, this exercise may help you transform your anger into creative, vital energy.

## Exercise #4

### *Moving Through Your Anger*

Close your eyes and allow yourself to feel your anger. Exaggerate or amplify whatever you are experiencing—tensing tight muscles or moving the energy, for example—and feel what happens in your body as you do this. What sensations are you aware of? What images do you see in your mind's eye? What phrases, words, or voices do you hear internally?

If feelings or images arise that are frightening or repugnant to you, remember that these are in your mind, they are not reality. Imaging that you are acting violently, even doing it symbolically, does not mean that you would do anything similar in reality. Rather than censor your images, breathe into your belly, say to yourself, "This is simply a thought," and allow yourself to enter the imaginal world of your shadow character. By using a creative art process to enliven a shadow character, you actually disempower it and re-empower yourself.

***Choose as many of the following as you desire:***

#### FIRE BREATHING

Stand with your feet shoulder width apart, knees slightly bent. Breathe in and out through your nostrils, allowing them to flare. Begin to breathe out through your mouth, making any sounds that want to come. Allow your body to move in whatever way feels good for you, whether it be jumping around, punching into the air, or flailing around. After a few minutes, return to your original standing position, close your eyes, and breathe deeply into your belly.

## TEMPER TANTRUM

Begin in any way that feels good for you, whether it be lying on a bed, standing, or on the floor in a heap. Allow yourself to begin to move in whatever way satisfies your anger, as long as you do not hurt yourself, another person, or property. You may want to structure it by kicking or pounding on a bed or you may want to freely move your body, allowing surprises to emerge. When you feel finished, focus your attention internally, allowing yourself to take credit for what you have just done.

## FANTASY FIGHT

Begin to focus on whomever you feel angry with. Imagine what you would like to do to that person or those people. When you feel ready, allow yourself to do symbolically in movement what you have fantasized. You may want to wring a towel, punch a pillow, rip newspapers or old phone books, break recycling bottles in a container, whatever feels satisfying for you that would not hurt you, another person, or property.

## COLLAGE

Find visual images and words that express the anger you feel. Cut them out of magazines and put them on a backing. Hang your collage some place where you can see it, take credit for what you have done, and appreciate this as a part of yourself.

## PAINT YOUR ANGER

Get big paper, paint, or whatever medium suits you. Without planning your painting, allow yourself to put down images and feelings as they arise. Choose whatever colors you are drawn to and let the color guide your hand. Continue painting until you feel finished. Do as many paintings as you feel like doing. Do not censor what you paint. When you are finished and they are dry, put one or more on a wall where you can see it, take credit for what you have done, and appreciate this as a part of yourself.

## YOUR HATE LETTER

In your journal or on a newsprint pad, let yourself write a hate letter to whomever you feel angry towards. Do not censor what you write as you are not going to send this. It is to help you let go of your anger and move out of the obsessive blaming on which you have been spending your energy. You might start your letter with, "Dear so and so, I am so angry at you. I feel like I can never forgive you. You had no right to…" Continue writing until you feel finished.

*When you have finished doing one or more of the above processes, check in with yourself and find out how your body feels, notice any changes in your breathing, sensations throughout your body, any emotional shifts, etc. Notice if you feel any differently toward the other person or about yourself. Do you feel energized, spent, scared, surprised?*

## PAYOFF

Explore what possible payoff you may be getting by holding onto your anger. It may be that you feel shy, frightened, or do not know how to set boundaries (feeling that you do not deserve to set them) and your anger helps you to do so. It may be that your anger keeps you from feeling your fear (and subsequent unpleasant feelings) that you are in some way bad and that is why you endured this terrible past. Discovering a payoff is an important step in transforming your anger. (Refer back to the questions under the heading Self-Work, before exercise #1 The Erotic Inventory, to help you discover your payoff.)

### *Write about your experience in your journal.*

You may want to go back to exercise #3, *Revisiting the Garden of Innocence,* and find out how your experience differs now that you have released some of your anger and let go of some of your blame. Hopefully, you have had a new experience of your anger—one that has energized you, cleansed you, or prepared you to drop into grief.

Just as many people feel frightened to confront their anger, they also feel afraid of their grief—fearing that it will consume and immobilize them. However, we can never truly let go of that which we have not mourned. If we quell our grief, we keep ourselves stuck in the past, preventing ourselves from experiencing ourselves fully in the present, and precluding ourselves from moving freely into the future.

## Mourning

When imagining how life could be if you were brought up in a state of innocence, you may have felt sad, even depressed. Just as depression keeps us from feeling our own anger, it also stops us from feeling our grief. By depressing ourselves, subduing our feelings, we ward off what we think is the enemy—feeling bad—when, in fact, we are preventing ourselves from feeling good.

Ironically, people describe depression as feeling bad. Yet, if we allowed ourselves to feel sad, we would more readily feel good. Yet, the sadness allows the feeling to be released—to flow out so that the more joyous feelings hidden behind the dam can be experienced. However, most of us are so afraid of feeling the pain of our grief, we would rather be depressed than take the risk. This is a travesty. The e-motion (energy-in-motion) of grief allows the waters of change to cleanse and fertilize barren ground. In fact, researchers have found that toxins are released through tears.

Unfortunately, most of us deny our grief, as if it were an aberrant behavior. When we were children, our grief was hushed up, squelched, or averted with some distraction, criticism, or food. The pain that we then experienced was from having to silence our grief, not from feeling it. Most of us have not had the experience of feeling sad, crying, even wailing until, of its own accord, the grief transforms into acceptance, understanding, forgiveness, even joy. Like anger creating a passageway to grief, mourning creates a passageway to acceptance—which is, in itself, a preparation for taking another step.

We have found that mourning for what we did not have is one of the best ways to begin healing our wounds. The greatest emotional wound—not to have been loved as we truly were—cannot heal without the work of mourning.

### Exercise #5

### *Mourning Your Sexual Innocence*

Get a representative sampling of photographs from throughout your life. They may be of you alone or with family or friends. Also, gather photos of your mother, father, and any other important people who affected your erotic development.

If you do not have photos or want some additional stimulation, you may draw images of yourself or other important people at different phases of your development.

Organize them chronologically.

Close your eyes and remember important experiences about yourself as an erotic being (both positive and negative).

Open your eyes and look at various pictures of yourself as a child, as well as photos of your mother, father, and other important people. Allow yourself to see and know what you do not ordinarily let yourself see or know. Feel any feelings that emerge as you do this, without stopping.

For your mother, father, and any other important person, choose a representative photo that supports you in getting in touch with what you did not receive from that person. Look at the photo and then, out loud or silently to yourself, tell that person what you did not receive from them and how sad you feel. Allow yourself to grieve in any way that feels right to you.

Now, choose one photo in which you can see your wounded child. Look at that photo and see what you do not ordinarily allow yourself to see. Begin to speak to that child, or to the wounded child within you. For example, ("I know how hurt you have felt and how you learned not to trust other people. I am so sorry. I love you. I will take care of you now.") Then, allow the child aspect to speak back and allow a dialogue to develop.

## Journaling Yourself to Health

Keeping a journal is always a helpful and important process when you are wanting to change certain aspects of your feelings, attitudes and behaviors. Writing journal entries about your thoughts, feelings, images, and/or inner dialogues—all of these are helpful in marking the progress you are making, and also looking at which blocks keep arising. For instance, as you write, you may begin to notice patterns or repetitive voices. You may discover that whenever you begin to feel your erotic nature stirring, some inner character or voice emerges who is against you enjoying yourself sexually.

*The following exercise will give you some ideas for how to use your journal.*

## Exercise #6

## Journaling

Let yourself write for a minimum of fifteen minutes without censoring or organizing what you write using one of these ideas that interests you:

*My personal definition of shame is...*

*I know I am feeling shame when...*

*My somatic (bodily) experience of shame is...*

*I shame others overtly or covertly in these ways:*

*I have been shamed in these ways:*

*Healthy sexuality is…*

*A sexy man is…*

*A sexy woman is…*

*What I want in lovemaking is…*

*What I don't want in lovemaking is…*

Whenever you feel the urge, look back over your past writing and notice if your attitudes or feelings have changed at all. If you have not censored your writing by trying to write what you think you should feel or would like to feel, but you have written what you truly feel, fear, or believe currently, you will see an accurate reflection of your inner and outer changes.

You may find that you have a complex set of feelings or attitudes about a particular issue. You may even become aware of conflicting feelings or beliefs. These may feel as if they are your own or you may identify them as voices of your mother, father, or other important people from your past. The following exercise will help you use these internal conflicts or dialogues to your advantage.

🌱   🌱   🌱   🌱   🌱

## A Dialogue with Shame

Remember back to the opening story in *The Power of Awareness* (Chapter 7) where I, Judith, confronted my sexual shame after molding clay. Perhaps you recognized a dialogue imbedded in my story between the voice of freedom and the voice of shame. Although most of us try to suppress them, we are constantly hearing or being affected by inner dialogues—reflecting the conflicts we experience about our feelings, attitudes, and behavior.

Notice if you identify with or experience anything similar to the following dialogue involving sexuality, freedom, and shame:

The voice of Healthy Sexuality: *I deserve my healthy sexuality. I deserve to feel pleasure, ecstasy, and fulfillment.*

The voice of Sexual Shame: *No way. You are disgusting for wanting this. Who do you think you are anyway?*

Healthy Sexuality: *I am tired of having to squelch my desires. I am tired of feeling shame when I act on them. I really want to change this.*

Sexual Shame: *Forget it! There is no way that you are going to change this. This is just the way you are.*

Healthy Sexuality: *I am so sick and tired of you. Why don't you just shut up and leave me alone.*

Sexual Shame: *Tough luck. I am here to stay. You can not get rid of me.*

Healthy Sexuality: *Leave me alone. Get out of here. It is okay to enjoy my sexuality!*

Sexual Shame: *There is nothing you can do to get me to leave. You are doomed to feel disgusting.*

While few people actually write down their inner dialogues, most people cycle in their inner dialogues and go nowhere fast—just like this one. Whether the issue is sex, work, food, or anything else, this lack of resolution is painful. Although this cycle can repeat itself ad nauseam, with the right strategy—consciously "processing" the material through *Dialoguing*—you can move out of the trap of the conflict. How? By learning to work with and discover the unity underlying the conflicts between these voices. It is really quite easy. However, it takes commitment and perseverance.

You may be wondering why your dialogues have not led to inner peace and resolution. You simply have not learned to ask the right questions or to create a valuable focus for moving through the conflicts. Furthermore, if you are like most people, you have assumed—consciously or otherwise—that life-long conflicts are irresolvable. Or, as in any competitive arena, one side must win while the other side loses. Let us consider an alternative.

Healthy Sexuality: *We have engaged in this battle for a long time with neither of us finishing the other off. What do you really want from me? Why are you torturing me?*

Sexual Shame: *I am afraid that your sexuality will know no bounds and that you will stop doing anything productive in your life.*

Healthy Sexuality: *I might go to an extreme for a while because I have felt so repressed, but I will not stay that way forever.*

Sexual Shame: *I'm afraid people won't like you for yourself but will just try to use you.*

Healthy Sexuality: *When I feel ashamed, I am more likely to get used because I am less aware. My attention is focused on my shame and negative feelings about myself. When I don't feel ashamed, I can be more alert and make better choices.*

Sexual Shame: *What will your parents say?*

Healthy Sexuality: *I can imagine! But I am no longer willing to let them rule my life. They can say or think what they will and I am still going to live my life my way!*

This approach to *Dialoguing*[2] helps people individuate—let go of the destructive attitudes of their parents and integrate the constructive attitudes as their own. The easiest way to begin this process is to choose two voices: one that is connected to your traitor—the part of you that is trying to put you down, criticize you, or in some way sabotage you, and the other is connected to your guardian angel—the part of you that supports you in expressing your essence, that believes in you, and wants you to individuate, self-actualize, and feel fulfilled.

As we explored earlier, each of these aspects of yourself are called self-styles or subpersonalities—ways that you express different parts of your personality as you relate to yourself and interact with people in your life.

Most people have well developed traitors and poorly developed angels. Think about yourself. You probably spend more time berating, pushing, shaming, and criticizing yourself than you spend appreciating, applauding, recognizing, or celebrating yourself. As a result, the self-styles you might call your *Put down, Piledriver, Pathological Perfectionist, Shamer,* or *Critic* are stronger than self-styles you might name your *Credit taker, Wise One, Higher Self,* or *Innocent Child.*

*Dialoguing* helps develop your underdeveloped aspects. Most people succumb to their traitor and feel miserable or cycle endlessly through the same material—and also feel miserable. By *Dialoguing* with regularity, persistence, and tenacity, you strengthen your inner angel. At first you may find that your traitor voices are strong—even pushy, articulate, and convincing while your angel voices are weak, tentative, even apologetic. As you practice—just like strengthening a muscle—your angel voices will get stronger and more articulate. You will soon find that they are able to stay centered amidst the trickery, conniving, threatening, shaming, and otherwise sabotaging voices of your traitor.

## Exercise #7

### *Angel-Traitor Dialogue*

Supplies needed: your newsprint pad or journal, one color crayon for your traitor and another color for your angel or your journal.

Without censoring, write the first voice that occurs to you. Write as much as that self-style wants to say at this moment or until the responding voice is ready to come in.

With your other color, write the response from the other self-style. Continue to let your traitor go through his/her normal undermining routine, allowing your angel to respond.

If you have trouble finding your angel voice, think of someone whom you know who could stand up to your traitor and imagine what that person would say. Use those words as if they were your own until you find your own words.

If you find that your traitor has a lot to say and your angel has hardly one word to say, have patience. Imagine that your angel is a new flower bud that needs care, attention, and water.

Have your angel voice ask your traitor what h/she wants from you, what h/she is getting from this, what h/she is fearful of or any other questions that come to mind. Allow your traitor to respond exactly as you hear it.

Let your angel voice make "I want" and "I don't want" statements to your traitor. Give your angel voice permission to set boundaries for your traitor. Tell him/her that you have had enough, that you will no longer let him/her rule the show, etc.

Find out what each character wants and what each character needs from the other to create a more harmonious inner relationship. They may even bargain together—for example, "I'll stop hammering on you if you clean up your room every day."

Continue Dialoguing until you feel ready to stop. If your traitor has the last word, remember that this is just the beginning. Eventually, your angel will get stronger and take the lead in your show.


As you practice Dialoguing, you may become aware of specific traitor and angel voices. Give them personal names that are meaningful for you. For instance, I, Judith, named my self-style that feels sorry for me, Poor Pitiful Pearl, based on a story in my family. As you begin to discern specific characters, let each of them talk as if you, and all your self-styles, are sitting at a round table having a discussion. Have fun with it! If you do have fun, you will be sending a message to your unconscious that change is pleasurable.

You may find that your conflict remains polarized and there seems to be no way out. One side represents the comfort zone and the other side represents risk—new territory. The familiar side (the comfort zone) may not feel good but as Dorothy in the Wizard of Oz says, "There's no place like home." The risky side, which is new territory, beckons with hopes, dreams, promises of fulfillment as well as lions, and tigers, and bears.

Arnold Mindell,[3] a brilliant therapist and theorist, describes the predicament between the comfort zone and the new territory as an edge—like a cliff overhanging an abyss. There is a figure waiting at the edge, trying to stop you from going over the edge into new territory. This edge figure holds the voices of fear, shame, gloom, and doom. "No, don't do it. It is disgusting. It is horrible. If you do it, your parents will hate you. Nobody will want to be around you." The voices of these edge figures are the many voices of your traitor. Often, you can recognize an edge figure as a parent, grand-parent, or some other important person of your past and present.

On the other side of the edge is another edge figure beckoning you to enter new territory—to risk, to change. "Your time has finally come. Do it! You can trust. It's okay to make the leap." It expresses an angel voice, gently guiding you into more enlivening and enriching life experiences.

One way to support yourself to go over an edge, to take the risk and try new behavior is to take on the role of the edge figure and amplify it. Like Dialoguing, the following exercise often helps you break a stalemate by providing some missing information—what is making it so scary or seemingly impossible to move forward.

## Exercise #8

### *Becoming an Edge Figure*

When you become aware of an edge figure or a traitor voice that is thwarting your progress or otherwise getting in your way, put your paper down, stand up, and allow yourself to become that character.

Move the way that character would move. Make sounds or talk the way he or she would talk. Amplify this behavior—exaggerate it or do it as subtly as you want.

As you explore this character through amplification, allow it to transform in any direction.

If you do not try to control how you think this transformation should occur, you are more likely to stumble upon valuable surprises.

If you start crying, yelling, wretching, or spontaneously doing any other cathartic process, do it for as long as it feels good to you or until it changes. If you find that you begin to do or say things that you might consider strange, give yourself permission to explore and discover what treasures might be hidden beneath the surface.

The more you know about negative self-styles or edge figures, the more you can keep them in their place. Your knowledge and awareness disempowers their ability to sabotage you when you least expect or desire it. It also helps you harness the power of benevolent self-styles or edge figures.

🌾　🌾　🌾　🌾　🌾

# The Power of Declaration

You are expressing your potency when, in *Dialoguing,* your angel makes a statement of desire (I want or I don't want), intention (I will, I won't, I plan to), or demand (You must or must not). Declaring yourself, standing up for yourself, is a milestone in the healing process. When you declare yourself, you are making a statement about your intention and commitment. You are also sending a message to your unconscious about who you are and what you are about. Declaration often emerges in relation to others—like a spouse, child, boss, or friend. "No more piddling around, this is who I really am!"

Declaring yourself to authority figures is often the scariest. Anyone who has considered standing up to their parents—or has actually done it—knows this raw fear. For most people, taking the bull by the horns and facing the fear is extremely empowering.

Though most people consider taking this action in relation to parents, few people imagine declaring themselves to God or a Higher Power. Unconsciously (and consciously for some), most people hold God or a Higher Power responsible for the state of their own and the world's suffering. "If you are so almighty and powerful, how could you let these horrible things happen?" Furthermore, growing up in our androcratic society with a harsh, judgmental God—most of us are waiting to be punished, often for our "unholy" (sexual) thoughts, feelings, or actions.

The act of declaring yourself as a healthy, vibrant erotic being to the spirit of God or the Goddess (or, if you are agnostic or an atheist, declare yourself to the creative forces of nature), can have very beneficial effects. Use the following exercise to find your version of, "I am a healthy sexual, alive, vibrant human being. I love my body, my sexuality, and my lust."

## Exercise #9

### *Listen God*

You can do this by writing a letter or speaking out loud.

Tell God, a Higher Power, or any authority figure who has lorded over your aliveness and sexuality negatively, that you no longer agree to accept this shame.

Say or write what you will not put up with any longer and what you intend to do, feel, or think.

Pay attention to how you feel as you speak these words. Allow yourself to experiment with what words are appropriate for you currently

🌾      🌾      🌾      🌾      🌾

# Deep Reflections

Sometimes, in our groups and workshops, we pass out mirrors so the participants can explore their reflections. The reactions are often dramatic. Some people respond in mock jest: "Oh no, not the mirror. Anything but that." But as we observe them taking part in the exercise, we know that their joking actually masks their fears—the ones we all face.

Each of us must work with ourselves to embrace this figure in the mirror who holds the key to our self-love or lack of it. Most of us gravitate toward our self-hatred when looking in the mirror, finding all the ways in which we do not fit the cultural ideal. The pursuit, when looking in the mirror, is to find self-love.

## Exercise #10

### *Self-Reflections*

*Supplies needed: A hand mirror and if you have it, music that opens your heart.*

Place your mirror where you will be able to reach it easily. Get in a comfortable position and close your eyes. Breathe deeply and allow yourself to sink into the floor, chair, bed, etc.

As you relax, allow yourself to become quiet. Feel your inner attention moving deeper inside yourself to a place of pure being. Breathe deeply.

From this sacred place of pure being, imagine looking at yourself and seeing your essence.

Imagine that the love from your eyes and your words could heal all of the wounds that keep you from living your essence more fully.

When you feel ready, take your mirror in your hand and slowly open your eyes, allowing yourself to look at yourself from the deepest place in your being.

Talk to yourself out loud, saying all the sweet and loving words you always wanted to hear.

Allow your eyes to be soft and unguarded, looking deeply inside yourself with love and compassion.

When you feel complete, put your mirror down and write a description of your experience.

🌿　🌿　🌿　🌿　🌿

# Body Image

Attempting to heal sexual shame without a deep connection to our bodies is like trying to fly without wings. We lose touch with the very source of our being. If we do not live in our bodies, where can we truly call home?

Most of us feel ashamed of the way we look. That's often what we confront when looking in the mirror. In healing our shame, it is vital that we come to terms with the body that we have been given and that we have helped to create. Unfortunately, we have to contend with Madison Avenue's and Hollywood's images of what a sexy man or woman looks like currently. We would have different ideas about the ideal image if we were living in a different time or in a different culture.

But, being here now, we must make peace with and appreciate the magnificence of our own bodies. The following exercise can support you in developing a more loving attitude toward your body.

## Exercise #11

### *Healing Body Image*

*Supplies needed: a full length mirror, a pencil, crayon, or chalk, and a drawing pad.*

Without clothing, look at yourself in the mirror for about one minute.

Turn away from the mirror and get your drawing materials.

With your eyes closed, draw your body as you remember it.

Stop drawing when you feel finished or when you have opened your eyes to peek.

Because it is impossible to render a realistic drawing using this technique, it becomes a way to start appreciating the shapes of your body.

Whenever sexuality has been shamed, there is bound to be shame about the body, genitals, and bodily functions. The first step in healing shame about your genitals is to familiarize yourself with them. The following exercises will help you further your knowledge of your own body, and perhaps, take away some of the feelings of being a stranger to yourself. After you have explored your own genitals, you may want to do the same exploration with your partner.

## Exercise #12

### *Genital Revelations (For Men)*

*Supplies needed: A hand mirror and a few pillows for support.*

Stand or recline on your pillows in a comfortable position without any clothing.

Look at your penis—examine it and notice its shape, color, and texture. Do the same with your scrotum. Using your hand mirror, look at the underside of your scrotum, penis, perineum, and anus.

Now, use your hands to explore your penis and scrotum through touch, noticing how different parts of your genitals feel to your fingers and inside you. Feel how your penis extends inside your body towards your rectum—that it is longer on the inside than it is on the outside. Use ample lubrication.

Find which strokes feel pleasurable on the shaft of your penis, over the glans, on the ridge of the glans.

Explore your anus and find out what kinds of touch feel pleasurable to you. (Many people have never explored their anus and feel tremendous shame about touching themselves and being touched there. So now take the opportunity to explore your anus.)

If you feel so inclined, make an open and/or closed eyed drawing of your genitals or sculpt them.

## Exercise #13

### *Genital Revelations (For Women)*

*Supplies needed: A hand mirror, a few pillows for support, a speculum if you can obtain it, and a flashlight or a strong directional light.*

Without your clothing, lay on a bed or sit in a chair in which you can partially recline. If you are lying down, use pillows to prop yourself up part way.

Position your hand mirror so that you can see your genitals.

First look at your external genitalia noticing the various shapes, textures, and colors.

Now, use your hands to examine yourself, feeling the different textures with your fingers and experiencing the various internal sensations.

Then, gently spread your labia apart and once again, notice the various shapes, textures, and colors. Locate your clitoris, your vaginal opening, and your urethra. Gently, lift the hood of the clitoris so that you can see the clitoris itself.

Again, use your hands to stroke and massage yourself, feeling the different textures with your fingers and experiencing the various internal sensations.

Reach inside your vagina and gently stroke the walls of your vagina. You will find that the vaginal wall is mostly smooth, except for a ridged area located behind your pubic bone on the front wall (the belly side of the vaginal chamber). This ridged, spongy tissue is called the urethral sponge and swells during arousal. Here you will find your "G" spot (named after the German physician von Grafenberg who first wrote about it). This is an area the size of a pea, which also becomes engorged during arousal and forms a protuberance that presses against the vaginal wall, producing highly pleasurable sensations. Since you will not be able to feel it if you are not aroused, simply become familiar with the general location of it.

When you have explored, stroked, and massaged your external and internal genitalia to your satisfaction, wash your hands and get ready to look inside your beautiful flower.

If you have access to a clean speculum, carefully insert it and lock it in place. Holding your flashlight in one hand and your mirror in the other, look inside your body to see what your vaginal canal and cervix look like. (Your cervix looks like a big thumb with a small opening (os) at the bottom.)

If you feel so inclined, make an open and/or closed eyed drawing of your external or internal genitalia or sculpt them.

🌿    🌿    🌿    🌿    🌿

# An Exotic Flower

In the early seventies, I, Judith, finally found female health practitioners who would answer my questions about my vaginal secretions with other than patronizing and palliative responses. For years, I was told by more than one gynecologist, "If your secretion is not yellow or foul smelling, don't worry about it." When I assured them I was not worried, I only wanted to know what was going on in my body when my vaginal secretions were clear and thin, viscous and stretchy, or paste-like, they would invariably assure me that everything was normal and that women had a variety of secretions during the month.

Not only did I feel patronized, I felt frustrated that I did not understand what was happening in my own body. I also felt angry at the medical profession for keeping this information to themselves, cheating us women from having knowledge and understanding of our basic functioning. This withholding of information was definitely a way to keep women beholden to and dependent on the doctor authority who was usually male.

Lest you think I was an angry feminist, I want to assure you that I was not. I was a young woman trying to learn about myself and my body. During adolescence, I had asked my mother these same questions. She, however, did not have answers. I found this astounding. However, now that I know about sexual repression and the dispropriation of knowledge to women by the medical profession, I am no longer surprised.

In Berkeley, California, I finally found women who were teaching other women about the mysteries of their bodies—making it not so mysterious. I was overjoyed. With a group of young women in our twenties and thirties, I learned about female anatomy and physiology—much more than I had learned in my pre-med Anatomy and Physiology class at the University of Wisconsin. I received the information for which I had been searching, and wonder of wonders, I finally saw what the gynecologist had been examining—my internal genitalia.

I also had the privilege of viewing other women's genitalia—external and internal. All of us were surprised by the differences among us—each woman's labia and cervix had a different color and shape, and our clitorises were situated differently. Though this might sound obvious to you, I was amazed that each of us looked as different on the inside as we do on the outside.

This experience gave me a greater appreciation for the beauty of our genitals. The inspiration for Judy Chicago's artwork was obvious. I, too, saw each woman's genitals as an exotic flower unfolding.

# Masturbation

Just as women have been denied information about their external and internal genitalia, both men and women have been denied access to that most personal and precious act—masturbation. Perhaps no one has done more for bringing masturbation out of the closet than Nancy Friday. *My Secret Garden* (1973) broke open the myth that women did not have sexual fantasies while masturbating, exposed the so-called "rape fantasy" and interpreted it as a means for women to handle their guilt about being sexual, and, perhaps most importantly, made masturbation a topic of discussion.

*Men In Love* (1981) exposed men's desire for women to be lusty, sexually potent, and even to bring themselves to orgasm. In *Women On Top,* her latest book on the topic, Friday brings us the fantasies of a generation of women who have been raised masturbating, who have Madonna as their idol, and who know that sexual pleasure and masturbation are their birthright.

However, those of us who grew up before the sexual revolution of the seventies, have probably experienced some degree of shame when we reached between our legs. Not that growing up after the sexual revolution has necessarily been an antidote to shame. Quoting Friday,

*"Here is the most natural thing in the world—our own hand on our own genitals, doing something that gives us pleasure and harms no one, practicing the safest sex in the world…*

She goes on to suggest that,

*we feel guilty as thieves, our sense of self lessened when it should be heightened by mastery and self-love."*[4]

Though she is speaking about women, the same holds true for men. Historically, it has been accepted that men do masturbate, though it has been severely frowned upon. Hence, men suffer from shame and guilt also. Their masturbation has been hidden and rushed, lest someone walk in and find them in the act—not exactly great practice for sustaining erections. Even with all the taboos, most men are quite familiar with masturbating—they have done it most of their lives.

Besides the shame and guilt males experience with masturbation, there's another quagmire. They question, "What's wrong with me that I can't get a woman (or man) to help me get off?" It arouses feelings of inferiority and lack of attractiveness. The internal logic goes: "If I were more desirable, I wouldn't need to take the matter into my own hands." After the pleasure and relief of orgasm, loneliness and doubt often ensue. Many women, on the other hand, have not allowed themselves to masturbate. They do not know what gives them pleasure, or how to do it. They still suffer from the sewer phenomenon.

Also, many people either forget or have never learned that their entire body is an erogenous zone and can, in fact, produce orgasmic sensations. Women and men who have been paralyzed from the waist down are capable of having orgasms from non-genital stimulation! The following exercises are designed for men and women who are not familiar or comfortable with masturbating, for those who experience guilt or shame, for those who rush through it to climax, and for those who focus exclusively on their genitals.

## Exercise #14

### *Self-Pleasure*

Set aside time for yourself in which you will not be disturbed. Get in a comfortable, relaxing setting—perhaps a warm bathtub or your bed.

Begin to experiment with stroking your entire body lovingly, except your genitals. Explore which strokes feel good, which feel exciting, arousing, or just soothing. Use lots of oil as you massage and stroke yourself.

Stroke your nipples, underarms, inner thighs, neck, face, all of your body, searching for areas which produce pleasurable sensations. Do not rush. If you find a pleasurable stroke, do it at least ten times before changing it, giving yourself time to become aroused.

When you have explored, stroked, and massaged your entire body to your satisfaction, begin to explore your genitals in the same way. Start with the area around your genitals—your pubic hair, your anus, and perineum (area between genitals and anus) and for men, your scrotum. Find out what feels good, what feels exciting, arousing or just soothing. Use an ample amount of a water-based lubricant, as you try out various strokes—a light touch, firm, long strokes, etc. Remember to stay with the same stroke long enough for your body to accept it and resonate with it.

## WOMEN

Enter your vagina slowly by softly caressing your outer labia. Gradually, work your way in until you are circling around your clitoris. Try holding your clitoris between your thumb and forefinger, and roll it gently between your fingers. Use a lot of lubrication as you experiment with a variety of strokes.

If you have not already added your PC Squeeze and Release, begin to do so now. Also, remember to breathe and allow your sexual energy to flow through your Inner Flute, bringing music to each chakra. Allow yourself to make sounds as you breathe and experience pleasure. Keep breathing into your soft belly, and letting your sounds come from deep down in your belly.

Experiment with stroking your nipples with one hand as you stimulate your clitoris with the other.

Or experiment with finding your "G" spot, also called "sacred" spot if you are highly aroused. Using your third finger, insert it into your vagina and locate the tissue where you feel ridges. Begin to stroke side to side like windshield wipers or up to down with your finger curled toward you or circling around the inside circumference of the vaginal wall. When you find your sacred spot, you may feel the sensation of having to urinate. That is normal. Maintain the same stroke until you feel pleasurable sensations. Do not be surprised if it takes you several practice sessions with yourself to locate your sacred spot and move past any discomfort to pleasure.

When you become adept at stimulating your sacred spot, with your other hand, caress your entire body. Allow yourself to make sounds and to undulate your spine or move in any way that feels pleasurable.

## MEN

After you have caressed your entire body, and awakened the area around your penis, begin to stroke the shaft of your penis, using ample lubrication. Start gently, then more firmly. Hold your hand around the shaft, moving from the base up to the tip and all the way down to the base. As you speed up, use a milking motion, making sure to stimulate the sensitive ridge around the glans. Notice which part of your penis is most sensitive.

While one hand is milking the shaft of your penis, use your other hand to stroke your scrotum, perineum, anus, inner thighs, belly, and nipples.

Touch your nipples. Men tend to forget that their nipples can be as sensitive as women's. Have an attitude of the Zen Beginner's Mind as you try new ways of touching yourself.

Experiment until you feel pleasure.

You can squeeze your PC muscles and release. Remember to breathe and allow your sexual energy to flow through your body. Allow yourself to make sounds as you breathe and experience pleasure. Keep breathing into your belly, and letting your sounds come from deep down in your belly. (Squeezing your PC muscles during masturbation can be good practice for delaying orgasm during intercourse.)

### WOMEN AND MEN

As you pleasure yourself, remember to breathe deeply, move your pelvis freely, and open your jaw, allowing sound out.

Bring yourself to orgasm if you wish, or just allow yourself to feel aroused. Remember that you can do whatever you want, for as long as you want. If you begin to pressure yourself to climax, remember that this exercise is about giving yourself pleasure, not about bringing yourself to orgasm.

If you want to raise your pleasure quotient, rather than letting yourself release into orgasm, stop stimulating yourself, breathe up through your Inner Flute to your Third Eye, and hold your breath. When you exhale, follow your breath down your Inner Flute to your genitals as you relax your entire body. Breathe in this way several times, then begin to arouse yourself again. After you repeat this cycle two or three times, allow yourself to surrender to your orgasm if you so desire.

🌿     🌿     🌿     🌿     🌿

# Water on the Knee

When I (Judith) was eight years old, a girlfriend told me that it felt great to let water pour down on her vagina while taking a bath. I tried it and, indeed, it felt great. This became my favorite way to masturbate, though I did not even know the word.

Though I felt afraid that someone would wonder why the bathtub was running for so long, I continued the practice regularly, into my early adolescence. Then came a fateful day. I was about twelve years old and I went to the doctor because my knee was bothering me. Since I was a dancer, my knees were of great concern to me. I waited with trepidation for the doctor to make his diagnosis.

When he delivered it, I was stunned: I had water on my knee!

I was mortified. I am sure I turned several shades of red as I blushed with shame. I had been found out. Now the doctor and my mother knew my secret.

My bathtub pleasuring came to an abrupt halt. Only several years later when I learned that water could not reach my knee through my vagina, would I once again allow myself this sweet pleasure.

# Good Vibrations

When I (Daniel) was 13 years old, a friend suggested that we buy a vibrator together. We would alternate using it at our own houses. I was willing to give it a try. When my turn first came, I turned it on with trepidation, hoping the noise would not arouse the curiosity of my family: it's one thing to be caught with your pants down, but quite another to have a machine attached to your penis. I decided that this was an experience I could live without, so I was very cautious when I used it.

I took my penis in hand and put the vibrator on it. I had never had an orgasm during my waking hours—nocturnal emissions were my only forays into release. (When my mother questioned me about the wet sheets, I felt shame and offered no explanation. No one had ever told me about "wet dreams".)

As the machine vibrated, I remember feeling foreign sensations. It was incredible! When I ejaculated, my experience of pleasure changed forever. And I orchestrated it—with a little technological assistance. But there was evidence. I shot semen everywhere. The floor. The walls. I even hit the ceiling. I learned that pleasure was always available—whenever I wanted it—but, I had to keep it secret.

I'll never forget when some other kids—so-called friends—somehow caught wind of our machine. One of them yelled out to me in a crowded schoolyard, "Hey, Berg, how's the machine." I couldn't find a hole big enough to crawl into. Nonetheless, my friend and I continued to exchange the machine for quite awhile, until it eventually broke. Although we did not replace it, masturbation continued—and still does.

Masturbation is a common practice for most men. The theme of masturbation—and the feelings that accompany it—has emerged in all of my men's groups. Someone will test the waters by broaching the subject. Slowly, others will admit to masturbating as well. Despite their shame, they will acknowledge their practice of it—even with pornography. Many are surprised to find that all the men masturbate. They have kept it secret due to shame.

# Healing Through Sexual Fantasies

As you may recall from the last chapter, we tend to view our sexual nature within moral terms. If we are aroused by something which is unacceptable to our belief system, we question our goodness, rather than our belief system. The construct of normal versus abnormal is foremost in our minds. We are forever questioning, "Is this okay?" which means "Is this normal?" which means, "Am I okay, normal, lovable, even worthy of being alive?"

This response is directly related to shame. It curbs our erotic impulses. The following exercise is designed to aid you in legitimizing and freeing your fantasies. If you did *Honoring Your Fantasies*—Exercise #6 and *Revealing Your Fantasies*—Exercise #7 in *Freedom through Acceptance* (Chapter 8), you are ready to try this. If you have not done them, we recommend it. If you have not reached a level of accepting yourself as you are currently, it is difficult to give yourself permission to go further.

## Exercise #15

### *Freeing Your Fantasies*

Create time and space for yourself in which you will not be interrupted.

Set a mood which you find aesthetically pleasing and which arouses your senses. Use candlelight, dim, or colored lights, incense or other sumptuous aromas, massage oil, music, soft and sensuous fabrics, foods with pleasing tastes and textures, and/or erotic literature, movies, or pictures.

Allow yourself to begin making love to yourself, caressing yourself and stimulating yourself in whatever way feels good for you. Remember that your entire body is an erogenous zone if you permit it to be.

As you begin to fantasize, if your critic or judge begins to comment, set a boundary by telling that character, "You are no longer in charge. I am free to fantasize about whatever

I like." If this is not enough to release the critic or judge, then dialogue to create space for your fantasy. Then, give your fantasy permission to fly. Anything goes, as long as it is arousing to you.

Whenever your internal judge tries to shame you, dialogue with that character, then return to your fantasy.


As you practice this, you will find that your shaming voices become quieter and your fantasies become more exciting. Metaphorically speaking, you are opening the door of the cage, and the birds and beasts—your fantasies—are taking flight. Share your fantasies with your partner or with a trusted friend when you feel ready.

One way to know if you still feel shame about a fantasy or behavior is to imagine telling it to various people. If that seems easy, do it with some of those people. If you find that you can easily tell your partner, try telling someone who you care about but are unsure about their reaction. This is vulnerability. Now, broadcast them to the whole world. Just kidding!

It is not necessary to reveal all of your fantasies to prove that you have healed yourself of shame. But it can be a measuring stick for you. As your shame lessens, so does your fear, hesitance, and list of reasons why it is none of their business. When you do not feel ashamed, you will feel free to tell or to remain silent. Neither choice will have an emotional charge. There will be nothing to defend, rationalize, or prove.

🌿   🌿   🌿   🌿   🌿

# Self Love (Judith's story continued)

I was seven years old when I remember having my first fantasy while I masturbated myself to sleep. In the fantasy, I am in the second grade class at my school and the teacher asks who would like to play being the baby today. I volunteer and am told to go to a back room where I lie down on a cushioned table without any clothes on. Then all the other children are allowed to come to the back room and play with the baby. They come to my room and very lovingly fondle me, the baby.

This became a favorite fantasy of mine as a young woman. I realize in retrospect, that this was my way of getting over my shame about masturbating. By being a baby, incapable of taking care of myself, I could not be responsible for what everyone was doing to me.

All through my twenties I was aware that I could come to orgasm more easily with my partner if I were having a fantasy of being forced to climax against my will. I would hear myself repeating, "No, no, no," until I reached orgasm. I often wondered why I was shouting "no" rather than "yes" when I clearly wanted to be sexual and I most certainly wanted to have an orgasm. As I worked on myself in and out of therapy, I became aware of the shame and guilt I was still carrying about my sexuality.

If I said "no" in my fantasy, the part of me that felt guilty had a voice. She was trying to stop this outrageous behavior. She was trying her best to keep me pure. But she could not stop this man. It was his fault I was having an orgasm. I was not responsible for it. It was not my fault that I was being forced to feel so much pleasure.

In this way, the "good girl" tried, but she could not control the show. Despite her shame, I still had sex and I still had orgasms. But even so, my "sexy woman" was not free. It was not until I faced all my shame and guilt squarely that I found myself saying to my partner, "Yes, that's it. Just like that. Don't stop."

No longer guilty or ashamed of my sexuality, I find that I no longer create a fantasy that renders me helpless or irresponsible. My freedom is ever expanding. Because I can love myself, my love for my lover intensifies. Fear and shame have taken wing. I can look deep into my lover's eyes and say, "Yes!" as waves of orgasms wash over me.

## Supporting Change

Because the process of change is so elusive, and yet so important to understand if we are to create the love we want, we are including the following two sections, *Confronting the Opposition* and *Celebrating Your Erotic Successes and Integrating Your Changes*. The first deals with the many ways we sabotage ourselves—and how these self-styles can be used to our benefit. The latter addresses how we can support and encourage ourselves to go over edges and expand our pleasure quotient.

As each of us takes more personal responsibility for ourself, for what we bring to the relationship, for how we react to our partner, for how we contribute or collude, we will be able to create healthier, more erotic relationships. Then the healing and the joy that comes through the relationship, from our partner, is an added benefit rather than something necessary for survival.

## Confronting the Opposition: Passivity

Oftentimes, we feel defeated in the face of an enemy perceived as too strong. Sexual shame seems like that formidable a force. Many people react to these forces by giving up; and when they give up, they also become apathetic. "What difference will it make anyway?" Giving up and not caring is understandable, yet given the desire to heal, nothing is more deadly. It leads to numbness, hopelessness, and despair—hardly inspiring states of being. You must remember what your life is really about—despite the setbacks along the way.

Disempowering patterns lead to passivity—the tendency to be inert and helpless. Two opposing yet equally disempowering patterns exist here: 1) feeling miserable and resigned to living in a black hole; 2) waiting for life to be magically transformed into something more grand. In the former there is no expectation, while in the latter, there are unrealistic expectations.

Wouldn't it be great if the emotional and sexual wounds we received in childhood magically disappeared as we grew older? Who could argue with a Higher Power who solved all of our problems without conscious work on our part? Imagine if this Power interceded, eradicated the problem at its roots, and cleansed us of any remaining trauma.

Although you know this to be a fantasy, a childish part of your unconscious may keep wishing and imagining that it were so. Perhaps you harbor the secret hope that somehow, you can achieve what you most desire without taking any risks. So, when risking is necessary for change, some part of you dissuades yourself from moving forward.

Others become passive because of their internal critical voices. Questioning your ability to be significant, competent, or lovable, these voices discourage you from making the changes you most desire: "Why bother? This will never work. Nothing else ever has." That voice is the one that needs the most healing. Do you hear an inner voice saying, "There's no way out of this"? Does it say, "You've always been this way and you always will be?" Does it say, "You don't deserve any better than what you're getting?"

Or perhaps you don't hear any voices, but just have a feeling that your life won't change. Or you have images of staying stuck. Through whichever channel these hopeless messages descend, you must learn how to transform them. Believing and accepting these inner messages of hopelessness maintains their power over you, your freedom, and your happiness.

Can you remember a time when you believed there was no way out of a situation, and yet you somehow managed to create success? We are only limited by what we stop ourselves from imagining. What's most important is to take positive action in the face of doubt and fear. That's how we shape a positive personal destiny.

Remember, it is never too late to heal your sexual shame. I, Judith, focused on healing shame since my early adulthood, while I, Daniel, didn't make significant progress until my mid-thirties. It hardly meant that I, Daniel, was not being sexual. However, the shame I felt—at least on some level of my being—effectively stopped me from experiencing deeper levels of genuine intimacy and sexual fulfillment.

## Stop Should-ing on Yourself

Life is filled with paradox. At the same time that taking action is crucial to healing, the healing mindset is more important than any action. It is great to have dreams of who you "could" be. But beware of when the could turns into shoulds: "I should meditate!" or for some, "I 'should' meditate *more!* " "I 'should' clean up my diet!" "I 'should' exercise more." "What's wrong with me for not working on myself more?" "I should be further along on the path. What's wrong with me for still getting stuck in this place?" How about this one? "I should be working on healing my shame more." The list goes on and on. Paradoxically, this strategy uses shame to help heal shame. How effective will this be? Not very! Please stop *should-ing* on yourself. This only leads to more shame.

Nothing is more important in the healing process than having compassion for yourself. The endless driving and striving to be better by overcoming obstacles—and being harsh with yourself when you do not live up to your expectations—is truly a major detriment in the healing process. It defeats the purpose!

In Thomas Moore's groundbreaking book, *Care of the Soul,*[5] he reveals how the obsession with changing, healing, and getting better does not support the soul. He raises important issues. Let's not focus all our attention on results without enjoying the essential process.[6]

## Honoring Our Own Pacing

Ironically, by honoring our indolence, our lack of caring and attention, we open ourselves to more freedom of choice than ever before. This is because our shadow side needs to balance our endless striving—our addiction to perfection. There is an aspect of most people which is always trying to be the best—and intolerant of any aspects which do not have the same motivation. Consequently, they experience an inner struggle. One way for the sloth (or whatever you want to call it) to communicate with the endless striver (or changer) is through letter writing. Here is an example:

Dear Changer,

*Please get off my back and leave me alone. I do not want to get better. I do not want great relationships. I do not want to work on healing my sexual shame. I do not want anything you want. Stop trying to inspire me to grow, to become self-realized, to heal shame or anything else. I do not want to change my diet. I do not want to exercise. I do not want to meditate. I do not want to love. I do not want to work on myself. I do not care about having great sex.*

*I am okay exactly as I am. I like being a couch potato who eats chocolate cake. I like being unpresentable, unfashionable, and unhip. I do not want to change.*

Sincerely,

*The Inner Toad*

The following exercise can help you confront and combat aspects of yourself that are against your making any changes:

## Exercise #16

### *I Do Not Want to Change*

*Supplies needed: Your journal or a large newsprint pad and jumbo crayons.*

Before writing your letter, close your eyes and allow yourself to contact the part of yourself that is tired of working so hard to change.

Pay attention to how your body feels and responds to your thoughts and feelings about working so hard. Exaggerate those movements in your body. Let yourself make sounds that go with the movements and feelings.

Staying in the character of the aspect of yourself that does not want to change anymore, begin to say phrases and sentences that express this position.

Now, take out your paper and begin to write your letter. You may want to write your letter to your mother, father, God, or your own internal pusher. Write to whomever elicits the strongest feelings of resistance in you.

If you are using large newsprint and crayons, try using your unaccustomed hand, as that supports the flow of uncensored material. Allow your writing to be as big as feels good for your hand. The more you allow your feelings to come out in the way you move your hand across the page, the more pleasurable this kind of writing feels.

When you feel finished, find a name for this inner character and sign your letter.

Notice how you feel after doing this project.

Many people find their sense of humor when writing this kind of letter. This helps them to back off from compulsive pushing and be more gentle with themselves.

Another way to work with these parts of yourself that are against change is to enter into a dialogue between them and the pusher aspect of yourself. Keep dialoguing until you strengthen the angel voice who supports you to go at a pace that feels good and right for you. Use any of the creative arts processes we have suggested in other exercises with the focus on a part of yourself that is against change.

As you acknowledge and give this self-style permission to be, your internal conflict will decrease. Ironically, you will probably make the changes that you desire more easily. The Tao of change.

🌿    🌿    🌿    🌿    🌿

# Letting Go of Victimhood

Acceptance encourages us to stop being victims. Regardless of whether we believe in the notion that we create and choose our life experience, albeit unconsciously, we definitely choose the way we respond to these situations.

However, our present behavior is often based on choices we made as young children in our family of origin. Those decisions may have made sense in the family system in which we were brought up, because we gained acceptance, safety, security—the payoff. But they no longer make sense in our current situation. Yet, like an old tape, we keep playing them.

If playing the victim happens to be the way you keep yourself stuck, the first way to get yourself out of the trap is to find out what your positive payoff is for playing the victim. When you discover that, you can develop a strategy for addressing that specific issue more directly.

For instance, you may realize that your payoff for playing the victim is that you stop yourself from trying to change, thereby insuring that you do not try and fail. Digging deeper, you become aware that you harbor fears about your competence. If you were to address the issue of your competence and your fear of failure directly, you might develop a strategy in which you built in success by taking very small steps. In that way, you could heal and expand your self-concept, so that you truly felt competent.

Then, failures are not feared but are looked at as valuable learning experiences. When you use your experience to grow in this way, there is no longer a need for playing the victim and the behavior drops off.

## Celebrating Your Erotic Successes and Integrating Your Changes

Many people are good at developing a plan of action and implementing it. When they complete the project, they are on to the next one and the next, and the next. They seem successful, yet they do not feel satisfied. Something is lacking.

Other people develop a plan, begin to execute it, and get discouraged. It is not happening quickly enough. The rewards are too nebulous. Each experience is exciting, even satisfying, yet, for some reason, there is no follow-through. Again, something is lacking.

These are two possible scenarios of many. In both of these, what is missing is taking the time to celebrate each success and integrate the changes into the newly expanding self. Without celebration and integration, lasting change rarely occurs.[7]

Yet, most of us feel shy about celebrating ourselves and few of us even understand how to integrate new learning in any other way than doing what comes naturally. The following story of a men's group exemplifies how foreign these ideas are to most of us.

Eight men were sitting in a circle. I, Daniel, gave them the instructions for the process. One man turned to the person on his left and asked the question, "What are you ashamed of?" That man responded and passed the question onto the next man. In this form the same question was passed around the circle many times. Responses flowed easily: "I'm ashamed of how I undress women with my eyes." "I'm ashamed of not having a more prestigious career." "I'm ashamed of not taking better care of myself." It could have gone on all night.

Then I switched the question. The men were shocked when they heard it. "What are you proud of?" The question seemed painful to answer. The men dug deep. The responses trickled out: "I'm proud of my body." "I'm proud of how good a father I am." "I'm proud of how successful I am." And then a man spoke a truth that forced others to stop and nod: "I'm really ashamed to acknowledge or talk about what I'm really proud of."

These men are hardly different from most people. Most people are taught to hide their personal gifts as if honestly acknowledging and expressing them would make them appear conceited or self-important. Ironically, instead of feeling proud of their greatest strengths and virtues, many of us feel ashamed and embarrassed.

Carl Jung discussed this phenomenon in relation to psychotherapy clients. He noted that clients will tell their therapist many horrible things about themselves early on in the treatment. However, they will resist to the last day acknowledging their positive strengths and attributes. The unwillingness to embrace one's personal value and beauty lays at the heart of neurotic behavior. Something needs to change.

We have been raised on the questionable principles of puritanical religions and child development experts who teach self-negation under the rubric of, "What is good for the child." We have learned to hide our self-love and appreciation so profoundly that it is difficult to unearth it. Indeed, the term self-love is often synonymous with masturbation.

One of the biggest problems we face as people is that we have unlearned—been conditioned out of—celebrating our joys and successes in life. We have learned to feel ashamed of them. As you work with the following exercises, be aware of any feelings of shyness, shame, criticism, and any other self-sabotage that may arise. You may want to write them on another sheet of paper. Then come back to your credit taking focus.

## Exercise #17

### *Hooray for Me!*

*Supplies needed: your journal or a large newsprint pad and crayons.*

Each day write a list of statements taking credit for yourself. The statements might begin with, "I like that I…," "I take credit for…," "I am proud that I…"

There is no right way to do it. However, what is vitally important is that you do it regularly. Just like strengthening any muscle, you must give it regular exercise. Celebrating helps you to take credit for how much you have accomplished. It creates positive feedback for the parts of yourself that have worked so hard.

A variation of this exercise is to write a list of complaints as well. You may not write more complaints than credits, but you may write more credits than complaints. Complaints can be anything from, "I don't like that…, I never…, I can't…." Sometimes people complain about too much pleasure! Many people do not think that they should complain. Yet they do. This variation allows the complaints to come out.

Besides writing a list, you can write a poem celebrating yourself. Be creative and let yourself have fun. Hang your list, poem, or letter in some prominent place where you will see it and read it frequently.

You can also write in your journal using some of the following ideas to focus your writing: what I did, how I did it, what I like that I did today, my self-work today focused on…. If you want to complain, use a reverse focus: for example, what I did not do, how I did, or did not do it, what I do not like that I did today. You will probably be surprised at how much fun you can have celebrating yourself or even complaining.

There are many ways to take credit or to celebrate yourself. You can draw pictures of yourself celebrating, buy yourself a flower or something that feels celebratory. Another way is through movement. Performers take bows as a way of taking credit. The audience applauds, which is their way to show appreciation and to give credit for a job well done. At sports events we cheer when someone excels. When children do well, they often receive pats on the back. We jump for joy. All of these are movement patterns that support your body, and hence, your whole being, to celebrate and to take credit.[8]

At first, you may feel silly doing these movement patterns as it is not common in our culture to see people who are not performers taking a bow, or to see someone begin to clap for him/herself. However, if you continue to experiment with these movements, you will probably experience greater joy and satisfaction with yourself—and certainly, less shame.

## Exercise #18

### *Take a Bow*

Stand with your feet parallel, about shoulder width apart.

Let your knees bend slightly to take stress off of your hamstrings and to let your pelvis drop into place.

Stand tall, letting your head move forward and up. This insures that you do not tilt your head back, which many people do when they try to stand tall.

Imagine lengthening and widening your body as you breathe in and out of your belly.

Think about something you want to take credit for. Then, slowly, curl your spine, starting from the top of your head, letting each vertebra move up and over. The effect is that you are hanging over, much like a candy cane. Keep curling over until the small of your back is the highest point of your body.

Let your shoulders and your arms relax, so that your arms are hanging down, your fingers brushing the floor.

Stay there for as long as it feels good for you.

When you are ready to, begin to uncurl upwards, stacking each vertebra of your spine on top of the lower one until you become erect.

Not only does this help you to take credit for what you feel good about, it helps integrate your body. If you are feeling anxious or frightened, this movement pattern will center you and help you feel more grounded.

Celebrating can be spontaneous. In fact, as you heal the shame that binds you, you will probably find yourself feeling more energetic and joyous than ever before. While on the path of recovery, opportunities arise which light the path and reveal markers that show how far you have traveled. Our responsibility is to be alert to the possibilities and allow them to develop as they occur. In this way, we organically celebrate our newly expanded self. So, be on the lookout to allow for and celebrate the expected and the unexpected.

# Integration

One reason that so many people work so hard to change but do not seem to get very far stems from a lack of understanding the importance of integration. We know that when children learn new information, they practice applying the newly acquired skill immediately. They tell friends and family about it. They use it in imaginative play. They draw pictures about it. They dream about it. These are natural ways that children integrate new information to make it their own.

We adults, on the other hand, often collect experiences. We have a profoundly moving experience, perhaps we become aware of an old pattern, or we finally take a risk and attempt a new behavior. We tell our partner or a good friend. But many of us do nothing more than that. As a result, what we have just experienced does not become integrated into us. As a result, we have to experience it again, and relearn it. No wonder we often feel frustrated with the slow pace of our change. We are thwarting our own progress.

So, with a little bit of attention, this is easily remedied. When you have just done or experienced something that you value and that you want to integrate, do one or more of these ideas as frequently as possible:

a. *write in your journal*

b. *do creative arts projects—pictures, collages, sculptures, songs, poems, etc.*

c. *post reminders*

d. *celebrate yourself*

e. *re-visit artwork that you have previously done and notice your reactions*

## Stepping into Relationship

One of the greatest rewards for building a solid relationship with yourself is that it expands your horizons with other people—most notably your lover. As you remove inner obstacles to pleasure, you are able to fly higher with your beloved. Clearing up shame and pain allows you to experience the sweetest fruits life has to offer—straight from the garden. No punishing God here!

Now that you have focused on your own erotic awakening, the next chapter, *Healing with Your Beloved—and Beyond,* will help you realize your potential with your lover.

*10*

# Healing with Your Beloved—and Beyond

*If we heal the shame that keeps us from being authentically ourselves, we free ourselves to create relation-ships…that fulfill both our need to be deeply connected to another and our need to be deeply connected to ourselves.*

Christine Brautigan Evans, *Breaking Free of the Shame Trap*

We arrive in adult relationships often reeling from past hurts, yet still filled with dreams and desires of great love and healing. As we move through life—as if a divine or demonic force were at work—we recreate situations with present lovers which are eerily reminiscent of past relationships. It is as if an invisible compass were at work, guiding us into territory which initially appears unfamiliar, yet later reveals itself as the same old place.

When present situations awaken past wounds, we tend to respond with anger, depression, helplessness, or hopelessness. "It wasn't supposed to be that way. This time it was going to be different." But then it wasn't—once again.

Take heart! Relationships experts Gay and Kathlyn Hendricks put it this way: "Nature's therapy process is to put us in situations that resemble past situations in which we have been traumatized. It has to work that way; otherwise, how else would we ever free ourselves from the grips of those issues?"[1]

Re-creating seemingly negative past situations simply means that some life lesson has not been learned. There is some skill or attitude that we must master. The good news is that these re-created situations are actually an ideal place in which we can heal.

It follows that since emotional scars develop within families and other close ties, the antidote naturally occurs within similar environments. This is not a terribly exciting option to most people. Who wants to risk experiencing pain when it seems avoidable?

Many people choose the seemingly safer course of holding back their expectations about relationships—life has made them "realists." They have learned to live by the motto, "nothing ventured, nothing lost." Even though they make themselves less susceptible or vulnerable to pain by diminishing their expectations about intimacy, their safe solution is flawed: for in doing so, they also make themselves less open to pleasure and fulfillment. In the process, part of them dies. Perhaps you can relate to this. However, there is no way around it if you are committed to healing. As Carl Jung believed, the deepest healing comes through your emotional wounds. The first step, as usual, is awareness.

# Your Parents' Insignia

Generally, we can learn a lot about our own relationship difficulties by exploring how our parents handled their relationships. Without awareness, we are doomed to repeat the past—not only our own, but also our parents. Many people awaken to realize that they've created relationships which are strangely reminiscent of their parents' relationship. If their parents had a fulfilling and exciting relationship, this would not be a problem. However, few people strive to have relationships like that of their parents.

Rather than blame or shame ourselves for any similarities between our own relationship and that of our parents, we can learn how our unconscious beliefs and identification with them, if unchecked, serve to re-create what we most want to avoid. Therefore, if we are interested in changing particular patterns, it behooves us to become aware of behavior patterns which stem from our parents. You may be surprised at what you learn by doing the next process.

## Exercise #1

### *What Your Parents Lack*

Take your journal or pad and create four columns.

Label each of the four columns with these headings:

**I Lack**      **I Feel**      **I Feel**      **I Do**

Close your eyes and take a few deep breaths.

Allow images to emerge of your mother.

Imagine or remember two or three ways that your mother experienced a lack of intimacy or eros in her life, or both. Write those ways under the **I Lack** heading ("closeness," for example).

Imagine or remember how your mother feels when she lacks each of those experiences and write them under the **I Feel** heading ("sad," for example, when she lacks "closeness").

Then remember or imagine how she feels in reaction to her first feeling and write it down under the second **I Feel** heading ("angry," for example, when she feels "sad" about lacking "closeness"). There is a second **I Feel** heading because we rarely experience and express single emotions. Since most people are uncomfortable feeling vulnerable, we express a secondary feeling which leaves us feeling less vulnerable. These secondary feelings are actually defensive reactions—designed to protect us from our own fears and feelings of inadequacy.

Under the **I Do** heading, write her behavioral reaction to the secondary feeling ("I withdraw," for example, when I feel" angry" rather than feeling "sad" about lacking "closeness").

| **I Lack** | **I Feel** | **I Feel** | **I Do** |
|---|---|---|---|
| Closeness | Sad | Angry | Withdraw |

Another way to read this is: when I lack closeness, I feel sad. Rather than feel or express my sadness, I feel angry. When I feel angry, what I do is withdraw.

Another example might look like this: when I lack sexual satisfaction, I feel scared. Rather than feel scared, I feel angry. When I feel angry, I criticize.

| **I Lack** | **I Feel** | **I Feel** | **I Do** |
|---|---|---|---|
| Sexual satisfaction | Scared | Angry | Criticize |

After you have completed this process for your mother, then repeat it for your father.

Then go through and circle any patterns that are similar for you.

When you have completed the above, read your **I Do** column with your **I Lack** column. (In the examples above it would sound like this—"I withdraw when I do not experience closeness"; put another way: "In order to get the closeness I desire, I withdraw." The second example would read, "When I lack sexual satisfaction, I criticize." Put another way: "In order to feel the sexual satisfaction which I desire, I criticize.")

Our behavior is related to fulfilling a lack. However, the behavior of withdrawing will not fulfill the lack of closeness just as the behavior of criticizing will not fulfill the lack of sexual satisfaction. These behaviors are dysfunctional, but, because every behavior we engage in is an attempt to resolve something, we can assume that these behaviors are logical—albeit in a dysfunctional way—to some part of ourselves.

It is obvious and reasonable to imagine that if we are lonely and want company, rather than sit home and drink, a healthier, more functional behavior would be to call a friend. If we lack physical closeness, a healthier and more functional behavior would be to ask for a hug or to cuddle. If we lack intimacy, a healthier, more functional behavior would be to make an emotional connection with someone.

Most of us do not take the reasonable, more functional path. Even though we may not be happy, we take the path of least resistance. Though we are unhappy, at least we are not a sitting duck. In other words, though we experience a lack, it feels too risky or vulnerable to communicate our desire to fulfill this lack more directly. Instead, not liking to feel vulnerable, we send a message that says, "We do not want it anyway!"

Then we are safe. Unhappy, unsatisfied, but safe. Generally, we are unconscious of this process. If we are conscious of it, we may be ashamed of our behavior or feel self-righteous and vindicated.

Most people are surprised to discover how similar their own lacks, feelings, and behaviors are to at least one of their parents. It is not surprising in that you learned some of your limiting patterns and beliefs from them. This negative programming is part of your family legacy. Does that mean you are stuck with these dysfunctional patterns and beliefs? Not at all.

By recognizing and becoming aware of when you are enacting unconscious familial patterns, you can have some choice about whether you want to continue these patterns or not. You can take a look at your typical behaviors and assess how effective they are in fulfilling your lacks. Once you are aware, you can then choose a more empowered action to replace a more dysfunctional one. Ask yourself, "What empowering actions **(I Do)** can I take when I experience one of these lacks in the future?" Perhaps, rather than withdrawing, you could tell your partner that you are not feeling close and want a hug. The more aware you become of these patterns, the more you can communicate a message that might bring the fulfillment you desire.

Choosing empowered actions in our intimate relationships can help us challenge and change deeply held fears and beliefs, such as, "I have been so hurt in the past that I can not trust people and will never allow myself to risk being vulnerable again." But we must choose vulnerability in our intimate relationship if we want to experience fulfilling lifetime love.

## Choosing Vulnerability

The paradox about shame is that we want to hide what we most need to expose—our vulnerability. Perhaps nothing can be as scary as being vulnerable. That vulnerability was sometimes abused by important others, and now—as if an incomprehensible plot were at work—we need to reveal it to heal the wound. When we are willing to be vulnerable, we *do* open ourselves to risk. But we also open ourselves up to the highest level of pleasure and fulfillment—and to greater potency.

We face a conundrum. The instinct to avoid pain is built into the deepest levels of our biological and psychological make-up, thus reinforcing a difficult-to-resolve paradox: The very experiences that make life enjoyable and pleasurable—emotional and physical intimacy with loved ones—become tinged with extreme pain. No wonder the healing process seems so mixed with confronting the things in life we most dread!

When we express to others how much we want to be loved or nurtured, feel weak or undeserving, sexually desirous or undesirable, or fear abandonment and loss—the fears of rejection become heightened. Shame begs us to keep quiet—to keep our desires and fears to ourselves.

Perhaps you believe that you have already tried sharing your most vulnerable feelings and it failed miserably. Perhaps you are content with your limited expectations. Most probably, you felt hurt in the past when you let yourself be vulnerable. Perhaps, you now feel ashamed of the desires and fears you keep close to your heart. No one can blame you for being wary now. But we intend to show you how vulnerability can be remarkably positive—how it can actually help you heal your shame, empower you, and help you create lifetime love.

The following story is an example of a couple who were headed for disaster but saved the day by becoming more vulnerable with each other. Telling secrets—those little and big things you withhold—is a major piece in being vulnerable.

## Empowerment Through Vulnerability

Scott experienced the pain of withholding information the hard way. Scott and Susan have been together for eighteen years and married for sixteen years. They have three children, aged fourteen, twelve, and nine. They came to therapy initially to deal with an attraction Scott developed outside of their marriage. Scott had hired a new employee, Carol, to whom he felt increasingly attracted. He also felt ashamed of this.

Susan began to sense that Scott and Carol were sexually attracted to each other. She noticed that Scott mentioned Carol's name at home frequently, and that he stayed at the office later than before she worked there. Susan felt threatened. Unlike many women who discount their own perceptions or are afraid to speak their concerns, Susan confronted Scott about her feelings and intuitions. Scott listened but then played down his level of attraction to Carol. As the weeks passed, Susan persisted and finally, after much prodding, Scott acknowledged sheepishly that indeed his attraction to Carol was stronger than he had previously admitted.

Scott told Susan he had never been sexual with Carol—which was true—nor had it ever gotten close to being sexual. Nevertheless, he admitted that he experienced a certain ease and warmth with Carol that he was not feeling with Susan. He felt attractive when he was with Carol—something he was not experiencing with Susan. Susan felt very hurt, angry, and distrustful.

When they entered counseling with us, we worked on re-establishing trust and uncovering the roots of their emotional distance. We suggested that they talk about what troubled them in their relationship. Some examples from Susan were: "You don't pay enough attention to me." "You keep leaving projects incomplete and I have to constantly pick up after you." "You don't help out enough with the children." Some examples from Scott were: "I feel like I need to beg for sex." "I wish you would not spend so much money." As they cleared the air, they revealed past secrets—many of which the other had already suspected. One from Susan was: "I'm not happy with how much money you make." One from Scott was: "I wish you would lose some weight." This process continued over weeks and months.

After they made peace with the hurt and anger activated by these disclosures, they were able to look into each other's eyes without that familiar distance, without shame—and with more integrity and love.

However, the truth-telling process was not complete. In a session without Scott, Susan revealed a big secret—one that she felt ashamed and fearful of, and had kept from him since the beginning of their relationship. She admitted that she did not find him sexually attractive. She realized that with-holding this secret had created distance between them—having experienced the benefit of the other truth telling—but she was terrified of his reaction. Would he leave her? Would he be devastated? How would she handle his reaction?

But finally she was ready. With fear and hesitance, she told him. Holding her breath, she await-ed his response. After sitting in silence for several minutes he responded, "I do feel hurt. I can't say that I didn't suspect it. If you're willing to stay with me under these circumstances, I have no inten-tion of leaving." She breathed more easily. He did withdraw for a short time. However, he eventual-ly opened up to her more than ever. She felt immensely relieved after having revealed a secret she had withheld for years.

Then, something magical began to happen. She began to find him much more sexually attrac-tive. They became more intimate and experienced greater sexual satisfaction. So much of her energy had been consumed by withholding this secret that there was little left to feel any potential attraction.

*Revealing secrets can awaken dormant erotic potential.*

Susan's increased attraction related to more than revealing the secret. Knowing how Susan felt, Scott worked on improving those things he was able to change and Susan responded positively. There are some things we can do to improve our attractiveness to our partner, while there are other things we cannot change. So telling secrets can help the other person take a more pro-active approach to change—whatever the desired change may be. At least, they know where the discontent lies and they can make a choice about what action they want to take.

Scott and Susan's relationship improved profoundly. The ease, warmth, and subsequent sexual attraction that Scott had been feeling for Carol, he now felt more strongly with Susan. Had anyone told Scott or Susan that their relationship would become more exciting and fulfilling by revealing their secrets—and then working through the unresolved issues—they never would have dreamt this possible. Revealing their secrets—feelings and fears they had withheld—saved the day.

## Tell Your Secrets

Most of us have learned to hide, to hold secret what is most precious to us—and this includes our shame. But these secrets are building blocks, no matter how small and insignificant they may appear. They can either build bridges or walls. Most people use them to build walls.

We decide that it's no big deal to withhold something that keeps parading through our mind. Or we somehow cannot find the right time to say it. We do not want to hurt our partner's feelings. We have a whole list of rationalizations that make it okay to remain quiet—and invulnerable.

The only problem is that each time we decide to remain safe and quiet, like Susan and Scott initially, we cement another invisible brick in the wall between us. As we build the wall higher and thicker, we find that we have little to say to our partner, who, not surprisingly, is no longer sexually appealing anyway.

These seemingly minor fears, feelings, desires, and hurts that we so readily decide to withhold, become secrets. We do not generally think of them as secrets. Yet, what are they if we find all sorts of reasons for keeping them to ourselves?

Secrets are poison! Nothing fosters a sense of separation and alienation as much as maintaining so-called deep dark secrets or even "white lies." There is a saying in Alcoholics Anonymous: "You are only as sick as your secrets."

So sharing the feelings and fears you have withheld is a significant step in the vulnerability process. For most people, this starts with the feelings and fears we have about the other. "I'm afraid *you* don't love me." "When you do not take good care of your personal hygiene, I feel both turned off and that you really don't care about my feelings."

Though these kinds of feelings and fears are difficult to express, most people feel even more vulnerable when revealing feelings and fears about themselves. Such statements as, "I am afraid that I'm unlovable" or "When you don't look good, I think it reflects poorly on me. It brings up my fears that I'm not enough." These feelings are often so painful, they flit across our consciousness and disappear from our awareness. We only stay conscious of our discontent with our partner—which is not as painful or as shameful. Nor must we remain as vulnerable. But we pay a big price—we create distance, disharmony, discontent, drama, and damage.

# The Healing Relationship

In a healing relationship, both people feel free to explore secret or taboo aspects of themselves in the presence of the other. By putting shame into words, we can step outside its power over us. It no longer needs to be our dictator—ordering us to withhold vital aspects of ourselves. Sharing rather than hiding becomes the fulcrum of self-forgiveness. This is emotionally risky business, no doubt, but the alternative of emotional isolation will no longer suffice.

Here is a process that can help you challenge old patterns of fear and withholding.

## Exercise #2

### *Fearful Revelations*

Sit across from your partner.

Look at your partner and ask the following question: "What are you afraid of?"

Your partner answers and you respond with "Thank you." For example, "What are you afraid of?" "I am afraid that you might reject me if I initiate sexually." "Thank you."

Then your partner asks you the same question, you answer, and your partner says, "Thank you."

Continue going back and forth with the same question for at least ten minutes or until it becomes difficult to think of answers. At that point, continue for at least five more minutes. Often the most important information emerges when the familiar has already been played out.

When you both feel complete, close your eyes and silently review what you have just said and heard. For about two minutes, think about these three questions:

What did you reveal that was the most meaningful for you?

What was most significant to you that you heard from your partner?

What did you think but not say?

Now, open your eyes and talk about the above three questions.

After this process, partners or group members (if this is done in a group) will often say, "I realize I'm not alone. Other people have the same feelings and fears as me." Most people are preoccupied with hiding their wounds from the outside world. By doing this exercise with your partner or in a group, most people are surprised that what seems most frightening turns out to be most healing. Frequently after doing this exercise, partners feel closer, better understood, and amazed at the similarities between them. The most frequent reaction sounds something like, "I never knew you felt that way, too!"

❦     ❦     ❦     ❦     ❦

## Choosing Vulnerability

For me, Daniel, I grew painfully tired of withholding what I believed were my deep dark secrets—my fears, jealousies, and insecurities. Without prodding, I made a decision about twenty years ago that ultimately changed my life. I began telling people when I felt jealous of an attribute or characteristic they possessed. I started sharing the doubts I had about myself. I began revealing my greatest fears to others. No one laughed.

Before I began exposing my vulnerabilities, I could hardly look people in the eyes. I was consumed with shame, and was terrified that people would find out how angry and unhappy a person I felt like inside. Ironically, my behavior revealed more than it concealed. My stooped head, avoidance of eye contact, and lack of friendliness were dead give always. Nonverbally I was communicating, "I don't feel good about myself. Keep away from me."

I shudder to think what my life would be like if I had not started and continued expressing my vulnerability. I am sure that I would be isolated, alone, and enraged. Instead, I have many close friendships and a real feeling of community. I certainly would not have the kind of lover relationship I have with Judith now. I know and recommend the power of self-disclosure.

## Revealing Shame

Shame exists in the shadows. Until recently, it has been taboo to even talk about it. But we have found that the more you acknowledge your shame to yourself and then express it to others, the more you will grow as a person.

The preceding exercise *(Fearful Revelations)* is ideally suited for embarking on this journey of revealing and healing your shame—simply by changing the question to "What are you ashamed of?" After working with the above question, you and your partner might pose a question that either of you generate or explore some of the following questions which we have found to be helpful in dealing with shame:

"What are you afraid of in bed (or in relationship)?"

"What do you stop yourself from doing or saying?"

"In what ways do you feel (or fear that you are) sexually inadequate (aberrant)?"

After working with any of these questions in the format we suggested, please remember to talk about what was most important about what you revealed, what impacted you most about what your partner revealed, and about anything you thought of saying but chose not to express for any reason. Though this discussion does not ensure that all your feelings and reactions will get addressed, it does create a container for those that are most charged, significant, or scary.

Finding out about your partner's vulnerabilities often elicits strong reactions of compassion, love, and tenderness. Revealing your own vulnerabilities may also be an expression of how you have wronged your partner. Expressing your sadness or remorse for past attitudes and actions is an important ingredient to healing erotic wounds.

## Making Erotic Amends with Others

Two of the most important steps in 12-step recovery programs have to do with making a searching and fearless moral inventory (Step 4) and making direct amends to such people wherever possible, except when to do so would injure them or others (Step 9).[2]

Just as we suggested that you make amends with yourself, we suggest that you do the same with those people whom you feel you have wronged. Most people carry shame about how they have handled matters of the heart. I know that I (Daniel) have been responsible for a good deal of pain suffered by past lovers.

I realized while writing this book that I had never fully expressed my deepest remorse for how I had handled breaking up with my ex-fiancée—even though I had apologized innumerable times. Though the event occurred over nine years ago, I still felt some shame and sadness about my behavior. I reached out to speak with her again about how I had handled the situation.

Once again, I acknowledged my feelings of fear which had given rise to my behavior. In times past, I had always held back to some degree. However, this time was different because I really let myself experience the depth of my feelings and communicated my grief to her without reservation. I know that I will never act that way again and I have forgiven myself. She has also forgiven me. I still feel sorrow for what happened but I no longer feel burdened by shame.

Like Daniel, you may feel ashamed of yourself for something you did with your current partner or a past lover. It is never too late to make amends. However, making amends is not synonymous with confession. Though confession may expunge your guilt, it will not eliminate your shame. Shame ceases when it is healed.

To avoid using amends as a means to purge yourself at your partner's expense, we suggest that before making amends with your partner, present or past, you do the following:

*Look for any pay-offs you may have gotten at the time of your action(s).*

*Explore any unconscious motives you may have for revealing your secret currently. For instance, if you feel hurt and angry at your partner, or if you are harboring resentment, telling your secret may be a way to retaliate or inflict pain. If you become aware that this is the case, address these issues with your partner before you attempt to make amends.*

## Defense from Shame

Unhealed shame can prevent you from admitting you have wronged someone, knowingly or unknowingly. It is also at the root of defensiveness. For instance, your partner gives you feedback about yourself, makes a request of you, expresses a like or dislike. You feel attacked. You quickly and vehemently come to your own defense—you explain and justify yourself. Your partner may ask you why you are being so defensive when h/she was only making a suggestion. Or you blank out. You feel confused, like your mind has turned to cotton candy. You look at your partner as if h/she were from a different planet.

Both of these reactions are defensive. When you react defensively to your partner, chances are you are feeling ashamed that what has been said is true—at least in part. If there were not some truth to it, why would you have such a strong reaction? If you were not afraid that it might be true or ashamed that it were true, you would be able to respond in a normal tone of voice as if you were saying, "Please pass the salt." When you feel your blood pressure rising, hear your voice becoming strident, feel your jaw tightening, see red, go blank, recite a list of rationalizations, there is more going on than you might like to believe. Some part of yourself believes, or is afraid, that was has been said to you is true! And you are probably ashamed of that.

If you are shame based, you may be feeling ashamed of yourself right now as you remember times when you defended yourself. Perhaps feeling ashamed helps you to feel like a good person, if you believe a good person should feel ashamed. However, it does not help you heal your shame. Nor does it help you become less defensive. Nor does it support your relationship in becoming more fulfilling on every level. Quite the contrary.

One of the most healing attitudes you can take for your relationship is to treat shame as a respectable feeling. That would mean that you no longer need to defend yourself from feeling ashamed. You could hear something about yourself that might be less than desirable, and admit that there is a part of yourself that feels ashamed that it may be true. You could even entertain the idea that something was true about you that made you look less than noble.

Though it may sound easy, most people have a difficult time assuming this attitude when they are in the thick of it—feeling ashamed, defensive, and protective. Since shame arises so easily in lover relationships—not only about sexuality per se, but about not feeling significant, competent, and lovable—it is extremely important to be able to react non-defensively to your partner's suggestions, feedback, or requests.

The following exercise can help you work with your defensive reaction or eliminate it completely.

## Exercise #3

### *What If It Were True?*

Write a list of three ways in which you believe your partner's behavior is negatively affecting your relationship, even if it is a small effect. Include one item that relates to your erotic relationship—sexual or emotional.

Take turns as the reader and the responder. Read one item at a time and allow your partner to respond before changing roles.

As the responder, when your partner reads one statement, pay attention to your somatic responses. Describe those to your partner, the reader, without interpreting them. For example, "My stomach is getting tight" rather than "I'm feeling anxious."

Breathe deeply and tell yourself silently anything that will help you quiet your readiness to defend yourself. Then, regarding your partner's statement, ask yourself the question, "What if it were true? How am I doing this in our relationship?"

(At this point, you are in research mode doing emotional archaeology. If you try this statement out hypothetically, you have the opportunity to find out what may be true about your partner's statement. If you defend yourself, you shut down the research mode, thus precluding yourself from learning anything new.)

When the responder has found some truth in the reader's statement, change roles and repeat this until you are finished.

If you have not found at least a grain of truth in your partner's statement, you are probably defending yourself against something you feel shame about unconsciously. Ask yourself the questions, "What would I think or feel about myself if that were true about me?" "What might my partner think or feel about me if this were true?" "What actions or responsibility would I feel compelled to take if I believed this were true?" If you are feeling stuck because you do not believe you do what your partner has referred to "in that particular way," look at how you may be doing it in other aspects of your life or relationship.

The more you are able to let go of defensiveness, make a hypothetical inquiry, and become vulnerable, the more readily you will resolve conflicts, avert them, or dissolve them. As you develop your skill in conflict resolution and dissolution, you will be free to experience the natural eros between you. Then, when you meet in an erotic embrace, there will be nothing to defend, nothing to prove—only the joyful ecstasy of meeting your beloved.

🌿　　🌿　　🌿　　🌿　　🌿

# Let's Talk About Sex

Being open about sexual feelings and fantasies tends to stretch people's outer limits of expressing their own truth. The culprit is once again shame—and the fear which emerges from this shame. We've learned to feel ashamed of our sexual desires and fantasies—and so, when confronted with the possibility of speaking them, many of us gasp for air. Our throats tighten and the words just won't come out. How do you open that blockage? It helps to breathe deeply for sure. But what's most important is the decision to just do it! Simply open up your mouth and let the words flow…or stumble out.

Of course, it helps to create a context for this. For example, "Honey, I love you and want to feel even closer with you. I want both of us to experience even more satisfaction in our lives. That's why I think it's important for us to talk more about it." (Of course, you can always point to the fact that we recommend it in the book.)

Your partner may think that something's wrong if you communicate your desire for a change—particularly if that partner is a man. Remember to use the communication tools you already know as well of those you have been learning in this book. Vulnerability is what's needed here, not defense. Strange as it sounds, vulnerability is power. Your partner is more likely to hear you if you communicate your request from a vulnerable position. Even though it may feel scary, it will serve you to let go of self-righteousness, feeling undeserving, or like a victim to uncover and express your vulnerability.

Like the immediacy of sex, the immediacy of communication about sex can bring pleasant rewards. When you express your feelings and desires in the moment, rather than hours or days later, the phenomenon of "who said or did what" is less likely to occur. If you focus on expressing *your* feelings ( I feel sad, scared, jealous, etc.,) rather than on making the other person wrong, you are more likely to experience success and satisfaction.

The following three exercises will take you on a sexual communication journey—spanning the range from before sex to after sex. We have found this communication particularly helpful in transforming our own sexual relationship. Often extraneous thoughts or images arise during intimate embraces, taking lovers light years away from each other. Communication can form a bridge back into the shared world. There need not be shame for emotionally leaving the erotic encounter—thinking about work, fantasizing about a different person, or whatever—the key is learning how to come back and be present.

However, many of us are filled with shame, guilt, and fear, making it difficult for us to tolerate feedback—which we construe as critical. And this is what makes it almost impossible to ask for what we want, to say no without feeling guilty or responsible, or hear no without feeling rejected. So the following processes are very important in changing these limiting patterns.

## Exercise #4

### *Sex Talk Before Sex*

Before you start being sexual, take turns telling each other how you feel about talking about sex in general. Is it comfortable? Uncomfortable? Let your partner know what is uncomfortable for you to talk about.

Next, tell your partner what you would like, specifically, from your sexual encounter. You can use the kinds of words you are most comfortable with, but you cannot avoid being specific. Rather than using language that devalues sex, talk about your sexual organs and sex in words that sanctify it or elevate it to a noble place. (For names that you might want to use, refer to Chapter 3—*Eastern Sex for Western Lovers.*)

For example:

*I like it very much when you fondle my (balls, testicles, scrotum).*

*My yoni wants your lingam to enter more slowly.*

*I want you to touch my anus only when I'm close to orgasm (coming).*

Let your partner know if talking specifically like this is comfortable or uncomfortable for you—but find the easiest way for you to do it, and do it! The important thing is that you and your partner know what you're talking about. (A point of the exercise is to learn to be specific when discussing your sexuality).

Also, clearing up what each partner wants and doesn't want before you have sex will set the parameters so that something objectionable to one partner is less likely to occur during sex. (If and when it does occur, then use your communication skills to process it.)

You can do the preceding exercise without including the next one, or you can combine the two.

## Exercise #5

### *Sex Talk During Sex*

During your sexual encounter, take turns saying specifically what you want, what you like, what you don't want, what you don't like.

One person at a time is the Giver and one is the Receiver.

The Giver begins by doing what feels good and right to him or her, keeping in mind what h/she knows about the Receiver.

The Receiver's responsibility is to say what he or she likes, what the Giver is doing that feels good or not so good, and if there's anything the Giver should be doing differently. Sometimes, when you are not yet comfortable asking for what you want, talking from the position of your vagina, penis, or other part of your body makes it easier to say. For example, rather than asking, "Would you suck my nipples?" you might say, "My nipples are aching to be sucked."

The Giver responds as lovingly as possible, without resistance.

Then switch roles as many times as you want.

When you are comfortable expressing your likes and dislikes, and asking for what you want, and you are also comfortable hearing the same from your partner without going into a self-putdown, shame, or becoming angry, incorporate these skills into your free-form lovemaking without taking turns.


If feelings of shame, anger, fear, sadness or any other emotions arise during this experience, they can also be included. Touching or being touched are some of the most powerful, vulnerable experiences we have as human beings. Being touched in a way that you most desire—if you have never or rarely had this experience, can arouse feelings of grief and relief—not to mention joy!

A person may cry during this time, and the other person may become totally confused. "Am I doing something wrong?" Or you may feel upset that your partner is not touching you like you have specifically requested. When you tell your partner, he or she may want to blame you in response: "I'm doing exactly what you told me. What's wrong with you?" Again, the way through is vulnerability. What does it bring up for each of you to feel unlovable, incompetent, or insignificant?

Please be patient with yourself and with your partner. Since we are so unfamiliar with allowing our vulnerability to be seen by others, it can be scary to feel so exposed. So breathe deeply and let yourself move into new territory.

## Exercise #6

### *Sex Talk After Sex*

After the sexual encounter, review what happened. Taking turns, tell your partner what you liked and what you didn't like. Again, be as specific as possible. Use language that conveys the sacredness of the sexual encounter, rather than degrading it.

Most of us have taboos that are often unconscious when it comes to talking about sex explicitly. Even with an intimate lover, most of us say, "I'm looking forward to doing it tonight," rather than, "I'm looking forward to sucking your delicious penis (lingam, wand)."

We are reluctant to say, "I love the way your vagina, (yoni, moist cave) tastes," so we say, "This feels so good."

Remember, be specific. "I liked how you touched me" does not give much information. However, you communicate a lot of information when you say, "I liked it when you kissed me gently under my arm," or, "The way you slowly massaged my nipples felt wonderful." If you feel more comfortable speaking from the position of your body, you could say, "My yoni loved how sensitive you were as you stimulated my clitoris."


These exercises de-condition us from patterns of shame and support us to speak more freely about our sexuality. They help us to become educated about our partner's desires and dislikes. The more comfortable you both are talking about your erotic dreams, desires, fears, fantasies, etc., the more easily you will move into the dynamic synergy that awaits you. Also, the more you know about your beloved, and the more h/she knows about you, the more you can work together as a team, co-creating the kind of intimate, erotic relationship you desire.

🌿   🌿   🌿   🌿   🌿

# The Healing Power of Fantasy

As you feel less and less shame in your life, you may consider sharing your most intimate fantasies with your partner. When fantasies are viewed as a symbolic x-ray of the deepest yearnings of the soul rather than with moral judgment, they become an avenue to enrich a relationship.

In *Women On Top,* Nancy Friday describes sexual fantasies as "the complex expressions of what we consciously desire and unconsciously fear. To know them is to know ourselves better."[3] And to know our partner's fantasies is to be let into one of the deepest chambers of their being. As you listen to your lover's fantasies, receive them as if you are being given a jewel. If you feel scared, disgusted, angry, or sad hearing your lover's fantasy, please reserve judgment and take some time to look into *yourself* and find out what is being activated within you unconsciously. Remember that your reactions tell more about you and your inner life than they do about your partner.

Erotic fantasies are the complex design of our psyche to overcome the guilt/shame/fear/anxiety we experience in relation to being sexual. Our fantasies contain the key that can unlock our arousal and allow us to feel pleasure and reach orgasm despite the guilt/shame/fear/anxiety we may feel. So, as you and your partner share in these precious and private (perhaps exclusively private until now) dreams and fantasies, remember that this may be an important means for accessing the depths and breadth of your sexuality. It is also a key to healing the guilt/shame/fear/anxiety you are holding in your body and psyche.

Most people keep their fantasies to themselves because they fear a negative reaction from their partner. One such man was Serge. He experienced fantasies of making love with teenage girls, although he was clear that he would never act on these fantasies. He was afraid to tell his wife, as he perceived her as critical, judgmental, asexual, and lacking empathy. When he garnered the courage to reveal these fantasies to his wife, his worst fear was realized. "That's disgusting!" she spat out as she looked at him with revulsion.

Her reaction reflected what was obvious. His marriage was in trouble. It was not satisfying, nor did it provide him with a safe haven to explore his inner life. Her continual judgment of him and lack of understanding became untenable and the marriage ended in divorce.

Luckily, their story is not the rule. When people realize that fantasies are symbolic representations of their inner life and not external reality, it becomes much easier to accept the unusual or bizarre.

Please allow yourself to unhinge from the traps of fear and judgment. It helps to accept your own fantasies first but since that is not always the case, do not be surprised if your partner reflects an opinion similar to your own critical voice. However, revealing your vulnerable feelings is a sure way out of this trap. Tell your *first truths first.*[4] For instance, your conversation might start like this:

You: "I want to tell you about a sexual fantasy I have had but I am afraid of your reaction. By not telling you, I keep feeling ashamed and afraid that you will think less of me if you knew. That is keeping me from being more intimate with you. I am aware that I'm keeping myself protected."

Saying your first truth first, before you tell the content of your fantasy in this case, helps create a safe space. Your partner knows you are afraid, sees your vulnerability, and will probably listen more empathically. By leading with your vulnerability, which is also your truth, you are setting the stage for a more intimate exchange. It takes courage and self-awareness to drop below the level of superficial judgment about fantasies—whether they are your fantasies or those of your lover's.

Fantasies need not—in fact *should not*—be taken literally. Though many women enjoy fantasizing about being forced to come to orgasm—the so-called rape fantasy—we have never heard of a woman who really wanted to be raped or mutilated! The notion that a woman who fantasizes about being overpowered actually wants to be raped is tantamount to believing that men who fantasize about women with sexually voracious appetites are sex maniacs.

Both fantasies are the psyche's clever design to help you overcome the guilt/shame/fear/anxiety you hold consciously or unconsciously about being a sexual creature. If you and your partner regard your fantasies in this light, you will be able to reap the rewards that the wonderful world of fantasy offers.

The following exercise for healing shame between partners involves one partner telling a sexual fantasy that h/she has used to masturbate or while making love.

## Exercise #7

### *Exchanging Fantasies*

In a relaxed setting, tell each other that you are going to disclose very private fantasies.

Before telling your fantasy, you may want to tell first truths first. You may be afraid of your partner's reactions, etc. Take your time and give yourself permission to prepare the ground before revealing what has been so fearful for you.

When listening, it is best to listen with curiosity, interest, and love. If judgments emerge, you do not need to focus on them. Simply notice—like in various forms of meditation—and keep coming back to your breath and your feelings of love for your partner.

When you have finished sharing your fantasy, talk about any feelings of shame you experienced or fear about your partner's reactions. Listen to his/her reactions, and breathe deeply, treating yourself with love and compassion.

Simply having your partner listen without judgment can be very healing, because you are, in effect, saying, "I'm showing a very vulnerable, very intimate part of myself, and if you don't judge me for it, then I can trust you enough to divulge other equally or more vulnerable feelings."

And the more you can bring all of yourself into the relationship—including aspects of yourself for which you have felt shame—the more you will develop trust, openness, and intimacy. Not surprisingly, the more you will be setting the stage for being lifetime lovers. Here is an example of a couple who took this risk.

## A Risk Pays Off

Jack was feeling distant from his wife, Sharon. Sharon couldn't quite put her finger on it, but she sensed that something was wrong. It turned out that Jack was having repeated fantasies of making love to a woman with whom he worked. Although he had never acted on his desire, he was nonetheless feeling ashamed and terrified to reveal his inner life to Sharon. He had all kinds of rationalizations: "It will just hurt her." "She'll get pissed at me and lash out." "It won't do any good to talk about it, so what's the use?"

Yet it kept eating at him. He found himself feeling more and more guilty—and, increasingly more distant from Sharon. He was stuck! Fortunately, he had some friends who knew something about intimacy. He confided his dilemma to them and one of them offered some simple advice: "Tell her!"

He really got it. He couldn't keep up the charade any longer. With great trepidation he gingerly broached the topic. After dropping the perceived bomb, he anxiously waited for her response. "Will she call me a heel?" "Will she kick me out?"

Slowly she spoke: "I knew that something was wrong and I kept waiting for you to tell me. I'm actually relieved to hear this. I was imagining that it was a lot worse." He was shocked. This revelation opened the door to a closer and more loving—and erotic—relationship than they had ever experienced. She asked him about the fantasies he had about this other woman, and despite his strict Catholic upbringing, he revealed every intimate detail. Sharon was far more open to fulfilling his fantasies than he ever imagined possible.

And guess what? He stopped fantasizing about the other woman. Such is the power of communication.

# What's Under the Fig Leaves?

As we have previously discussed, shame shuts down curiosity. More than likely, shame stopped you from feeling or following your curiosity about your lover's body just as it stopped you from exploring your own body. Now, having acquainted yourself with your own body and genitals in the last chapter, it's time to get to know your partner's—intimately.

It is most important in these exercises that you use an experimental approach. We call this "workshop sex." We spoke about this briefly in Chapter 1, *Out of the Pits*. We've borrowed this name from Stan Dale because we found that it is effective in keeping people out of goal-oriented, orgasm driven, performance focused, and routinized sexuality. If you get stuck, anxious, depressed, or otherwise out of a state of grace, breathe deeply, and do whatever it takes to find a relaxed state inside yourself and to feel connected to your partner. Remember, these exercises are about healing with your beloved and going beyond—increasing your pleasure quotient.

## Exercise #8

### *Let's Play Doctor*

Set aside uninterrupted time for yourselves—at least one hour. Take a shower or bath, and create a sacred space using incense, music, flowers, or whatever feels special to you.

Pleasuring yourself in front of your partner is an edge for many people but is well worth tackling. We recommend that you take turns watching each other masturbate, so that you can learn more about the kinds of touch your beloved enjoys. Also, a great deal of shame can be healed through this kind of sharing.

Take turns being active and receptive.

**The active partner:** Recline on pillows so that your back is supported and you can still make eye contact with your beloved. Explore your own genitals while your partner watches. Let him/her study the landscape of your genital anatomy. Then, when you feel ready, begin to arouse yourself.

**The receptive partner:** Allow yourself to look with all your curiosity. Learn about your partner's anatomy. Then, as your partner begins to arouse him/herself, find out whether h/she wants to be touched or not. Some people feel comforted by a hand or foot touching them and others are distracted. As your partner becomes comfortable masturbating in front of you, you can add excitement by participating in his/her masturbation. (We address this more extensively in Chapter 11, *From Monotony to Sizzling Sex.)*

When you watch your partner masturbate, do not hesitate to ask questions if you are curious about something h/she is doing—depending on your partner's arousal level, that is. If h/she is highly aroused, talking about what h/she is doing at that moment may be difficult—especially if masturbating in front of you is a new activity.

Another fun variation to this exercise is for the two of you to masturbate together, simultaneously. You can time your orgasms to come together. This is a great exercise for healing shame and promotes intimacy if the two of you are making eye contact or talking as you masturbate together.

Because there are so many taboos in our culture about looking and about masturbating alone or in front of someone, overcoming these obstacles can be quite a challenge. Take your time and remember, one step at a time. One of the benefits of allowing your partner to watch you masturbate is that h/she will become more familiar with and knowledgeable about how to arouse you.

## Exercise #9

### *Becoming Familiar with Foreign Territory*

Create a sacred space for yourselves with music, incense, flowers, etc. Make sure that you will have uninterrupted time of at least one hour.

As the receiving partner, you begin by getting comfortable on pillows, breathing deeply, making eye contact with your partner, and inviting your beloved to become familiar with your genitals.

The active partner begins by making eye contact, verbally accepting the offer, and making gentle physical contact for the purpose of connecting.

Begin by stroking your beloved's body in much the same way you stroked yourself before masturbating. Before you stimulate the genitals, use a gentle touch to arouse and eroticize your beloved's entire body.

When you sense that your partner is ready to have genital stimulation, begin to arouse him/her around the genital area. If you are not sure, ask.

Use the focus of exploring his/her genitals, just as you did your own in Exercises #12 or #13 in Chapter 9, *Awakening Your Erotic Self.* Use a soft touch as well as lots of lubricant because the tissue of your genitals is delicate. Make sure your nails are well clipped or, if they are long, use extra care.

As you look and caress, talk to your partner's penis or vagina. Tell it that it is beautiful, that it has a place in your relationship, that it is loved and deserving of pleasure.

Some people like to give their genitals personalized pet names, others like to use the sanskrit names lingam (tongue) and yoni (womb), or the Tibetan term vajra (thunderbolt or scepter of power). Other names for the penis and the vagina are listed in Chapter 3, *Eastern Sex for Western Lovers.* Use humor and have fun as you try out different names to find out what appeals to you.

### For the Receptive Partner

As your beloved is exploring and massaging your genitals, watch when possible, breathing deeply, and feeling. (Some people like to set up mirrors so they can get a better view.) Allow yourself to notice all the various emotions and thoughts that move through you. If you feel afraid or ashamed, breathe deeply, allowing your breath to help you through these feelings. Allow your genitals to speak to your partner, saying what feels good, what is desired, or what you would like a bit differently. For instance, you might say, "My yoni wants you to explore deep inside it. Please come in slowly." "My lingam want you to use a firmer touch as you stroke it."

Sometimes the receiver wants to stop when an uncomfortable sensation emerges. These unpleasant sensations often come from blocked energy stored from past traumas. If you can allow your partner to give you emotional support through the discomfort, you will have an experience of healing your vagina or penis from all the past traumas you have experienced. These traumas might be from overt sexual abuse or for women, they might be from a practice of being entered when you are not fully lubricated and ready, or not having complete orgasms. For men, the traumas may be related to sexual abuse, the pressure of performance, pushing or trying to delay ejaculation.

### For Men

As you bring your focus of attention to your partner's genitals, begin to stroke the pubic hair and the vulva lightly, then the labia—major and minor, and finally, the clitoris. Make sure you use a lubricant while massaging the clitoris. Find a stroke that is pleasing to your partner and stay with it until you feel your lover's body asking for something more. She will lift her pubic bone toward you if she wants more pressure, or pull it away if she wants less pressure. She may begin to rock her pelvis back and forth quickly if she wants you to speed up. When her movement changes, you can vary your stroke, and pay attention to her feedback. If she moans with pleasure, stay with your new stroke. If you get negative feedback—none or a grimace or a "no"—ask her what she would like you to do. A simple rule of thumb which is often forgotten is: If you don't know, ask!

When she is highly aroused (she may or may not have begun to have clitoral orgasms), slide your finger into her vagina slowly and begin to familiarize yourself with the inner chamber. As you explore, massage the tissue gently. Feel for the area behind the pubic bone that has ridges. If your partner is highly aroused, this will be engorged. Search for her "G" spot, also known as "sacred spot," which is an area the size of a pea, located between half an inch and two inches from the vaginal opening. Experiment with a rhythmic stroking (like windshield wipers, a beckoning movement with crooked finger, or going around the inner circumference as if you were stirring) while you apply gentle pressure to this area. When first feeling their sacred spot, some women experience mild discomfort—a burning sensation or the feeling of having to urinate—which passes if you gently continue your rhythmic stroking while she breathes into the area. This will enable your partner to relax and surrender as she moves into the release from a vaginal orgasm.

Many women often need at least twenty to thirty minutes of sacred spot stimulation before they experience the full release of vaginal or uterine orgasms. So men, have patience and perseverance. When a women experiences the depth of release and satisfaction from this magnitude of orgasm, you, too, will reap the rewards. A woman who is thus satisfied is likely to be more loving, more nurturing, more erotic, and more relaxed.

However, many men and women give up, feeling discouraged. They are unable to find the "G" spot or find it, then lose it, or lose patience with themselves or their partner. Please do not give up. Use the focus of "workshop sex," being present, feeling pleasure, and being intimate. Your exploration may not end in orgasm, but you will have gotten to know your lover a little bit better. Appreciate orgasm as a possible outcome, not as the goal.

When you have mastered this phase, you can try variations such as stimulating the clitoris and "G" spot simultaneously. As women grow in their capacity to experience pleasure throughout their body, they are better able to handle the intense sensations of these mixed orgasms. Also, you can add oral stimulation to your loveplay if you and your partner enjoy it. Many women enjoy having oral stimulation of the clitoris while one or two fingers are inside the yoni.

**For Women**

As you prepare to focus your attention on your partner's genitals, begin to caress his belly and his inner thighs. Do not be surprised if he does not develop an erection as most men require direct stimulation of the shaft of the penis in order to do so. Use ample lubrication and begin to move your hand up and down the shaft from the base of the penis to the tip, using firm pressure. When your partner's penis becomes erect, you can vary your strokes, experimenting with what you saw him do in the previous exercise. Many men enjoy having their scrotum caressed while their penis is being stroked. If you are not sure, ask your partner what he wants.

If your partner loses his erection, enjoy his "soft on." Since most men have a tendency to pressure themselves to perform and maintain their erection, the more you can relax and enjoy his soft penis, the easier it will be on him. Remember workshop sex, pleasure, and presence. Orgasm may occur as an outcome, but it is not the goal.

Most men require a firmer or faster stroke rather than a slower, more gentle stroke to regain their erection. Experiment and also ask your partner.

If you and your partner feel comfortable exploring anal stimulation, this can be very advantageous to the man. His prostate gland can be palpated by crooking your finger under his pubic bone. Stimulation of the prostate helps a man gain more control of his ejaculatory response as well as loosening some of the tension that many men hold in their groin.

Make sure to use a lot of lubrication and enter very, very slowly, stopping to allow the anal sphincter muscles to relax and accommodate to your finger. Some men enjoy this stimulation tremendously while others find it highly uncomfortable. If your partner relaxes and enjoys this kind of stimulation, find out what strokes, rhythms, etc., feel good to him. If he feels uncomfortable, support him to focus his breathing into the area of discomfort—imagining that he can breathe into the spot where he feels your finger.

As a man reaches the point of no return, his scrotum becomes tight and his testicles move up close to his body. If you want to support him in raising his pleasure quotient, rather than moving through to ejaculation the first time, stop before he reaches the point of no return. He can tell you and you can ask.

At that moment, you should stop your rhythmic stroking and press on his perineum while he breathes up his Inner Flute and holds his breath while focusing on his third eye (see Chapter 3, *Eastern Sex for Western Lovers.)* After he exhales, relax your pressure on his perineum and resume your stimulation. When he is ready to ejaculate, use the strokes that you know he enjoys the most.

### For Men and Women

Before you complete, tell your partner's yoni or lingam (or whatever names you have chosen to use) that you are preparing to depart. Give thanks to the Emperor or Moist Cave for being available, receptive, or whatever other thanks you want to convey. Ask your beloved's penis or vagina if it is ready to have you depart. If the answer is "no," find out what it needs to be ready for you to finish.

Share your experience with your partner. Then, before you switch roles, wash your hands well since the anus has bacteria that are not beneficial for your eyes, mouth, or partner's genitals.

# Your Right to Pleasure

Shame prevents people from telling their partners what they like or don't like, and what they want or don't want. It creates a feeling, deep down, that you do not deserve to have pleasure. Therefore, you do not ask for it because that would exacerbate the feelings of shame for wanting it.

I (Judith), have worked with many women over the years who have had difficulty talking about an unpleasant sexual experience with their partners. When we explored what stopped them from saying something, they often said, "Well, I was at least having *some* pleasure. I was afraid that if I said something, he and the pleasure would stop altogether."

This is the way it is often rationalized. Carlene expressed it poignantly. "I'm afraid that he will be offended or feel hurt. So I stop myself from saying anything. I don't want him to question his masculinity. But when I look more deeply, it's coming from a place in me that doesn't feel I deserve much pleasure."

Fabulous lovemaking that gets better over time as well as real intimacy are only possible if both people feel comfortable asking for what they want and feel free to say what they do not want. The following exercise will support the two of you in this endeavor.

## Exercise #10

### *Reclaiming Pleasure*

Set aside uninterrupted time with your partner—an hour is preferable. Just as in the previous exercise, take a bath or a shower, and create a sacred space.

Take turns being the active and receptive partner.

As the receptive partner, your responsibility is to ask your partner to pleasure you exactly as you want. Whereas the previous exercise focused on exploring your genital anatomy and learning how to pleasure your partner, this focuses on your capacity to ask for, give, and receive pleasure.

As the active partner, your charge is to enjoy your lover and have fun as you give him/her what is being requested.

As the receptive partner, your charge is to ask for your heart's desire.

Important for both of you is making sure that you do only what feels good for you. Remember to take risks to stretch your own limits and breathe through those feelings of shame, fear, or feelings of incompetence.

If and when you say what doesn't feel good, also say how you would like it to be—softer, firmer, longer strokes, etc. If you do not know what would feel better, first say what does not feel good, then explore what feels better. Perhaps you might say, "Try doing the same movement with more pressure so I find out if that feels good. That is better but my lingam still wants something else. Would you use more lubricant. Ah, yes, that's it. Thank you."

Allow yourself to make requests that might seem outrageous. "I would like you to kiss every inch of my body." "I want you to peel off my clothing as you whisper sweet words in my ear." "I want you to wear sexy lingerie and dance for me." "I would like you to stimulate my "G" spot until I am ready to come to orgasm and then stimulate my clitoris as well." Have fun and allow yourself to ask for what you have longed for and dreamed about.

When you are the active and passive partner, express any feelings of shame that arise as well as your feelings of pleasure.

As the receiver, when you feel your pleasure quotient reached, tell your partner. Decide whether you are ready to stop for now or if you want your partner to continue to stimulate you, supporting you to expand your tolerance for pleasure.

Before the active partner completes, talk to your partner's yoni or lingam, asking if it is ready to have you depart. Remember to depart slowly and with the same reverence that you have been using as you give pleasure.

Take turns sharing the way you have done in previous exercises.

When people feel a lot of shame, it is often difficult to be on the giving or the receiving end of the above exercise. You can look forward to your ability to give and receive pleasure expanding as you heal your shame. As you begin to live without shame and experience your erotic connection continuously, you will be re-vitalized and energized by the synergy that happens between you and your partner, you and many people with whom you interact, you and nature.

*An exercise that fosters this kind of joyous synergy, which we call* The Shameless Lover, *follows:*

## Exercise #11

### *The Shameless Lover*

Together, explore each other's body, including your genitals. Your only goal is to feel pleasure and enjoy each other, not to "have sex." Use the attitude of "workshop sex."

Use a spirit of play and discovery, and don't be afraid to let humor come in.

Use some of the skills you have developed to stimulate and enhance your arousal—remember the PC Squeeze and Release, breathing through your chakras, and others that have been helpful for you.

Use your entire body to explore your partner. Besides touching with your fingers, you might stroke your partner with your cheek, your hair, your lips, your tongue, even your genitals—any parts of your body that interest and excite you or your partner.

Use a water-based lubricant, body oils that have been developed for lovemaking, feathers, silk scarves, fur, special foods, or anything else that strikes your erotic fancy.

If you slip into shame or routine, remind yourselves that this is about pleasure and that you both deserve to experience lots of it.

Let each other know how different kinds of touch and stimulation feel—what feels good, what feels not so good, and what would feel better.

Be sure to share when feelings of shame and pleasure arise.

Also, if you feel gratitude toward or delight in your partner, show it and say it. Your partner cannot hear this acknowledgment too much.

*The Kiss, by Constantin Brancusi, 1912*
*Philadelphia Museum of Art: The Louise and*
*Walter Arensberg Collection*

Touching each other in an exercise like this doesn't mean that you or your partner always wants to be touched or stimulated in this way. But it supports both of you in becoming more comfortable talking about sexual feelings, expressing your feelings more easily and clearly, asking for what you want, and receiving and giving pleasure—all vital to healing shame and being lifetime lovers.

## Celebrating and Integrating with Your Beloved

Just as it is important to celebrate your own successes, it is equally important to celebrate the successes that you and your partner share. As you heal and expand your erotic relationship, celebrating all of the steps along the way can add to your pleasure and enhance your effort.

There are as many ways to celebrate as there are people. You can create a ritual to celebrate steps that you have taken or you can celebrate spontaneously. A ritual might be as simple as taking a bath, preparing a special dinner, taking a walk—with the expressed focus of your conversation being remembering and taking credit for all the changes you have both made. Or you might decide to go dancing—celebrating your erotic relationship. You might send your lover a card or flowers or leave a special note where h/she is sure to find it. I (Judith), was having lunch with a group of women at a professional training seminar,

*The Kiss, by Auguste Rodin, 1886–98*
*Alinari/Art Resource, NY*

when one of the women reached into her purse for her wallet. She found a surprise love note from her beloved!

A spontaneous celebration might occur while you are lying with your beloved, talking about the sweet lovemaking you have just experienced. Sometimes a simple statement of appreciation, or some kind of credit-giving statement can create the celebration. For example, "Thank you. You were so present during our lovemaking today. I want you to know how much I appreciate that and how much I appreciate you." If it is cause for a joint celebration, "We were great! Our lovemaking was spectacular tonight." If you prefer the nonverbal route, you might decide to do something special for your lover during lovemaking that expresses your appreciation. Of course, your celebration need not be limited to lovemaking. You can celebrate breakthroughs in communication, a heightened feeling of emotional intimacy, or the completion of a physical project well done.

If your partner has difficulty taking in your appreciation, you might remind him/her that there is no need to respond, you simply want to express your love and gratitude. The more the two of you celebrate together, the more you will feel inspired to continue your practice—and continue to take risks, expanding your edge. And, as your relationship blossoms, many of you will look back and laugh at "the way it was."

## The Power of Groups

To augment the work you are doing individually and with your partner, you may consider joining a group. This can enhance your ability to create intimacy with your beloved. Some people prefer to join a group of individuals while others find it more satisfying to join a group of couples. Currently, there are a wide variety of groups to choose from, particularly if you live in a major metropolitan area. While some people prefer 12-step support groups, others may gravitate to therapy groups. Still other people may prefer weekend or week-long workshops. Of course, they are not mutually exclusive. Whatever your pleasure, the similarity is that you have the opportunity to reveal yourself in the presence of others and to learn from your peers.

This exposure in the presence of others can catalyze remarkable healing. Again and again, we witness this phenomenon in our own group work. Often, people's wounds are revealed through their critical and punishing inner voices. For example, "I'm absolutely pathetic. No one could possibly love me." We often have people who have made these kinds of statements look around and make eye contact with other members of the group—breaking through the isolation that their shame engenders. When participants share these wounds in groups, and make contact with other people, the healing process is in full force. And the healing is not only for the person revealing themselves. The other members of the group profit as well. One person's work creates community healing.

When you are in a group or class, the group or community with whom you are studying becomes a quasi-family in which you learn new ways of approaching intimacy and sexuality. Since we learn about intimacy and sexuality through our social educations—even if it has been less than adequate—groups are ideal for this re-education process. When a group of people adopt attitudes in which sexuality is sacred, and when they participate in processes together that deal with sexual shame, healing occurs from that alone. When people heal their wounds, they no longer expend energy on internal conflicts. They are then free to create, enjoy, and manifest their highest dreams.

## 12-Step Recovery Programs

The healing nature of groups can be witnessed in 12-step recovery programs. Inspired and designed to confront people with situations which they both psychologically dread but need for healing, these social milieus challenge people to reveal what they most want to hide. From gambling, to alcohol, to drugs, these environments expose the shadow side of any obsession.

According to Gershon Kaufman,[5] the power of 12-step programs lies primarily in their treatment of secondary shame. By providing people with a forum to share their shame about various addictions in the presence of others who are likewise revealing themselves, the hidden pain of the leper—the perception that you are all alone—is dynamically resolved. However, the deeper level shame which stimulated the addiction in the first place, is not necessarily dissolved. Practicing the processes in *Lovers for Life* will be invaluable for this deeper healing.

## The Way of Shame in Sex and Love Addictions

Sex and Love Addicts Anonymous comes closest to our territory of sexual shame. Referred to as SLAA, people attend who believe they are using love and sex addictively. As wonderful as love and sex can be, if you find yourself continually having one-night-stands, affairs, thinking about sex constantly even though you may not be engaging in it, needing sex to feel loved, or preoccupied with getting love, you are a good candidate for an SLAA group.

One woman credited a good deal of her recovery to her work in SLAA. She referred to herself as a "sexual anorectic." Although she was always preoccupied with sex, she never acted out sexually. Her focus, whether she was in a relationship or not, was always on: "Is that person sexually attracted to me? Am I going to sleep with him? I wonder what sex would be like with him?"

She was always fantasizing. She found that she got herself into very inappropriate relationships with partners who, like herself, put all their emphasis on sex.

What she found in the SLAA program was that she was not alone, that she was not strange or perverted, and that she could heal. She found hope that she might eventually be in a healthy, intimate relationship. In her recovery, she unearthed memories of early sexual abuse that she had repressed as a young child. Reclaiming her sexuality as a healthy woman became a process of first acknowledging her sexual wounds, realizing that she could change, and then integrating her sexuality into her sense of herself as a whole woman.

Another big part of the SLAA program is having a sponsor. Like in any 12-step recovery program, the sponsor becomes a coach, a friend, and a mentor—somebody who is there at any time to help you avoid the pitfall of whatever your addiction happens to be.

## Healing Shame in Men-Women Groups

In our ongoing intimacy groups, we frequently found that the theme of sexual shame underlies many fears and conflicts. Most people have had fantasies and/or experiences which they think are unspeakable. They feel very ashamed and think they must be perverted. When they share their shame about having these sexual fantasies or feelings, they remove the burden of secret shame. Almost invariably, the members of the group respond in a much more understanding, compassionate, and accepting manner than the person imagined.

During a group meeting in which people were talking about their feelings of shame and guilt about sexuality, Tom, a fifty-seven-year-old, recently divorced man, stood up and told this story about both shame and pride:

> *"For my whole life, I was ashamed of my penis. It would pop up in excitement when I didn't want it to. I felt embarrassed when I thought that people could see that I was aroused. I always tried to keep it down.*

*Recently, I had an experience in which I was lying in bed and I saw my penis erect in the mirror across the room. For the first time in my life, I felt proud, excited, and happy to have a penis.*

*I had just started masturbating and this time, I really felt a sense of ownership and love for my penis. I actually stood up with exultation. Finally, I truly loved my penis. I knew that it was this gorgeous, wonderful part of myself."*

Tom's face was radiant and his body jubilant. The other men in the group were spellbound as they listened. Tom's sharing catalyzed a deep exploration of sexual shame.

A thirty-three-year-old man sat awestruck. "God," he said, "I really envy you. I have always felt the shame part of it, but never the pride." All the other men expressed feelings of awe and envy. One by one, they revealed how they masturbated quickly because of their feelings of guilt about masturbation. They all remembered their adolescent fear that their mother would walk into the room and "catch" them. So they learned to hide their masturbatory behavior. They masturbated quickly, just to release sexual tension. But they still felt ashamed. These feelings of shame persisted.

They revealed to the women how vulnerable they had felt as adolescents when their penises became erect at inopportune moments. Each man had his own painful story.

This prompted the women to begin speaking about their feelings of guilt when men became aroused. Many women described how they felt responsible for the man's erection and believed that they must have done something to provoke it. Even if they did not intend to, somehow, they were responsible. Other women admitted that they *wanted* to be responsible for the man's erection. They wanted to believe that they were so sexually attractive to the man that he could not help but get aroused.

Joe said, "You know, you can take responsibility, but the fact is that sometimes I get hard when riding on a bus. The bus goes up and down and my tight jeans rub against my penis, and I get an erection." George commented, "It doesn't always happen because of a woman. It could be somebody touching me accidentally, it could be just an image I'm having internally." The men all nodded knowingly.

Carolyn expressed amazement that so many men felt so ashamed of their penises, of their erections, and of their sexuality. In reaction to her, Steve said that he could not believe that she would say that. He reminded her of the conversation they had at lunch, in which she described her pattern of being very seductive with men, pulling them toward her, feeling excited that she could control them with her sexuality. Then, when she felt as if she had them, she pushed them away, called them animals, and accused them of perpetrating a crime of seduction.

As Carolyn and Steve unraveled what had happened between them, it became apparent that although she was aware of her pattern of pulling men toward her and then pushing them away, she was not as conscious of the shame and guilt that she felt. Nor was she conscious of the men's guilt on which she played.

Carolyn's revelations catalyzed a significant process for Steve. He got in touch with feelings of deep pain at having been lured in by women and then, just when he started feeling attracted and aroused, pushed away by them.

I, Judith, got up and started acting out the process that was unfolding. First I played the seductress. Then I quickly switched to the "good girl," saying with outrage, "I can't believe what you are doing. You are an animal. I would never do anything like that. My mother would not approve."

And that is exactly what he had experienced—hooked by a seductress, spit out by a bitchy miss goody-two-shoes. The other men who had also experienced this said that they felt like a victim. They never had understood where it was coming from in the woman. They had not felt able to defend themselves against it, and feared that they, indeed, were somehow guilty of a heinous crime.

The women nodded knowingly. All of them were familiar with the pattern—feeling lusty, acting seductive, attracting the man, feeling guilty, pushing him away, and blaming him for his lechery.

Though men and women alike were acutely aware of their pain, they also felt joyous. Uncovering these patterns, expressing their shame, crying and laughing together was exquisitely healing. Blame gave way to vulnerability. Self-righteousness gave way to understanding and compassion.

## Celebrating Eros in a Group

As members of a group become more trusting of themselves and the group process, celebration naturally occurs. We encourage this through dance, verbal processes, and using other creative art forms. We may put on lively music and ask each member to dance in the middle of the circle, or interact with each member while the rest keep the rhythm and support what is unfolding. Many people use this form to allow their erotic nature to emerge, some shyly and quietly, others boldly and with exuberance. They are not sexual per se, but rather express their life force energy.

We have asked people to share what they feel proud of and then to celebrate their accomplishments. This is usually far more challenging than expressing what's "wrong" with them. So a significant part of the work is to take credit and honor yourself. We explored this in the last chapter—*Awakening Your Erotic Self.*

Sometimes, participants will spontaneously celebrate themselves. This is not only profoundly healing for the celebrant but equally valuable for the other groups members. The previous story of Tom celebrating his penis is an example of spontaneous celebration. Phallos and Eros were united at last. Not only was Tom healing a very deep wound, it was ultimately healing for everybody to hear this story. Although the men initially felt envious, Tom's experience became a beacon of light for how they could relate to their penises. As time passed, many of the other men were able to celebrate their sexuality as well.

## Challenging Revelations

Frequently, in our groups, we would split up into smaller groups of four, each having two women and two men. We did this when we wanted to give participants an opportunity to reveal aspects of themselves about which they felt shame—and to bridge the distance between men and women by helping them learn more about each other. Using the format from Exercise #2 in this chapter, *Fearful Revelations,* we would substitute one of the following questions:

*"What do you desire sexually?"*

*"What stops you from being more emotionally intimate?"*

*"What do you stop yourself from doing or saying during lovemaking?"*

*"What do you stop yourself from doing or saying that generally creates emotional distance from other people?"*

*"What excites you most about relationships?"*

*"What turns you off?"*

*"What do you feel ashamed about yourself as a sexual being?"*

Just as in the first exercise, we asked the questioner to say "Thank you" after the respondent had revealed his/her treasure. When we were finished, we asked them to talk about what was important to them about 1) what anyone in the group had expressed; 2) what they had revealed; 3) and about anything they thought of saying but chose not to for any reason. These discussions invariably support people in feeling less shame, more accepting of themselves, and more aware that they are all human—with similar fears, feelings, and longings.

# Practice Makes Perfect

Whether you focus your healing work on yourself, within your relationship, or in a group, the most important ingredients in determining how successful you will be lie within yourself. Your level of commitment, your desire to become more aware and conscious of yourself, your tenacity and resiliency, and your attitude are the determining factors. As you heal your shame, you will find that your erotic nature begins to unfold and blossom on its own.

Yet the road can be bumpy. There are valleys between the peaks. As we (Daniel and Judith), worked on our sexuality, we experienced moments of relief, of ecstasy, and then we would plunge back into a black hole. Once in the hole, we would creep tentatively toward each other, afraid to explore new territory, only wanting respite from the agony of separation, fear, and despair. Then we would regain our courage and begin again.

As you might remember from Chapter 1, *Out of the Pits*, as a result of our own failures and successes, we developed techniques and tools that helped us take our erotic relationship to great heights. However, we found that having a great experience was not enough. We needed to integrate the principles and tools to develop mastery if we were going to have a fabulous and lasting erotic relationship.

The next section deals specifically with the inevitable challenges to being lifelong lovers. You, yourself, may not have experienced all of them; however, you have or will likely be challenged with most. Perhaps no cliché is more true than "an ounce of prevention is worth a pound of cure." By working with the next four chapters, you will position yourself for ongoing relationship success. Stack the deck in your favor! Don't wait to be dealt a lousy hand.

The next chapter, *From Monotony to Sizzling Sex*, explores ways of dealing with a common erotic malady in long-term relationships—boredom and monotony in the bedroom. In it, you will learn multiple ways of turning routine or disinterest into an erotic garden. Learn about multidimensional lovemaking and marvel at the creativity and pleasure released from what may have seemed like a dry well.

*11*

# From Monotony To Sizzling Sex

*Through spontaneity we are re-formed into ourselves. It creates an explosion that for the moment frees us from handed-down frames of reference, memory choked with old facts and information and undigested theories and techniques of other people's findings. Spontaneity is the moment of personal freedom...of creative expression.*

Viola Spolin, *Improvisation for the Theater*

One of the biggest complaints we hear from long-term couples is that their lovemaking becomes too predictable and familiar over time. It may be pleasurable and even exciting, but the same routine always happens. It becomes monotonous. Even if they have satisfying orgasms during habituated lovemaking, they do not get to express their erotic creativity. Nor do they feel the depth of satisfaction that can be experienced from the melding of uninhibited sexuality with spiritual connection. When only a limited range of eros is expressed, they eventually feel frustrated and bored.

Wouldn't it be limiting to simply be a one-dimensional character with no changing facets—someone who always ate the same food, wore the same clothes, read the same books, visited the same places, thought the same thoughts, and made love the same way?

When we resist (or don't even feel) the urges to explore, to take risks, and to be vulnerable, a routine sets in and the formula for success which has worked once becomes a formula that we continue to use. For example: Jack knows that if he touches Jane in a certain way, she gets turned on. And Jane knows that if she touches Jack in a certain way, he gets turned on. It is mechanically effective foreplay, and prepares them for intercourse. But because it is effective, they ritualize it. That is, they tend to repeat it by rote every time they make love.

Of course, by repeating this over and over again, it gradually loses its power to excite. Jack and Jane may feel that they are "just getting old," or that "the honeymoon is over—you've got to expect that." But that is not the case. They have just trapped themselves in a routine, mired themselves in a rut. Ruts are common to all aspects of life, but perhaps they are more disturbing when it comes to sexuality.

Why do we become stuck in ruts and fail to explore other possibilities? The answer is shame, fear, and lack of knowledge. When we maintain familiar sexual habits, we live within the "comfort zone." We save ourselves from risking being ignored, humiliated, or rejected for trying something new—and possibly failing.

This should not be a cause for alarm, because it is reversible. As we heal our shame, our fear and judgment decrease. Then we can move into new territory with excitement rather than trepidation. With a little imagination, any couple can restore the sparkle to their love life—or develop it in the first place.

We want to support you in putting more spontaneity and fire into your sexual relationship—to move from monotony to sizzling sex. To experience this, it helps to take risks. You may awaken aspects of yourself which are currently asleep. That is part of the healing and the fun of developing yourself into the luscious, exciting, and erotic multifaceted person that you truly are.

## Entering the Erotic Other World

To keep romance and eros alive, it is essential for partners to create a sensual world, where practical concerns disappear in warm embraces. You may want to refer back to Chapter 3, *Eastern Sex for Western Lovers,* in which we addressed the importance of creating a sacred space. Remember, there is no right way. But it is important that you create an environment which supports the emergence of eros.

We (Judith and Daniel) know how difficult it can sometimes be to turn off daily life when entering the erotic world. We also know how valuable it is. We view it as a primary element in fanning the flames of passion in a long-term, committed relationship.

Like many of you, we are married, have a child, and own a house. We also run a business together. Because we have a full plate, there are always details to attend to about something. So when we meet between the sheets, it is important to turn off the work-a-day world of *doing* and to enter the sensual world of *being.*

I (Judith) often take a few minutes to relay messages, bring Daniel up to speed on certain projects, or otherwise empty my mind of mundane details that I want to pass on from the day. I know that I will not be able to lose myself in eros if thoughts of work, household chores, or any other practical concerns are laboring in my head.

I (Daniel) listen patiently (and sometimes impatiently) to Judith as she passes on her messages and informs me on the state of various projects. Since it is easier for me to slip into the erotic world, I support Judith by stroking her body as she completes her list.

Then we hold each other and melt into each other's body, allowing our breathing to synchronize. Sometimes we lie together, just breathing for quite a while, before we begin to stroke each other and awaken our sexual energy. We have an agreement: nothing needs to happen other than us just being together. It takes away the pressure of having to have magnificent sex.

You can experiment to find out what works for the two of you. Since people make transitions differently, and men and women tend to have different timing leaving the ordinary world and entering the erotic world, it is important to find rituals that work for both of you. As you experiment, allow yourselves to have fun. Remember, this is not a competition, nor is it about finding the "right" way. Let your focus be on finding *many* ways to join together in entering the erotic world.

## In the Flow

When you are "in the flow," be it in sports, performing, doing a creative arts project, teaching, or making love, your experience of yourself is profound. While in this state, many people describe their experience as connected with God, feeling one with the universe, tuned into something greater than themselves, ecstatic, timeless, spacious, boundless, and blissful. What could be better!

Perhaps you have experienced this state with your beloved or with a past lover. Perhaps while doing some of the exercises in this book, you experienced this together. For most people, it is an experience that *happens to them.* They do not know how to bring it about. This chapter is designed to help you create this ecstatic state together at will.

# Freeing Your Multidimensional Lover

Once the two of you have let go of the world of doing and entered the world of being, you are ready to experience what we call *multidimensional love-making*. Multidimensional lovemaking occurs when partners allow themselves to express different aspects of themselves during the act of love. It is lovemaking that moves fluidly from one state to another, from one mood to the next. Rather than following a routine, in multidimensional lovemaking, partners shift in and out of roles as they respond to their own internal changes or to their partner's subtle verbal and nonverbal signals.

They expect the unexpected. For instance, partners may be caressing each other tenderly, anticipating sleep. Unexpectedly, one person's moan of pleasure alerts the other to a particularly sensitive spot or an increased level of arousal. As if on cue, the other responds with heightened passion. What was a tender embrace turns into a sexual encounter, now locked in a deep kiss.

One partner's tongue begins exploring the other's mouth as if entering a cave for the first time. The other, sensitive to a somewhat unusual sensation, becomes more receptive, welcoming the explorer, who in turn responds to the welcome by becoming even more focused on each cavernous nook and cranny. Another moan, and the couple transforms into snakes wrapping around each other. On and on it goes through several metamorphoses, fluidly switching from one state to another, moving with a mind of its own. Neither partner tries to force it into a mold, or make it follow a program. Their erotic dance is free, free to become whatever the moment brings.

*Dance of Passion, by Phil Dizick, Bronze, 1978*

So multidimensional lovemaking is not about learning a recipe or about developing a skill—other than the skill of following your inner guidance and your imagination and responding to your partner's cues. Multidimensional lovemaking is the ultimate experience of "being in the flow." It is an expression of the multiple aspects of your inner lover. Set your multidimensional lover free. Enter the theater of love. It requires a bit of daring but offers rewards of passion, delight, and ecstasy.

## Accessing Your Inner Characters

Who isn't amazed at the startling abilities of some actors and actresses to transform themselves into different characters? Consider Dustin Hoffman, who played a lusty young man in *The Graduate*, a neurotic single father in *Kramer vs. Kramer*, a street savvy person in *Midnight Cowboy*, a mentally retarded man in *Rain Man,* and an ancient Indian in *Little Big Man*. In each of these roles he was absolutely convincing.

It's been said that great actors and actresses do not "act out," they "act in." In other words, they can access the inner aspects of themselves that are like those of the characters they portray. They "identify" with their roles. They are essentially accessing different "self-styles" (refer to Chapter 2, *Eros Unveiled*).

Haven't you been able to literally experience what other people are feeling occasionally? Tears roll down your cheeks during an emotional movie scene. You shudder when you hear how a friend was nearly hit by a car. The movie or the real-life situation touches something in you and awakens dormant feelings. These feelings reflect a vital dimension of humanness, the experience of empathy—an inner aspect of you resonates with the other.

# The Inner War

When we teach people about their inner psychological make-up, most of them are initially disbelieving when we suggest that every person has multiple aspects—that we each have a host of different personalities within us. Most people like to perceive themselves as one unified person. However, when you consider the inner conflicts we often feel, it is easy to see that inwardly we speak with more than one voice.

In *Eros Unveiled,* when describing the Inner Lover, we talked about the idea that we have many subpersonalities or self-styles within us. These inner aspects provide the richness and excitement of theater when we consciously allow them to unfold and present themselves.

For example, one self-style is seductive and is eager to initiate the theater of love. Another self-style is fearful and feels rejected easily. That character is reticent to be seductive. An inner battle ensues:

**The Seductive One:** *This seems like a good time to initiate. Let's see what can happen.*

**The Fearful One:** *I don't think you should. But, if you do, at least be subtle so that if h/she isn't interested, it won't be obvious that you are hanging out on the line.*

One voice wants to go for it, the other wants to play it safe.

Our inner tension builds but the curtain remains drawn at the theater of love. We are stymied by the inner aspects of ourselves which are engaged in endless conflict.

# Creating Inner Harmony and Excitement

Most of the time, at least some of our inner characters are operating at cross-purposes. You can easily verify this by asking yourself if there is anything that you feel you *should* be doing but are not. Invariably, you will be able to come up with many examples.

The conflicts among our inner characters cause us to experience great stress and pain. Resolving these conflicts can bring about beneficial physical and emotional healing. It also allows us to enter the theater of love and become multidimensional lovers.

How do you do it? The first step is to become aware of the situation. Simply recognizing when an inner conflict develops can help you turn your attention from trying to deny discomfort to creating long-lasting conflict resolution. Then, using various techniques you can discover what each of your subpersonalities are attempting to accomplish and find ways to get them to work together.

For example, Dan and Elise entered couples therapy during their engagement to address a variety of issues that were surfacing as their wedding day drew near. Developing themselves as lovers was high on their list. During one session, Elise expressed concern about feeling awkward and uncomfortable when Dan suckled at her breast. At first she found it arousing, but if he suckled for a sustained period of time, she would gently steer him away from her breast.

However, Dan did not want to be steered away. He enjoyed himself and he could tell that she was enjoying herself as well—that is, until something seemingly turned her off.

As we unraveled her inner drama, Elise revealed that when Dan suckled at her breast, she began to think of him as a child and herself as the mother. Since this was not a role she wanted to occupy in daily life with Dan, she felt uncomfortable. She believed that if she were to indulge in her feelings of pleasure and allow him to suckle, she would be taking on a maternal role that would carry into their life outside of lovemaking. To complicate matters, she was ashamed that she felt aroused and maternal at the same time. Elise became paralyzed from her inner conflict and rather than becoming vulnerable and disclosing her dilemma, she began blaming Dan for wanting to suckle.

The way out was entering the theater of love and developing multidimensional lovemaking. First, it was important that Elise and Dan realized that the roles they took on while making love were similar to actors and actresses playing parts on stage. Second, they had to learn that they could occupy a certain role for a period of time and then change to another role, just as if they were having a fantasy. Third, they had to let go of rigid images they had about how lovemaking should be and adopt an attitude of being in the flow.

Elise felt tremendous relief when she realized that they could enter the world of fantasy and take on different roles as their love theater unfolded without negatively affecting their relationship. Much to her surprise, by allowing their inner characters to have a voice and to interact, she soon learned that there were untold positive effects. As their lovemaking became more spontaneous, it also became more exciting. They found that their lovemaking became a stage for their deep inner stirrings to emerge. They became comfortable with the idea that many characters lived inside them, so that when a character emerged, they supported its emergence. As their deepest desires were played out, their intimacy blossomed.

After discovering the joys of multidimensional lovemaking, in part by letting go of shame, Elise had an ecstatic experience: "I was making love with Dan by candlelight, and his face looked like the god Pan. I just let myself enter into that fantasy, and I became a nymph. "

Interestingly, tantra embraces the use of fantasy in lovemaking. In tantra, you are seen as a soul, so there is a recognition that various manifestations of the personality may emerge as you are engaged in lovemaking. You may see your lover in some other kind of form. Tantra encourages lovers to join each other in fantasy as these various forms unfold.

The next exercise is designed to support you in creating your own theater and developing the skills of a multidimensional lover. We have found that the use of gloccolalia—making sounds that use the cadence of the spoken word or that use a foreign or animal rhythm of speech—together with dramatic improvisation, develops spontaneity, a sense of play, and promotes inner freedom. It can also be a whole lot of fun. And these are key ingredients to multidimensional lovemaking.

## Exercise #1

### *The Dialogue of Gloccolalia*

Stand facing your partner. Take a few long, deep breaths together while making eye contact.

Partner A begins by making sound language (gloccolalia), gesticulating, and moving in character with the sounds.

Partner B responds in whatever way h/she wants. This is also with sound and movement.

Partner A responds and so on as if the two of you were carrying on an improvisational theatrical skit or dialogue. Since you do not know what your partner is going to do, or how you are going to respond to it, there is no way to rehearse. There is no way to be wrong or make a mistake. Whatever you do is okay.

Allow yourself to be as wild, crazy, passionate, tender, silly, humorous, serious, angry, afraid, sad, or sexy as you dare. This is a way to push the limits of your comfort zone and play. Have fun and take risks. Act out what you normally do not allow yourself to do.

Allow the improvisation to go for at least ten minutes before stopping. Then let partner B initiate and see what happens differently.

When both people have had a turn initiating, talk about your experience together. Remember, this is not a review of what the other person did "wrong," it is how you felt when you or your partner played various parts.


Do not be surprised if this exercise brings up conflictual issues—for yourself or between you and your partner. Also, do not be surprised if the two of you stop the exercise shortly after you have begun. You can feel quite vulnerable, and many people look at each other and say, "This is silly. Let's not do it." If you look deeper, you may become aware of shame—in this case, the fear of being humiliated. We challenge you to go further.

When you improvise in this way, even though you are playing, your fears, hopes, and reactions are still yours. If you do get stuck—whether you are paralyzed or in a fight—try using the same form to move out of it. But tell your partner what you would like him/her to do differently. Then talk about your experience being as vulnerable as you will possibly allow yourself. Remember, you are on the path together.

Hopefully, your experience improvising with gloccolalia was fun. As you play with this form, allow yourself to be more and more authentic as you act, sound, and respond. In this way, the more vulnerable aspects of yourself will feel safe enough to emerge as well. The same spontaneity, willingness to go into the fantasy play, and freedom to become any kind of character are the skills that you will use as you enter the theater of multidimensional lovemaking.

The following exercise can provide you with a taste of multidimensional lovemaking, even though it is planned. Although it lacks the spontaneous element, it can still help you free your inner aspects and experiment with stretching your limits.


## Exercise #2

### *Acting In*

For the woman: At some point during lovemaking, imagine yourself to be the Mother, at another point you might be the Little Girl, and at other points the Wild Animal, the Erotic Nymph, or the Sleazy Hooker. Let yourself be anyone you want to, as long as it is not harmful to your partner.

For the man: At some point you might imagine yourself to be the Sensitive Poet, the Cosmopolitan Lover, the Cave Man, the Little Boy, or whatever you feel might be fun and exciting, as long as it is not harmful to your partner.

For both of you:

Let you imagination run free: you might feel yourself to be some kind of animal or even, say, a beautiful flower.

Don't be alarmed if your imaginary roles become cross-sexual; there are both male and female aspects to each of us. So, for example, the man may momentarily become a woman, and vice versa. The same goes for androgyny; you might feel yourself to be both male and female at the same time.

If you are in sexual union, and you become aware of an image of your lover, say, as a god or goddess, it could be that the image of your lover is of your same gender—it can be a wonderful experience to allow yourself to go into that image, deeply, fully, to allow your lover to become that god or goddess.

When this happens, there is no need to talk about it in the moment, unless you want to. Your partner may not be aware of the specific content of your fantasy, but he or she will often psychically pick up the energy of it—and the two of you can begin a dance that is otherworldly and often ecstatic.

In multidimensional lovemaking there is tremendous fluidity between you and your partner and among the roles that each of you can play, moment-by-moment.

You can practice by pre-arranging your roles or allowing them to develop spontaneously. They are whatever each of you, individually or together, want them to be. As you feel free to enter your fantasy world and bring it into your lovemaking, monotony will be replaced by sizzle, excitement, and passion.

🌿   🌿   🌿   🌿   🌿

# Erotic Fantasies

Another way to add sizzle to your lovemaking is to enact your fantasies with your beloved. You might gasp and say, "No way! It was one thing to tell my fantasy, but act it out? H/she would think I was crazy and would never agree to that."

Consider that you might be wrong. What a loss to not even try! Perhaps there is a way you can allow yourself to follow your impulses (those that do not harm anyone) without having to worry about how you might be perceived. Take a risk! Allow your beloved into the deepest chamber of your soul. Have fun and enjoy the ride!

In *Eros Unveiled,* we talked about adopting a "dance attitude" in which all life becomes an art experience. If you do this, your lovemaking takes on the quality of fine art, and your sexual relationship becomes a stage on which to play the theater of your self. If you use this attitude during your sex play, your fantasies will flourish, and the many facets of yourself which may have been lying dormant will come to life.

# Erotic Imprints

Many people's fantasies involve psychic erotic imprints which we talked about in Chapter 8, *Freedom Through Acceptance*. If you remember that your fantasy is just that and is NOT necessarily something you really want to do or be done to you, it is possible to turn it into theater. This is possible only if both of you stay out of judgment and condemnation.

In *Freedom Through Acceptance,* we talked about Harry, a man in his forties, who aroused himself with a fantasy that involved a psychic erotic imprint from his early childhood. When he understood that the abuse he had experienced at the hands of his babysitter had created a psychic erotic imprint, and did not mean that he was perverted, he welcomed the fantasy.

Sharing this fantasy with his partner was possible after he stopped shaming himself for having it. Asking her to participate was still difficult because he did not know how she would receive it. He finally took the risk. After addressing her feelings of anger at the babysitter and sadness for Harry, Nancy was ready to enter the theater of his fantasy.

First, she had to separate reality from fantasy. By participating in Harry's fantasy, she had to remind herself that she would not be perpetrating a crime. She would simply be joining his erotic fantasy world. Second, she had to recognize that just because she played the part of the sexually inappropriate babysitter, this did not mean that she would do something like this in life outside of the fantasy world. Giving herself this inner freedom allowed her to move on to the third step. That was to find the character within herself that could act out such a role.

## The Theatre of Your Self

For this, Nancy had to access one of her self-styles that would do something dishonorable. Though she knew she would never do anything like his fantasy in her waking life, she was aware and accepting of herself enough to recognize shadow aspects of herself that would or had done something she considered naughty. She drew on these experiences to play the character in Harry's fantasy.

The notion that she would arouse him by acting surreptitiously also excited her. One Saturday afternoon when Harry was taking a nap, Nancy seized the opportunity. Quietly and deftly, she loosened his pants and began to stimulate his penis. Harry took the cue and feigned sleep. Nancy went to town.

Using a lubricant, her fingers wrapped around the shaft of his penis, she moved up and down rhythmically. With her other hand, she fondled his testicles, caressed his inner thighs and his belly. Harry showed no signs of being awake—that is, other than his erect penis. Before the point of no return, Nancy stopped what she was doing and pressed on Harry's perineum. He still feigned sleep.

She aroused him once again, this time using her mouth and her tongue. Still no sounds, no movement other than that of his erect penis—and a little heavy breathing. Once again, before the point of no return, she stopped and waited, pressing on his perineum.

Nancy slipped out of her jogging suit. She leaned over, got the lubricant, and poured some into her hand. While one hand resumed her efforts on the shaft of Harry's penis, her other hand found her clitoris. She massaged it gently, then rolled it between her thumb and forefinger. She let out a little moan. Harry still feigned sleep.

When Nancy felt her vagina pulsing with life, she kneeled over Harry, inserted his erect penis into her vagina, and began moving up and down slowly. As she moved up his shaft, she squeezed her PC muscle, pulling him into her; then, as she moved down his shaft, she softened her PC muscle, allowing his penis to fill her.

She began to move faster. Harry's eyes remained closed. She felt his gluteal muscles tighten and she knew he was about to climax. Finally, he opened his eyes and smiled for a moment. Then, his body convulsed in a powerful and delicious orgasm, his deep moans filling the room. "That was perfect," he whispered, while he pulled Nancy closed to him. "When can I join *your* fantasy?"

Interestingly enough, Nancy's favorite fantasy had some similarities to Harry's. It was not based on a traumatic experience. But it did involve another man—in this case a stranger—who was portrayed as the greatest lover on earth. This is Nancy's fantasy.

The first scene varied. Sometimes it started in Nancy's office, sometimes on a secluded beach, at a park, alone on a small island, or in her own bed.

The second scene was always the same. She would take a short nap and begin to dream about an unrecognizable yet familiar man coming to her and making love to her in the most sumptuous manner. He would caress every inch of her body until every molecule was aroused. He knew exactly what to do to drive her to a state of ecstasy. He would continue to bring her to orgasm after orgasm until she dissolved into the blissful state of oneness with the universe.

The last scene also varied. Sometimes he would enter her and they would continue to make love until the two of them became a vibrating mass of energy, with no distinction between their bodies and the cosmos. Other times, he would hold her until she fell fast asleep.

Since Harry and Nancy had a healthy attitude about sharing in each other's fantasies, Harry had only to deal with some feelings of jealousy that the ultimate lover of her fantasy was someone other than him. He decided, without telling Nancy, that he would compete with her fantasy lover—and win. He did not wait long to try his luck.

Nancy stretched and yawned. It had been a busy day. She had been on the go since eight that morning. She would get to the paperwork on her desk, but first she would take a short nap, a little pick-me-up.

She stretched out on the couch, dropped her head back on the cushion, and before she realized it was fast asleep. As she slept, she dreamed of her familiar but unidentifiable lover coming to her in the night. It was dark and she could hardly see his face. But she could feel his body pressing against hers. She brought her hands to his head, entwined her fingers in his curly hair, and smelled his familiar, delicious aroma.

He kissed her gently. Slowly, his tongue found her tongue, and they melted into one. Just as slowly, his lips and tongue found their way around her ear, down her neck, and to her erect nipples. She shivered with pleasure. He licked and sucked her breasts with surety and enjoyment. She could feel her clitoris awakening. Her vulva was pulsating, already wet with anticipation. Her yoni longed for his mouth.

Gently, she moved his head off of her breasts, pushing him downward. He would not be hurried. Once again, his lips and tongue began a slow journey downward—down her stomach, over the soft curve of her belly. until his face was buried between her thighs. She couldn't stand waiting much longer. Her clitoris was throbbing, wanting to be enfolded by his warm, moist tongue.

In her dream now, she was naked. Her dream lover was playing her like an instrument. Her strings were quivering under the touch of his tongue. She wanted him so badly. Her pelvis arched towards him, begging him to satisfy her. His tongue was licking and bathing the lips of her vagina, then probing deep within in it, and finally, flicking across her throbbing clitoris, sucking it, driving her to ecstasy.

Suddenly she was yanked from her slumber into the reality of her office setting. She sat upright, wide awake, her body quivering in orgasm.

"Oh God!" she said, realizing that she was no longer in her dream world. She was wide awake in the real world and Harry was with her, his head buried between her legs, his dancing tongue bringing on waves and waves of undulating orgasms. She laughed with delight as she realized what he was doing.

"Don't stop!" she said, her breath rapid, her gutteral moans of ecstasy filling the room. "But a little harder. Don't go faster, just harder."

He responded immediately, pressing more tightly against her, his tongue a moist and nimble tool of pleasure that swept her into sweet oblivion once again.

Her pelvis moved involuntarily, a slow, rhythmic swiveling up and down, up and down. She let the delicious feelings spread through her.

She knew her beloved was also lost in the pleasure of stimulating her—his head was moving up and down, following her own movements perfectly, so that no matter how she thrust her pelvis, his tongue was right with her.

And now she wanted him to be even more gentle. "Softer, even softer. Yes." She hardly had to tell him before he was responding. She knew he wanted to please her and would do anything she asked. Her heart swelled with gratitude and love for Harry. These thoughts were lost as another wave of orgasms spread through her body, leaving her limp.

"Come inside me," she whispered.

Without moving his mouth, his fingers found their way inside her wet and slippery yoni, searching for her sacred "G" spot. Rhythmically, his fingers swept across her sacred spot, deftly massaging, almost milking her juices.

Her audible moan let him know that he had found the right place. Changing images swept through her mind. She remembered when they first met and they were young. Then she imagined that she was a flower and he was moving deep inside the center of the flower. Then she became liquid lava. Suddenly, the two of them were birds, flying gracefully, silhouetted against the moon. Fireworks were going off inside her—brilliant, light bursts of colored energy. She was cells bursting with life, singing to the stars!

She surrendered willingly to the onslaught of sensations that filled her body. She felt out of control, deliciously out of control, and totally safe at the same time.

As each successive wave of orgasms swept over her, she opened more deeply, until she felt that she had reached the core of her being. Deep, guttural moans of pleasure filled the room as her entire body undulated as if it would never stop. Then, finally, her entire body trembling, the last orgasm cascaded through her—her sweet liquid gushing forth.

It was good, it was so good!

Finally she lay in a state of ecstatic exhaustion, utterly, completely content.

After a few moments, she felt his head come close to hers, felt a tender kiss on her lips. She chuckled—his nose was wet.

"You were wonderful," she said.

"So were you," he replied. It was like me having the orgasms with you."

"How was the timing with my finger?"

"Perfect, just perfect. Should I do the same for you? Do you want me to?"

"No, my love, let's wait until tonight or tomorrow. You're so drowsy now, why don't you just…"

She was asleep before he could finish his sentence, and he kissed her lightly on the lips once again, and pulled a throw over her.

"I love you," he whispered, and softly tiptoed out of her office.

This was not an unusual occurrence for these lovers—with few exceptions, all of their sexual encounters were events of sublime passion, of total giving and receiving. And the bond it wrought between them was something to behold.

As well as knowing what your partner wants and becoming adept at doing it, sizzling sex depends upon the right attitudes: when you and your partner allow yourselves to be vulnerable; when you are both able to reveal your private fears and desires to each other; when you are both able to freely express your imagination, your fantasies, and your secret longings in a safe, secure environment then a marvelous, erotic energy is available to heighten your sexual encounters and turn them into transcendent experiences.

The ecstatic power within you lies waiting. Be adventuresome, be vulnerable, be open, be free—and watch your sex life change from monotony to sizzle.

## Exercise #3

### *Enacting a Mutual Fantasy*

Tell your partner that you want to share a fantasy you have and that you would like to incorporate it into your love theater in some way. Get your partner's agreement that he or she will enter your fantasy world, will allow you to direct him or her, but will only do what feels reasonably comfortable for him or her.

You become the director and lead role while your partner plays the supporting role. As director, you set the stage in any way you want. When you feel ready, tell your fantasy to your partner. In the role of director, it is up to you to tell your partner exactly how to act in the supporting role.

If you feel that your intent is not understood, a good way to get your idea across is to show your partner what you want.

As the two of you move into the fantasy, make sure you both ask for and give each other feedback.

#### Director

You are allowed to and supposed to make corrections. It is okay to say such things as, "When you do this, please be more gentle," or "Look this way instead of that way." Making statements of appreciation always helps. For instance, "That's it. You're doing it just the way I wanted. Thanks."

If you ask your partner to do things that you know h/she doesn't like to do, you will probably not have the kind of experience for which you are longing. You might ask your partner to do things that are a stretch for him or her, but do not take this as an opportunity to treat your lover as a master might abuse a slave.

#### Supporting Partner

You are allowed—in fact, encouraged—to ask such questions as, "Am I doing it right?" or "Is this what you had in mind?"

Remember, in the supporting role, only do what you feel comfortable doing. If you try something and find that you don't feel good about doing it, stop. If you are uncomfortable joining into your partner's fantasy in a particular way, it does not mean that anything is wrong with you or that anything is wrong with your partner. If you start going into blame or self-deprecation, stop what you are doing, breathe deeply, and find out what is going on under the blame. It's likely to be fear or shame.

After you find out what fears about yourself are triggering your feelings, then come back to your partner's fantasy and explore how you might participate in a way that is more comfortable for you.

In the supporting role, you have an opportunity to serve your lover totally. When you enter into your lover's fantasy fully, you are giving yourself and your partner the experience of your unfettered "Yes." If you are feeling yourself holding back, find out what you need to do to surrender into this position of the giver.

When your fantasy theater feels finished, talk together about how this experience was for you, what you liked and what you didn't like, what you would do the same and what you would do differently.

This process can be great fun and deeply satisfying if you enter in with the attitude of play, a "dance attitude," or remember that you are creating your own theater. Few people allow themselves the pleasure of asking for their heart's or soul's desire. Please, take this opportunity to indulge yourself.

It can also be very challenging for both people. Few people have been schooled in this type of relationship exploration—so be compassionate and playful with yourself and your partner.

If you or your partner has been sexually abused as a child, as a survivor, you may have difficulty entering into some of the fantasies that you or your partner imagine. Please do not use this to go into shame or blame! Whether or not you are conscious of the abuse, your body stores the memory of it in your cells. So, if the fantasy you hear or begin to enact is similar in *any* way or reminiscent of the abuse perpetrated, you may have an unexpected and surprising somatic emotional reaction.

You may choose to use many of the exercises in the preceding chapters to heal the shame that you experienced. However, we recommend that the adult who was abused as a child seek therapy or find a support group to address the feelings and subsequent beliefs and behaviors that were established after experiencing sexual abuse. If available, the partner can find support from a group for partners of survivors or a therapist familiar with abuse.

Also, if someone is always enacting the same fantasy, then it may be useful to discover what is driving the fantasy. It may be valuable to ask yourself what is wanting to be fulfilled through this fantasy. For example, if a man always wants to be a suckling child, we might find if we looked more deeply into this, that he wants more nurturing in his life.[1] Once aware of this, rather than attempting to get this need fulfilled in the sexual arena alone, he could focus on developing other ways of being receptive and receiving nurturing.

If your fantasies involve attractions to people other than your beloved (which many people's do), these, also, can be used productively in developing your erotic bond. We address this specifically in Chapter 13, *Handling Other Attractions*.

                                  ✌   ✌   ✌   ✌   ✌

# Erotic Accessories

As you and your partner enacted a fantasy together, you may have used or at least felt the desire to use props or costumes. Just as in the theater where props and costumes help the actors and actresses create a mood or an effect, they can help you set the stage for the theater of your erotic relationship.

As various facets of yourself show themselves, experiment with using props, costumes, or other erotic accessories with the same attitude of play, a "dance attitude," or creating your own theater.

If you have had any shame about your sexuality, you probably have not ventured into a store which sells sexual enhancement products. It's never too late. Make an adventure out of it. Go with your partner to an adult store or, if you prefer, a lingerie department. If you don't yet feel comfortable doing this, there are catalogues you can browse through together in the privacy of your own home. Or be creative and find sensual textures, fabrics, feathers, music, etc., around the house to use in your love theater.

## Exercise #4

### *Sexual Enhancement Exploration*

Go to an adult sexuality shop, a lingerie shop, or a store that you would not otherwise frequent, or procure a specialty catalogue.

Buy something that has to do with sexual or sensual pleasure. It may be body oils, sexy lingerie, a vibrator or erotic pictures.

Back at home, with your partner, explore and play with the sexual enhancement things you have gotten.

Use these props and costumes to help yourselves focus and develop the facets of your multidimensional lover. Imagine that you are creating a cast of characters as you experiment with various props.

If you begin to have feelings that you are doing something that is shameful, or something that is naughty, dirty, bad, or silly, use this as an opportunity to heal your shame. You may tell your partner that you are having these feelings so your partner can support you, or you might want to work internally with yourself as you are engaged in this sex play.

Keep using your sexual enhancement items as you feel these shameful feelings. As you do, search within yourself for another voice to come in and say, "This is my birthright, this is really okay."

Find the part inside you that really does believe that. It's not just enough to say it, but you've got to find the part inside that really believes it, even if that part is only one percent of you right now.

🌿  🌿  🌿  🌿  🌿

## Adding Spice and Surprises

If you think of your erotic relationship as theater, the first act would be to set the stage and focus on building the tension (building arousal), the second act would be your actual lovemaking, and act three would include the climax and dénouement. There are no limits to the number of scenes you can have in each act. For instance, act one might include five scenes, all building arousal: scene one might start at home getting dressed to go out; scene two might be eating dinner at a romantic restaurant; scene three might be dancing at a club; scene four, driving home; scene five, undressing each other in front of the fire or in the bedroom.

Besides adopting a *dance attitude* and using props, changing the stage set can add zest and interest. Experiment with building arousal and making love in different places and at different times. Surprise each other. If you are the kind of person who completes a project before moving onto the next one, stop in the middle, find your beloved, and enter the theater of love.

Let your imagination soar! If you enjoy intrigue, place clues that your partner must find to move on to the next step. If surreptitious sexuality turns you on, there are ample opportunities to build your arousal if you allow yourselves. Some of the favorites couples have told us are: in the back of a dark movie theater; at a romantic restaurant with long tablecloths; at a dinner party when the other guests are in a different room; or in a hot tub with friends, blanketed by the dark night.

While some couples enjoy being risqué, other couples prefer more traditionally romantic gestures. For example, something as simple as putting a flower or love poem on your partner's pillow may bring out the passionate lover in him or her. For others, it might simply be holding hands during an automobile trip.

Many people wait for their partner to initiate the theater of love. You both may be waiting for a long time. If initiating a new approach feels too risky for you, talk to your partner first and make a plan together. However you do it, remember that the goal is to have fun and enjoy yourself. By cultivating your erotic relationship, you will reap the rewards of greater intimacy, aliveness, spiritual connectedness, and peace.

## Position Yourself for Love

Just as fantasies, a change of scenery, props, costumes, and accessories can add zest to your lovemaking, so can experimentation with various positions. You can experiment and create positions on your own or find a book that appeals to you.[2] We are, however, suggesting that you explore the multitude of ways that your bodies can join using the same dance attitude or theater approach that you have employed previously. So, rather than searching for the best position to achieve orgasm, imagine that you are developing a repertoire of steps that you will join together in your lovemaking dance.

It can be both fun and instructive to practice various positions with your clothes on as well as without clothes but prior to arousal. Use the focus of how each position feels—physically, emotionally, spiritually. Look for positions that

Indian Miniature, Erotic Scene
Snark/Art Resource, NY

encourage relaxation and contact. Pay attention to what inner aspects or self-styles arise when you are on top, underneath, face to face, front to back, etc. Notice which positions foster intimacy, which foster arousal, which create intrigue, etc.

You can use this information to amplify whatever might be happening during your theater of love. For instance, the man may enjoy entering his partner from behind and find that he becomes highly aroused in this position. The woman, though, may feel unconnected to him in this position if they use this position before she feels a heart connection. However, after the woman feels connected emotionally, she may enjoy this position both for the physical stimulation it offers and for the self-style she might access while using it.

## A Good Fit

As you experiment with various positions during lovemaking, you will be adding the dimension of "fit." Many couples find one position that works and that's what they use. Besides being boring to use the same position each time, the woman may not be receiving adequate stimulation for orgasm and the man may be receiving too much stimulation to control his ejaculation.

If the woman has a shallow or small vagina and her partner has a long or large penis, certain positions will be painful for the woman, as the penis will hit and bruise her cervix. Similarly, if the woman has a deep, large vagina and her partner has a short or small penis, he may not get the stimulation he needs and penetration may be difficult to maintain in certain positions.

Another aspect to fit is the arousal factor. If you have explored each other's genitals, you may have discovered that the woman's clitoris is close to or far from the entrance to her vagina. Similarly, if you have explored her sacred spot, you may find that it is deep in the vagina or close to the vaginal opening. As you play with a variety of ways to join in your lovemaking, take enough time to let the woman find out if the position will stimulate her clitoris or sacred spot. Many women find that some positions feel better than others when they are in different states of arousal.

Men have a similar process to discover. Most men in our culture have not been schooled in sexual techniques for controlling ejaculation. However, experimenting with and finding out which positions offer more or less stimulation can be a step toward developing more control.

Though some women have clitoral orgasms easily and quickly, it takes a longer period of stimulation for the deeper orgasms of the vagina and the uterus to take place. As the two of you become comfortable experimenting with the myriad of ways that human bodies fit together, you may explore ways to support the ecstatic experience of mixed orgasms. As you experiment, look for positions in which there can be penetration of the woman's vagina either manually or with her partner's penis so that she can receive clitoral stimulation by her partner or herself as well.

Some guidelines when exploring different positions and developing your repertoire are:

*Look for positions in which the two of you can totally relax and melt into each other while sexually joined. This harmonizes your energy and makes for a richer, fuller, and more ecstatic experience.*

*Discover which positions are highly arousing and which are mildly arousing to each partner so that you can choose how much stimulation you want at a given time.*

*Find positions in which the woman can get vaginal and clitoral stimulation simultaneously.*

*Find positions in which the man can get stimulation of his penis, scrotum, and anus simultaneously if he enjoys this.*

*Find positions that support each partner's rhythm. Since it usually takes longer for the woman's flame to heat up, find positions that gently support the kindling of her flames.*

*Determine which positions are best for developing emotional intimacy and a feeling of connectedness.*

*Find out which positions support both of you in moving energy up from your lower chakras to your higher chakras.*

Practice these positions and become familiar with them so that you can move in and out of them effortlessly. Give them personalized names if you like so that you can speak your own language

*Koryusai print, Shunga oban yoko-e, ca. 1764–1788*
*Art Resource, NY*

as you do your love duet. Then, like the dancer, actor, or athlete who practices and rehearses endlessly, they must forget about technique and dance/play when they are on stage performing or in the tournament.

So it is in lovemaking. Ecstasy can only move through bodies that are unblocked and unfettered with conflict. So learn the positions and techniques, and integrate them so that you

*Erotic Scene. Attic red figure cup by the*
*Briseis painter. Pompeii about 490 B.C.*
*Erich Lessing/Art Resource, NY*

have truly mastered them. Then forget what you have learned—be spontaneous.

As you work with the exercises throughout this book, we hope that you experiment and devise your own ways to replace monotony with sizzling sex. This can only make your love theater more exciting and rewarding. Then, as you feel safer with each other and more satisfied, you can take even more risks, expand your pleasure quotient a little more. And as you bring eros into more aspects of your life than lovemaking, the same ecstatic quality of your lovemaking can flood your life.

The next chapter, *Why Monogamy?*, explores one of the most frightening issues that couples face. We believe that the monogamy vs. non-monogamy question, whether clearly established in some relationships or hazily understood in others, constitutes one of the most dramatic challenges to being lovers for life. That's why we are devoting an entire chapter to exploring this crucial issue.

# 12

# Why Monogamy?

*The emotional benefits of long-term monogamy are…profound. Couples who have grown to love and trust each other over the years form an unparalleled support system. Their shared history, their steadfast commitment, and their appreciation of each other create a vast reservoir of peace and contentment.*

Patricia Love and Jo Robinson, *Hot Monogamy*

Most couples feel challenged regarding the potentially thorny issue of monogamy. The very concept can arouse fear-based behavior: clandestine affairs, addictive flirtations without consummation, avoidance of all contact with attractive others, or the old-style morality-based monogamy with its feeling of sacrifice and being trapped. In each of these scenarios, there lacks the sacred, open union of an inspired lover relationship.

Understanding the history of monogamy may prove helpful in correcting some potentially errant courses of practice. Archaeological, anthropological, and theological research provide documentary evidence from the Bible and the beds of civilization—Sumer, Babylon, Canaan, Anatoloia, Cyprus, and Greece—that married men and women freely participated in the sacred sexual rituals without compromising their fidelity.

*…despite the fact that the concept of marriage was known in the earliest written records, married women, as well as single, continued to live for periods of time within the temple complex and to follow the ancient sexual customs of the Goddess."* [1]

You may recall that as late as the first century B.C., women who participated in the sacred sexual customs of the goddess were still thought to make excellent wives. In these goddess cultures, the *qadishtu*, many of whom were women of wealth and property, passed their inheritance of property, land, and titles to their children. Since society was organized matrilineally, knowledge of paternity was not an issue.

However, the Levite laws of the Israelites, believed to be written by scholars about 1000–600 B.C., were focused on insuring knowledge of paternity. These laws demanded virginity for all Hebrew women before marriage and then fidelity—but only for the wife. Infractions carried the penalty of death by stoning or burning.

The rape laws which were written at the same time restricted women's autonomy as well and made her the wife and property of the rapist. The divorce laws made it easy for a husband to dismiss his wife if he so chose, but a previously married woman was considered undesirable. The likely result was very compliant and pleasing wives! These laws, which restricted women's sexual and economic activity, not only insured knowledge of paternity but probably were aimed at destroying matrilineal descent customs.[2]

The customs of the times supported this idea. Though it was considered shameful for a Hebrew woman to make love to a man other than her husband, Hebrew men were expected to have several wives—as many as they could afford. And unless the other woman was married or betrothed, a lack of fidelity on the part of the male was assumed.

And so the concept of morality—and immorality—was devised. Starting with the Levites, then picked up by the Christians, it became shameful for women to serve the goddess—to engage in sex before marriage and then, outside of the marital bed. Before that time, in some cultures, married women and men practiced monogamy—except for the sacred rituals of the goddess. However, both men and women celebrated the festivals and it was considered sacred for the married man to make love to a qadishtu (not his wife), and for the married woman, as a qadishtu, to make love to a married man (not her husband).

The new morality formed the basis for the double standards we still have today about pre-marital virginity and sexual fidelity. Here we also find the beginning of the attitude of shame toward sexuality. So, when we talk about monogamy, it is important to remember that monogamy as we know it today began as a way to achieve total sexual control of women and of their wealth and status. Morality and shame became the means to this end.

# What Is Monogamy?

Monogamy. Think about it. Few words elicit such strong reactions. Monogamy actually means "the custom or condition of being married to only one person at a time" and "the condition of having one mate for life." Though by definition the word does not imply anything about sexual partnering with others, it has come to be understood as "mate-fidelity."

Moralists love the word, as if its practice predicts one's virtue as a human being. Still others reject it categorically, as if it were handed down from the pulpit of religious dogma, or the politicians of "family values." The controversy rages on today.

Whether people accept or reject monogamy, it has become increasingly clear to us that many people disagree on how to practice it. While interviewing large numbers of people about their beliefs and practices regarding monogamy, we shook our heads in disbelief more than a few times. The magnitude of different interpretations was nothing short of startling. On one extreme, socializing with people of the other sex constitutes a breach of monogamy. On the other extreme, it's okay to be overtly sexual with other people as long as there is no actual intercourse.

What exactly is monogamy to you? What are your associations? Where are the boundaries of monogamy? The following process can help you clarify your definition of monogamy.

## Exercise #1

### *Monogamy is...*

Close your eyes and take several deep, full breaths.

Say the word "monogamy" to yourself and out loud.

Allow any images of monogamy to emerge.

Ask yourself these questions:

*What is my definition of monogamy?*

*What does it mean to be faithful?*

*What does it mean to be committed to someone?*

*What are my core beliefs about monogamy?*

*What did my parents believe?*

*Do I want to practice monogamy with my partner? If so, how would I like to practice it?*

Whatever emerged for you during this last exercise is important to share with your partner. We are not in the business of moralizing. Rather, we are here to simply present some possibilities which have worked for large numbers of people. You and your partner must ultimately make your own decision. But we can tell you this: You and your partner had better get clear about what each of you means by monogamy. That's why sharing your understanding of monogamy is so important to a long-term relationship.

# For the Times They Are A-Changing

Changes in social conditions at the end of the twentieth century are catalyzing a shift from the freewheeling sexuality of past decades toward a new monogamy. Helen Singer Kaplan, the noted sex therapist, refers to it as *High Monogamy*. It's not the ball-and-chain version of our parents and grandparents, which was based more on "shoulds" and "have to's" than on true love and intimacy. It is founded in the realization that greater intimacy, creativity, spiritual growth, and sexual ecstasy is available in a one-to-one relationship that endures over time.

The movement toward this new monogamy is not an isolated affair. Lots of couples are doing it. They are doing it because they believe it is the best way to keep love alive. They are bonding with each other through choice, not addiction. They are longing for greater intimacy, for relationships that provide not only a haven, but a laboratory for self-development and spiritual evolution. They are trying to capture and foster more of the richness life has to offer—including the experience of sexual ecstasy. Even some of our most famous bachelors like Warren Beatty, John Travolta, and Hugh Hefner, long considered womanizers of the highest (or lowest) order, are now saying yes to monogamy.

# Sex and Monogamy

Monogamy and monotony have been linked because of a questionable belief: sex is more exciting and fulfilling with strangers—and becomes duller over time with the same partner. As you know, we challenged this latter view in the last chapter.

If you never commit to anyone, your fantasies of the exotic other can remain undiluted by mundane life details with a mate. Always searching for the "new and improved" to re-stimulate a boring life, the latest sexual partner holds the promise of phenomenal erotic excitement. A familiar relationship cannot possibly hold a candle to the new fantasy. A composite of this belief can be summarized like this: "It was great in the beginning, but now the thrill is gone. I guess we just got used to each other. Anyway, you can't expect sex to be as exciting as when we first met. It would be better with someone new."

But if you talk to couples who have embraced their relationship as a path to deeper love, intimacy, and sexual fulfillment, you will hear a very different story. Love and sexual fulfillment increases geometrically with greater trust, intimacy, and yes, familiarity.

An old friend of ours, Glen, who has been in a twelve-year monogamous relationship, expressed it this way:

*I can only make love when I'm in love. I've had sex with lots of different women. Some of them I really liked, but it was never as exciting and stimulating as with Alice. Our sexual satisfaction has increased as we have grown to know and love each other more.*

Perhaps this can be an inspiration for you.

## Dis-Ease with Disease

In the 1970s, herpes, gonorrhea, and syphilis cast a shadow over the sexual landscape. However, as feared as they were a generation ago, today they seem pale in comparison to AIDS. By the mid-1980s, people were becoming terrified of this new, deadly epidemic. Casual sex started losing ground to a growing awareness that if you sleep with the wrong person, you might die.

At first, AIDS seemed to affect only the socially disenfranchised, such as gay men, intravenous drug users, Africans and Haitians. But that was a short-lived illusion. More and more cases began appearing in the heterosexual population. The AIDS virus hit colleagues at work, acquaintances, friends, and relatives. Today, most people have known at least one person who has died from AIDS. For many, AIDS has profoundly altered their views about life, death, and relationships.

One watershed event in AIDS awareness was the announcement by basketball legend Magic Johnson that he was retiring because he had tested positive for the HIV virus. When tragedy befalls our heroes, it evokes deep feelings of vulnerability within us all.

Johnson was at the pinnacle of his life, a sports superstar, admired and respected by millions. Yet, perhaps he had unconsciously succumbed to the cultural myth that heroes were invulnerable. Despite warnings that had been issued about the dangers of unprotected sex, particularly with large numbers of partners, he continued to act as if he were immune.

Johnson's announcement initially shocked many heterosexuals who were still following multi-partner patterns of sexuality into breaking through their denial. "If it can happen to him, it can happen to me."

Unfortunately, denial is the foe of awareness. Young people, in particular, continue to fall prey to the illusion that they are invulnerable. Surveys taken in 1992 indicated that the majority of sexually active adolescents were consistently engaging in unprotected sex.

Among more mature and prudent adults, sexual adventures have been curtailed because of the newly obligatory conversation with potential lovers about their past sexual partners. Situations that seemed like great opportunities in the 1960s set off warning lights and red flags in the 1990s. Just as things are warming up, many people have learned to stop and ask: "When was the last time you were tested? Do you carry proof of your negative test with you? Who have you been with since you were tested? How do you know for sure that h/she/they are not infected? Are you willing to bet your life and mine on it?" Obviously, these questions hardly flame the coals of passion.

Some people have become so terrified of the potential consequences of sexual relationships that they have chosen the safe but lonely course of celibacy. Others have chosen to abstain until they find a partner with whom they are considering a committed relationship. Either way, it is clear that for many people, promiscuity is not an option anymore. For most people, the free and easy sexual exploration outside monogamy has come to a screeching halt.

# The Inevitability of Sex

Although many people have halted their sexual adventures, their desire for sex has hardly been quenched. Human beings are hardwired with sexual desire. When outward possibilities for fulfillment diminish or disappear, people automatically look for alternative pathways. Some people escape into a private inner world of sexual fantasies. Others indulge in "phone sex." Still others follow their fantasies and their desire for sexual contact into the outer world—looking for the magic of recognition in the depth of someone's eyes, enjoying the arousal stimulated by the contour of a thigh. In whatever form, people crave physical and sexual excitement.

The AIDS epidemic has not killed the archetype of deep desire and longing for union with a soulmate. Yet for many disillusioned seekers of the perfect relationship, the possibilities for passion, intimacy and friendship with the same partner have seemed like the naive delusions of dreamers.

But what if it were possible to have it all with one person? What if a long-term, committed relationship could become the path to a life of deep emotional, physical, and spiritual fulfillment? What if the issues that seemed like obstacles previously could help open the door to deeper levels of intimacy and ecstasy? What if you really could be lovers for life?

# Reviewing the Sexual Revolution

Nostalgia buffs to the contrary, the sexual revolution has produced mixed results. For some, it was a passage of liberation—an introduction to openness and freedom. For others, the decades of unbridled sex left emotional scars. For many, it marked an abrupt change from repression to licentiousness; out of the freezer and into the fire, with no transition period in between. In many cases, the quick jump proved devastating.

This was particularly true for people whose backgrounds had instilled in them guilt and shame about their sexuality. Without resolving these issues, they plunged directly into the sexual stew that began bubbling some thirty years ago. Today, disappointed and disillusioned, many people are still grappling with these issues.

# Open Relationships

Non-monogamy was once considered a panacea for romantic relationships, whether or not they were stagnating. However, having multiple partners opened Pandora's box to the point where most couples felt engulfed by pain.

Despite the so-called "age of sexual enlightenment," many people felt ashamed when they discovered they had feelings of jealousy, rage, fear, and distrust. Although the concept of allowing their lovers to have sex with other people sounded liberating in theory, in practice it often led to alienation and estrangement.

The reality of their lover's kissing, fondling, sucking, or having intercourse with anyone else hardly inspired feelings of love, trust, and intimacy.

The new morality of that time gave a twist to traditional morality's "should nots": Instead of, "You should not play around outside the relationship," the new proscription went, "If you really love him (or her), you should not feel possessive."

Non-monogamy probably ruined more relationships than it strengthened. Many people who believed that the capacity to choose who they slept with would enhance their personal freedom ironically found themselves enslaved to endless guilt and insecurity. Some who got involved in open relationships were unwilling to set boundaries because of peer pressure. They feared that they would be considered "unenlightened," "uncool" or, worse yet, "uptight."

In those wild times, most people seemed to forget that they had the right to say <u>no</u> to people with whom they did not want to make love. Women were sexual with men even when they really did not want to be. Men felt obligated to be sexual regardless of whether or not they felt desire. Other men took it for granted that a woman would jump in the sack after the first date. Even in 1985, I (Judith) went out with a man who told me—after I had refused to sleep with him on our third date—that I was the first woman he *hadn't* slept with after the *first* date. He was proud of it! Then he tried to denigrate me for turning him down.

## Sexual Idealism vs. Reality Testing in Non-monogamy

*Reality testing* is finding out what happens when we actually act on our professed ideals. It is taking an honest look at what is really true, as opposed to what we wish were true. Imagining how we might respond to a hypothetical situation is quite different than being confronted with it in reality—as you have no doubt discovered.

Henry, one of the leaders in the Human Potential Movement, and his colleagues conducted their own personal experiment with completely open relationships—those in which partners agree that they may have other sexual relationships without the permission of their primary partners. Theoretically, he thought that was what sounded ideal, to help each other "realize themselves" fully.

His lover was the first to experiment. When she came home one night and announced that she had had intercourse with another man, Henry had his first experience of incongruence between thought and feeling, head and heart.

Although he said, "That's fine, dear; you've done what we said; I understand and, my, aren't we advanced," his stomach was not nearly so calm or assured. In fact, it was tied up in knots.

Using all the therapeutic techniques they knew, they attempted to understand and resolve the feelings this incident had aroused. They explored any withheld feelings they may be having toward each other—her feelings of hostility and his insecurities about his masculinity. They went into their feelings about their parents, other lovers, their childhoods. In the language of the time, "It got heavy."

As Henry tells it:

*Our talk went well. By evening we had worked it through so that I felt good about her again. We began to make love but to my dismay, I had no erection. I realized then that truth was in my body.*

They continued to unpeel the layers of the onion, attempting to find the answer that would bring Henry's body and mind back together. Each night, after revealing more fears about each other and about themselves, they would begin to have sex, each time finding a slightly less droopy penis. "It was like the angle of my penis was the answer in the back of the book," Henry recalls.

His level of erection became his measure for whether or not they had resolved all the issues between them. Finally, after five nights, he became erect enough to enter her.

Henry discovered that his failure to "get it up" was due to his fears and childhood feelings of insignificance. If she could so readily substitute someone else in his place as her lover, how important was he really?

Even though his words said, "Fine, dear," and he consciously believed that he wanted to have this degree of freedom in the relationship, his flaccid penis declared his deepest truth. It said, "I'm hurt. Since I'm not sure you want me, I'm not going to take part in this relationship." From this experience, Henry decided monogamy was preferable. It was easier on the stomach.

Another story about reality testing took place in the Berkeley, California of the 1970s—one of the most sexually free spots on the planet at that time. It involved an acquaintance of ours named Jim.

Jim lived in a communal living situation with eleven adults and seven children. They rented an old mansion in the Berkeley hills for their commune. This wasn't a hippie commune—they were all fairly mature, professional, working adults with no glaring hang-ups and with normal children. They had come together because of their ideals—that they could find a better way of living and sharing their lives. On many occasions, they talked rationally of their intentions and agreed to share as much as possible. This included cooking, house maintenance, money, child-raising and—by mutual consent—sex.

Jim had arrived with his *significant other,* Anna, with whom he had been living for three years. Their relationship had been close and loving, and they had each been free to pursue other interests—except that they had both voluntarily opted for monogamy. Now they had agreed to open the relationship.

They quickly became close friends with several of the other adults in the commune. One man, in particular—Mel—became Jim's closest friend. Jim and Mel spent many hours discussing what they wanted to accomplish with their experiment. They tried to outdo each other, explaining how open they were, and that they had placed absolutely no restraints on the sex life of their partners.

Though Mel was in a relationship, Jim thought that he was constantly on the lookout for someone prettier and sexier. He found it in Jim's Anna.

They all spent many casual hours together, arms around each other, occasional kisses, chatting and getting to know each other. It was obvious that Mel was attracted to Anna and that she returned his interest.

One evening, Mel came up to Jim, put his hands on Jim's shoulders, looked him straight in the eye and said, "Look, I'd really like to make love to Anna, and I think she wants to do it. Are you sure it's okay?"

"Yes," he said, "enjoy yourselves." And he meant it. Of course, it was a bit surprising to him that Anna had wanted to make love with Mel, too. And he had been noticing that she was acting cooler toward him in bed. Well, there was nothing to do but to let them make love. He was committed to the social experiment.

He couldn't help watching them walk up the stairs to the bedroom, arm in arm, obviously looking forward to it. They stopped for a moment and kissed—a long, lingering kiss. Jim noticed that Anna was pushing her hips tightly up against Mel's groin, all the while doing a little hip wiggle.

"Damn," he thought, "she'd never done that while kissing me!"

After a few moments they walked into Jim's bedroom and shut the door. He thought to himself, "I should go out, get away from here for a while." But he didn't. Instead, he walked up to the steps and sat down in front of the bedroom door. It was quiet inside.

He stayed there for about ten minutes. He kept telling himself, "It's okay. She has the right. Stay cool." But he couldn't stay cool. Mel had known how much he loved Anna. Why couldn't he keep his hands off?

Then he heard the sound of Anna's guttural moans—the kind she made only when she was about to have a very intense orgasm. He gritted his teeth, put his hands over his ears, then listened again even more closely. Neither of them were holding back now, and cries of pleasure echoed through the hallway around him.

Finally, he could no longer stand the sound of it and he got up and ran out of the house, tears streaming from his eyes. He jumped on his motorcycle and rode it through the streets of Berkeley that night. He was so angry and hurt that he almost got into a fist-fight with the Hell's Angels. By the time he raced up the winding road back to the commune, it was time for the regular evening meeting. Everyone was there, including Anna and Mel sitting next to each other, holding hands.

"All right," he said in a loud and angry voice, "listen up. I don't care what we've agreed to or whatever I've said. From now on, I will personally beat the living shit out of anyone who fools around with Anna again! That means anyone!" And he glared directly at Mel.

The room became totally silent, and he was dimly aware of the shocked expressions looking back at him. After all, he was the founder of the commune. He was the one who had encouraged maximum sharing, and now he was the one who had dropped this bombshell.

He grabbed Anna and pulled her upstairs after him. "Stop it," she cried, "you're hurting my arm," but he kept pulling her. When they were alone together, he held her and said, "Okay, it's your decision. It's me alone or I'm leaving. Do you understand? I can't go through this again! Take your choice!"

Well, Anna made her choice, and her choice was Mel. The commune began to split up shortly after that. Jim learned a hard and humbling lesson.

Our last story involves Gary and Barbara. This loving couple almost lost their relationship because of conflicts generated by Gary's desire to be sexual with other women, and Barbara's fear of that.

At the beginning of their marriage they had no agreements about being sexual with others. Gary was the first to try a sexual relationship outside the marriage. Barbara considered doing the same, but she just couldn't follow through with it.

Later, when Gary became emotionally as well as sexually involved with other women, Barbara suffered tremendous pain. Feeling that her personal territory had been invaded, she expressed great anger toward Gary: "I hate you for wanting this with someone else," she told him during that unhappy period. "How could you share that kind of intimacy and cheapen our experience."

She knew that she was reacting from a gut-level survival instinct. Yet when she judged herself, her intellect overrode her heartfelt convictions. "I should be more enlightened," she berated herself.

Gary also believed that "Barbara was the one having problems." They both believed that her inability to be sexual with more than one partner or feel good about Gary being sexual with another woman stemmed from her background of sexual repression. They both told themselves that "if only Barbara would do more work on herself and change, the problem would be solved."

So whenever Barbara felt jealous, angry, mistrusting or depressed, they processed…and they processed…and they processed! And of course, when Gary felt frustrated, sad, or afraid that he could not have what he wanted, they processed…and they processed…and they processed!

Needless to say, they were miserable. Disenchanted with processing their feelings constantly, they were also frustrated that they had no time to simply enjoy each other. Something had to change!

After much soul searching, they realized they were in a no-win situation. Their disparate beliefs became apparent as they explored what was keeping them from moving forward.

They had tried Gary's approach and it had led to endless analysis and pain. Perhaps Barbara's approach would be more fruitful. However, in order for them to adopt Barbara's approach wholeheartedly, they both had to let go of the picture that Barbara was the "identified patient" because of her sexually repressed background.

Gary and Barbara agreed that if they wanted a highly erotic, deeply nurturing relationship, they had to have complete trust and safety. That meant staying within the monogamous relationship. This necessitated a paradigm shift. They had to get on the same team and approach this difference between them as a challenge to be solved by both of them rather than the one who was "wrong."

And as they did, lightness came back into their relationship. They did little processing. Their sexual freedom within the marriage deepened. Gary felt overjoyed at the way Barbara blossomed as a lover. Their lovemaking soared to heights he had not thought possible.

Barbara felt relieved that she, or her sexually repressed background, had not been the cause of their problem. As her feelings of trust deepened, she found that she was quite free sexually. And she felt ecstatic! Then, paradoxically, Barbara felt so much love for Gary and felt so secure in their relationship, she reversed her position. She decided that she wanted to give him the gift of freedom—complete freedom. She thought, "Perhaps having another lover is a special fantasy for Gary, perhaps he will feel more fulfilled. If I can give this to him and not suffer, I want to be able to do that."

Gary, on the other hand, found that he now wanted greater intimacy if he were going to become sexually involved. When Barbara and he were no longer dealing with jealousy, fear, and doubt, their emotional and sexual intimacy deepened.

As Gary experienced the source of his sexuality bubbling up, he began to question if it were possible to have this same level of gratification from sex with someone outside the union.

Though they prefer not to label their relationship as monogamous or otherwise, they have found the rewards that come from this level of commitment. They now enjoy spectacular lovemaking.

## Pulling Back

If the goals of the sexual revolution were fulfillment, then the results were dubious. Certainly, momentary excitement reached a feverish pitch at times. However, as these examples illustrate, the deep satisfaction that most people yearned for was rarely achieved. The two-headed dragon of jealousy and emptiness propelled many people to reconsider the price of so-called freedom.

In the midst of this re-evaluation, many couples returned to traditional monogamy. In 1980, before anyone had heard of AIDS, *Cosmopolitan* magazine surveyed 106,000 women about their attitudes toward sexuality: "So many readers wrote negatively about the sexual revolution, expressing longings for vanished intimacy and the now elusive joys of romance and commitment, that we began to sense that there might be a sexual counterrevolution underway in America." Though it was the in thing to be single or divorced during the sexual revolution of the 1960s and 1970s, more people got married in the 1980s and have stayed married. This trend has continued into the 1990s. However, despite the fear of AIDS and the work of the Religious Right, the counterrevolution has not shoved sex back into the closet with the other skeletons.

Some positive changes in attitude and behavior have persisted. Sex is discussed more openly and readily than previously. Accepting women as sexual beings with sexual fantasies is now part of the mainstream. The search for eros, initiated en masse during the sexual revolution, is continuing.

## Cocooning

The relationship between monogamy and the increasing importance of our homes was pointed out by future forecaster Faith Popcorn. In *The Popcorn Report*,[3] she suggests that people today are much less inclined to leave home for work or play than they have been in the past. She labeled this trend "cocooning."

We are seeing an upsurge in home businesses, cottage industries, and home delivery services. People are fed up with too much traffic, too much noise, too much congestion, too much crime, and too much stress. Muggings, gang violence, drive-by shootings, car-jackings—all contribute to the belief that it's safer to stay at home.

Because people are staying at home more, they are interested in improving their home environment. They are getting the latest electronic equipment for work, entertainment, and physical fitness.

So, what does this have to do with monogamy? Since many of us are spending more time at home, we are together in our relationships for longer periods of time and we are looking to our partner to fill the gap of excitement, stimulation, and fulfillment that once came from outside the home.

## No Time for Fooling Around

Another factor in the monogamy movement appears to be time, or more specifically, the lack of it. Time seems to be speeding up. Computers, modems, fax machines, answering machines, car phones, and pagers all contribute to a pace and lifestyle which is becoming faster and more complex. There's more to do and less time to do it. Not surprisingly, consumer demand for take-out food and pre-prepared meals has sky-rocketed in the 1990s because everyone wants to save time.

Our lethargic economy has also contributed to this phenomenon. The increasing number of households with two working parents or single parents who work discourages multiple partnering. As a culture, we seem stretched too thin for extraneous romantic interests. Talk to practically anyone and the message is clear: People are on overload. They want their down time for themselves. And what better way to spend time than to be intimate with your loved one? As a culture, our tendency to cocoon and preserve what little time we have for ourselves make us ripe for passionate monogamy.

## Choosing the Big M

The nineties are clearly a time in which there are many different converging reasons for choosing monogamy, all reinforcing the value of a long term, one-on-one sexual relationship. Many couples who choose monogamy out of fear are discovering its advantages, and then remain committed to it by preference.

Though some of us take refuge in monogamy to avoid the emotional pain that can come from open marriages, anxiety over AIDS, or the existential despair of overwhelming loneliness, there are others who are inspired to practice monogamy because of the treasures it holds.

Like beautiful gardens, great relationships take time and energy to make them truly flourish. You cannot put in a few minutes here and there. You need to tend them diligently. Any gardener knows that you have to continually cultivate the soil, water, fertilize, pull the weeds, and control for insects. And gardening doesn't hold a candle to the conscious energy needed to create and maintain great relationships.

We do not view monogamy as a choice based on morality or on fear. It's a matter of practicality. We feel that within a monogamous relationship, we can achieve the highest level of sexuality and intimacy. It can be a path of spiritual evolution—one that more and more couples are following every day.

We do not deny that it is often an uphill journey at times, but considering that the destination is High Monogamy, we find it a path well worth traveling.

However, choosing monogamy is not enough to overcome the temptations of other attractions. And repressing these desires usually brings disastrous results: resenting your partner, laying your own erotic impulses to sleep, or just experiencing an overall sense of irritability. You need a good plan to handle these attractions when they do arise—without feeling guilty, ashamed, or closing down emotionally. How can you harness the erotic energy generated by other attractions and bring it into the sanctity of your own lover relationship? That's precisely the question we will answer in the next chapter—*Handling Other Attractions*.

# 13

# *Handling Other Attractions*

*Many of us do expect that once a commitment has been made, we automatically become immune to anyone else's charms and that we are somehow "off limits." You may then assume any feelings you share with, develop, or still retain for another person must be love, which has to be consummated.*

Suzie Hayman, *The Good Sex Guide 2*

## Nocturnal Intrigues

I (Daniel) recently visited with a new friend. Judith was at home that evening taking care of our son. My new friend, Jack and I were sitting out on his woodsy deck, overlooking Mt. Tamalpais in Marin County, California. We were discussing all kinds of interesting topics when his wife, Nancy, arrived home and joined us on the deck. Since Jack was already occupying the only chair, she sat right next to me on the chaise lounge.

The summer night grew cooler so Nancy and I shared a blanket together—partly because it was easier not to move, and partly to show how "cool" we were. With friendly feelings, we each put an arm around each other.

Even though it was quite cold, I started feeling a warm sensation. The sensation continued to grow. Soon I felt downright hot. My erection starting straining against my pants. Mr. Honesty here was having some serious questions about what to do. Should I say something to them or pass it off as just another erection? How was I going to handle this? How open would I be?

I am absolutely committed to truthfulness in my relationship with Judith—and that includes telling her about my attractions toward other women. In fact, I told Judith the next day. But with my new friends, it was not so cut and dried. I did not know if they were as committed to having truthful relationships as I am. I thought about one of our cardinal rules: when in doubt whether or not to say it—then say it.

I took a deep breath and mentioned how strange it felt to be turned on by another man's wife. They both laughed and it was truly no big deal. Just my brief reference to the taboo subject of sexual attraction allowed us all—or at least me—to feel more comfortable and close. None of us made a drama out of it by imagining that this attraction needed to be acted upon or that it was anything other than my feeling a spark of sexual energy.

## Sexual Energy Is a Big Plus

Speaking of sexual energy, when I (Judith) asked my parents, Ruth and Martin, how they have managed to keep their relationship so vital after being married for 45 years, they looked at each other and laughed. "Sex!" they responded together.

Mom, an attractive and physically fit woman in her mid-sixties, proceeded to reveal their shared secret. When my father sees a woman he finds attractive, he comments freely to my mother. If the woman is still within range, Mom checks her out and gives her own evaluation. "That," she says, "has allowed our sexual energy to stay lively, rather than depressed from years of Dad pretending to find only one woman attractive."

As a child, I remember parties at which my father was flirting with women who were good friends of our family. Similarly, my mother flirted with the men and they with her. All of them were close friends. There was nothing secretive or seductive about their behavior. Nothing changed when a partner entered the room. He or she would be brought into the easy-going banter and camaraderie.

The partners, all of them husbands and wives of long duration, obviously had juicy, monogamous relationships. They were openly affectionate with each other and I never doubted that these couples loved and cherished their spouses. I never remember seeing or hearing a scene of jealousy or the use of sexual attraction to humiliate or offend anyone.

It was obvious that sexuality played an important part in the lives of these couples. It appeared that they enjoyed and were confident of their maleness and femaleness, so much so that they felt secure when their partner flirted with another.

As I thought about those couples who filled our home during my childhood, I realized that they are all still married, except those whose spouse has died. Some of the couples were high school sweethearts, yet their marriages stayed vital and sexy for half a century.

## Dealing with Other Attractions

Catherine Johnson, in *Lucky in Love*, describes the qualities of marriages in which both partners feel they have a happy marriage.[1] She interviewed 100 couples who had been married for seven years or longer and found that most happy marriages are held together by a powerful and enduring sexual bond "even when partners do not fully realize it."

When asked about the importance of fidelity, most of the couples said they had a strong belief in monogamy and practiced it steadfastly. Fidelity, they felt, was the basis for building a happy relationship. It was a matter of course for them, as routine as putting on a coat on a cold day or brushing their teeth after breakfast. Many of the couples in Johnson's study were aware that secrets corrode a relationship. Some said they chose monogamy because of that.

Though even the happiest couples openly admitted they could be tempted, they consciously did not cross the line. They "flirted," but talked themselves out of the attraction before it became too strong. As my (Judith) father used to say, "Don't put a stumbling block before a blind man." These happy, thriving couples understood this axiom and stopped themselves long before they might be blinded and stumble.

One man, who described himself as being "as horny as the next guy," avoided any situations in which he might be alone with an attractive and willing female. His strategy was to nip a compromising situation in the bud, before he was forced to say yes or no. "I just wouldn't want to be unfaithful," he said. "My kids would see me as a lesser person if I did that, and there isn't a piece of tail in the world that's worth giving up happiness for."

One woman in the group had devised her own strategy for avoiding infidelity. When faced with a man to whom she felt sexually attracted, she asked herself who she would choose if she met both him and her husband for the first time on the same day. Since her husband always won hands down, she knew that her attraction to the other man was mainly due to the newness of the situation.

What about couples who were less conscious of the danger of unexpected attractions, and found themselves involved before they knew what had happened? One woman described in Johnson's study found herself falling for a colleague, and stood on the brink of transgressing. Quickly, she telephoned her husband. Hearing his voice anchored her in the reality of her marriage and how much she loved him—and the moment passed.

As these couples testify, it is important not to act on other attractions but to keep breathing until they pass. Acting on these attractions almost always leads to a disaster (remember Chapter 12— *Why Monogamy?*). And spending time processing hassles over potential lovers—either your own or your partner's—hardly leads to a deep and abiding feeling of intimacy. While acting on other attractions is clearly a transgression for most, simply feeling attracted to others often arouses fear, doubt, and shame.

## The Power of Openness

Even people who have committed themselves to telling their partner the whole truth about everything become faint at heart when faced with revealing their feelings of sexual attraction to others. More often than not, in organizational seminars and psychological counseling, we have heard both men and women gasp and croak, "You're not suggesting I tell my partner *that*, are you?"

"Yes, even *that*," we say. Then we usually hear a litany of beliefs about the damage that might occur in the relationship if *that* truth were told: "He couldn't handle hearing that," "It would hurt her feelings," "He wouldn't understand," "It could destroy our marriage," "What good would that do?"

After accepting the fact that their motivations to remain silent, although altruistic, largely stem from their fears of being unable to cope with their partners' reactions, most people swallow hard and decide to tell even *that*.

The results are consistently successful. It is not always evident immediately, as some partners do use this information as a reason to feel hurt, betrayed, or suspicious. However, when both people realize that feeling a sexual attraction is not synonymous with acting on it, but rather that both people are juicy, sexy people. Then they can both relax, have fun, and enjoy their sexuality. In fact, many couples become closer as a result of discussing other sexual attractions.

Early in our own relationship, when Daniel first risked telling me that he found a particular woman attractive and that he had found himself feeling aroused in her presence, he was surprised and grateful to find that I was not hurt, angry, or fearful.

I was more interested in communicating openly than I was in the actual event. Since I did not react negatively, Daniel was free to experience his own feelings and reactions more fully. He was clear that he was not going to act on his desire, but he felt guilty about feeling aroused and attracted to someone else. By the time we were through talking, Daniel's guilt feelings had dissipated.

I let him know how much I appreciated his sexuality and that I fully supported him in casting off his shackles of shame and guilt. We both felt closer to each other than before we began our communication. Suddenly I looked more beautiful and sexually attractive to Daniel than I had been only a few minutes earlier! He had freed up his energy by telling me the truth about his attraction, as well as his guilt, rather than withholding it and turning it into a secret between us.

When I (Daniel) experienced a sexual attraction and withheld this information from Judith, I found myself feeling less attracted to Judith. Guilt is a real turn-off. But when I eventually expressed these feelings, I found my natural attraction to her resurfaced. Had I continued to handle it on my own, rationalizing that it was not significant because I had not acted on it, the temporary wall between us would have grown thicker. But once I told her, there were no secrets to sustain any walls between us, and our natural attraction was free to spark. It was another example of what we have said over and over again in this book: secrecy and withholds diminish your erotic experience.

Gay and Kathlyn Hendricks, co-authors of *Conscious Loving,* have experienced a similar phenomenon, as they recounted in a personal interview. "As I (Gay) learned to tell the truth more, I became a more sexual person. And as I learned that Kathlyn was committed to hearing and telling the truth, I felt more sexually attracted to her. It was a happy surprise to know that the more we celebrated the truth in the moment, the more sexual I felt."[2] Gay and Kathlyn call this approach "high fidelity."

## Playing with Other Attractions

In the last chapter we recounted Henry's experience when he was involved in a "no-secrets" relationship. His reaction to his partner's candor about her relationship with another man had rendered him temporarily impotent.

Many women and years later, he deals with that kind of candor differently. He and his wife now feel free to ask or tell each other when they are attracted to someone else. That allows them to acknowledge any attraction they might have, enjoy it, and even be flirtatious. Neither asks the other to deaden their sexual attractions. Yet, because they have agreed to be monogamous, they are both clear that they will not act on their sexual attractions. The result is a relaxed feeling between the two of them. Neither feels threatened when the other is away for extended periods of time. Both can feel love for and eroticism toward others without feeling guilty or suspicious.[3]

## Conscious Couples and Other Attractions

Most happy, vital, monogamous couples who consciously deal with outside attractions tend to have four things in common:

*They allow their partners to be sexually attracted and attractive to other people.*

*They have fun with and enjoy their sexy feelings toward others.*

*They are truthful with each other about their attractions.*

*They use the spark of the flirtations to add spice to their own relationship.*

In the following exercise we outline a way for partners to get used to being open about outside attractions. You may want to vary it, but we think it's a good beginning:

## Exercise #1

### *Acknowledging an Attraction*

Sit together facing your partner. Decide who will be the first communicator and who will be the first responder.

***First communicator***—Tell your partner what your intention is in acknowledging an attraction you have, or had such as, to become closer, to clear up a misunderstanding, to practice telling the truth, to alleviate guilt, or anything else that is important for you. If you become aware that part of your intention is to get back at your partner, to get his or her attention, to find out if he or she cares, tell those also.

*Responder*—Thank your partner for taking a risk, being truthful, vulnerable, or whatever feels true for you. Then tell how you feel hearing what your partner revealed such as, "I appreciate your desire to feel closer to me and I am afraid of what you might tell me."

*Communicator*—Tell any fears you have about sharing your sexual attractions such as, "I'm afraid you are going to feel hurt and get angry at me."

Remember, most of us do not talk about our sexual attractions because we have been punished for telling the truth. So be patient with yourselves and supportive of one another as you reveal what you have been unwilling to tell or hear until now. Keep sharing your fears until you both feel ready to move on.

*Communicator*—Tell your partner who you are or were attracted to and any of the circumstances about the attraction such as where, when, and for how long. Tell all the details you have been most afraid of revealing. Express them in terms of what has attracted you, *not* in terms of putting down your partner or comparing your partner to your other attraction.

*Responder*—Keep breathing and paying attention to the reactions in your body as your partner talks. When your partner is finished speaking, take time to digest what you have heard. Take a deep breath, and tell your partner how you feel. If you feel yourself going into a defensive reaction such as anger, self-putdown, becoming numb, or any reaction that feels negative before your partner is finished, ask your partner to stop.

*Take some time to talk about what is going on for you such as, "I'm beginning to feel resentful, that somehow I'm not enough for you." If you find that you begin to attack or blame your partner with statements such as, "You don't appreciate me. It's your problem that you don't think I'm sexy," breathe deeply and look for your own vulnerability. In this example, you might state it as "I'm often afraid that I'm not sexy."*

*Communicator*—Tell your partner how you feel now after having revealed an attraction, how you feel about yourself for having done so, and how you feel about how your partner responded.

*Responder*—You become the communicator and begin the process again.

*When both of you have had an opportunity to be the communicator and the responder, take time to talk about what you have learned from doing this exercise.*

The first time you let something out of the closet, it often stumbles out in a clumsy way. So be patient with yourself and your partner. Hearing that your lover has been sexually attracted to someone else often activates fears that you have effectively kept hidden until now. Fears of abandonment, sexual inadequacy, and rejection are commonly triggered. Be gentle and compassionate with yourself as you allow yourself to uncover these wounds in your self-concept. Remember, you can only change and heal what you are aware of.

🌿    🌿    🌿    🌿    🌿

# Fantasies: Virtual Infidelity or Spice?

There is a big difference between being tolerant of your partner's sexual attraction to someone else and tolerating your partner actually making love with this person. But how about when your partner has fantasies about making love with someone else with no intention of acting on it?

Many of us enjoy sexual fantasies in which we play the protagonists of a pleasurable rendezvous. But very few of us tolerate images of our mate making love to another—fear and jealousy crop up. How can you utilize the power of other attractions—both yours and your mate's—and harness these within the context of your relationship? Well, some couples have found that when they share their fantasies about being sexual with others, their sexual relationship is actually enhanced.

Robert, a man in his mid forties, often had sexual feelings and fantasies about other women, but had never told his wife. He was afraid she would feel hurt, angry, and rejected. He was also afraid that he would not be able to cope with her reaction. When he heard some couples talking about how they were able to share these fantasies, he was excited by this new possibility. In fact, these couples believed that if they did not tell each other, it would create separation between them.

With trepidation, he went home and told his wife. Much to his surprise, she was very accepting—so much so that they started acting them out together during their lovemaking. She would occasionally simulate a woman to whom he felt attracted. Their sex life became more stimulating because he took a risk and shared his sexual fantasy life. We witnessed this in the story of Harry and Nancy in *From Monotony to Sizzling Sex*.

Some people feel that they are being unfaithful when they use fantasies of real or imaginary people while masturbating or making love. Jeff likes watching pornographic movies (so do a lot of other adults—porno flicks account for a big part of sales and rentals at video stores). His wife, Grace, does not mind. However, Jeff feels like he's cheating on Grace when he masturbates to pornography because he forms an attachment, however fleeting, to the images of other women while he is aroused. In Jeff's case, porno flicks allow him to satisfy his desire to experience other women sexually, if only through video.

Without supporting or condemning pornography, our general attitude is, if one or both partners use pornography as a turn-on, it should be out in the open and not a secret. Also, if the use of pornography enhances the relationship, fine—but if it keeps a couple from finding out why their sexual relationship is not satisfying, and keeps them from improving it, then pornography can be a real detriment to closeness.

Porno flicks are only the beginning—virtual sex is no doubt coming. According to futurist Faith Popcorn,[4] we are starting to have electronic entertainment centers in our homes that will provide us with virtual experiences of all kind. Why not sexual?

This may be a great way to derive pleasure for yourself, but how will your partner feel if he or she is left out? That's all the more reason good communication skills will be necessary. If things are going great between you, then it may not be so difficult to hear that your partner made virtual love with a stranger when you come home from work!

# Fantasy and Monogamy

Some people are quite creative in their ability to realize their fantasies and still stay true to monogamy. David Steinberg, the editor of *The Erotic Impulse* and *Erotic by Nature* told me (Daniel) how he and his partner fulfilled one of his favorite fantasies. David, like many committed men, still fantasized about picking up female strangers and making passionate love to them. Most men and some women in monogamous relationships grieve the loss of this titillating possibility. However,

David imagined a way that he could experience the best of both worlds. He suggested that he and his partner role play a stranger fantasy. His lover agreed.

They decided to meet at a singles bar as two people who did not know each other. They would take separate cars, have different identities and not break character until after they got back home. Here's what happened:

First David went to the bar and started hanging out with the guys. A short time later, his lover entered the bar in a provocative and revealing outfit. They exchanged glances like two strangers who were interested in each other. She went to a table alone. He slowly walked over to her—feeling the excitement of the encounter—and introduced himself.

They exchanged fictitious names and identities. They then flirted to arousal, left the bar together and jumped into the back of his van. There they made passionate and furious love together—as strangers. After their lovemaking, they exchanged phone numbers, kissed good-bye and drove separately back to their home. They both loved it.

Although their experience may not be appealing to you personally, perhaps it can inspire you to be more bold in expressing your own fantasies.

## To Be or Not To Be (Present)

Should you have fantasies about an attractive other *while* making love to your partner? We have found that when people fantasize about others while making love with their partner—without telling their partner—emotional distance is created. Although our discouragement of this might sound at odds with our recommended use of fantasy, it is quite different to be in your own fantasy world than it is to share that fantasy world with your partner.

The difference between fantasizing about another person without telling your mate vs. telling him or her can be profound. In one case, it creates separation through secrecy and in the other a deeper level of connection can be created. Doing fantasy enactments—provided your mate agrees to the arrangement—can be an invaluable strategy for lifetime lovers.

We interviewed a couple, Jennifer and Mark, who are in a monogamous relationship and chose to handle this second possibility in a most creative way. Jennifer had been traveling in Bali and met a man toward whom she felt a strong attraction. He was also in a monogamous relationship, however they spent lots of time together over a two-week period. She felt quite frustrated about being unable to consummate their relationship. On her flight back to Hawaii, where she and Mark live, she grieved the loss of being able to make love with other men—in this case, with David.

Once back, she shared everything with Mark (notice the truthfulness). She kept thinking about David, however, and was having a hard time emotionally disconnecting from him. Mark was remarkably understanding. Rather than blame Jennifer for feeling so strongly toward another man, Mark suggested a way for her to bring this erotic energy back into their relationship. He suggested to her, "I will wear the mask of David when we make love."

For Mark, it wasn't a role play. He did not intend to become David or be anyone other than himself. Rather, he supported Jennifer to project her images of David onto him and he would be an available screen. Mark told us,

*If Jennifer could get a response from me that she had never gotten before, than she is helping me expand myself. Besides, it was allowing her to do what she wanted and needed to do. If all it would take to renew her earliest passion was to think of this man while she was making love with me, then it was worth it.*

He thought that whatever David reflects and brings to the surface for her, then he could be that also. It just may be more dormant in him. And, indeed, that is partially what happened. Mark reported,

*That first week after she got back was one of the most awesome sensual, sexual experiences we had ever had. The fantasy about David unlocked something that was real between us. Well, maybe fantasy isn't real but it is a key to unlocking what is real.*

By including the feelings generated in this other attraction, Jennifer and Mark became closer than they had ever been. Jennifer told us that the experience of Mark wearing the mask of David allowed her to free herself from this other attraction—and bring her erotic energy back to Mark. They are a great model for using the erotic energy stimulated by other attractions.

If you are going to fantasize about making love with someone else while making love with your partner, clue your partner into your intention. Ultimately, your partner needs to be included in your fantasies without being replaced by some fantasy partner.

We have found that when people fantasize about another person, without telling their partner, h/she can sense that they are not altogether present. This is true even if their partner cannot articulate it. If you do not alert your partner, he or she will pick up on your distance.

Perhaps you believe that your partner cannot sense or feel your lack of presence in these circumstances. Even if you have not cultivated your ability to sense human energy, you are aware, on some level, if your partner is really present. Similarly, you can tell whether a friend is really listening to you deeply, or if they are preoccupied or uninterested.

In an informal experiment performed at the New York Open Center in 1984, biologist Rupert Sheldrake had test subjects sit facing a blank wall. A group of observers sat behind them. A test subject was then picked at random, and the observers were asked to stare at the back of his or her neck for ten seconds. This procedure was repeated several times. The test subjects had no rational way of knowing whether they were the one being stared at during each trial. Yet, when questioned separately, they were able to report with a statistically high degree of accuracy (over seventy percent) when they had been the focus of the observers' attention. We can indeed sense the attention or inattention of the people around us.[5]

While the strategy applied by Jennifer and Mark may suit some of you, others may find it undesirable. They do not want to "wear the mask" of anyone else. A client of ours once said to her husband, "If we are making love and you are dreaming about another, who is the we? Are you really here with me?" This woman felt their connection—or lack of it—was palpable.

A colleague of ours who also believes that fantasizing about others while making love with your partner drains the intimacy from lovemaking, has developed a different tool to resolve this potential quagmire. He uses a meditation technique to harness the energy generated by his sexual fantasies with others. Rather than feel ashamed and repress it, he redirects his energy to his partner.

He allows himself to be aroused by someone he sees during the day, talks with, or reads about. Then, during lovemaking, he uses conscious discipline to channel that energy towards his partner. This takes a great deal of intention and commitment. Yet, by doing this rather than draining energy from the relationship, his fantasies add sizzle and connection. You might find tremendous value with this technique.

## Exercise #2

### *Redirecting Your Sexual Energy*

Separate the sexual sensation or emotion you experienced from the person that gave rise to the experience. Realize that your desire and the object of your desire are distinct from each other. For instance, if you are a man, perhaps you were excited by a woman with a gorgeous pair of legs you saw on the subway going home, and you fantasized what it would be like to explore them further. At night, while having sex with your partner, the image of the woman with the sexy legs comes to mind. It is tremendously exciting. With conscious discipline, you re-create the image of those sleek legs, feel the sexual energy that image stimulates, and then focus that energy into touching or imagining your partner in the present moment.

You allow the feeling and the energy of the fantasy to build, then pour it into your real-life relationship and leave the image of the fantasy figure behind. Now you are passionately making love with your partner using the sexual energy you had available to you from your fantasy.

Using this technique, you can be a sexual being all the time, while maintaining a relationship that is monogamous mentally, emotionally, spiritually, and physically. This technique requires some rigorous mental discipline, but you may find that you can focus your sexual energy into your primary relationship rather than diffusing it through other attractions. This enriches and energizes the partnership, which has the most potential to offer you practical, real-life rewards. What a wonderful gift to give your lover and to receive for yourself!

ᘓ   ᘓ   ᘓ   ᘓ   ᘓ

## Attractions in the Workplace

The lady in the subway with the sexy legs was a passing fancy, and it is unlikely you will ever see or be tempted by her again. But what about your relationship with a person to whom you are attracted in your job situation? How in the world are you supposed to deal with this tricky subject of sexuality with him or her? Perhaps you have even thought of transferring to another division in the company, of changing jobs or anesthetizing yourself. On the other hand, it feels pretty good when that sexual current travels through your body. Anyway, changing jobs takes too much energy or is a bit too impractical.

Today, more men and women are working together as peers than ever before. Married and single, they are working long hours together, frequently traveling together as business colleagues, and experiencing the triumphs and disappointments that partners who work together feel. Because we are sexual creatures, sexual attractions inevitably arise.

Let's look at other attractions contextually. If you are sexually attracted to someone who passes by, it is quite different than if you are attracted to someone with whom you work or who happens to be your lover's friend. Whereas a smile, or some other respectful display of appreciation—acknowledging the person as a sexual being rather than a sexual object—may be all that is necessary for the casual passerby, that will not solve your dilemma with the person you see on a regular basis. What do you do?

There's no protocol, but it is imperative that we create one. As we flounder, the number of sexual harassment lawsuits grows. The personnel manuals get thicker and are replete with how to and how not to talk to or behave with your supervisors, subordinates, and co-workers, but employees still spend a lot of time around the water cooler.

In my (Judith's) work as an organizational consultant, I witness many men and women struggling with their feelings of being sexually attracted to co-workers—or not sexually attracted to those who are sexually attracted to them. Neither group knows how to handle their feelings. Nor do the office spectators. All three groups waste an inordinate amount of time, energy, and money trying to avoid the issue.

However, a solution exists, but it requires a cultural shift—a paradigm shift to linking, to gylanic principles—in the way men and women, employers, and employees relate. It is being practiced by many pioneering people. The solution is simple: talk about your attractions. Talk to the person involved first. Let him/her know what you are feeling and ask if h/she shares similar feelings. Then decide together how you want to handle the outcome. Since many people in the office may be aware of it if the attraction/flirtation has been brewing for some time, it is useful to let them know what the two of you have decided. That cuts down on water cooler talk.

It helps to create an open atmosphere and start the shift by having the entire office attend a seminar such as *The Human Element*,[6] which I, Judith, facilitate. If some people are reticent to attend, those who are interested start the ball rolling. When only one half of a team has attended, people report noticeable shifts in morale, productivity, and in the way people relate to one another, regardless of position. When trust is established and people feel free to speak about what is on their minds, the topic of sexuality can be handled like any other important topic.

Open communication about sexual attractions results in creative and inspired working relationships. Everybody wins with this solution. The involved pair are free to put their energy into their jobs so they and the company profit. With the relationship out in the open, their co-workers can also stop worrying about the situation and concentrate on their jobs as well. And the pair go home to their husband, wife, or significant other more energized and stimulated by their work instead of being drained by it—so their families benefit.

On the other hand, if you are attracted to a colleague and he or she is not attracted to you, or even aware of your feelings, it can be awkward to even mention it—for the recipient of your feelings may not take the subject seriously enough to want to discuss it with you. Persistence often pays off in these cases. Find creative ways to bring it up in a friendly non-threatening manner. Ultimately, people will listen.

In the long run, honest communication is the best policy. Several years ago, I (Judith) led a seminar for a work team from the armed forces. There was a lot of talk in the hallways and the restrooms about the colonel and his secretary. Many people were certain they were having an affair, though no one had ever talked to either of them about it. Their sexual attraction to each other was palpable. When they finally got up the courage to acknowledge their attraction, they also clarified that neither of them wanted to act on it because they were both happily married.

Their work team was visibly relieved. Now that it was out in the open, they began asking questions, going over last year's history in an attempt to make sense of it and come to terms with feelings they had experienced. When all the misunderstandings due to silence and secretive behavior were cleared up, the whole team benefited.

For another team from a manufacturing corporation, a similar situation was unraveled. The differences were that the man was not married and the pair were peers. Had Linda been single, Steven would have liked to pursue a romantic relationship. Given that she was married and wanted to stay that way, she and Steven agreed to maintain boundaries around their sexual attraction. Having brought it out in the open, they both felt free to enjoy the sexual energy between them without having to act on it. Both reported feeling greatly relieved by gaining clarity about their relationship. Their work relationship continues to flourish years later.

This kind of relationship, called "More than Friends, Less than Lovers" by David Eyler and Andrea Baridon,[7] has been documented in a study conducted by researchers at the University of Michigan. Twenty-two percent of the managers questioned reported being involved in a relationship of this type. They also found that these relationships generated a great deal of creative and productive energy, which benefited the work pair as well as the company.

Men and women are going to be working together more and more in the future. A recent study at the University of North Dakota found that productivity was enhanced when work teams included both men and women. Since women and men are destined to work together, and sexual attractions are here to stay, it behooves us to harness the creative energy from men and women who learn how to communicate openly about their attractions.

Rather than pretending that there is no attraction (pushing it into the shadow which creates problems which we have elaborated), we suggest that work couples be open about their sexual attraction with each other and with their respective romantic partners. This idea of a "sexually energized but strictly working relationship" seems to be intuitively understood by women and approached skeptically by men. In the end however, men who have embarked on such relationships have touted their virtues, as well.

## Inner Male and Inner Female

The intimacy developed by being open and vulnerable, as described above, is not important when the attraction is to a casual passerby, since you are not in a significant relationship. However, the benefit that you can derive by looking more deeply into your attractions, even to the stranger on the street, is enormous. Besides simply enjoying your sexuality, this exploration can give you insight into yourself.

One way to understand other attractions is through what the psychoanalyst Carl Jung called the anima (the female aspect of a man) and the animus (the male aspect of a woman). Living within the psyche of every man and woman, these inner figures are commonly projected onto passerby's, acquaintances, friends, or work mates. So, a way to think about the people who attract you is to regard them as your anima or animus projections. They often represent ways to fortify undeveloped aspects of ourselves.

A woman will be attracted to men who reflect some aspect of their internal male or animus. It could be an aspect that she identifies with, or an aspect that she does not identify with, but would like to develop. Yet another possibility is that the men have qualities that she does not identify with and does not want to experience because they are distasteful to her. But a less evolved part of her gets hooked.

Sally has always been attracted to men who are extremely self-involved, comfortable with taking but not very skillful at giving. Her ex-husband epitomized this kind of man. Though she consciously did not want to be with a man who fit that profile, she found herself repeating this destructive pattern. When Sally first considered that these men may mirror her inner male, she looked at her history for evidence.

She recognized that her past lovers all bore striking similarity with her own father (which Jung believed laid the foundation for animus projections in a woman). She had internalized this kind of man so deeply—epitomized by his difficulty in giving—that she questioned whether she was worthy of being cared for or receiving anything herself. As she visualized and articulated the kind of man for whom she truly longed—attentive, concerned, generous—she also became clear about her fears of ever finding this kind of man.

Sally's story has a happy ending. She worked through these issues to the point that she became attracted to a more giving and attentive man—the kind of man she had hoped to meet. He and she talk openly about their hopes and their fears. Sally still grapples with her difficulty in asking for help and allowing others to support her. She continues to look for the unconscious payoffs that come from believing that no one can be fully present with her or support her. But, as she acknowledges the truth about the self-involved men of her past, she finds herself being less attracted to them and more attracted to her fiancé.

## Why Certain People Are Attractive to Us

If you ask yourself the following questions about people who attract you, you can learn a lot about yourself:

*What qualities does this person have that I find attractive?*

*How do I treat those qualities in myself?*

*What role do these qualities play in my life?*

*Do I accept these qualities, reject them, or limit them?*

*What aspect/s of myself have been blocking these qualities from emerging from me?*

*How can I develop these qualities in myself?*

For example, a woman might find a man who has rippling muscles sexually attractive. Besides merely enjoying the catlike sensuality of his body as she watches his biceps flex, she could allow herself to become aware of what his muscles represent to her. The answer may be sensuality. Then she might focus on how she holds back her own sensuality for fear of appearing too sexual. Going back into her history and remembering the myriad of mixed messages she received from her parents and her culture, she may understand why she developed negative feelings about letting herself appear too sexual.

Consciously, she would like to express her sexuality more. But what would people think? That she was a whore? Guilt and shame run deep. However, she does not want her dress or behavior to be determined by her fear of disapproval, whether it is from the outside, or from the internalized voice of her mother. She is committed to feeling fully free.

So the action she decides to take is to start by becoming aware of when she suppresses or diminishes her sexuality. One way to do this is to write voice dialogues between the part of herself that wants to be liberated and the part of herself that wants to remain a "nice girl." (Refer back to *Awakening Your Erotic Self*, Chapter 9, for exercises using dialogue work.) Then she may go shopping and try on the kinds of clothes she has secretly wanted to wear, just to experience how she feels wearing them. Perhaps she may buy something and wear it, exploring how it feels to expand her sense of herself and her possibilities.

## The Deeper Significance of Crushes

Sometimes attractions turn into crushes. Sometimes crushes turn into obsessions. If this happens and you are faced with a serious attraction that is long lasting with a neighbor, co-worker, or friend, it is even more important to explore the questions above. It is more likely that the person to whom you are attracted represents an undeveloped aspect of yourself. If you are in a committed relationship, the following questions are also helpful to explore:

> *What qualities does this person have that you feel are lacking in your partner? How have you and your partner addressed this?*
>
> *How does this person treat you differently than your partner? How have you and your partner addressed this?*
>
> *How does this attraction affect your ability to be intimate with your partner?*
>
> *How do you use your attraction to avoid intimacy?*
>
> *What fears about yourself arise if you imagine yourself fully committed in your relationship.*

Use these questions to work on yourself and then to discuss your attraction with your partner. Also, consider that you are having an affair, although unconsummated, and acknowledge this to your partner. H/she will probably not like hearing this but it will validate the intuitions and feelings h/she has had. If you are afraid to broach the subject on your own, we recommend that you seek couple's counseling. Another useful approach is to go into your own individual counseling with the purpose of understanding yourself and your motivations—especially if you have a pattern of consummated or unconsummated affairs.

There's no question that it can be scary to address other attractions, whether you are the person experiencing the attraction, or the person who suspects your partner is experiencing it. If you are experiencing attractions that arouse secrecy in you, it's time to face the music. If, on the other hand, you suspect that your partner is carrying on an intrigue, it may serve you to address your concerns.

Even the little concerns can be valuable to address. You need not hide your feelings of jealousy, if you suspect your partner feels attracted to someone else. Of course, this doesn't give you license to blame or shame your partner by venting your life's insecurities on him or her either. There's a middle ground. In the following story, a couple reaches great heights after simply talking about the jealousy of one partner.

# A Risk Paid Off

They sat together on the floor, their backs resting against pillows, and stared into the flickering light from the fireplace. Phil sighed. He felt a sensation of inner warmth and love for Sandra that was so intense it brought tears to his eyes. He gave her hand a tender squeeze, and she returned it.

How wonderful it was that they were able to talk out their problem. *His problem*, he thought. He was the one who was jealous the night before at the party. It had seemed to him that Sandra paid too much attention to the host. And then as they were leaving, she rushed over to him and gave him a big hug. A little too friendly, Phil thought. But he didn't say anything. He just stewed. Until this evening, when he finally brought it up.

It hadn't been easy for him. He tended to avoid confrontation. But he and Sandra had been working with a therapist to improve their communication skills. When he brought up his feelings of jealousy, Sandra didn't laugh at him, nor did she become defensive. In fact, she said she was flattered that he cared about her enough to feel that way. Then she went on to explain that, of course, she was flirting with their host the previous night. But he was an old friend. It was playful, and it didn't mean she wanted to have an affair with him or that she loved Phil any less.

Phil brushed at his eyes with the back of his hand. It was such a relief getting this cleared up. Intellectually, he knew Sandra hadn't been making a pass at the host. But that wasn't the real issue. It was his feelings—his jealousy and his doubts—that he felt ashamed of and had troubled him. And he was able to talk to her about those feelings, revealing his vulnerable side. So, what began as *his problem* changed to *their problem*, and they worked it out the only way such a problem can be solved—together.

He leaned toward Sandra and kissed her gently on the neck, just under her ear. "Oh, that's nice," she said. She turned toward him and their mouths met. Their kiss was unhurried, lingering. Their tongues met, blending leisurely. As they kissed, their hands explored each other's bodies. This was familiar territory, but they touched, searched, probed, and caressed as though for the first time.

Phil parted from Sandra for a moment to throw another log on the fire. When he turned back, he saw she had spread the quilt on the floor and was starting to undress. He was out of his own clothes in seconds. As he drew near her, he could see her smile in the flickering light. He finished undressing her, covering her with soft kisses as he removed her clothes. Then he laid her gently on the soft quilt and continued covering her body with kisses mixed with licking and sucking.

He knelt between her legs and slowly lowered his head until it was between her thighs. He began to lick her inner thighs, switching from one to the other at an easy pace. Finally, he wrapped his arms around her legs and barely, ever so barely, touched his tongue to her vaginal lips—just enough so she could feel it and know he was there. Then he began to work his tongue into the warm, slick fold of her vagina. He licked at the inner lips, then moved upwards until his tongue was flicking gently, very slowly, at her pulsating clitoris.

He lay flat on the quilt now, sucking and licking as contentedly as a baby at the nipple. Somehow he lost track of time, engulfed in the present, his mind at ease. Sandra's hips began to move, almost imperceptibly at first, and then stronger and steadily faster. Her breathing began to quicken and she was moaning in delight. He could feel her thighs pressing harder against his head. As her body began to quiver, her moans got louder and she began to pant, he moved his tongue as fast he could, sustaining it until Sandra's body began undulating in orgasm. After the peak of her orgasm, Phil slowed his tongue to make slow circles around her clitoris, pressing hard against it, then almost imperceptibly. Sandra's body quivered with a few more orgasms, then went limp.

Gently, she drew Phil's head up to hers and whispered in his ear, "Be in me." In one smooth motion, he gathered her up, and pulled her onto his lap, and slid his erect penis into her moist cave until he could go no deeper. She wrapped her arms around him and brought her mouth up to meet his. Their bodies were pressed against each other so tightly she could hear Phil's heart beating. They breathed together, their mouths locked in a deep kiss.

Phil knew that Sandra had started running energy through her Inner Flute because each time she inhaled, she squeezed his Wand as if she were trying to suck him up into her. Oh, how he loved to be inside her moist, welcoming vagina. He, too, began running energy up to his crown chakra. This was new to both of them so they both felt a bit awkward. They lost the rhythm and started laughing. Phil lost his erection and slid out. Sandra reached down and placed his beautiful penis between their bellies. Slowly, they began to breathe and rock together. Within minutes Phil regained his erection and slid back in.

As if in a dance, they shifted positions. Sandra was on top, moving up and down exactly the way Phil loved. Without thinking, Phil knew that Sandra would reach orgasm several times in the course of their coupling. He, too, would have several little "cums," before the final explosive orgasm drained him of his seed and his strength.

But he was in no hurry. Nor was she. Locked together, they moved slowly and gently, engulfed in the pleasures of their bodies and the depth of their love for each other. They had a long evening ahead of them—and a long life, too.

At long last, Phil lay his head down on Sandra's breast, one nipple in his mouth. Sandra whispered, with a hint of humor, "Do you still feel jealous?" A sleepy "No, honey. I love you," and Phil fell asleep like a baby in her arms. Sandra smiled. They were once again as close as close could be.

# Tools for Handling Sexual Attraction

Here are some general guidelines, based on what we have presented in this chapter:

1. If you have other attractions, acknowledge them to yourself.

2. Be open and honest about your attractions, both with your partner and with the person to whom you're attracted.

3. Agree with your partner on clearly-defined boundaries in your relationship, and agree on methods for maintaining these boundaries.

4. Share your fantasies with your partner, if your partner wants to hear them.

5. Exercise your ability to ask for what you want and your ability to say no.

6. Use your other attractions to learn more about your own erotic nature and about your feelings regarding your relationship.

7. Enjoy your sexuality and the spice and the energy of other attractions, knowing that you do not have to act on them.

Handling sexual attractions is obviously one of the greater challenges to being lifetime lovers. But an even greater challenge is overcoming the harmful effects of one or both partners stepping over the line—having an affair. We will suggest some strategies for working through these obstacles in the next chapter, *Getting Through the Hard Times*. As you well know, there are a host of other potential difficulties in lover relationships that have nothing to do with attractions or affairs. We will cover some major ones in the next chapter as well.

Every relationship faces potential dissolution at times. However, it is possible to move beyond the instability. It takes a deeper level of commitment and the willingness to risk even more. We cannot let our comfort zones lull us into apathy. We must face the challenges directly. *Getting Through the Hard Times* will provide you with more tools to handle obstacles when they emerge.

*14*

# Getting Through
# the Hard Times

*Through Love all that is bitter will be sweet.*
*Through Love all that is copper will be gold.*
*Through Love all dregs will turn to purest wine.*
*Through Love all pain will turn to medicine.*

Rumi, from *Look! This Is Love: Poems of Rumi*

## Aftermath of an Affair

Sarah, a well-dressed woman in her mid fifties, ran her hands over the glimmering silk. The skimpy teddy revealed her curves beautifully. "It's a little racy," she thought, "but that's what I want. The sexier the better."

After she changed back into her street clothes, she left the dressing room and paid the saleswoman. She glanced at her watch. She had other errands ahead of her. Her next stop was the bookstore. She had a pretty good idea what she wanted, and she headed right for the section on relationships, looking for how-to books about sex.

She leafed through a dozen or so, finally choosing four that she thought would suit her purpose. After paying for her selections, she was off on her next errand—a visit to an adult book store. This was really pushing her limits. Acutely embarrassed and uncomfortable, she stood among the men with raincoats draped over their arms. She glanced at several porno magazines, finally picking three that he might like.

She could feel herself blushing when she picked out the sex toys from the glass case by the cash register. But, she had made up her mind—and she was going to go through with it. The man behind the counter seemed indifferent to her, as though well-dressed, middle-aged women routinely procured porno magazines and massage oil there.

Relieved to get out of the seedy atmosphere, Sarah headed home, stopping at her favorite gourmet shop for champagne and caviar. That seemed to do it. She was ready to set a mood that would captivate him, that would stir his erotic nature.

All this was part of her plan. She had conceived of her plan two days earlier, when—on her fifty-fifth birthday—she had discovered that her husband was having an affair. Betrayed, mortified, and furious, she confronted Paul. She knew there had to be a reason; he had never before been unfaithful in their thirty-five years of marriage. She wanted answers! He had none. The affair had been going on for two years. What was so different about their life that would motivate him to pursue another woman now?

After much self-examination, the answer suddenly became apparent. Two years ago, their oldest daughter had divorced and returned to the family home with her year-old child. "When my daughter and grandchild arrived," she told us, "I put all my energy and attention into taking care of them. The affair began a few months after they arrived. I discovered it two weeks after they left, when I started paying attention again. I put two and two together and figured that my lack of attention had created conditions in which he chose to have an affair. I reasoned that if I began paying attention to him again, I would see a change."

Shocked as she was, Sarah still took firm action. She made it clear to her husband that she wouldn't tolerate his affair. She exacted a promise from him that he would see the other woman the next day for the last time. He must either end the affair, or she would leave him. He repeatedly insisted he was committed to the marriage and had not intended to hurt her. Reluctantly, Paul agreed to cut off the affair as she had demanded.

Even after extracting his promise, she was consumed with suspicion and mistrust. "I found myself calling his office several times a day, asking his secretary where he was. I didn't want to live like that but I couldn't help myself. My anger and jealousy showed me how much I really valued him. I did not want this other woman to take away my husband."

For the next step in her plan, Sarah arranged for the two of them to get away on a special four-day weekend. It was just in time to celebrate their thirty-fifth anniversary, only two weeks away. She was determined to "become a better lover than this whore" whom her husband thought was so sexy. By the time their getaway came around, she would be ready to deliver the rest of her message. By then she would have finished her crash course in sexuality. She would choreograph the weekend as though it were as exciting as an affair. She was going to compete and win.

## Reawakening Sexuality

Sarah's story had a happy ending. Not only did Sarah win back her husband, but in the process she discovered her own sexuality. Paul was the only sexual partner she had ever known. Born in 1929, she married just after her twentieth birthday. A virgin on her wedding night, she knew virtually nothing about sex or her own body. She had never masturbated because she had learned from her mother that good girls did not do that sort of thing. Sex had been okay, nothing to rave about. Her husband was a generous lover and often asked her what he could do to please her, but she simply did not know. She was a stranger to her body when it came to sex.

In retrospect, she describes herself as having been "sexually depressed." She had grown up with an unconscious belief that women were not supposed to enjoy sex. Her mother was a product of the Victorian era and though she was a passionate, lively woman, she was uncomfortable with anything sexual. The movies Sarah saw as an adolescent and young woman had all gone through the censoring bureau. "Husbands and wives slept in twin beds. Society did not acknowledge the sexual part of people, particularly women." Paul had complained that she never initiated in sex. Now she knew why. Her shame stopped her body from being turned on.

By the time the four-day weekend arrived, Sarah had become friends with her body and her sex organs. With the help of a mirror, she looked at her vagina. She learned to masturbate, she found her G-spot, and she used a vibrator for the first time. She learned about the changes and fluctuations in her body so that she could be aware of what she wanted and what to ask for. She read her books carefully. By the end of her second week of self-created basic training, she was ready!

# Better Than a Honeymoon

Their four-day weekend was better than their honeymoon. Sarah initiated lovemaking. Paul loved it and so did she. She knew what felt good and what felt even better—and she told him. She was not shy. At last he was getting the lover he had always wanted. They made love, ate, danced, and made love some more. She felt delicious, succulent, and satisfied. Even though it had taken her this long to find her sexuality, she still had a lot of life ahead of her. Boy, was she going to enjoy it!

Sarah and Paul celebrate their forty-seventh wedding anniversary this year. "You have to create your own passion," Sarah says. "Then, together the two of you can play with it and enjoy it." Now the frequency of their lovemaking waxes and wanes. As Paul, who is approaching seventy-seven, falls asleep earlier, they have sex less frequently. She smiles with pleasure when she talks of him. "When it happens, it's great, so I don't experience a loss."

# Views from the Other Side

We also had the good fortune to interview Paul. His view of the affair was somewhat different than his wife's. Though he did not attribute his affair to his wife's sudden lack of attention, he did say, "She didn't give a damn if I were there or not." Besides, he wanted someone more aggressive and his wife had not heeded his sexual requests over the years. The woman he began seeing clandestinely was more adventurous and sexually aggressive, and he liked that.

When we asked him why the affair began when it did, he responded simply, "I met her at a workshop and one thing led to another."

"But why then?" we persisted, "You've been to similar workshops before."

"Well, this woman was holding me in this workshop, and I became aroused. Then I thought, why not? I didn't think there was anything wrong with what I was doing."

"Then why didn't you tell your wife?" we asked.

"I didn't think she would approve," he responded sheepishly.

And was he ever right. "When she reacted so strongly upon learning of the affair," he said, "I realized that Sarah really cared. So I promised that I wouldn't see my friend again."

Although he would still like his wife to be more aggressive sexually, he is appreciative of the changes she has made and is happy their marriage is stronger than ever. "I never considered leaving her for a minute," he declared emphatically. "I knew she was the woman for me from the moment I laid eyes on her," Paul said as he smiled with a twinkle in his eye.

It is probably quite apparent that Paul did not engage in the level of self-reflection that Sarah did. Unlike her, he did not use the affair as a catalyst for his personal growth. He never became conscious and aware of what motivated him to begin the affair. Nor did he search to understand the ways that he had helped create conditions in which an affair was an option. But even though Paul never really dealt with his part in understanding the affair, he did return to the marriage with one hundred percent emotional investment.

# Morals of the Story

There are several morals to this story. One is: if someone hands you lemons, make lemonade. Sarah could have bemoaned her fate, caved in and felt like a victim. She could have resented and blamed her husband for emotionally and sexually abandoning her, ruining their marriage and her life. Instead, she chose a response which took the relationship to an unprecedented level of pleasure and success. She became proactive rather than reactive.

Another moral is: it's never too late to change. Our heroine could have believed that she was over the hill. She could have become despondent and depressed, helpless to change herself or her marriage. She could have had an affair herself to get back at her husband and teach him a lesson. Instead, she chose a response which enriched and expanded her, and added value to her relationship. She changed her beliefs about women, sexuality, aging, and herself.

And yet another moral is: before you take the speck out of the eye of another, take the beam out of your own eye. Sarah could have berated Paul for his infidelity, called him names, and kept up the drama for years. She could have stayed in the safe zone of blame without asking what role she played in the drama. Instead, she chose to become aware of how she might have unconsciously and unintentionally colluded to co-create the unhappy circumstance.

Perhaps there was a hidden payoff in the lack of attention she had been giving her husband. Perhaps she felt more free to give her attention to her daughter and granddaughter if he were occupied with other interests. Perhaps his other interests saved her from feeling guilty about withdrawing her attention from him. At any other time in their marriage she might have been curious and asked questions about what he was up to when he began spending Thursday evenings "doing his own thing." But she asked nothing.

At the time she had felt glad that he was doing something on his own, since he had never previously done this in all the years they had been married. He was not one to go out with the guys, socialize with co-workers, or seek entertainment alone. The fact that suddenly he wanted to set aside Thursday nights without telling her anything about his plans did not seem strange to her at the time. The fact that she did not ask questions did not seem strange to her either.

In retrospect, both seemed strange. It was as if she had been in a trance. Relieved to have more time and energy for her daughter, unconsciously and unintentionally, she looked the other way when suspicious signs appeared.

Another moral: hold a vision of the big picture when calamity befalls you. In other words, don't throw the baby away with the bath water. She could have felt so betrayed that she decided her marriage was over. False pride could have led her to divorce him, saying, "Who does he think he is? I'm not going to let him do this to me again." However, she and her husband had a strong foundation of love and friendship. She knew what she wanted from her marriage and she worked to create it.

Affairs are not the only hard times some couples face. However, they tend to challenge people in the most primal ways. The following story involves a couple, Ben and Susan, who handled an affair entirely differently.

# Time to Remodel

Ben and Susan entered therapy after Susan's affair was discovered. Their relationship was in shambles. They described their marriage as a house that had been gutted by fire. They struggled with the decision of whether to abandon the charred ruins (get divorced), or use the opportunity to remodel and build what they had always wanted.

Even though they knew that remodeling entails a lot of dust, dirt, and discomfort, they decided to do it anyway. Throughout their work in therapy, Ben and Susan used this metaphor to help them endure the stress and pain of tearing down the parts of their relationship which no longer served them. It also helped them to withstand the fear of the unknown as they explored new territory together. As part of reconstructing their relationship, they actually remodeled their bedroom to reflect the erotic relationship they had always wanted.

They delved into all the old patterns which they had accepted as "just the way it is." With a lot of attention and intention, they learned to be more vulnerable with each other, to be more direct in what they wanted from each other and the relationship, and they worked through the resentment and fear the affair had stimulated.

# There is Hope

As these couples demonstrate, learning how to navigate through life's challenges is the ultimate test of success or failure. Perhaps nothing is worse than the anguish of love gone sour. Everyone has suffered the pain of relationship blues. And when we are in the middle of it, it is difficult to imagine any way out.

When you are feeling hurt, resentful, victimized and misunderstood, it's not easy to view the situation objectively. Nor is it easy to look at your partner and see the good with the bad—or the potential for change. Yet the stories of couples like these show that the hard times can be extremely fertile periods if used well.

It is easier if both people are committed to move through the difficulties—which, of course, need not be limited to an affair—but it is quite possible to begin the process alone. You can begin by simply saying something like this to your partner: "This does not feel good to me. This is not what we are about as people. Let's get off it and find out what is at the bottom of our defensive reactions." To do this, you must abandon your position of self-righteousness, or role as the victim.

The next time you have a squabble or feel badly about what is happening in your relationship, try this exercise we call "Let's Get Off It."

## Exercise #1

### *Let's Get Off It*

When you become aware that you are acting defensively or you are simply not feeling good about the way you and your partner are relating to one another, take a few deep breaths and let them go. Close your eyes if that helps you to sense and center yourself. Then get in touch with your desire or vision for the relationship.

Open your eyes, look at your partner and say your personalized version of, "I want to work this out. However, how we are dealing with it does not feel good. Let's do it another way. This is not serving us."

If your partner responds favorably, take a few minutes to look at each other without talking and touch each other in any way that feels good to both of you. If your partner continues an abusive or defensive pattern, keep breathing and ask what you would like from him or her. If your partner does not stop, tell your partner that you are going to take care of yourself by taking time alone, being quiet, or whatever works for you. This also gives your partner time and space to cool off. When you are both ready, go to step four.

Now make a statement of your commitment to go the distance and to find out what is really being triggered for you at the self-concept level. This might sound like, "Let's find out what is really going on for both of us that is causing us to become so irritated by each other."

Complete the process by making credit taking statements for yourself and giving appreciation to your partner for the work you have both done. They might sound something like this. "I'm proud of myself for not reacting to you as I so often have and I am very appreciative that you were so open as well." Even a very general statement can do wonders. "I feel glad that we were able to get out of blaming each other and become more loving" is one example.

We (Daniel and Judith) use this process whenever we find ourselves in the middle of a negative pattern. Sometimes we are able to get out of the negativity immediately. Other times it takes us several hours or days to get to the bottom of what is going on between us. We have found techniques like these invaluable for keeping our relationship sweet and supportive over the years.

Here's a good rule of thumb about when to use the last exercise: when you feel certain that your lover is surely the villain, and it is difficult to imagine what you ever saw in this person who is glaring at you. Don't wait for your partner to begin the process of reconciliation and re-connection. He or she may be waiting for you to begin.

An effective and humorous way to address the "you first" dynamic is to play the following game. It is usually fun and can take the pressure off of a highly charged situation.

## Exercise #2

### *You First*

Begin by staring each other in the eye. One of you begins by saying , "You first."

The other person says, "No, you first."

The two of you continue going back and forth saying, "No, you first" ad infinitum or ad nauseum, whichever comes first. Allow yourselves to use any tone of voice and body movement you want. Exaggerate and play with both your sounds and your movement. Let yourselves make faces, be ferocious or funny, however you feel moved as the process unfolds. If either of you have a history of physical violence or are afraid of violence, make sure you agree on ground rules, such as no touching, before you begin.

Denise and Lenny frequently became adversarial and stuck in an emotional stand-off in which neither of them were willing to take responsibility for how they were co-creating the situation. Neither were willing to become vulnerable in any way. Each felt sure their position was the right one, and refused to move until the other showed empathy or understanding.

As they began to play "You First" during a counseling session in our office, their anger erupted. Denise stood with her hands on her hips, her nose barely a half-inch from Lenny's nose. Lenny grabbed Denise's shoulders. Glaring at each other, between clenched teeth, they spat out the words like bullets. Suddenly their noses touched. Magic happened. They stuck out their tongues. They began to laugh uproariously at the absurdity of their postures. "You First" ended in a warm embrace.

This experience became a reference for Denise and Lenny whenever they got stuck in their adversarial positions. Simply by saying, "You first," or by sticking out a tongue, either one of them could initiate gales of laughter. Then, with their dispositions restored, they could address the issues at hand.

# Changing Positions Fluidly

Perhaps no skill is as important in moving through hard times as the ability to shift stuck positions. When couples get locked into their respective corners, like two boxers, they often engage in a fight to the finish. They lose the ability to see what's happening outside the ropes. And this ability is essential to changing the damaging dynamics—the capacity to fluidly shift from one state to another, from one psychological position to one that may feel radically different. This capacity is really part of the multidimensional lover.

Nisha Zenoff, an internationally acclaimed process oriented psychologist, attributes many of the problems we have in relationships to our inability to shift roles and remain fluid in our relationships. "We have so much pain because we get stuck in a limited role and lose our ability to *see the bigger picture."*

She describes how we can avoid this quagmire by developing fluidity. She describes this as, "being able to move in and out of different roles, fully occupying one position when you are in it, and when you are not, being able to watch various roles from an observer position." The key to learning how to shift out of a stuck position is to "notice something you haven't noticed such as changing signals, dreams, visions, feelings, sensations or body postures."

By developing the ability to shift positions and by strengthening your observer/meta-communicator, you can prevent unnecessary pain, and you can catapult your relationship to glorious heights. And once again, vulnerability is the key. Moving off your position requires courage, vulnerability, and trust—of yourself and your partner. This ability to shift positions is critical, particularly when external events challenge your relationship stability.

So external events can catalyze difficult times, and some of these events are even positive in nature—like the arrival of a new child. Newborn infants and older children can intensify relationship challenges dramatically. The following story involving our own experience attests to this.

# From Lovers to Parents

We (Daniel and Judith) felt blessed! Amidst the horror stories of many people's relationships —tales of joyless, hopeless, and despondent unions—we felt buoyed against the pitfalls of romance gone awry. Looking into each other's eyes, pressing our warm bodies against each other, we felt lucky almost beyond belief. Despite the challenges we faced, we had each other. While misunderstandings, abandonment, betrayal, and mistrust seemed like the norm in many relationships we observed, ours flourished, month after month.

Of course we had our spats and quarrels, our hurts and pains. Yet we had a deep, abiding belief that we could and would move through it all. Even though we had our sexual problems, and areas of tension which occasionally drove us to frustration and filled us with despair, we still felt basically optimistic and clear-headed. We were able to resolve or dissolve conflicts as they arose.

Then our son was born. Who would believe that such a sweet, innocent, and delightful little fellow could change our relationship so completely? Probably most people who have had children, that's who. Quarrels turned into heated arguments and spats turned into prolonged fights. We were shocked and disbelieving that we—these loving and conscious people regarded by many as a model couple—had fallen so profoundly from grace. There were times when we literally felt hatred toward each other and the unutterable came to the foreground: the possibility of divorce.

What happened? Seemingly minor problems became magnified. The same unwashed dishes, the same socks on the floor, the same forgotten chores, now aroused Judith's ire to a frightening pitch. "I will *not* be your mother" resounded in my (Daniel's) ears. It was not that I hadn't heard this before from Judith, but now she seemed to have no sense of humor, patience, or compassion. She had always been clear and communicative about what she would and would not do in the way of picking up after me, yet she was also gentle and tolerant of what I, too, perceived as my shortcomings. But, shortly after the birth of our son, she was giving me no margin of error.

Sure, I knew that I did not take responsibility in certain ways, yet I felt unappreciated for the contributions I was making to our family. I was working harder than ever, yet at the same time I practically lost the everpresent source of nurturing and support I had come to expect. Although I appreciated the boundless love my young son was receiving from his mother, I also wanted to be held and cherished myself.

I felt like a hurt, unwanted, and unappreciated appendage, a money-making machine. Not only was I missing the love I once had, I also felt unreasonably penalized by Judith's intolerance. I told her that I recognized my undeveloped aspects and was working on them, even though I found it difficult to imagine taking on more responsibility.

## Painful Contemplations

As we walked through the wooded hills of our neighborhood one cold Christmas day, the tension was palpable. Judith saw smoke rising from a neighbor's chimney and it reminded her of feeling betrayed. I had promised that I would have our broken fireplace repaired, yet had left the project unattended. It was symbolic of other incompletions.

Her hurt and anger filled the grayish silence. She wasn't shy. In no uncertain terms, she pointed out my failure and expressed her deep pain. She felt alone; that although I was providing financially for the family, I was not fully being a team player. Thoughts of divorce passed through her mind daily.

Rather than defend myself from Judith's wrath and disappointment, I listened. I walked. I did not respond. I allowed myself to sense how deep her pain ran, like a dark, underground river coursing through her life. She talked about the feelings of being a new mother. She told me how she felt unappreciated and insignificant when I promised to do something but didn't follow through.

It irked her that I could be so disciplined about my own physical exercise, yet skip attending to a whole list of things I had agreed to do for the household. She felt overburdened by the demands of a heavily nursing baby, her counseling work, and our new home. Even before the baby, she experienced conflict between acting responsibly toward others and taking time of herself. When I let things slide, she felt even more internal pressure. Hearing how her pain was related to my behavior touched me in an indescribable way. Rather than respond quickly, I told her I would take time to consider her words.

Over the next few hours, I pondered my deepest motivations. Why, whenever I walked into the house, did I become blind to what needed attention? This was quite a contradiction considering how acute my senses really were. What motivated me to completely "forget" promises I had made to Judith when in many other aspects of my life I was extremely responsible? Who did I expect to clean up my messes, really? I even wondered, Does this mean I don't love her as much as I thought I did? I realized that there must be an unconscious payoff at the source of my actions. What could it be?

## Are You My Mother?

I went off by myself and walked through the hills, trying to sort through my feelings. Later, when I returned, I was ready to talk. I was embarrassed to admit it, but Judith's criticisms were accurate. I was acting like Judith was my mother! My mother is a great lady and I love her dearly, but when I was growing up, she was quite intrusive. I had learned to turn her off as if she were an irritating TV commercial.

I remembered scenes from my childhood. My brother and I would be watching TV and my mother would walk into the room and tell us to take out the garbage. Without looking, we would respond in unison, "Yeah, Ma." Yet we both somehow "forgot" our chore and our promise. Miraculously though, the garbage disappeared.

Having mastered the ability to turn off my mother in childhood and adolescence—with little consequence—I was able to draw on this skill with my wife. But Judith would have none of it. She was shrewd and from the very beginning had been wise to my tricks. Now, with an infant to care for, she had less tolerance for my behavior while I, feeling left out and unappreciated, became more prone to these undesirable ways. It was altogether a bad mix. I realized that a pattern I had learned earlier in life was now contributing to the demise of my marriage.

## A Work in Progress

Sometimes motivation to change arises internally, without external pressure. This was not one of those cases. A giant boot was kicking me out of my comfort zone. I realized that changing my behavior—picking up after myself, doing the dishes, and more—would be less painful than staying the same. Potential divorce from my wife and less time with my child did not sit well with me.

But still there was a conflict. I could not simply *will* myself to change. God knows I had tried that before. This only works temporarily until the heat dies down. To get greater perspective on my lifelong tendency, I asked myself, "Why am I so reluctant to be more responsible?" To start with, I considered any payoffs to having a wife (mother) who was hurt and angry on the one hand, yet still cleaned up after me.

I discovered much to my chagrin, that I loved to have someone be my maid. I could go about my business, engage in the interesting parts of projects and then leave the clean-up drudgeries to someone else. I became aware of the unconscious belief driving part of this behavior: a woman's role is to take care of a man on all levels—androcracy in modern times.

Consciously, I did not conceive that I held this traditional male view. After all, I had been involved with men's liberation for many years, had done extensive research on the male sex role, and had led many workshops and groups to help men free themselves of limiting, archaic male roles. I had also developed a love and respect for women. Yet now I had something to lose—a maid. To let go of this male privilege was/is not easy.

Through much soul searching, I also became aware that I was afraid of being closer and more intimate with Judith. My behavior helped create a boundary or barrier between us which I unconsciously perceived as safe. I could avoid feeling vulnerable if we were engaged in a fight. Nothing like hassles to keep people apart.

Through dialoguing, I explored my self-styles that wanted to change and my self-styles that wanted to remain the same. After I had worked through this inner conflict—at least more than previously—I then made a deeper decision to change these old, dysfunctional ways.

Over time, as Judith and I both saw changes, the tension began to subside. I have learned to take greater responsibility for cleaning up my messes and this has had major benefits in my relationship. Have I completely transformed? Absolutely not! I forget and go back to past ways at times. But I continue to uncover more unconscious blocks to being responsible, and make more and more changes over time.

## The Chain Is as Strong as Its Weakest Link

Although the details may vary, we have heard similar stories from countless couples. When the first child arrived, regardless of whether the people were young or old, newly married or firmly established, the relationship was tremendously disrupted. In fact, each new child can amplify and exacerbate any latent or unresolved issues in the relationship—even the fourth or fifth child. A chain is only as strong as its weakest link, and any stress will test the strength of the whole chain. The responsibilities of parenthood are a sure way to find the weak links in the relationship.

Life is filled with challenges. When a baby is born, a partner loses a job or begins a new job, a home is purchased, or a parent or a child dies, everyone is tested. These positively or negatively charged events may stress one or both partners. If you are aware that your worst relationship challenges are likely to arise when one or both of you feels stressed, you can be forewarned, and prepared to meet them when they come.

## Memories of Sexual Abuse

Many people are becoming aware of being sexually abused during childhood. These memories often arise in the context of loving, sexual relationships. Whereas sex may be strained before the person becomes aware of past abuse, when explicit memories surface, sexual relations often come to a grinding halt. This is not only painful for the victims of the abuse; it is painful for their partners as well.

Both partners want and deserve support. Groups abound for people who were sexually molested as children. Support groups and educational workshops for the partners of these women and men are just beginning to form. Scott Nelson, Ph.D., a psychologist in Mill Valley, California, has been instrumental in bringing attention to this group. His workshops and support groups are designed to aid the partners in dealing with the rejection, projections, and abandonment they experience.

Since both partners experience a myriad of feelings and reactions during recovery, any kind of support group and/or counseling to which the couple avails themselves can be helpful. The more both partners use all the exercises and skills developed in the previous chapters, the more easily they can move gracefully through something as trying as sexual abuse memories.

## Differences in Desire

Another challenge some couples face relates to differences in sexual desire. The challenge with different desire levels is that it can cause massive separation between the partners. Typically, one partner feels resentful and deprived, and associates the rejection with being unloved, insignificant, and/or incompetent. The rejected partner often withdraws emotionally, prompting the other partner to feel threatened and defensive.

But it doesn't have to be this way. There are ways of dealing with these differences which are actually bonding. What can partners do when one partner wants to have sex and the other does not, particularly when this is a pattern? Let's look at how different couples solved this problem. We'll start with the story of Arny and Beth.

Arny and Beth have been married for twenty-four years. They came into couples therapy, both in pain, almost ready to separate. Arny was angry at Beth. Beth felt hurt and was angry at Arny. He said that she never wanted to make love and he was ready to find a woman who liked sex.

"She used to like sex," he said, glowering at Beth. "She never turned me down. Now it's rare if she says yes. I don't know what's gotten into her." Beth turned to us and groused. "He wants sex every night and sometimes I don't. What's so wrong with that?" There was nothing wrong with that—but the context of the situation was poorly framed.

Slowly, we unraveled the roots of their conflict. In his late forties, Arny was in the throes of a mid-life crisis. He was not as successful as he had hoped to be by this age. Though he was an avid runner in good physical condition, he was feeling less attractive as he grew older. A new sports car had not solved his problems. His relationship with his three children, ages fifteen, seventeen, and twenty, ranged from "mediocre to horrible" in his opinion. It seemed to be getting worse as the children got older.

Beth, also in her late forties, was facing her own mid-life crisis. She had been a full-time mother and homemaker until three years ago when she had gone back to school to get a graduate degree. Exposed to younger women and men with newer ideas, she began to question some of the assumptions on which their marriage was based.

Until recently, she had never even considered turning him down. She had sex with him whether or not she felt like it. Over the years, rather than risk crossing him or hurting his feelings, she had learned to feign interest—often faking orgasm. Now, she was struggling with a desire to be her own person, to let go of her children and create a life for herself. She no longer wanted to be complacent or passive, yet she didn't want to lose her marriage.

As they expressed some of their hurts, fears, and hopes to each other, it became apparent that though they had had some differences, their goals were similar. They both loved each other and wanted to stay together. They both wanted lovemaking to be exciting and pleasurable. They both wanted to support the other in moving into their mid-life with the same kind of teamwork they had used throughout their relationship.

It was both painful and touching when Beth revealed she had been faking orgasm. Arny went through a myriad of feelings. He was outraged that she would lie, hurt that she didn't trust him, fearful that he was not a good enough lover, and—finally—curious and empathetic about her feelings.

They explored their beliefs and feelings about marriage, sex, gender roles, and each other. Gradually, as Beth let go of some deep, unconscious shame and guilt she was carrying about her sexuality, a breakthrough occurred—she was starting to view sex as a natural, positive, healthy function. As a result of this, it became okay for her to tell Arny that though she was not feeling aroused, she would support him while he masturbated.

Beth began kissing Arny's body as he masturbated, and found that she was becoming aroused, herself. She also began to masturbate and found that her sexual appetite grew as she became more familiar with her body. On his part, Arny worked to separate his feelings of competence and lovability from Beth's response. He came to realize that she was not rejecting him as a person when she turned him down; she was simply saying, "I'm not feeling sexual now."

This reassured Arny and relieved some of the need he felt to have frequent sex. Arny paid more attention to the emotional side of their relationship. Through sex workshops, Arny and Beth are continuing to learn about each other. They still struggle at times, but they are headed in the right direction.

## Handling the Situation

Here's a potentially simple solution to different desire levels. The less desirous person in the couple can *help* their partner satisfy him or herself. By participating in the act peripherally, the *helper* can assist the more desirous person without having to become more engaged than feels good for him or her. Paradoxically, the less engaged person may feel their own juices begin to flow through this participation—although it's optimum when there is no expectation for this to occur. This next couple dealt with this type of situation elegantly.

Carla was already in bed when Angelo got home. He tiptoed into the room and undressed quietly. He had been hoping she would still be awake when he arrived. He had been thinking about her throughout his shift. He had worked later than usual, picking up overtime that would come in handy, with his vacation only two weeks off.

As he slid under the sheets, Carla turned her head. "Hi, Ange," she said sleepily. "Hi, darling," he said, leaning forward and kissing her lightly on the mouth. He breathed in deeply. God, he loved her smell. And there was something special about it when she had been sleeping. He didn't know what it was, but it always excited him. As he thought about that, he realized his penis was getting erect. He reached for her hand and brought it towards him until it touched his penis.

"Look who's with me," he said. Carla made a small giggling sound. "Oh, Ange, honey, not tonight. I'm just really worn out. Maybe in the morning okay?" "Yeah," Angelo said, "I guess so." He turned onto his side, his back toward her.

Carla could hear the hurt and disappointment in his voice. She moved toward him, pressing against him, taking pleasure in the presence of his muscular body. She nuzzled her head against his shoulder. "Why don't you take care of it now, and I'll be with you," she said. She pushed her hand between his legs from behind and gripped his scrotum softly."

Angelo sighed with the pleasure of her touch. Then he lowered his hand until it was gripping his penis. Slowly he began to stroke it, and he knew it wouldn't be long before he came. After a minute or so, the familiar sensations began to stir, and he ejaculated with a loud expression of pleasure.

Angelo had put in a long, hard day, and now he allowed himself to drift into a deep, peaceful sleep. Carla curled up next to him, enjoying the feel of pressing her breasts against his strong back. In a moment, she, too, was asleep.

## Enjoying the Soft Times

As prominent as the erect penis may be, the soft member is often excluded from any club. Both men and women tend to have judgments about it, wishing they could will it into its heightened state. But, as we all know, it has a mind of its own. Working with the various states of penile arousal can be an art form. The next couple's story may prove insightful.

They had been lying in bed together, reading. Joan's book was a better-than-average romance novel and she had slowly begun to get horny. She put her hand between Darryl's legs and felt his penis. It was tiny and soft. Darryl kept reading, pausing only to say, "Hmmm, what's happening?"

"Just checking the territory," she said with a smile. He laughed and went back to his reading. She began reading her book again, too, but she kept her hand on Darryl's penis, working it slowly until she began to get a response. The stirring of his penis increased her excitement. She set the book on the bed and, while still holding onto Darryl, Joan began to rub between her own legs.

Eventually Darryl's penis became erect. He set his book down and moved into her arms. Her vagina was already soaking by now, and she guided him into her. But something wasn't quite working. He continued to move in her, but his penis had lost it's firmness. It had slipped out once, and he had difficulty getting it back in.

Finally, Joan had to face the facts. She was a lot hornier than Darryl was. When they were first married, it had bothered her that Darryl's libido didn't seem to be as strong as hers. For a long time, she had put up with it, figuring that that was life. The rest of their relationship was great, so she figured she could live with this aspect.

That changed, though, after she had attended a women's group. In the group, Joan spoke about her situation and said she had become resigned to it. One of the other women laughed. "No way, Joan," she said. "You've got a right to an orgasm." Then she told Joan what she could do.

Now, in bed with Darryl, she thought about what she had learned that day and how it had made such a difference in her friend's life. She pulled Darryl's mouth to hers and gave him a kiss. "Honey, I think you're a little tired," she said, "Let's try something else." Darryl smiled. "I think you're right," he said.

He withdrew from her and lay on his back while she straddled him. His penis was almost flaccid now and Joan reached down and gripped it at the base. She slid her hand up toward the head, forcing the blood to engorge the last inch or so. That part was rigid enough to be inserted in her vagina. She repeated the procedure a few more times, stopping when she figured his penis wouldn't get any harder.

Then she reached down with both hands and spread her vaginal lips wide, revealing her swollen clitoris. "That's so pretty!" Darryl said. He was staring at her vagina, not so much with lust as with curiosity and delight. Joan smiled at him and began to move her hands up and down, massaging her clitoris with the lips of her vagina. As she masturbated, she rocked back and forth, feeling pleasure in the contact of her body with Darryl and in his adoring gaze. Finally she felt the orgasm beginning.

"Now!" she said. Darryl leaned his head forward and began to suck the nipple of one breast while he massaged the other, pinching and kneading it gently between his fingers.

Joan clenched her thighs tightly against Darryl's hips and moved her hand rapidly up and down until the orgasm peaked. The wonderful feeling spread through her body and it lasted and lasted, tapering off gradually with each stroke of her hand. Again and again she moved her fingers over her clitoris, milking each drop of pleasure from the lingering sensations. Then she fell forward across Darryl's body, and their mouths met in a deep kiss.

Moments later, she reached up and turned off the light. She and Darryl talked for a few minutes, then gradually they both drifted off to sleep, locked in each other's arms.

## Feeling Unloved

One of the common problems that prevents couples from having sizzling sex is that one or both of them may feel unloved. This feeling is often masked by other problems. For example, the man may feel that they are not having sex frequently enough to satisfy him. This may be due to the fact that each partner's sex drive is different, or to any number of reasons.

But the man's dissatisfaction is often heightened by thinking that the reasons his partner doesn't want to have more sex with him is that she doesn't love him. This, in turn, arouses his deeper feelings that he is unlovable. She, on the other hand, may feel that she is inadequate or lacking in some way because she isn't able to respond to him as frequently as he would like.

Because he feels rejected, he becomes less willing to be vulnerable, and withdraws emotionally. His partner senses his coolness and responds by desiring sex even less often than before. The result is a stand-off.

It is essential to address the self-concept issues of both partners. If the man understands that his partner still loves him, even when she is not ready for sex, then he will not feel so rejected by their differing sexual appetites and will not react by distancing himself. When the woman understands that he feels hurt, but is still being warm and loving, she will be more ready to compromise and help find a solution. When each of them feels loved and wanted, then the specific problem issues—whatever they may be—are more easily solved.

## A Recipe for Success

No matter what situation you and your partner face, there are certain skills which can ensure success. Used diligently, these skills can transform your relationships. Moving back and forth between your own intense feelings of anger, jealousy, fear, or disappointment, and the meta-position or witness position is the key. The meta-position is when you step out of your personal reaction to the relationship and get a larger perspective on what is really happening. If you have access only to your own immediate experience without having any perspective on the relationship, you are bound to encounter defensive reactions. Your partner may accuse you of being self-centered or uncaring. In this instance, they may be right.

On the other hand, if you are able to have perspective on the relationship, but are unable to experience your own personal reactions fully, you will have a tendency to lose yourself or give yourself away emotionally—and then feel resentful. Transformation can only come when you are aware of and responsive to yourself as well as having perspective on the relationship. Here is a model to aid you in moving through hard times, if they should arise.

# Experiencing Yourself

*When in the position of experiencing your feelings, doing the following may serve you well:*

### Feel Fully

Allow yourself to feel (that does not mean act out) whatever you are experiencing without trying to stop or restrict the flow. Remember that e-motions (energy in motion) have a life of their own and will change organically if unfettered by have tos, shoulds, or musts. Pain comes from trying to stop a feeling from moving through its natural pathway.

### Behave Congruently

Let your behavior match how you feel inside. If you are feeling angry, hurt or scared, allow your behavior to reflect that instead of acting tough, victimized, confused or apathetic. On the other hand, beware of habitual patterns of angrily blaming others. Behaving congruently is not a license to react defensively or act abusively.

### Communicate Responsibly & Respectfully

Make direct feeling statements such as, "I feel furious," or "I feel unloved by you," rather than pass off blame filled judgments as feelings, such as, "I feel that you are mean and uncaring. You are a total ogre." Whenever the words *that* or *like* follow the word feeling, you can be sure that a feeling will not be forthcoming. Even if you are furious, hurt, or scared, be respectful of your partner and of your relationship. Do not become emotionally or physically abusive.

### Express "I Want" Statements Clearly & Directly

Deliver clear statements about your likes and dislikes as well as what you want and do not want, instead of simply complaining. The more direct and clear you are, the more likely you are to receive what you want.

# The Four A's of Perspective

*Moving into the meta-position, or witness position, you are able to view the experience from a broader perspective. From this vantage point, you can use what we call 'The Four A's':*

### Acknowledge Involvement

You can see the drama that has unfolded as a play in which you are participating rather than simply as an unwilling victim.

### Accept Co-creation

Then, you can look for how you are participating without blame or self-criticism. This in no way means that you are responsible for your partner's behavior, for each of us is always responsible for our own actions. It has to do with recognizing your part in the play and understanding how your behavior might affect your partner.

### Assess Unconscious Motivations

After acknowledging that you have a part and accepting how your part helped co-create the drama, you are ready to look for what might be going on under the surface of your consciousness.

Without blame or shame, begin to explore what possible reasons you might have had for your behavior—and what possible reasons your partner might have had for his or hers. Remember that you are not trying to be right, but rather to understand the situation more deeply. If your conclusion is that you are an angel and your partner is a villain, look again. Remember, this does not mean that you are asking for what you got but rather that you might have some hidden pay-off for having the behavior continue or for not addressing it.

### Act From Empowerment (Alive Action)

After the two of you come up with some possible pay-offs and unconscious motivations for your behavior, the next step is to decide what kind of action to take. From the perspective of the witness, or the meta-position, it is possible to be extremely creative in solving a problem. Rather than reacting to the intense emotions of the moment, ask yourself, "Where do I want to go from here? What do I want to achieve? What course of action will help me achieve my goal? How can I develop the skills required to pursue my plan? How can I insure that I am taking care of myself and my feelings as well as the relationship?

From this meta-position, we are free to peruse the situation as it unfolds and continuously make adjustments in our plan of action if need be. If I think that a certain course seems valuable but, once into it, find that it doesn't feel good or match my desires, I must be free and able to change my plans. Like steering a sailboat, I must be at liberty to adjust my sails or change my course to meet the ever-changing conditions of the sea. This is especially true when dealing with traumatic or highly charged situations. How I think I am going to feel is not necessarily how I end up feeling.

# Better than Compromise

Joan, forty-four years old, and just remarried, had told her husband, Art, that she did not mind if his grown children joined them on a long awaited vacation. As the departure day grew nearer, she became increasingly more uncomfortable with her decision. She had been looking forward to a romantic holiday without any obligations or scheduling. She imagined waking up each day not knowing what they would do, and deciding leisurely together over breakfast.

Art's children had other ideas. They were eager to know what the schedule would be. Joan wanted to please them since she believed that her pleasing them would please Art, whom she loved dearly. However, she began feeling resentful of the children and of Art.

When she finally told Art about her concerns, the two of them used the Four A's and were able to find a new solution that felt better for Joan—and also worked for Art. The two of them would start the vacation without the children, who would join them on the fourth day. Thereafter, they would join up with the kids at noon. Joan felt relieved as did Art, who also wanted time alone with his beloved. The kids were amenable to the solution, since they understood their father and step-mother's desire for time alone.

If, despite your attempts to stay in touch with your own feelings yet keep perspective on the relationship, you find yourself knee-deep in the mire, here are a few quick reminders to get you back on track.

## Quick Techniques for Turning Around

Remember the following:

*The two of you are on the same team.*

*You share a common desire to experience a relationship that feels good.*

*Both of you are simply trying to survive the best way you know how.*

*It's better to have the relationship work well than to be right.*

*If you think there are only two options, look again. There are always more possibilities.*

*Creative problem solving can* only *happen when you have figured out where your emotional charge is coming from at the self-concept level.*

*Sexual intimacy deepens as the two of you become more open and vulnerable with each other.*

In this chapter we have presented some tools and methods for overcoming potential conflicts. Beneath each of these methods, however, lies a principle. If an affair has occurred, openness and vulnerability are called forth. It isn't necessary for partners to have perfectly matched sexual desires, or to submerge their own desires for those of their partner. What *is* necessary is the commitment to working together, to solving problems and creating solutions *as a team*. The degree to which you commit to this will be the degree to which you will experience the joys of being lovers for life.

In the last chapter, *Erotic Mastery*, we provide a map to help you remember the various aspects of creating and sustaining a long-term lover relationship. You will be able to use it as a handy reference guide in exploring any relationship concerns which arise in the future. Hopefully, it can be a relationship bible for you throughout your life.

# 15

# Erotic Mastery

*Mastery is not perfection, but rather a journey, and the true master must be willing to try and fail and try again.*
George Leonard, *Mastery*

*Erotic Mastery* will be a refresher course for *Lovers for Life*. Although we have addressed all the aspects of mastery previously, we will now share our 24 principles systematically—principles which you can refer to again and again. This will help you integrate them more fully into your lover relationship. After each principle, there are references to related exercises throughout the book. In cases where there are no exercises, we direct you to the chapters and headings in which the material is covered.

Although love and sexuality are natural and instinctual, erotic mastery is an acquired art—not an innate ability. We recommend that you use *Erotic Mastery* as an opportunity to continue working with the material. Besides, there's no shame in practicing the basics time and time again. Repetition is the mother of mastery. Even if practice doesn't make perfect, it sure makes you better.

A wise saying used in 12-step recovery programs is an apt motto for a healthy, happy, lifelong relationship: "Progress, not perfection." The partners in such a union are not competing with outsiders or each other. They work together as a team. They are not looking for a final payoff; their reward is continuous. It comes from the enjoyment of living, loving, and working together—experiencing each day fully. Process-oriented rather than goal-oriented, they live their lives on a path of mastery.

Developing mastery in a relationship is not reserved for extraordinary people only. It's available to all who desire it, if they are willing to live the principles. True masters never allow circumstances to stop them. They are unstoppable! Though we cannot guarantee mastery, we can assure you that if you continually apply these principles, you will experience more and more success in your lover relationship—not to mention the rest of your life. We hope that this book will be a resource that you can turn to many times over the years.

## A Reminder

We have presented a tremendous amount of material in *Lovers for Life,* hoping to coach you in your erotic awakening and development. However, we want to emphatically remind you that mastery does not occur overnight. It takes time!

Perhaps you felt discouraged when you did not experience immediate success doing different exercises. Did you give up? Did you tell yourself or your partner that it simply was not worth it? If so, remember the importance of confronting the opposition (Chapter 9, *Awakening Your Erotic Self*). At times, we all get discouraged. We must learn how to use so-called "failure" as an ally.

# Stages of Mastery

There is a profound model of learning, or achieving mastery which encompasses all skills—applying as much to sexuality or music as it does to sports or carpentry. Here are the four stages of mastery:

### Stage 1–Unconscious Incompetence

At this stage, you are not even aware that you lack competence. Although it has been said that ignorance is bliss, you may find yourself repeating painful and limiting behavioral patterns. A common phrase from this stage is, "I don't know how I got myself into this predicament again!"

### Stage 2–Conscious Incompetence

You feel painfully aware that you lack the competence you desire. Although you are aware of your ineffectiveness, you feel unable to change it—yet! At this stage it might seem that "ignorance was bliss," but there's no going back. Now that you face the important choice of accepting the challenge or throwing in the towel, it helps to remember that this is simply a painful and uncomfortable stage. A typical statement here is, "I did it again. I can't believe it. I thought I knew better than that. Am I ever going to get it right?"

### Stage 3–Conscious Competence

You have accepted the challenge and learned the basics of some particular skill. However, you literally must think about every step involved, or else you will be unsuccessful. It takes a lot of concentration and effort. For example, after you have learned how your partner really likes his or her body touched, you still have to think about every move. Lovemaking does not feel very spontaneous because your new skill is not second nature. In this stage, people often say, "I did it, but it takes a lot of work. Is it ever going to feel easy?"

### Stage 4–Unconscious Competence

You have practiced and learned the basics to such a degree that you no longer have to think about it. You have integrated the new skill into your repertoire of knowledge and it is a part of you. This stage is mastery. Now you are able to improvise and go with the flow without being concerned about the technique or the form—that automatically comes with you. People say, "Of course I can do that. That's easy and fun!" From this position, they often forget how hard they have worked to get there.

We are not born into a state of mastery or unconscious competence. We must apply ourselves continuously if we are to enter this state. While it might not sound exciting, unconsciously competent lovemaking is exquisitely fulfilling. As is unconsciously competent conflict resolution! If we approach the goal of unconscious competence obsessively, we will never reach the destination. Paradoxically, like a Zen koan, we must let go of our attachment to doing it right and enter a deeper state of being and flow.

Although we will limit our exploration of mastery to sexuality, intimacy, and communication, you can apply these life-changing strategies to all areas of your life. Whichever stage you currently occupy, take heart. Know that with strong commitment and an effective strategy, you can become masterful.

# Principles of Erotic Mastery

The following principles of erotic mastery can help you maintain a high level of eros in your relationship—if you apply them. You will find that many of these principles overlap each other, addressing different shades and colors of erotic mastery.

We know that you will be excited with your progress if you consistently follow this path of erotic mastery. Here are the 24 powerful principles of this path:

1. *Redefine Sex as Connection*

2. *Be Present—Let Go of Results*

3. *Adopt a Dance Attitude*

4. *Practice the Art of Loving*

5. *Sanctify Your Relationship*

6. *Be on the Same Team*

7. *Tell Your Truth*

8. *Know Thyself*

9. *Lead with Vulnerability*

10. *Give and Receive Feedback as a Gift*

11. *Keep Learning and Growing*

12. *Ask—You Deserve It!*

13. *Befriend Yourself*

14. *Develop Support Systems*

15. *Be Fluid in Your Roles*

16. *Include Your Fantasies*

17. *Accept Responsibility for Your Own Arousal*

18. *Breathe*

19. *Sexercise*

20. *Commit to Practice*

21. *Acquire Knowledge, Then Transcend Technique*

22. *Believe that You Can Succeed*

23. *Redefine "Failures" as Opportunities to Learn*

24. *Celebrate Your Successes*

## Principle #1: Redefine Sex as Connection

Staying in intimate, immediate contact with your partner fuels your love and turns mere physical sex into true lovemaking. When you focus on the love connection between you, you literally transcend most performance anxiety—and experience much more pleasurable contact. Sexuality integrates with life, enhancing intimacy during every moment. What is sex really? Where does sex begin and end?

When you expand your definition of sex, it may become more than you have assumed it to be. If you think of sex as the physical manifestation of your love, sex becomes an avenue for discovering new and satisfying ways to express your love and receive your partner's love.

Your erotic experience need not be limited to the bedroom. A glance, a gentle nod, or a soft touch can be either a prelude to lovemaking or it can turn a mundane discussion about household matters into a shared experience of intimacy. The emotional and spiritual connection between you can infuse your entire life with eros. Lovemaking becomes a way of life rather than a circumscribed act.

If you place more value on the emotional and spiritual connection in your relationship than on having orgasms, you are likely to experience the pleasant paradox of greater sexual satisfaction.

## Principle #2: Be Present—Let Go of Results

Lovemaking is an art. When we allow it to speak—even sing—through us, we experience its ultimate pleasure. Most of us have experienced the pleasure of being totally present in lovemaking—if only for brief moments. At such times, the world dissolved into a pool of sensuality. Life seemed perfect. It's possible to exist at that erotic level whenever we make love.

The more you stay in the present and "smell the roses," the more excitement, pleasure, and potency you will bring to your lovemaking. Orgasms will naturally occur without hindrance or pre-occupation.

Staying present was my (Daniel) most important erotic lesson—remember Out of the Pits. My preoccupation with getting the desired results used to turn sex into work. Not much fun! When I learned to enjoy the raw feeling of my fingers touching Judith's body without any goal in mind, I literally transformed my relationship to eros.

The key to being present and moving through performance pressures is to stay sensitive to your own desires and pleasure. If you do not feel pleasure in your own sensuality, you will lose—or never establish—the connection with your partner. Giving to the other person while staying in touch with your own sensations is a hallmark of presence.

You can quiet your mind-chatter and help yourself be present by focusing your attention on your physical sensations, whether it is your breathing, your energy centers, your tactile sensations, or any other somatic sensation. Whenever you realize that you are engaged in mind chatter, bring your attention back to your somatic experience. By focusing on yourself in this way, you will ultimately give much more to your partner—and get more yourself.

## Principle #3: Adopt a Dance Attitude

Your sexual encounters, indeed, all your life experiences become art when you adopt a dance attitude. This occurs by entering into a state a heightened awareness which can only happen when you turn off your mind chatter and become present—and when you focus your attention on the process, rather than the product. Then your appreciation of form, texture, color, movement or any other aesthetic becomes prominent. You delight in the curve of a hip and your expression of that delight—be it in your eyes, your sound, your caress—becomes part of your dance attitude. Rather than having sex, you are dancing a love duet.

Your daily life becomes your love theater. You are sad, and you do a crying dance. Your partner does a holding dance, giving you support to express your grief. You and your partner are angry and you do a fighting dance, then a dance of reconciliation. You and your partner feel loving and you do a love dance or duet. When you live your life as art, you feel enlivened. It is as if you are awakened after a deep sleep, appreciating your life for the beautiful, magical miracle that it is.

## Principle #4: Practice the Art of Loving

Love is both an emotion and an intention. By focusing your attention on opening your heart and developing your inner lover, you will experience more love than you can imagine—for yourself and for others. Cultivate your inner lover and your garden will bloom. The fragrance and the beauty of your blossoms will attract the bees. By asking the following questions you can bring forth your inner lover:

*How can I be more loving in this situation?*

*How can I appreciate myself or my lover more?*

*How can I experience a greater love affair with all life?*

*How can I bring more love into my life?*

*What would I do differently if I responded to my partner (or myself) with love?*

Remember these questions as you are touching your lover, looking at your beloved, speaking or even thinking of him/her. Remember these questions when you are evaluating and judging yourself. Think of your heart as a funnel through which all of your feelings, intentions, and behaviors pass. Imagine that your love flows fluidly through your fingertips, your eyes, your voice, the energy that radiates from you—and is received by your partner.

As you open to your erotic nature more and more, your entire life will reflect your loving intentions. People will naturally gravitate to you. Remember the Herman Hesse line, "Love must have the strength to become certain within itself. Then it ceases merely to be attracted and begins to attract." Grow your love that strong.

## Principle #5: Sanctify Your Relationship

Who among us does not take people for granted at times—including our lovers? Feeling gratitude and appreciation for your lover, on a regular basis, sweetens the love between you. It turns the ordinary into the extraordinary.

Find ways to enhance the sacredness of your relationship. Holding hands and making a prayer before meals, meditating together, and taking silent walks in the woods are a few possibilities. Simply by turning your attention toward the sacredness of your relationship, you will be nurturing the spiritual aspect between you and your lover.

And, of course, this is true for sexuality. Find rituals that enhance your sacred union. There are plenty to choose from in this book as well as other books and tapes. You can also create your own rituals.

## Principle #6: Be on the Same Team

Being on the same team reflects the partnership model, in which decisions are made consensually and sexuality always takes place within an I-Thou framework. Neither holds the other as an object to be manipulated for personal gain. Egalitarian by nature, these relationships stand the greatest chance to be successful over time.

It is challenging to move beyond the habitual patterns of self-recriminations or blaming others. However, whether you are dealing with sex, money, or any other issue, conflicts are more easily resolved when you and your lover are on your team. When there's a communication break-down, no one is to blame—but both of you are responsible. The concept and practice of co-creation applies here. In co-creation, both parties acknowledge and express how they have contributed to the problem and consequently, how they can contribute to the solution.

Being on the same team also reflects a spiritual aspect of relationship and helps crystallize the sacred union into a work of art. It helps us transcend any tendencies toward self-righteousness and haughty individualism—and connects us with the underlying unity woven throughout our relationships. It makes all the difficulties worth it in the end.

By committing yourself to being on the same team, you focus your attention beyond what's good for you alone. You make a pledge to yourself and your partner to consider how your actions will affect the totality of your relationship. This translates into consulting your partner about your intentions and actions—moving beyond the individualistic, doing everything on your own mentality. The bottom line is that it feels great—and it works!

# Principle #7: Tell Your Truth

To sustain eros and intimacy for a lifetime, you must be truthful with your partner. If not, it eventually catches up! When we have asked people at seminars, "What qualities make for a healthy relationship?" the words trust and truth always top the list. Secrets obscure the real love between partners and dampen sexual desire as well.

Relationship experts Gay and Kathleen Hendricks agree. They tell couples, "when you withhold, sexuality is the first thing to go." Gay has advised some male clients, "A mature man makes a commitment to one person; and tells his partner everything. When you tell your truth, your penis gets longer."[1] For some men, this sounds like a good reason to be honest.

Aspire to be present and open about who you are—including your fears, fantasies, likes, and dislikes. It will speak volumes about your commitment to intimate connection. When you are telling your truth, remember "first truth first." Relaying your fears about your partner's reactions may help you become ready to expose your vulnerability. Remember to breathe, before, during, and after you have garnered the courage to tell more than you previously have told. Truth often is revealed in layers. Give yourself permission to express each new truth as you become aware of it.

## Principle #8: Know Thyself

Just as telling the truth is paramount in developing and maintaining intimacy, knowing yourself is key to creating and sustaining passion and interest. The more aware you are of yourself, the more depth you experience and express, and the more possibilities you have. Rather than limiting yourself to your persona, by increasing your self-awareness, you can reclaim aspects of yourself that you discarded when you were a child. As you incorporate what were shadow aspects into your newly expanding self, your repertoire of choices grows. So does your spontaneity and your feeling of freedom.

Rather than using awareness to incriminate, shame, or blame yourself or others, adopt an attitude of searching for a treasure. If your motivation is curiosity or a desire to change, as you uncover information, you may feel sad, angry, etc., but eventually, you will feel excited and relieved. Each relic yields information that can help you create the changes you desire. You can finally understand why you do the things you do. That knowledge can unlock your inner power. You can change decisions you made when you were young and take charge of your life—not only your behavior but your feelings as well.

With increased awareness, you experience a decrease of confusion. You feel perplexed less and more like a friend to yourself than a stranger. You have less knee-jerk reactions. You respond less defensively. You won't make up as many stories about your partner's feelings or behaviors. You'll make less assumptions. Probably, you will like your partner more and h/she will like you more.

## Principle #9: Lead with Vulnerability

Being vulnerable opens the gates of love. You can then be seen, heard, felt, and touched in the most intimate ways—and experience this with your partner. Your deepest visions of love can be realized. Certainly, it's a risk to open yourself, yet ultimately, the rewards are only available through acts of vulnerability. Laying down your armor may activate your fears, but it frees up your arms for reconciliation and more love.

Remembering that what you really want is love will help you catch yourself playing the "blame game." Most people would rather be happy than right. If you win these fruitless battles, you get to live with a loser. So the best way through "he said-she said" quagmires is to be vulnerable. There are always different ways of interpreting a given situation. In fact, each one of us perceives the world through our own experience. None of us have a monopoly on the truth.

Be aware of your deepest fears, doubts, and insecurities—and acknowledge them to your lover. Frequently, these are activated by your partner's behavior—or at least your perception of it. Your partner never *makes* you feel hurt, angry, or rejected. His or her behavior simply activates these pre-existing feelings in you. Recognizing these unpleasant feelings requires that you first be vulnerable and open to yourself. Since most people are self-critical, this is no easy task. Dropping your defenses and becoming vulnerable takes courage, for you are likely to experience difficult feelings, images, or thoughts that you have about yourself. Furthermore, feeling or expressing vulnerability does not necessarily resolve the problem; however, it removes the defenses so that the real concern can be addressed. Then you can become allies trying to resolve the challenge together, rather than enemies seeking to win a battle.

## Principle #10: Give and Receive Feedback as a Gift

It seems simple enough. If you want to understand, just ask. If you want to inform, just speak. Feedback is essential to both teaching and learning. We must occupy both positions in our intimate relationships—the giver and the receiver of feedback. Although asking for or giving feedback can arouse strong feelings of vulnerability in both you and your partner, it can also lead to a deep experience of intimacy.

Be open when your partner gives you feedback, whether or not you ask. There may be times when your lover's feedback is not motivated from love, however, you nonetheless have an opportunity to learn something. Allow your natural desire to grow to be stronger than any tendency to defend yourself.

When your lover requests that you change something in your lovemaking, please do not view it as an attack on your competence—or use it as evidence that you are a failure. See it as valuable feedback—an opportunity to learn.

Your partner knows more about what makes him or her feel good than you do. Some people (men and women) derive great pleasure from having their nipples sucked; others (again, men and women) like to have their anus touched during sex; others, (yes, it's still both men and women) are titillated by having their toes licked. Of course, not all issues of feedback involve sexual matters. It may relate to any aspect of your relationship.

If you do not ask, and your partner does not tell you, it's likely that you will never know how something could be enhanced or corrected. What a loss! By restricting yourself from giving or receiving this important feedback, you cut yourself off from an essential resource. Don't miss this important opportunity by allowing fear or shame to control you. Ask questions that can lead to greater pleasure and joy for both of you.

If we knew everything in the universe, including what our partners feel, think, or desire—and our partners could fulfill our every request without even asking them, we would not need to ask any questions. And vice versa. Until this time arrives, let us enjoy the intimate process of giving and receiving feedback.

## Principle #11: Keep Learning and Growing

Seek to learn from teachers and coaches in the sacred art of sexuality and the subtle nuances of communication. Whether it be learning from a tantra teacher or relationship counselor, taking workshops or seminars, it is valuable to seek sources that can expand your horizons.

There are also many excellent books, tapes, and videos which can help you enhance your emotional and sexual experience. In some bookstores, there are entire sections designated exclusively for intimacy and sexuality. You may not find all of them appealing, so be discerning. There is enough information available so that you can find something which suits you. Who knows? Your partner may even be a teacher in disguise. Perhaps you can even be a role model for others.

Don't stop yourself from seeking information because you are afraid that you are insignificant, incompetent, or unlovable. Don't let the fear of not knowing replace your curiosity with apathy. No matter how much you already know, there is always much to learn. Commit to being a lifelong learner.

## Principle #12: Ask—You Deserve It!

Our son has a children's song with the lyrics, "If you want something, you have to ask for it." What an important message! One that seems simple enough, yet few of us heed it. We stop asking for what we want because of fear and shame. Even many people who have been intimate partners for many years avoid asking for what they want.

Now is the time to take a risk. What have you really got to lose? When you're laying next to your partner, harness the courage to ask for what you desire. When you imagine something new with your partner, risk and try it. Asking does require taking a risk, but playing it safe never leads to satisfaction. It's fine to ask your partner to touch or hold you differently, or anything else for that matter. Your partner may not respond to your liking, but at least you tried.

Let's not let old family and cultural conditioning render us helpless to ask for what we really want. Even if we don't feel wholeheartedly deserving, we can build up our inner fortitude by requesting more. Although our vulnerability may rise in increasing degrees of discomfort, we will expand our boundaries and create a larger comfort zone as we journey into the unfamiliar territory of requesting more.

It helps to explore which aspects of ourselves are opposed to receiving more and which support us to go further. By facing whoever in us has learned that we do not deserve satisfaction or fulfillment, we can begin to heal this split within ourselves. For many of us, the first place to start is getting in touch with what we want. How can we ask if we don't know what we want? For a variety of reasons, we have learned not to listen to ourselves. We lose awareness of what we want or don't want—until we give ourselves permission to tune into and listen to our inner selves. First, we hear all the voices that had been silenced previously. Then, we learn to discriminate. We gain access to our intuition, to our inner guidance, and we begin to live in a state of grace.

The more we allow ourselves to know that we have wants and desires (and this necessitates healing the shame that squelches these impulses), the more we can ask for what we want. Let's not let our fears of being judged, rejected or humiliated for expressing your desires stop us from asking. If we ask, we just might get what we want.

## Principle #13: Befriend Yourself

Rather than feeling stymied by your internal conflicts, learn to use them to your advantage—and your partner's. We all have many voices or self-styles within us. Some people have learned to harmonize their inner aspects while others struggle to make the simplest decision.

Imagine that your entire cast of characters sits around a table making decisions. Everyone is there except those unsavory characters whom you have locked into the closet (your shadow). Yet, somehow, these characters slip out and run the meeting. Your efforts to have a more positive outcome are thwarted once again, thanks to your self-saboteurs ruining the show. Mastery seems impossible, as does feeling hopeful or content.

Remember that the inner struggle can be used to create greater vitality and aliveness. By focusing on what the different characters want and need from each other, you can avert the habitual in-house fighting that leads nowhere fast. Use dialoguing to create this inner dynamism. Only by harmonizing these different voices can you truly make friends with yourself. Since most people have well developed "traitor" voices who criticize, denigrate, and push them, make it a priority to cultivate the "angel" voices who believe in you and have your best interest at heart.

It can be very powerful to use a mirror. By befriending your reflection, you can peel away deep layers of self-loathing. Saying "I love you" to your mirror image may arouse feelings of foolishness or irrationality. However, by acting "as if" you were truly talking to your own friend in the mirror, you can affirm your highest intentions. By focusing on befriending yourself, you will gradually experience positive changes in your self-confidence, self-esteem, and self-image.

## Principle #14: Develop Support Systems

We all experience difficulties or challenges in our lives. Unfortunately, most of us have learned to "handle" them all alone. Out of fear or shame, we hesitate to ask for support, thus depriving ourselves of valuable resources. Self-sufficiency is admirable and valuable. However, when it is used to veil fears of feeling undeserving of other people's support, or validate beliefs that accepting support means that you are weak or incompetent, it is deleterious. You deserve support. Please, don't let anything stop you from receiving it. The power of joining people who have similar goals, values, and practices can be vital to your success.

More and more people are coming together for mutual support through self-help groups, workshops, and classes. People's needs and desires for community are rising like the phoenix. There are many groups and centers that focus specifically on erotic development. Various tantra teachers offer workshops across the country as do sexologists from a variety of orientations. Often communities evolve from these workshops and centers which function similarly to support groups. They provide a safe haven for people to change their old beliefs about sexuality—often shame-based—and adopt a healthier, more fulfilling relationship to both their sexuality and to their partner.

Many people stop themselves from registering for a workshop or joining a group because they believe that those who attend are weird or perverted, or that the workshop must involve licentious sexuality. For the most part, nothing could be further from the truth. Do some research before you sign up. Ask the questions that will provide you with the information you desire. Keep searching until you find what you want. But don't let fear and shame stop you. If you feel cautious, proceed with caution, but, proceed.

Some couples experience great support in joining a couples group. They find that their relationship challenges are not bizarre or unusual. And they learn new ways to handle various difficulties which emerge in their relationships. There's no need to do it all alone. That's a model which is rapidly disappearing.

## CHAPTER 10

See the following sections: *The Power of Groups; Twelve Step Programs; The Way of Shame in Sex and Love Addictions; Healing Shame in Men/Women Groups; Celebrating Eros in a Group,* and *Challenging Revelations*

## Principle #15: Be Fluid in Your Roles

Allow your natural instincts, intuition, and imagination to guide your expression. Free yourself from rigid limiting roles—both in and out of bed. Whether you are a man or a woman, you can be tender, compassionate, fiery, intense, strong, weak, mellow, or nurturing—depending on your mood. You can initiate or follow your partners' lead, depending on the shared atmosphere between you. Don't let old male or female conditioning control your personal freedom and expression. Limiting yourself to rigid roles stultifies your relationship whereas fluidly shifting among a multitude of roles enlivens your relationship.

Consider that lovemaking is the physical manifestation of your love. As you allow yourself greater freedom and fluidity in your lovemaking, allow those changes to permeate your relationship. Interacting with your beloved outside of defined roles presents challenges since there are no recipes. Yet there are also rewards. You may find yourself making love all day!

Let yourself be parent or child, mother or father, sister or brother, god or goddess lover, or friend with your lover. Don't let fear or shame be your confidante. By allowing yourself to be spontaneous, you can follow the ebb and flow of your multidimensional lover. Explore! Experiment! Have fun! In and out of bed.

## CHAPTER 9

## Principle #16: Include Your Fantasies

Accept your fantasies and bring them into your relationship—including lovemaking. Remember that fantasy and reality can be quite different. It's not a crime to fantasize. As long as you do not physically or emotionally abuse your mate by enacting your fantasies, then why not? Beware of shaming yourself for your fantasies.

Find safe ways that you and your partner can enact both of your choice fantasies. This is another way of giving form to your multi-dimensional lover. Fantasy helps establish new potential avenues of expression. Limitations in reality originate in limitations in fantasy. As you expand your willingness to include more of your fantasy life, especially with your partner, you will feel a heightened sense of pleasure and prowess. Remember, your imagination is where great sex begins. Why not use one of the most powerful sources of sexual arousal to your benefit—and your partner's?

## Principle #17: Accept Responsibility for Your Own Arousal

Just as we are ultimately responsible for our own feelings, we are also each responsible for our own sexual arousal. Learn more about your own body so that you know how to arouse yourself. Don't just wait for your partner to turn you on. Get involved. By learning more about what arouses you, you will become far better at communicating your likes and dislikes to your partner. You will be able to impart the subtle nuances that can help your partner drive you wild. Your partner will feel like a hero.

## Principle #18: Breathe

Whether we are learning to give or receive love, to touch while maintaining eye contact, or stay current, be present or vulnerable—breath is the magic ingredient that brings it all together. In some religions the words breath and spirit are synonymous. When we breathe deeply and fully, we allow the spirit to move through us. This is inspiration. And this makes love all the more exciting. This is the reason we placed such importance on breath in Chapter 3—*Eastern Sex for Western Lovers.*

Learn how to focus your attention inward and follow the sensations of your breathing. This is a basic skill for both developing self-awareness and creating sexual ecstasy. Similarly, learn how to direct your breath to relax and let go of useless stress. It will also enhance the quality of your orgasms. Just as soft, full-bellied breathing allows you to feel your emotions more deeply, it also allows you to experience pleasure throughout your entire body—not only in your genitals.

When lovers breathe together in a relaxed state, their hearts will be more open and they are more likely to experience long-lasting, whole body orgasms. So breathe, feel, relax, and look forward to more satisfying orgasms, inner peace, and greater intimacy.

## Principle #19: Sexercise

Most of us are aware of the benefits of physical exercise, yet few of us realize the benefits of sexercise. What is sexercise? It's a name we have given to some of the practices we have shared with you—practices related to enhancing your sexual energy. For example, both men and women can benefit from work on their PC muscles. This helps a woman become more aroused, and enables her to stimulate a man more deftly. This pleasures him, and by adding his own PC squeeze and release, he is able to maintain his erection, which in turn, helps him stimulate her more. Talk about a marriage made in heaven—an ascending spiral of pleasure!

In addition, by mastering your ability to move energy through your chakras (up your Inner Flute), you will heighten your sexual experience and make beautiful music together. So will loosening up your pelvis and you spine. Your orgasms will be enhanced. Also, the more flexibility and strength you have, the more possibilities you have for discovering new and stimulating positions. These sexercises will also help you experience a profound spiritual connection with your beloved.

## Principle #20: Commit to Practice

What separates the wannabe from the master? The answer is commitment—and lots of practice. That's how we acquire mastery. Yet, *how* we practice is just as important as *whether* we practice. If we go through the motions without being present, our practice is useless. As Moshe Feldenkrais, a brilliant thinker and researcher discovered, we derive more benefit from doing a single movement pattern with awareness than if we do the same pattern with mindless repetition. This holds true for practice of all kinds.

Becoming masterful at lovemaking, like any endeavor, demands some degree of practice. Arrogance can crop up, reflected in the belief that "I don't need to practice lovemaking." It may be true that you don't need to practice, but if you do practice, you are guaranteed to become a more pleasing lover and experience greater pleasure yourself.

Practice in lovemaking can range from verbal communication exercises that involve no touching to actual sexual intercourse. You may practice certain positions, movements, or breathing techniques. Maintaining the practice means to stay focused on the intended exercise while also staying connected to the bigger picture—experiencing your physical, emotional and spiritual connection.

For example, during a practice session if you are working with a particular position, and you suddenly feel inspired to try something new, forego the temptation to leave the form. Continue with the exercise you chose to work on. You might wonder, "Doesn't that stymie spontaneity?" Yes, for the time being. But the intention in practicing is to stay within a particular form until you find freedom within it. Freedom through discipline! Could you imagine if one dancer followed his or her inspiration and began improvising during a choreographed duet?

There will be many times when you will simply be exploring with your partner, with no intention to practice. If you have practiced with awareness, you will find that your ability to "go with the flow"—as a direct outgrowth of your practice—will be enhanced. The greatest improvisers are the people who have mastered the basics—and practice is the means whereby we master the basics.

Sometimes your progress will astonish you. You will feel like you could practice forever. At other times you may feel as though you're not advancing at all, possibly even regressing. Those can be the most frustrating times. But don't let the frustrations stop you from practicing. Take a break, do something to regain your sense of humor, and get back on the pony.

## Principle #21: Acquire Knowledge, Then Transcend Technique

To become erotically masterful, you must become knowledgeable. Learn the basics about female and male anatomy, techniques to enhance orgasms, positions which add interest to your lovemaking, the various likes and dislikes of your lover, and how to move sexual energy through your chakras.

Yet, if you focus only on acquiring knowledge, you will never become masterful. Paradoxically, the key is to learn your theories well, and then forget everything you know. A person can be overly concerned about the information and lose touch with simply being present. That is why someone can be a technically knowledgeable lover, yet still not be a great lover. When the heart, soul, and intuition are not present in the experience, lovemaking  becomes mere physical activity—sporting sex.

To create ecstatic lovemaking, we must transcend technique and knowledge. Great musicians understand theory and composition, and have acquired technical mastery of their instruments. Yet, it is only when they allow their inspiration to flow that they can move their listeners deeply.

Let's say a concert pianist has decided which pieces she will play for this particular concert. They are complex pieces, and performing them will be stretching her limits. Day after day, month after month, over and over again she practices. In her practice sessions, she achieves technical proficiency. Then she is free to explore her feelings, her interpretation of the musical score, and this is when she truly comes alive—when her playing moves the audience to tears and rapture.

The same is true for lovers. Learning tantric techniques, PC muscle control, sacred spot stimulation, and your lover's personal likes and dislikes is valuable. It helps you journey into pleasurable and satisfying territory. Yet, if you rely on knowledge without following the natural sensations and reactions of your lover, moment to moment, you will miss the most important "data" of all. For only in the subtle movements of the immediate experience can true sensuality and connection emerge.

Sensation becomes the teacher. To live on this edge, we must be open. Openness emerges from trust. Trust not only in our partners, but perhaps more importantly, in ourselves. And if we are primarily focused on being a "successful" lover, we are not in a trusting state. We are efforting—trying to prove something to somebody. The irony is that when we are in this self-conscious mindset, we remain the technician. To become the artist, we must trust ourselves enough to let go and surrender to the moment.

## Principle #22: Believe That You Can Succeed

There's nothing more powerful than belief. As Henry Ford once said, "Whether you believe you can succeed or you believe you can't succeed—you're right!" So if you believe that you will not succeed, you will find a way to fail. That's why it is so important to confront whatever parts of yourself are disbelieving.

We have all sabotaged ourselves in certain ways, despite our best intentions. We can put forth a massive effort and still wind up empty, simply because an unconscious belief stops us from experiencing success. The good news is that you need not be held prisoner by past limiting beliefs. But one of the age-old questions is: how can we believe if we do not already believe? In other words, how can we change self-limiting beliefs?

By experiencing small successes, we build bridges of *credibility* that give us a basis for believing we can be more successful. For example, let's take a man who sometimes has had trouble getting an erection during sexplay. Through counseling and practice, he is slowly learning to relax and not worry about it. He is learning to "let it be"—to enjoy his "soft-on"—and trust that it will take care of itself.

One night in bed with his lover, the man feels the old anxiety begin to take over. But this time he recognizes it and is prepared to deal with it. "Enough of this worrying about it," he says to himself, "I'm just going to enjoy myself—let my penis do what it wants."

A few minutes later, he feels the surge in his groin and feels a sense of confidence and satisfaction—it has worked. This man isn't over the hump yet; he will probably feel anxiety occasionally and have difficulty in getting an erection. But now he knows that relaxing, staying present, enjoying the process, and going with the flow can work for him—maybe not perfectly yet, but it can work! This creates a bridge of credibility that crosses the chasm between his previous disbelief and mistrust of himself and his goal—unwavering trust and belief in himself.

Practice, and create small successes. Build your bridges of credibility. Use your small successes to bolster your belief that what you want to happen will, in fact, happen. And it will!

## Principle #23: Redefine "Failures" as Learning Experiences

When you let go of the need to be perfect, you will be free to learn from your so-called "failures." Ultimately, there is only one failure: Giving up. Thomas Edison offers an important lesson from his own experience: After thousands of unsuccessful attempts to invent the lightbulb, critics told him that he was crazy to continue his pursuit. But he told them that those failures only inspired him. They had taught him what didn't work. That narrowed down the possibilities of what might work. He was downright excited about what most of us would call failure. After some 6,000 attempts, he finally created a light bulb.

Edison's failures were stepping stones to success. Similarly, learning what doesn't work in your relationship can be a stepping stone to developing mastery. You too can re-frame mistakes or failures as opportunities to learn something new. Making a mistake is not the problem. However, throwing in the towel is. Does reacting to your mistakes as if you had committed a crime or were a bad person really move you closer to success?

If you heed the inner voice that says, "Don't do it! Don't risk," you will stray from the path of mastery. We have explored this innumerable times throughout the book. It's that important! When the fear of failure is stronger than the desire to learn, growth is impossible. No matter how imposing your inner critic may appear, there is an angel inside of you that wants you to succeed. Develop your internal dialogue so that your angel aspects are in charge—not your fear and self-saboteurs.

## Principle #24: Celebrate Your Successes

And last but not least, celebration plays a significant role in the growth process. We have psychological needs to be rewarded for succeeding and going beyond our comfort zones. Yet even after completing an important project—or improving our love relationships—most of us give ourselves no celebratory self-acknowledgment for these accomplishments. Perhaps you know someone like this—maybe even you?

Celebrations after personal victories enhance your chances for future success. Why? Because it sends a message to your unconscious that a successful effort receives credit. Can you imagine if failure led to self-punishment and success led to neutral or negative reactions. What's the use of trying then? Pleasure will be short lived at best. Pain will be constant. If hard-won successful achievements do not lead to continued pleasure and inner satisfaction, you will tend to sabotage subsequent endeavors. However, by celebrating yourself, you are supporting the integration of new feelings, thoughts, and behaviors into your expanding sense of self. You are helping yourself to become the person you want to be.

Many people don't celebrate more because they have learned that celebrating is equivalent to bragging. This false humility is self-defeating. Since praise and celebration are vital to health, these people unconsciously look to others, particularly their partners, to furnish both—and then feel crestfallen when it is not forthcoming,

We have few healthy models of honoring our accomplishments and taking credit for our successes. So, without a model, become a pioneer. Experiment with taking credit for yourself and celebrating yourself. Take stock of how you have been improving as a lover, as a partner. Enjoy your accomplishments and give yourself credit for even the smallest accomplishment.

You can enjoy a lovely candlelit dinner to celebrate a positive shift in your relationship—or even a romantic get-away weekend. Create rituals of your own. Remember, feeling healthy pride in your accomplishments is a key to future successes. Celebration rituals boost your self-esteem and give you incentive to face greater challenges. Have fun and use your creativity. Celebrate the steps you take as a couple, and celebrate the accomplishments of your partner. These heighten your intimacy and increase the sweetness and love between you. They also help you become unconsciously competent!

# Hello to Mastery

Mastery is a lifelong process. The most essential quality that keeps us on the path is a love for learning—an innate desire to keep growing. The only person incapable of walking this path is the person who does not desire it, for whatever reasons.

Most of us feel like we have fallen off the path at times. The strong fire and desire we felt seems nowhere to be found. We forget. A good question to ask yourself during these darker times is, "How can I remember when I forget?" More than anything else, our success or lack of it will be determined by the openness of our attitudes toward life's possibilities. Let's open our eyes to life's magnificence—even when we don't feel like it.

# Last Reflections

Throughout *Lovers for Life*, we have given you our recipes for creating long term success in your lover relationship. These tools and processes are about much more than increasing sexual pleasure. They are about creating the type of relationship for which you have been longing; one that is intimate, passionate, trusting, loving, profound, deeply fulfilling—and lasting.

We have explored possibilities for healthy eroticism—where you rid yourself of ignorant, shame-based myths—and embody the lover within yourself. By honoring your inner lover, you open yourself to experiencing lifelong passion, trust, and true partnership with your lover. This sacred union rests upon truthfulness, commitment and effective strategies—the ordinary magic that brings rewards beyond your wildest dreams.

As you continue to develop skills to make love sweeter and sweeter, you will naturally live your dreams. Your relationship becomes an expression of your spiritual practice. You work together as a team and make your relationship a thrilling adventure—a work of art. When your relationship is viewed in this light, it never seems boring or stuck—although it may need to be reshaped and sculpted from time to time. Like any garden, it takes continued care.

*Lovers for Life* is about changing old, conditioned patterns and creating new, more positive ways of responding. These new habits will become automatic over time—unconscious competence.

We hope that we have helped open the door for you to experience the love you have always wanted. It has been our pleasure and honor to be your guides. May you live your dreams and experience the joy of being lovers for life.

Enjoy the adventure of life. You simply need to be open to exploring, learning, and practicing. There is a name for a relationship of this caliber: we call it *Lovers for Life*.

# Chakras and Sephirot: Ancient Medicine for Modern Times

## Chakras

The lowest *chakra,* the *muladhara,* is commonly referred to as the survival chakra in that it is said to contain our vital life force. It holds the energy for locomotion (i.e., to escape danger, and to gather food—all necessary tasks for survival). When this center is enlivened, people experience a zest for life and a strong connection with eros. Energy flowing through this chakra has a fiery quality.

After survival needs are attended to, preserving the species becomes paramount. The second chakra, the *swadhisthana,* holds the creative force. It also corresponds to our sexual center and is associated with giving birth. It is located at the genitals.

The next energy center, referred to by the Japanese as the *hara,* is located below the navel and is our physical center for balance and movement. Called the "movement center," "when your energy flows freely through this center you feel strength, vitality, and an aliveness that exudes from a healthy, relaxed body."[1] This energy center is not included in the Indian system as a separate center.

In the Indian scheme, the third chakra, the *manipura,* is commonly called the power chakra. Located above the navel, at the solar plexus, it holds the energy for taking charge, gaining mastery, and exerting personal power. Aïvanhov, a Rumanian spiritual master, describes the solar plexus as the "great doctor of our body."[2] It is said to be the "ancient brain" which holds the source of knowledge of the entire health of our body. This knowledge is the source of power. It is also the center of collective consciousness–how we know that we are a part of and belong to the entire universe. When your vital sexual energy is flowing freely through this chakra, you experience personal power in your ability to easily manifest what you desire in the world.

The fourth chakra, the *anahata,* is located over the sternum between the two nipples. Commonly called the heart chakra, it is the seat of compassion, love, devotion, and altruism. It is also considered the gateway between the physical energy of the three lower chakras and the more spiritual energy of the three upper chakras. When your energy is flowing freely through this center, you feel the desire to melt into your partner and merge—feeling the oneness between the two of you.

The fifth chakra, the *vishuddha,* or throat chakra, is found at the thyroid gland in the center of the throat. It holds the energy of communication, expression, and wisdom. When your energy flows freely here, you experience ease with communicating what you want—sexually and in all ways.

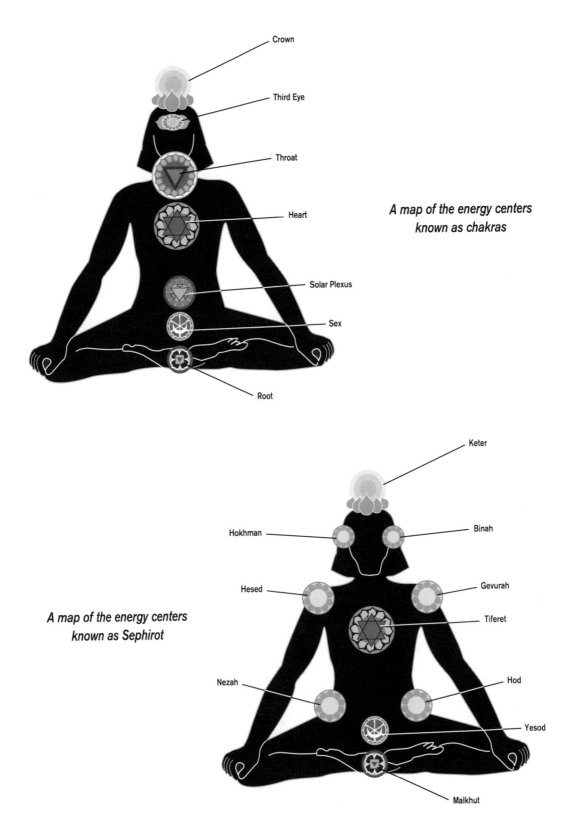

Crown

Third Eye

Throat

Heart

*A map of the energy centers known as chakras*

Solar Plexus

Sex

Root

Keter

Hokhman

Binah

Hesed

Gevurah

Tiferet

*A map of the energy centers known as Sephirot*

Nezah

Hod

Yesod

Malkhut

The sixth chakra, the *ajna,* is also referred to as "the third eye" and is located between the two eyebrows. Responsible for intellectual functions and clairvoyance, it also focuses the energy for the experience of pure consciousness, not necessarily connected to the physical body. The energy of the sixth chakra allows us to experience the inner guru. When your sexual energy flows freely through this center, you experience the spontaneity of your intuition and imagination.

The seventh chakra, the *sahasrara,* is known as the crown chakra and is located at the crown of the head, or a few inches above the crown. When energy moves up into this chakra, we are open to the experience of God. The halos depicted in Western artwork are representations of the white light or energy that emanates from spiritual beings at the crown chakra. The experience of freedom, unlimited power, and Unity consciousness are related to this chakra. When this chakra is open, your sexual union becomes a spiritual union as well. Your sexual experience feels ecstatic, expansive, and mystical.

# Sephirot

Unknown to most people, even most Jews, is the ancient Jewish mystical wisdom of the *sephirot,* designed for almost the same purpose as the chakras—to chart the relationship between human beings and the metaphysical nature of the universe. Each of the *sephirot* are manifestations of various aspects of God.

Similar to chakras, the ten sephirot designate energy centers of the body. At the positions of the solar plexus, heart, and throat chakras, there are complementary pairs of sephirot—each a set of harmonious opposites. Unlike chakras, which are counted from the bottom up, sephirot are counted from the top down.

Just as the chakras are depicted going up the spine of a person sitting in the lotus position, the sephirot are illustrated in the pattern of the archetypal human, called *adam kadmon.* In this configuration, the sephirot also represent the metaphysical pattern of the universe and the tree of life.

The texts which contain information regarding the sephirot as well as the interpretations have been fairly well hidden through the centuries. What has survived is written in code or symbol. Therefore, though ancient Jewish tradition incorporated this profound knowledge, it is not easily available. Tantra, however, though usually not part of the mainstream, was and is far more widely practiced.

The *sephirah* (singular for *sephirot), keter,* "infinity" corresponds directly to the seventh chakra and sits at the crown of *adam kadmon's* head. In that it represents God's essence, the "Oneness-of-All," and infinity beyond the realm of human experience, this sephirah can be experienced but the mystery—the numinousity of it—is understood through altered states of consciousness.

The second sephirah, *hokhmah*—the center of wisdom and universal harmony—and the third sephirah, *binah*—the region of laws and rigidity, representing justice and implacable, unrelenting severity—are equivalent to the sixth chakra. They sit at the right and left brain hemispheres and balance each other in harmonious opposition. *Hokhmah* is masculine, *yang,* active, pure abstract power, and logic. *Binah* is feminine, *yin,* receptive, pure intuitive power. They are considered to be the primary qualities that pervade all the universe.

The fourth and fifth sephirot, *hesed* and *gevurah,* are located at the right and left shoulders, another pair in dynamic harmony. *Hesed,* God's nurturing love, evolves from *hokhmah,* the masculine, above it. In *Hesed,* "the divine emanation manifests itself as mercy, clemency, indulgence, and forgiveness."[3] Gevurah, the power of God to move one into action, evolves from *binah,* the feminine, above it. Here, "the generosity and mercy of *Hesed* are transformed into militancy, strength of will, a consuming fire."[4] It is interesting to note that they involve their opposites in their synthesis.

The sixth sephirah, *tiferet*, sits at the heart and solar plexus and corresponds to the fourth and third chakra. Just as the heart chakra is the gateway between the lower three physical chakras and the upper three spiritual chakras, *tiferet* funnels and synthesizes energy between the purely metaphysical, more spiritual sephirot above and the more earthly and physical sephirot below. It is considered to be the region of beauty—in intelligence, purity, and light.

The seventh and eighth sephirot, *nezah* and *hod,* are the third dynamic pair and correspond to the center called *hara* in Japanese and Chinese traditions. They are located at the right and left hip sockets. Whereas *nezah* is dominance, *hod* is submissiveness. Though sometimes in opposition, together they create dynamic harmony. According to the spiritual master Aïvanhov, *nezah* is also considered to be the region of love. When the divine emanation fills *nezah,* it overflows into *hod,* which is said to be the region of the intellect, of concrete, practical knowledge, science and reason.

The ninth sephirah, *yesod,* sits at the genitals and corresponds to the sexual chakra. Like *tiferet, yesod* synthesizes the higher, more spiritual realms and funnels them down into the more physical realms. *Yesod* is considered the gateway between the spiritual realm and the material. *Yesod* is the region of life and purity through which every initiate must pass if his or her spiritual journey is to be successful.

The last and lowest sephirah, *malkhut,* is located at the feet. *Malkhut* translates to "God's kingdom," meaning the physical world of matter with hints of the spiritual realm. *Malkhut* needs an infusion of spiritual energy from above or it remains lifeless. It is also identified with *Shekhinah,* a Jewish name for the feminine, receptive face of God. This is because there must be an infusion of spiritual energy in order for God's spiritual process to unfold in the physical plane. This corresponds to the root chakra.

## Erotic Western Roots

Since many of us have roots in the Judeo-Christian culture, there are aspects of the Jewish tradition that may be enlightening regarding sexuality. Judaism as well as tantra views sexuality as sacred and as a path to the spiritual experience.

The Torah[5] recognizes the enormous spiritual power of sexuality. In fact, an entire section of the commentary on the Torah interprets the spiritual meaning of Song of Songs, the erotic love poetry of the Torah. A thirteenth century text, the Holy Letter *(Iggeret Ha-kodesh)* states that "sexuality can be a means of spiritual elevation when it is properly practiced, and the mystery greater than this is that secret celestial couplings unite according to a male-female pattern."[6]

Just as tantric practices are designed to replicate the experience of the union of the male/female polarity of God, Torah has a ritual sexual activity for the same. Growing up, I (Judith) often heard that it was considered a blessing, a *mitzvah* (literally, a commandment for your spiritual development) for a married couple to make love, and a double *mitzvah* to do it on the sabbath. It is regarded as a *mitzvah* because sexual union is the means by which the *neshemah,* the spiritual aspect of the soul or the Self, is restored to wholeness. Tradition has it that at conception, the *neshemah,* of each soul splits into male and female parts and takes residence in separate bodies.

*Thus, sexual union is a sacred act of returning to one's state of origin.*

On the eve of *shabbat,* the sabbath, sexual union is considered a double *mitzvah* because this is when God transforms from masculine to feminine. For six days of activity God is considered to be masculine, but on the Sabbath, the day of rest and receptivity, God is said to be feminine. Thus, by making love on Friday night, human beings are able to become united with God in perfect undif-ferentiated wholeness.

The sephirot embody the same pattern of male/female polarity and union. The lowest of the sephirot, *malkhut,* represents the material world, embodies the receptive, immanent aspects of God, and is identified with the *Shekhinah,* the feminine face of God. The other nine sephirot embody the male aspects of God and are considered to be the Holy Blessed One, *Kadosh Barukh Hu.* Being a microcosm of the whole, the sephirot reflect the idea that wholeness is created by the union of the male and female principle.

Jung, who was raised a Christian, describes the process of spiritual growth using similar princi-ples. Based on his cross-cultural studies of religions, he postulated that women must recognize and assimilate their *animus*—inner male aspect—and men must do the same with their *anima.* This, together with the recognition, acceptance, and assimilation of denied and disidentified aspects of the Self which Jung called the shadow, form a pathway to the emergence of the Self.

# Notes

## 2. Eros Unveiled

1. This technique was developed by Jeri Marlowe, MA, a Marriage, Family, and Child Therapist in the San Francisco Bay Area who specializes in sex therapy.

2. Nadine Stair, *If I Had My Life to Live Over,* as seen in *If I Had My Life to Live Over I Would Pick More Daisies,* (Watsonville, CA: Papier-Maché Press, 1992). Before publishing the poem, Papier-Maché initiated a search and continue to seek the author or a living family member, but none has been found as yet.

3. Creative Behavior was first defined by Schutz as unusual and satisfying behavior. Wm. C. Schutz, *Creative Behavior: Training and Theory Development,* unpublished paper, 1963. Schutz published this idea in *Joy,* (New York: Grove Press, Inc., 1967). This idea was developed by Eugene and Juanita Sagan at the Institute for Creative and Artistic Development. Creative Behavior was subsequently defined by Eugene Sagan as not the concern with an artistic product but a concern with the person having a certain kind of relationship or orientation to whatever experience he's having. This is the same as the "dance attitude" as defined by A. A. Leath. The Creative Behavior teacher uses a five-step process developed by Juanita Sagan. (Juanita Bradshaw Sagan, *On Founding a New Profession, the Creative Behavior Teacher.* Paper presented at the American Psychological Association Symposium, Washington, D.C. September, 1967).

4. A. A. Leath, Jr. "Manifesto for a New Theater, or Essays Celebrating Myself," *Creative Behavior and Artitstic Development in Psychotherapy,* American Psychological Association, September 5, 1967.

5. According to William Blank in *Torah, Tantra and Tarot, A Guide to Jewish Spiritual Growth* (Boston: Coventure Ltd, 1991). While Abraham embodies compassion and trust, Isaac is the epitome of strength and models the fear of God. Jacob's archetype reflects "splendid splendor" and teaches the importance of truth. After Jacob wrestles with the angel, he is blessed with the name Israel, "God-wrestler," adding the archetypal aspect of struggling with the ultimate meaning of human experience. Jacob's favorite son, Joseph, provides the archetype of the dreamer. He is gifted with precognitive dreams and rises to power because of his ability to interpret dreams. The four matriarchs of the Torah—Sarah, Rebecca, Rachel, and Leah—provide the complementary feminine elements to their husbands, balancing the masculine. "Just as the *I Ching* maintains that the entire workings of the universe result from the harmonious interaction of yin and yang, female and male energy, earth and heaven, so the Torah's archetypes balance their emphasis on yang archetypes with yin energy." Sarah is a spiritual woman who is filled with compassion. Isaac's wife, Rebecca, manifests strength. Jacob's first wife, Rachel, is the embodiment of the eternal feminine; whereas, his second wife, Leah, characterizes the woman who is elusive, ephemeral, always sought after but never attained.

6. Roberto Assagioli, *Psychosynthesis,* (England: Penquin Books, 1965).

7. Eugene Sagan, "*Self-Styles,*" an essay from *Parabolic Essays,* (Oakland, CA: Institute for Creative and Artistic Development, 1965). Self-styles are written about more extentively in Fred E. Newton, Jay Greenwood, and Juanita B. Sagan, *Alternatives to Failure: Resources to Improving Teaching.* (Mulloromak Educational Service District. January, 1985).

8. Walt Whitman, *Song of Myself,* vs. 1, *Norton Anthology of Poetry, Revised.* (New York: W. W. Norton, 1975), 816.

9. John Moyn and Coleman Barks, *Open Secret, Verses of Rumi.* (Putney, Vermont: Threshhold Books, 1984.)

10. Robert Moore and Douglas Gillette, *King, Warrior, Magician, Lover: Rediscovering the Archetypes of the Mature Masculine,* (San Francisco: Harper San Francisco, 1990), 126.

11. George Leonard, *Adventures in Monogamy*, (New York: Jeremy P. Tarcher, 1983).

12. Sam Keen, *The Passionate Life*. (San Francisco: Harper, 1983), 16.

13. Robert Johnson explores this brilliantly in his book *We: Understanding the Psychology of Romantic Love*. (San Francisco: Harper & Row, 1983).

14. Martin Buber, *I and Thou*, (New York: Charles Scribner's Sons, 1970).

## 3. Eastern Sex for Western Lovers

1. Blank, *Torah, Tarot & Tantra*, 96-97.

2. In the Jewish tradition of the Middle East, these energy centers were called *sephirot* (Hebrew for "spheres"). The two systems are similar with a few differences. In *Torah, Tarot & Tantra*, Rabbi Blank delineates the similarities and differences between these two systems.

   Both systems describe what happens in the mind and body as the experience of God unfolds. The *chakra* system emphasizes the internal, somatic experience whereas the *sephirot* system emphasizes the physically transcendent, metaphysical nature of reality.

3. Margo Anand, *The Art of Sexual Ecstasy*, (Los Angeles: Jeremy P. Tarcher, 1989), 163-168.

4. Anand, *The Art of Sexual Ecstasy*, 215.

5. Robert Frey, From interview, 1993.

6. Anand, *The Art of Sexual Ecstasy*, 385.

7. Wilhelm Reich, See *The Function of the Orgasm* (Vol. 1 of *The Discovery of the Orgone*). (New York: Orgone Institute Press, 1942, 1948). New translation: (New York: Farrar, Straus and Giroux, 1973). *Character Analysis*, (New York: Orgone Institute Press, 1945, 1949). (London: Peter Nevill, Vision Press, 1950). New translation: (New York: Farrar, Straus and Giroux, 1972).

8. Lori Grace, From interview, 1992.

9. Thomas Cooper, From interview, 1993.

10. A report of an Israeli study [Israel Ischemic Heart Disease Project] concluded that: "There seems to be a direct correlation between your wife's love and support and that heart of yours—the physical heart, that is... And how your boss feels about you also plays a role. The higher the appreciation, the less risk of a heart attack." from William Schutz, *Profound Simplicity*, (San Diego: University Associates, 1979), 103, taken from Prayers at Synagogue Stave Off Heart Attacks. Jerusalem *Post*, February 29, 1971.

## 4. The Wounds of Sexual Shame

1. Robert Karen, "Shame," *The Atlantic Monthly*, (February 1992), 42.

2. John Bradshaw, *Healing the Shame That Binds You*, (Deerfield Beach, Florida: Health Communications Inc. 1988), 48.

3. Alice Miller, *The Drama of the Gifted Child*, (New York: Basic Books, Inc., 1981), 100.

4. Alfred Ells, *Restoring Innocence*, (Nashville: Thomas Nelson Publishers, 1990), 51.

5. James Hillman, *New Age Journal*, (June, 1992), 139.

6. *The Erotic Impulse: Honoring the Sensual Self*, David Steinberg, ed., (Los Angeles: Jeremy Tarcher, 1992), xvi.

7. Alfred Ells, *Restoring Innocence*, 52-54.

## 5. The Roots of Sexual Shame

1. *The Holy Scriptures: According to the Masoretic Text*, (Philadelphia: The Jewish Publication Society of America. 1917), Genesis 2:16, 4-5.

2. Riane Eisler, *The Chalice and The Blade: Our History, Our Future*. (San Francisco: Harper 1987), chap. 6-8.

3. Elaine Pagels, *Adam, Eve, and the Serpent*, (New York: Vintage Books, 1988), xx111.

4. Pagels, quoting Augustine, *De Civitate Dei 14, 19-20*, 111.

5. Pagels, 117.

6. *Bhagavad Gita,* trans. Ann Stanford (New York: Herder and Herder, 1970), 22-23.

7. Gayle Pemberton, "A Sentimental Journey: James Baldwin and the Thomas-Hill Hearings," in *Race-ing Justine, En-gendering Power,* ed. Toni Morrison, (New York: Pantheon Books, 1992), 176, quoting James Baldwin, "White Man's Guilt," in *The Price of the Ticket* (New York: St. Martins, 1985), 410.

8. Eisler, *The Chalice and the Blade,* 8.

9. Eisler, 15.

10. Eisler, 20.

11. Barbara G. Walker, *The Crone: Woman of Age, Wisdom, and Power,* (San Francisco: Harper & Row, 1985), 12.

12. Walker, 10.

13. Raphael Patai, *The Hebrew Goddess.* (Detroit: Wayne State University Press, 1967.)

14. Eisler, 105. The letter *l* has a triple meaning. From English, it stands for the *linking* of both halves of humanity rather than their ranking. From the Greek *lyein* or *lyo,* it means both to solve or resolve (as in ana*l*ysis) and to dissolve or set free (as in cata*l*ysis). So here, "the letter *l* stands for the resolution of our problems through the freeing of both halves of humanity from the stultifying and distorting rigidity of roles imposed by the domination hierarchies inherent in androcratic systems."

15. Eisler, chap. 4.

16. Eisler, 48 quoting Marija Gimbutas, "The First Wave of Eurasian Steppe Pastoralists into Copper Age Europe," *Journal of Indo-European Studies* 5 (Winter 1973): 281.

17. Eisler, 53.

18. Though Christianity maintained Mary's status by allowing that she was the mother of the Son of God, she, alone of the Holy Trinity, was made mortal—and virginal.

    And, as Walker addresses in *The Crone,* our youth-loving, age-fearing culture can attest that there is a deliberate amputation of the Crone aspect—the wise woman and the reaper or destroyer—an essential part of the trinitarian Goddess. This is particularly interesting in that "the Crone was the most powerful of the Goddess's three personae. Seen in myth after myth as an old woman, she was yet stronger than any god. Under one of her Teutonic names, Elli or "Old Age," in a wrestling match she conquered even the god of strength, Thor himself. See Walker quoting H.R.E. Dasvidson, *Gods and Myths of the Viking Age,* (New York: Bell Publishing Co., 1981), 229.

    According to Raphael Patai in *The Hebrew Goddess,* (Detroit: Wayne State University Press, 1967), a similar struggle took place in early monotheistic Judaism in which the goddess had been held in the highest place of reverence. It was resolved somewhat differently.

    "The Goddess of the Hebrews, once the awesome Canaanite Asherah, had been officially suppressed, seemed to disappear. But she was in fact kept alive in oral legend, and then revived and preserved secretly in Kabbalistic writing (which was not available to women), described in rich detail by the rabbis of the twelfth and sixteenth centuries. They gladly imagined the Shekhinah, Lilith, the Shabbat, the Matronit, as deities. And Hochmah, goddess of wisdom, already had a place in the Bible. They stopped short at 'worship.' or overt prayer, but their devotion and reverence was as wholehearted as it was concealed." Alix Pirani, ed. *The Absent Mother Restoring the Goddess to Judaism and Christianity,* (London: Mandala, 1991), xi-xii. However, even in the mainstream of Judaism, the Goddess Asherah became the cherubim depicted on the holy ark. Also known as the Shekhinah, she is invoked and welcomed every Sabbath eve.

    Similarly, in India, goddess devotees protested and fought back when the Brahman priesthood tried to replace the original female trinity with three male gods, Brahma the Creator, Vishnu the Preserver, and Shiva the Destroyer. "They wrote in the Tantrasara that the Triple Goddess alone was the One Primordial Being, the Creatress of the three gods themselves… At the end of the world they would again disappear into her cosmic being." Walker quoting Amaury de Reincourt, *Sex and Power in History,* (New York: Dell, 1974), 167. Though far different than the early teachings of Jesus Christ, The Catholic Church has devalued sexuality, bodily functions, and women, relentlessly. Though they have been quite successful at instilling shame and mysogenistic values, they have been unable to squelch the ardent love that so many Catholics feel for their beloved Mary. See Eisler, chap. 9.

19. Barbara Ehrenreich and Deirdre English, *Witches, Midwives, and Nurses: A History of Women Healers,* (Old Westbury, New York: Feminist Press, 1973), 10.

20. Heinrich Kramer and James Sprenger, *Malleus Maleficarum,* trans. Montague Sumers (London: Pushkin Press, 1928), originally published in 1490 with the pope's blessings as the handbook for Inquisitors in hunting witches.

21. Walker, *The Crone,* 135, quoting Rossell Hope Robbins, *Encyclopedia of Witchcraft and Demonology,* (New York: Crown, 1959), 385, 464.

22. Starhawk, *Dreaming the Dark: Magic, Sex and Politcs,* (Boston: Beacon Press: 1982), 187. Witchhunts began sporadically in the late Middle Ages, bloomed in the Renaissance in the late fifteenth century. Persecutions increased througout the sixteenth century and reached their greatest ferocity in the early seventeeth century. The last of them, the Salem witchhunts, erupted in the late sixteen hundreds. This account of the witchhunts is based on Mary Daly, *Gyn/Ecology: The Metaethics of Radical Feminism,* (Boston: Beacon Press, 1978), Ehrenreich & English, *Witches, Midwives, and Nurses: A History of Women Healers,* Margaret Murray, *The God of the Witches,* Wallace Notestein, *A History of Witchcraft in England.* Rosemary Ruether, *New Woman, New Earth: Sexist Ideaologies and Human Liberation.*

23. Swami Nostradamus Verato, "To Russia with Love," in *Ecstasy Journal,* 11:2, (1993), 35.

## 6. Love, Sex and the Gender Dance

1. *Why Men Are the Way They Are,* (New York: McGraw-Hill, 1986), 101.

2. Merlin Stone, *When God Was a Woman,* (San Diego: Harcourt Brace Jovanovich, Publishers: 1976), 153-162.

3. Stone, *When God Was a Woman,* 160-161.

4. *Our Bodies, Our Selves: A Book By and For Women,* by The Boston Women's Health Book Collective, (New York: Simon and Schuster, 1971.)

5. Nancy Friday, *Women On Top: How Real Life Has Changed Women's Sexual Fantasies,* (New York: Simon and Schuster, 1991.)

6. Shere Hite, *The Hite Report on Male Sexuality,* (New York: Alfred Knopf, 1981), 160-161.

7. Diana E. H. Russell, *Rape in Marriage,* (New York, Macmillan Publishing Co, 1982), 17.

8. Russell, 22, 23. Worse still, in five of these states...this privilege has been granted to men who rape women with whom they have previously had voluntary sexual intercourse without cohabitation being required. One state, West Virginia, actually still grants some protection to men who rape their "voluntary social companions" even where there has been no prior sexual relationship.

   Even while defining rape conservatively, Russell found that fourteen percent of the English and Hispanic speaking women who were surveyed had been raped during marriage. Of those fourteen percent, ten percent had also been beaten by their husbands. In addition to those fourteen percent, twelve percent of the women surveyed had been beaten by their husbands but not raped. Other women of color were not included in the study.

9. Russell, 58.

10. Russell, 313, 314, quoting David Finkelhor and Kersti Yllo, "Forced Sex in Marriage: A Preliminary Report" (a paper presented at American Sociological Meetings, New York, August 1980), 29, 30.

11. The judge allowed his psychological counseling to be completed over the phone.

12. R. Emerson Dobash & Russel Dobash, *Violence Against Wives: A Case Against the Patriarchy,* (New York: The Free Press, 1979.)

13. John Gray, *Men Are from Mars, Women Are from Venus,* (Harper Collins, 1992), 17.

14. John Stoltenberg, *Refusing to Be a Man,* (New York: Nal-Dutton, a division of Penquin Books, 1989.)

## 7. The Power of Awareness

1. Kali is the ancient Goddess that destroys everything that is not lifegiving.

2. Rainer Maria Rilke, *Letters To a Young Poet.* (New York: Random House: 1984), 92.

3. Authentic movement is a discipline in which there is a mover and, most frequently, a witness. The intention of the mover is to listen inwardly and give bodily form to the energy, impulses, images, and feelings which arise from

the material emanating from his/her personal unconscious or the collective unconscious. As the mover is developing his/her inner witness, the external witness creates the safety necessary for the mover to journey into the unknown. The witness attends to the mover with the intent to "see" him/her while paying attention to his/her own inner experience.

## 8. Freedom Through Acceptance

1. Daniel Casriel, *A Scream Away from Happiness,* (New York: Grosset and Dunlap, 1972).

2. Friday, *Women on Top,* 19.

3. Friday, *Women on Top,* 20.

4. Stan Dale, *Fantasies Can Set You Free.* (Millbrae, California: Celestial Arts: 1980), 14.

## 9. Awakening Your Erotic Self

1. Sam Keen, *The Passionate Life.* (New York: Harper Collins, 1983), 35.

2. This technique is taught at the Institute for Creative and Artistic Development in Oakland, California and was developed by Eugene Sagan, Ph.D., and Juanita Sagan, MA, as a tool for working with self-styles.

3. Arnold Mindell, *The Dreambody in Relationship*, (New York: Routledge & Kegan Paul, 1987); *Dreambody*, (Boston, Mass.: Sigo Press: 1982), *River's Way: The Process Science of the Dreambody*, (New York: Routledge & Kegan Paul, 1985).

4. Friday, *Women on Top*, 31.

5. Thomas Moore, *Care of the Soul*, (New York: Harper Collins, 1992).

6. We'll cover this more extensively in *Erotic Mastery* (Chap. 15)

7. Techniques of celebration and integration are taught at The Institute for Creative and Artistic Development and described in the following papers: Sagan, Eugene. "In The Beginning," presented at the American Psychological Association, Sept. 1967 and published by the Institute for Creative and Artistic Development, Oakland, Ca.; Sagan, Juanita Bradshaw. *Editorial*, Institute for Creative and Artistic Development Newsletter, Vol. 10-11, March 1, 1968, ICAD, 1968.

8. These forms of movement celebration and integration were ritualized and taught by A. A. Leath at the Institute for Creative and Artistic Development.

## 10. Healing with Your Beloved—and Beyond

1. Gay and Kathlyn Hendricks, *Conscious Loving: The Journey to Co-Commitment*, (New York: Bantam Books, 1990), 42.

2. *Twelve Steps and Twelve Traditions*, The A.A. Grapevine, 1952.

3. Friday, *Women on Top*, 18.

4. This phrase originated and is used in The Human Element seminars. It is described in Will Schutz, *The Human Element: Productivity, Self-Esteem and the Bottom Line,* (San Francisco: Jossey-Bass: 1994).

5. Gershon Kaufman, *Shame: The Power of Caring*, (Rochester, Vermont: Schenkman Books, 1992).

## 11. From Monotony to Sizzling Sex

1. This is not to be confused with the feelings, images, and associations of being a baby that arise during lovemaking when a man or a woman is sucking a part of their lover's body. Because memory is stored as sensory information in our cells, when we move or act in a way that simulates these experiences, a chain of associations take us back to the original experience. When we use our mouth in lovemaking, this triggers associations that take us back to the gratifying experience of suckling at our mother's breast. This kind of natural regression can be soothing, relaxing, and very erotic.

2. See *The Art of Sexual Ecstasy* by Margo Anand; *Sexual Happiness: A Practical Approach*, by Maurice Yaffé and Elizabeth Fenwick; *Sexual Energy Ecstasy,* by David and Ellen Ramsdale; *The Joy of Sex* and *More Joy of Sex,* by A. Comfort.

## 12. Why Monogamy?

1. Stone, *When God Was A Woman*, 155.

2. Stone, 182-191.

3. Faith Popcorn, *The Popcorn Report,* (New York: Doubleday, 1991).

## 13. Handling Other Attractions

1. Catherine Johnson, *Lucky In Love*, (New York: Viking, 1992.)

2. From interview, 4/22/93.

3. From interview, 1993.

4. Popcorn, *The Popcorn Report.*

5. Though Sheldrake has not published this particular experiment, he discusses this phenomenon in his forthcoming book *Seven Experiments that Could Change the World,* (New York: Putnam, Riverhead Books, 1995).

6. *The Human Element* is a seminar created by Will Schutz that focuses on open communication in the workplace, teamwork, decision making, and conflict resolution. His newest book, *The Human Element: Productivity, Self-Esteem and the Bottom Line,* (San Francisco: Jossey-Bass, 1994), provides many case examples of the effects of this seminar.

7. David R. Eyler & Andrea P. Baridon, "Far More Than Friendship," *Psychology Today,* May-June 1992, v25, n3, 58-9.

## 15. Erotic Mastery

1. From interview, 6/93.

## Appendix

1. Margo Anand, *The Art of Sexual Ecstasy,* 171.

2. Omraam Mikhaël Aïvanhov, "Man's Subtle Bodies and Center," (France: Isvor Collections, Editions Prosveta, 1984), 65-94.

3. Omraam Mikhaël Aïvanhov, *The Fruits of The Tree of Life: The Cabbalistic Tradition.* (France: Editions Prosveta, 1989), 68.

4. Omraam Mikhaël Aïvanhov, 68.

5. Torah literally means "teaching" though it is often mistakenly translated as "law." It includes what is known as the Written Torah and the Oral Torah. The Written Torah refers to the first five books of the Bible, the Book of the Prophets, and the Writings. The Oral Torah is made up of interprations, elaborations, discussions, and commentaries on the Written Torah. The Written Torah is understood in the context of the Oral Torah.

   As Blank eloquently describes, Torah is the spiritual tradition of Judaism and the Jewish path to the experience of God. Because it is a spiritual text, the stories teach many lessons simultaneously. And as a spiritual text, it is a guide to those parts of the self which are not immediately obvious.

6. Blank, 107, 108 from Nachmanides (ascribed), Iggeret Hakodesh, *The Holy Letter.* S. Cohen, ed. (New York: KTAV, 1978), 48 (author's translation).

# A Message from the Authors

Dear Reader,

We hope that *Lovers for Life* has added richness to your life and shown you new possibilities for yourself—alone and in your relationship. We are committed to sharing the teachings in *Lovers for Life* and are asking for your support. If you benefited from *Lovers for Life*, we ask that you tell other people about it. Word of mouth is the most powerful tool for change. If we want to change our relationships—honoring love and truthfulness instead of hatred, fear, and deceit—we all must contribute. Besides potentially helping your friends, family and colleagues in their relationships, talking about the book helps you integrate what you have learned. Thanks for your contribution and support.

We continue to research what makes relationships successful and conversely, what damages or ruins them. We would like to know how *Lovers for Life* impacted you. We would also like to know what worked well for you and what did not.

We are interested in hearing about your personal history as well—how you learned about relationships, sex, and gender roles. We would also like to know what has contributed to your relationship successes or failures. We welcome examples of communication difficulties, including when you say or act one way but really feel another way. Biographical material would be helpful here. Anonymity is guaranteed. Please write or fax us this information.

Lovers for Life
P.O. Box 840
Fairfax, CA 94978-0840
Fax: (415) 457-8280

We are available to speak, lead seminars, and consult for your company, organization, or group. If you would like information about our seminars, a calendar of events, or information about other products we are developing such as an audio tape of the exercises in *Lovers for Life,* please contact us by mail, fax, or call us at:

(800) 372-8818
In California call: (415) 386-8338

We look forward to hearing from you. We welcome your feedback and suggestions.

Warmly,

Daniel and Judith